THE BILL OF RIGHTS

Government Proscribed

UNITED STATES CAPITOL HISTORICAL SOCIETY
Clarence J. Brown, President

PERSPECTIVES ON THE AMERICAN REVOLUTION
Ronald Hoffman and Peter J. Albert, Editors

Diplomacy and Revolution: The Franco-American Alliance of 1778

Sovereign States in an Age of Uncertainty

Slavery and Freedom in the Age of the American Revolution

Arms and Independence: The Military Character of the American Revolution

An Uncivil War: The Southern Backcountry during the American Revolution

Peace and the Peacemakers: The Treaty of 1783

The Economy of Early America: The Revolutionary Period, 1763–1790

Women in the Age of the American Revolution

To Form a More Perfect Union: The Critical Ideas of the Constitution

Religion in a Revolutionary Age

Of Consuming Interests: The Style of Life in the Eighteenth Century

*The Transforming Hand of Revolution: Reconsidering
the American Revolution as a Social Movement*

Launching the "Extended Republic": The Federalist Era

The Bill of Rights: Government Proscribed

The Bill of Rights

Government Proscribed

Edited by RONALD HOFFMAN

and PETER J. ALBERT

Published for the

UNITED STATES CAPITOL HISTORICAL SOCIETY

BY THE UNIVERSITY PRESS OF VIRGINIA

Charlottesville and London

THE UNIVERSITY PRESS OF VIRGINIA
Copyright © 1997 by the Rector and Visitors
of the University of Virginia
All rights reserved

Printed in the United States of America

First Published 1997

Akhil Reed Amar, "The Bill of Rights as a Constitution," reprinted by permission of
The Yale Law Journal Company and Fred B. Rothman & Company from *The Yale
Law Journal,* Vol. *100,* pages *1131–1210.*

⊗ The paper used in this publication meets the minimum requirements of the
American National Standard for Information Sciences—Permanence of Paper for
Printed Library Materials, ANSI Z39.48-1984.

Library of Congress Cataloging-in-Publication Data

The Bill of Rights : government proscribed / edited by Ronald Hoffman and Peter
J. Albert.
    p. cm. — (Perspectives on the American Revolution)
    Includes index.
    ISBN 0-8139-1759-X (cloth : alk. paper)
    1. United States. Constitution. 1st–10th Amendments. 2. Civil rights—
United States—History—18th century. 3. Constitutional history—United
States. I. Hoffman, Ronald, 1941– . II. Albert, Peter J. III. Series.
KF4749.B515 1997
342.73'029—dc21   97-2343
                                                        CIP

Contents

CONTENTS

Preface

THE United States Constitution today contains twenty-six amendments. The first ten of these, known as the Bill of Rights, were adopted within three years of the Constitution's ratification; the other sixteen have been added over the course of nearly two hundred years. This remarkable dichotomy in the constitutional experience of the United States has long engaged the attention of scholars, and it provides the larger context for the specific emphasis of this volume.

When the Founding Fathers finished drafting the Constitution in Philadelphia in 1787, they could not assume that the document would automatically be adopted. The fierce opposition its passage had ignited within the Constitutional Convention presaged similar storms of protest in many of the states by people who were quickly labeled Antifederalists. Believing that the proposed system of government did not adequately protect the rights of states and individuals, these men argued passionately in behalf of amendments to limit the powers of the new central government. The Bill of Rights that ultimately emerged from the process of negotiation between Federalists and Antifederalists has come to be considered the bulwark of the individual's liberty. But it remains unclear whether such an interpretation accurately reflects what the Founding Fathers intended.

Many men, both inside and outside the Constitutional Convention, believed that amendments were unnecessary. Some saw them as a means to make structural changes that would diminish the central government's power and enhance that of the states. As a consequence of political maneuvering during the ratification process, over two hundred amendments were submitted to the First Federal Congress that convened in New York in March 1789. The background of the concepts that were introduced, the motivations and philosophies of those who proposed them, the winnowing process that reduced the number of amendments to ten, and the mode of the ultimate adoption of the Bill of Rights are central issues for the history of the United States. And the fact that these principles have become an integral part of our definition of citizenship makes it essential that we explore, discuss, and understand their history.

This volume begins with essays by Lois G. Schwoerer and Donald S. Lutz that examine the antecedents of the Bill of Rights. Schwoerer focuses on the "lineages" of rights in the English experience—statutory enactments, common law precedents, natural rights philosophy, Commonwealth ideology, Lockean liberalism—and suggests how these influences were modified by the encounter with conditions in British America. Lutz complements Schwoerer by considering the various sources of the American Bill of Rights—English precedents, Antifederalist arguments, state bills of rights, and the like. Kenneth R. Bowling provides a chronological overview of the adoption of the Bill of Rights, and his conclusion—that the process elicited minimal controversy—establishes an underpinning for several authors who question the ultimate significance of the amendments.

One of these is Paul Finkelman, who examines the themes of anarchy and tyranny in Federalist and Antifederalist thought. He is persuaded that the Antifederalists—their fears of tyranny aside—ultimately came to accept the need for the stronger central government created by the Constitution. And the Federalists, notwithstanding their worries about anarchy, eventually accepted the Bill of Rights in the belief that it would not impede the authority of the new government.

Saul Cornell studies the nuances of "rights consciousness" and the consequent varieties of Federalist and Antifederalist thought, particularly the structuralists and the textualists among the Antifederalists—the one advocating fundamental changes in the framework of the new government and the other contending that the barriers written into the Constitution were sufficient guarantors of liberty when supplemented by a bill of rights. Paralleling this approach, Whitman

H. Ridgway looks at discrete local communities—Baptists in Virginia and Maryland, Quakers in Pennsylvania, urban mechanics in Baltimore, and rural yeomen in western Pennsylvania—to explore how issues such as religious freedom created support for the amendments; his essay concludes with an evaluation of James Madison's response to fears about the safety of rights under the new Constitution.

Michael Lienesch takes a more general approach, tracing the evolution of Antifederalist thinking on the subject of rights, state by state, from the close of the Constitutional Convention through the adoption of the Bill of Rights. He argues that the most important consequence of the Bill of Rights was political—that Congress, by adopting the amendments, firmly established the legitimacy of the new governing order. Akhil Reed Amar addresses related political and constitutional considerations, and his essay studies the Bill of Rights comprehensively to assess its impact on organizational structure and constitutional governance. Forrest McDonald, by contrast, argues that the Federalists were right in their original judgment that the amendments were unnecessary. He maintains that the Bill of Rights has afforded only minimal protection over the course of American history and that the amendments have proved particularly inadequate in times of crisis.

In a broad-ranging final essay, Bernard Schwartz contrasts the American and French experiences regarding bills of rights. He argues that Madison, in drawing up the American document, wisely decided to temper reason with experience, selecting colonial- and Revolutionary-era precedents that insured their enforceability in courts. But the French, in their enthusiasm to rebuild society, relied on pure reason in their 1789 Declaration of the Rights of Man and 1793 Declaration of the Rights of Man and Citizen. France's hortatory principles, Schwartz maintains, had universal resonance but contained no capacity for judicial or legal application.

The editors wish to acknowledge the contributions of the other participants at the U.S. Capitol Historical Society's symposium "The Bill of Rights: Government Proscribed," Jacob

PREFACE

E. Cooke, Kermit L. Hall, Stanley N. Katz, James T. Kloppenberg, Stephen Presser, and Suzanna Sherry. We would also like to acknowledge the assistance of Diane Koch in the preparation of this manuscript.

THE BILL OF RIGHTS

Government Proscribed

LOIS G. SCHWOERER

British Lineages and American Choices

FROM THE TIME of the first English settlement in America in the early seventeenth century, colonists insisted in their codes, charters, debates, and tracts that they were entitled to all the rights of Englishmen.[1] No American articulated the point more fervently than James Otis, who wrote in 1764, "Every British subject born on the continent of America . . . is . . . entitled to all the natural, essential, inherent, and inseparable rights of our fellow subjects in Great Britain."[2] Americans justified this entitlement on several grounds. In a debate in 1774 one spokesman advised that in claiming rights "it is necessary to recur to the law of nature [as well as] the British Constitution." Another responded, "Our claims are well founded on the British Constitution [alone]." Reaching for comprehensiveness, Richard Henry Lee declared, "[Our] rights are built on a fourfold foundation; on nature, on the British Constitution, on charters, and on immemorial custom."[3]

The author wishes to thank Sara Fentress and the staffs of the Folger Shakespeare Library and the Library of Congress for their assistance.

[1] For example, see Bernard Bailyn, ed., with the assistance of Jane N. Garrett, *Pamphlets of the American Revolution*, vol. 1, *1750–1776* (Cambridge, Mass., 1965), esp. pp. 112–15 for codes; Donald S. Lutz, ed., *Documents of Political Foundation Written by Colonial Americans: From Covenant to Constitution* (Philadelphia, 1987).

[2] James Otis, "The Rights of the British Colonies Asserted and Proved" (1764), in Bailyn, ed., *Pamphlets*, 1:444.

[3] Charles Francis Adams, ed., *The Works of John Adams, Second President of the United States: With a Life of the Author,* 10 vols. (Boston, 1850–56), 2:370. The remark did not exhaust the theories that justified rights. See John Phillip Reid, *Constitutional History of the American Revolution: The Authority of Rights* (Madison, Wis., 1986).

It has been argued that the strands in the British[4] ideological heritage that were most important to Americans in crafting their federal Bill of Rights were two mentioned by Lee—immemorial custom (that is, common law) and the British Constitution, as embodied especially in Magna Charta (1215),[5] the Petition of Right (1628), and the Bill of Rights (1689). It has been said that these documents were "the models in hand, or at least in mind," when colonists drew up their claim.[6] And, recently, a distinguished American constitutional historian (John Phillip Reid) has argued that the British Constitution was the *only* genuinely significant authority for those rights.[7]

In this essay I argue a slightly different case. In discussing selected British antecedents and precedents of the American Bill of Rights, I will make three general points. First, the British ideological lineage respecting rights was many-faceted. It contained several parallel and sometimes intersecting strands, including custom or common law, natural rights, statutes, country or Commonwealth ideology, and Lockean liberalism. We should think of British *lineages,* as in my title, not just of one lineage.

Second, all Anglo-American claims of rights reflected atti-

---

[4] The word *British* is meant to embrace *English* as well and is used in preference to *English-British.*

[5] For the role of Magna Charta in American ideology, see A. E. Dick Howard, *The Road from Runnymede: Magna Carta and Constitutionalism in America* (Charlottesville, Va., 1968). The place of the Petition of Right and the Bill of Rights in America has not been studied in detail.

[6] Eric Schnapper, "The Parliament of Wonders," *Columbia University Law Review* 84 (1984):1665. For discussions of the American intellectual heritage, see Bernard Bailyn, *Ideological Origins of the American Revolution* (Cambridge, Mass., 1967); H. Trevor Colbourn, *The Lamp of Experience: Whig History and the Intellectual Origins of the American Revolution* (New York, 1974); Howard, *Road from Runnymede;* Jack P. Greene, *The Intellectual Heritage of the Constitutional Era: The Delegates' Library* (Philadelphia, 1986); Donald S. Lutz, *Popular Consent and Popular Control: Whig Political Theory in the Early State Constitutions* (Baton Rouge, La., 1980); Reid, *Constitutional History;* and Gordon S. Wood, *The Creation of the American Republic, 1776–1787* (Chapel Hill, 1969).

[7] Reid, *Constitutional History.*

tudes toward larger political issues, such as the relationship between king and Parliament, the nature of royal prerogative and legitimate government, and the role of law. Claims to specific rights emerged out of practical political and legal disputes and not out of abstract theoretical disputations.[8] Although there are certain identities between Anglo-American claims and indeed identities among all subsequent claims of right entered elsewhere in the world in the nineteenth and twentieth centuries,[9] because earlier claims influenced those that followed, each is a product of particular political circumstances and political assumptions. Thus, each claim of rights offers its own perspective on the meaning of liberty and rights.

Third, Americans were not passive receptors of British lineages respecting rights theory and specific rights. Rather, Americans departed from that heritage to assert rights that had not been secured in Britain, however much some Englishmen may have desired them. In other words, Americans, following their English ancestors in their unique practice of writing down a claim, chose from among the strands in British lineages to create a Bill of Rights that contained unprecedented claims.[10]

British precedents and antecedents respecting rights are rich, complex, and old. Early concepts of rights were quite differ-

---

[8] Maurice Cranston insists upon the historicity of rights discourse and interest in specific rights in his *What Are Human Rights?* (London, 1973), p. 81: "A right presupposes a claim; if the claim is not made, the question of a right does not arise" (quoted in Edward Andrew, *Shylock's Rights: A Grammar of Lockian Claims* [Toronto, 1988], p. 19).

[9] A. Aulard, *Les Declarations des Droits de l'Homme* (Paris, 1929), counted sixty-four *national*, as distinct from state, declarations of rights up to 1929. Ian Brownlie, ed., *Basic Documents on Human Rights* (Oxford, 1971), collected fifty-four statements on human rights from the 1930s through 1969. Certain clauses in earlier claims, such as those claiming legal protections, appear in all subsequent documents.

[10] The practice of writing down a claim to rights and circulating it in print (when print became available) was peculiar to England. There is no document in the history of medieval European monarchies that is comparable to Magna Charta. The same is true for early modern Europe, if the

ent from what they are today, and although the word *right* remains, the meaning attached to it is not the same.[11] In English medieval law to have a right meant that an individual or a governing body or an administrative district possessed an authority or privilege not held by others. A right was an exclusive power or a privilege that was dependent upon property or status or gift; it was also sometimes referred to as a "freedom" or a "liberty."[12] For example, in the Middle Ages, the Roman Catholic Church in England enjoyed rights granted to it by English kings, and after the Reformation the Anglican Church also claimed certain liberties.[13] A freeman in a town who owned certain properties might possess the "right" or "liberty" to elect members of the town corporation, a power denied to a nonfreeman. A town might hold the right *not* to be taxed by the shire in which it was situated, whereas another town was subject to taxes.[14] Some individual rights were class-

---

Pacta Conventa of Poland is not counted. The few republican governments in Europe that influenced the colonists' thinking about *forms* of government did not have bills of rights. See Caroline Robbins, "European Republicanism in the Century and a Half before 1776," in *The Development of a Revolutionary Mentality: Papers Presented at the First Library of Congress Symposium on the American Revolution, May 5 and 6, 1972* (Washington, D.C., 1972), pp. 31–55. In the seventeenth century England passed on the practice of writing down the rights of its colonists in the charters it granted them, and the colonists continued it by including claims of rights in their codes and state constitutions.

[11] For the early continental development of rights theories, see Richard Tuck, *Natural Rights Theories: Their Origin and Development* (Cambridge, 1979).

[12] See the *Oxford English Dictionary* for the multiple definitions of the words *freedom, liberty,* and *right.*

[13] See Carl Stephenson and Frederick George Marcham, eds., *Sources of English Constitutional History: A Selection of Documents from A.D. 600 to the Present* (New York, 1937), pp. 25–26, 29–30, for examples of early charters granting certain rights to the church; see p. 606 for the Coronation Oath of 1689, which calls upon the monarch to confirm "all . . . rights and privileges as by law do or shall appertain unto" the Anglican Church.

[14] Ibid., pp. 96–97, 104, for examples of early borough charters. The *Oxford English Dictionary* gives examples of curious "rights" enjoyed by boroughs.

specific. Noble men and women enjoyed rights denied all other people, and male peers in the House of Lords claimed privileges for themselves as members of that body.[15] For hundreds of years, game laws "protected pheasants from peasants," because it was said that hunting was for gentlemen and "clowns should [not] have these sports."[16] Members of the House of Commons claimed certain "liberties" for themselves as members that did not extend to others or even to themselves outside the House. In the early seventeenth century such parliamentary rights as freedom from arrest and freedom of speech for members during parliamentary sessions were rights at issue between the Crown and the Commons. All the rights just mentioned clearly involve a form of possession and exclusivity. A central theme in the history of Anglo-American rights is how, why, and on what authorities the concept of possession and exclusivity was replaced.

In the early seventeenth century new meanings were added to these older concepts of rights, and from then on, for the next one hundred and seventy-five years or so before the American Revolution, the question of "rights and liberties" became a major issue in British political discourse. That question reached a point of high tension in 1628. Following a number of earlier inconclusive disagreements between Stuart kings and their critics over such matters as taxes and foreign policy,[17] Sir Edward Coke, the respected common law lawyer, led other members of the House of Commons in entering a

---

[15] Henry Scobell, *Remembrances of Methods, Orders, and Proceedings, Heretofore Used and Observed in the House of Lords: Extracted Out of the Journals of That House. By Henry Scobell, Esq. Cler. Parl. to Which Is Added, the Priviledges of the Baronage of England, Both In and Out of Parliament, Collected by John Selden, Esquire* (London, 1689), pp. 36–42, 65–66. Elizabeth Read Foster, *The House of Lords, 1603–1649: Structure, Procedure, and the Nature of Its Business* (Chapel Hill, 1983).

[16] Quotation in Edmund S. Morgan, *Inventing the People: The Rise of Popular Sovereignty in England and America* (New York, 1988), p. 24.

[17] For these earlier incidents, see J. P. Sommerville, *Politics and Ideology in England, 1603–1640* (London, 1986), esp. chaps. 4 and 5. Many of the same points made in the debate over the Great Contract in 1610 were repeated in 1628. See, for example, Elizabeth Read Foster, ed., *Proceedings in Parliament, 1610*, 2 vols. (New Haven, 1966), 2:188–89, 191.

claim to four allegedly immemorial individual rights: freedom from arbitrary taxation, freedom from arbitrary arrest
and imprisonment, freedom from billeting of soldiers in private houses without due process and compensation, and freedom from martial law imposed in time of peace on civilians
without parliamentary approval. Set out in a formal, written
statement, the Petition of Right, these rights gained legal status when Charles I reluctantly accepted the Petition.[18]

These rights are familiar to Americans, because in essence
they are part of our Constitution. What may be less familiar
are the arguments and theoretical implications that underlay
them, for they are foreign to our way of thinking. Drawing
upon medieval political and legal theorists such as Henry
Bracton and Sir John Fortescue (author of *De Laudibus
Angliae*), and citing such medieval laws as Fleta, the *Modus
Tenendi Parliamentum,* the apocryphal Laws of Edward the
Confessor, and, above all, Magna Charta, Coke and others insisted that the rights of Englishmen were part of the common
law and of an "ancient constitution" that predated the institution of monarchy.[19] Thus, rights were no gift of the monarch
and were beyond his or her power to withdraw. The nation's

[18]The text of the Petition of Right may be found conveniently in J. P.
Kenyon, *The Stuart Constitution, 1603–1688: Documents and Commentary*
(1966; reprint ed., Cambridge, 1986), pp. 68–71. Among the numerous
studies of the Petition of Right are: Lindsay Boynton, "Martial Law and the
Petition of Right," *English Historical Review* 79 (1964):255–84; Jess Stoddart
Flemion, "The Struggle for the Petition of Right in the House of Lords:
The Study of an Opposition Party Victory," in Clyve Jones and David Lewis
Jones, eds., *Peers, Politics, and Power: The House of Lords, 1603–1911* (London,
1986):31–48; J. A. Guy, "The Origins of the Petition of Right Recon-
sidered," *Historical Journal* 25 (1982):289–321; Linda S. Popofsy, "*Habeas
Corpus* and 'Liberty of the Subject': Legal Arguments for the Petition of
Right in the Parliament of 1628," *The Historian: A Journal of History* 41
(1979):257–75; and Frances H. Relf, *The Petition of Right* (Minneapolis,
1917).

[19]The classic study of the ancient constitution is J. G. A. Pocock, *The An-
cient Constitution and the Feudal Law: A Study of English Historical Thought in the
Seventeenth Century: A Reissue with a Retrospect* (1957; reprint ed., Cambridge,
1987), esp. chaps. 2 and 3. Stephen D. White, *Sir Edward Coke and "The
Grievances of the Commonwealth"* (Chapel Hill, 1979), examines Sir Edward
Coke's role and ideas in the passage of the Petition of Right.

rights had existed down through the centuries without break, for they had been confirmed in 1066 by William I, who was no conqueror. Exemplified in judicial rulings, legal maxims, and statutes, the common law possessed rare properties; it was on the one hand flexible (responding to changing customs and usage) and on the other compatible with eternal natural law.[20] Magna Charta, many times confirmed, was a statute[21] that, far from making new law, had simply declared the old common law and reaffirmed medieval laws.[22] It embodied (according to Coke's reading) subjects' rights, such as trial by jury and taxation by consent, that it had not originally possessed.[23] Magna Charta and other parliamentary laws restrained the king's sovereign power, Coke and others insisted.[24]

Common law and Magna Charta took precedence over Parliament, Coke was later read to mean. In Dr. Bonham's Case in 1610, Coke had said that the "common law will controul Acts of Parliament, and sometimes adjudge them to be utterly void."[25] We now know that Coke intended only to reassert that statutory law was based on reason and justice, but pertinent to my thesis is that eighteenth-century Americans used his remark in support of the doctrine of judicial review that they adopted.[26]

Yet the fact is that in 1628 Coke and others venerated Parliament, which they argued could trace its origins beyond the

[20] Sommerville, *Politics and Ideology*, chap. 3, esp. pp. 87–89, 91–92, 95, 98, 107. Pocock, *Ancient Constitution*, pp. 274–80.

[21] Technically, Magna Charta did not achieve statutory status until 1297.

[22] Pocock, *Ancient Constitution*, pp. 32–38, 44–45, 274–79. Janelle Greenberg, "The Confessor's Laws and the Radical Face of the Ancient Constitution," *English Historical Review* 104 (1989):611–37.

[23] Howard, *Road from Runnymede*, p. 91.

[24] Mary Frear Keeler, Maija Jansson Cole, and William B. Bidwell, eds., *Debates and Proceedings in Parliament, 1628*, 6 vols. (New Haven, 1977–83), 3:143, 495, 497, 503, 505–7 (Commons debates).

[25] Quoted in Howard, *Road from Runnymede*, p. 121.

[26] Ibid. Bailyn, ed., *Pamphlets*, pp. 100, 412–13, and references cited there on the meaning of Coke's ruling in Dr. Bonham's Case in 1610.

Conquest to the Anglo-Saxon Witenagemot. It was the only institution in the nation that had the responsibility to present grievances to the king, and the only body that could preserve law and the ancient constitution. As one spokesman put it, "The parliament is to redress grievances and mischiefs that happen." Another made the same point. "Let it be still our masterpiece to uphold parliament, for that we shall be able . . . to rectify whatsoever is amiss."[27] Because Parliament held such an important role, its integrity was essential. Since the sixteenth century, M.P.s had struggled to secure certain parliamentary rights that would assure open discussion of issues and protect members from arrest. The claim of freedom of speech went back to the reign of Henry VIII, when in 1532 the Speaker of the House of Commons began the practice of petitioning the king to grant M.P.s freedom of speech in debate.[28] As the case of Peter Wentworth in 1576 illustrates, the right of parliamentary freedom of speech was far from secure during the reign of Elizabeth I.[29] Yet in 1604 the Commons in *The Form of Apology and Satisfaction* described freedom of speech in debate and some other parliamentary privileges as "auncient" and "as our right and due inheritance." The *Apology* also enlarged the significance of parliamentary rights by saying (without regard to strict logic) that they extended to subjects: the "rights of the subjects of this realme chiefly consist in the priviledges of the House of Parlyament."[30] The 1621 Protestation also claimed the right of free speech for members of the House of Commons and declared that that *parliamentary* right was of great importance to *all* individual English subjects: "The liberties, franchises, privileges and ju-

[27] Keeler, Cole, and Bidwell, eds., *Debates and Proceedings in Parliament*, 3:143, 272, compare p. 277 (Commons debates).

[28] See Lois G. Schwoerer, *The Declaration of Rights, 1689* (Baltimore, 1981), pp. 81–84, and references cited there.

[29] Stephenson and Marcham, eds., *Sources of English Constitutional History*, pp. 364–65, 367–70, for the case of Peter Wentworth.

[30] Great Britain, Historical Manuscripts Commission, *Calendar of the Manuscripts of the Most Honourable, The Marquess of Salisbury . . . Preserved at Hatfield House, Hertfordshire*, 24 vols. (London, 1883–1976), 23:143.

risdictions of parliament are the ancient and undoubted birthright and inheritance of the subjects of England," it read.[31] In debate Coke made the same point: "The freedom of this House is the freedom of the whole land."[32] In other words, it was in Parliament that individual rights could be claimed and defended. These in turn depended upon parliamentary rights designed to protect M.P.s and the independence of the body from the king. Parliamentary rights lay *au fond* of the development of individual rights. For this and other reasons, the distant origins of parliamentary supremacy in Great Britain are found in the early seventeenth century.

The assumptions about the common law and the ancient constitution informed the debate over each one of the rights that became embodied in the Petition of Right. Coke's creation of the myth of the "ancient constitution" and his endowing Magna Charta with theretofore unacknowledged significance assisted parliamentary spokesmen in arguing that their claim was nothing new but rather simply a restoration of old law and specific rights that had *always* belonged to the nation. Thus, when an M.P., irate over financial exactions imposed on the subject, asserted that "the right of the subject is . . . bulwarked by the law of the kingdom," he meant that the right not to be taxed without consent of Parliament was provided by the "ancient constitution," the common law, and Magna Charta. When a peer insisted that the "sense of the Petition [of Right] is wholly comprehended in Magna Carta," he was expressing the belief that members were doing nothing but affirming the past.[33] Since "the scope and drift of Magna Charta was to reduce the regal into a legal power," it—that is, the law—protected the "liberties of our persons and [the] propriety of our goods."[34]

In the effort to preserve property from arbitrary taxation,

[31] For Protestation, see Kenyon, *Stuart Constitution*, pp. 42–43.

[32] Coke's remark is quoted in Morgan, *Inventing the People*, p. 24.

[33] Keeler, Cole, and Bidwell, eds., *Debates and Proceedings in Parliament*, 5:524 (Lords proceedings).

[34] Ibid., 3:127–28 (Commons debates).

lawyers and parliamentarians gave the word *property* more than one meaning. It meant not only tangible goods but also the constitutional right in those goods, the "propriety" in them, as the spokesman just quoted called it. Propriety itself was regarded as a property or possession and defended as such. Sir John Eliot declared that he feared less losing his property (that is, his money) than the right (the propriety) not to be deprived of that property except by consent of Parliament. As he put it, he feared most losing the "power in the law to preserve our goods."[35] Tangible goods and intangible constitutional principle were inextricably linked; if the subject were deprived of either one, his status as a freeman was imperiled, and England's government became an absolutism, operating outside the law.[36]

The idea that Englishmen possessed a property in their rights was wholeheartedly embraced by American colonists and applied directly to their own circumstances. In 1765 one colonist contested the Stamp Act in much the same terms used in 1628: "The burden of the tax is not the point," he said. "It is the laying it upon us, as we apprehend, unconstitutionally, a submission to which will be giving up our birthright, and entailing slavery on our posterity."[37]

Another notable feature of the debate pertinent to my argument is that when no precedent in common law could be found, as was the case with the charge that the Crown's use of martial law in peacetime violated an immemorial right, members were undeterred. They regarded the Crown's use of martial law as "of the greatest consequence . . . [because it] concerns our lives," and they simply claimed that it *was* an ancient right that the government was barred the use of mar-

[35] Ibid., 2:57, compare p. 55. The distinction between tangible property and the intangible property of a constitutional principle not to be deprived of property without consent of Parliament is underscored by a comment made regarding the ship money tax in the 1630s. One observer said, "Although our goods were not taken away yet the property was" (quoted in Sommerville, *Politics and Ideology,* p. 159).

[36] Sommerville, *Politics and Ideology,* pp. 148–51.

[37] Quoted in Reid, *Constitutional History,* p. 111. For colonists' devotion to the principle of property in rights see pp. 24–25, 71–73, 118–22.

tial law in time of peace.[38] This would not be the last time that Englishmen found in the "ancient constitution" what they needed to find to redress their own contemporary grievances.

The debate in 1628 was of uncommon importance in the history of mainstream rights discourse. It located that discourse in legal precedents, in the tradition of the common law, the "ancient constitution," and Magna Charta. It embedded the whole in a reading of history and law that was full of myth and fiction. Although weakened over the next century and a half, this common law tradition continued to lie at the heart of one strand of attitudes toward rights in England and Great Britain. Coke's works were well known in the American colonies and his views about rights deeply influenced the conceptual framework of the American Bill of Rights.

In the middle of the seventeenth century, during the decades of the Civil War and Cromwellian experiment, another strand in British lineages was introduced. The words *rights* and *liberties* took on different meanings, a development that well illustrates how time-specific the concept of rights is. Radical Leveller thinkers offered their own readings of English history and drew upon a different theory to justify their claim to subjects' rights. Although John Lilburne, the most famous of the Levellers, endorsed Coke's writings on common law and Magna Charta, his interpretation of the Charter was different; as one historian has put it, Lilburne "read the law of nature into Magna Charta."[39] But other Leveller leaders, such as Richard Overton and William Walwyn, flatly rejected the common law as the source of rights, decrying it as part of the "Norman yoke" that was imposed on the nation in 1066 by William I, who, they said, *was* a conqueror. They turned instead to the idea of fundamental laws that conferred on the people certain "inalienable" rights. These rights went beyond

[38] Lois G. Schwoerer, *"No Standing Armies!" The Antiarmy Ideology in Seventeenth-Century England* (Baltimore, 1974), pp. 29–31. Also White, *Sir Edward Coke*, pp. 251–53.

[39] William Haller and Godfrey Davies, eds., *The Leveller Tracts, 1647–1653* (New York, 1944), pp. 43–47. Also William Haller, ed., *Tracts on Liberty in the Puritan Revolution, 1638–1647*, 3 vols. (New York, 1934), 1:111.

Magna Charta and the Petition of Right, which only contained rights that, as Walwyn put it, had been "wrestled out of the pawes of . . . Kings."[40] Overton also dismissed Magna Charta as a "messe of pottage," declaiming that "justice is my naturall right . . . [given me] by lineall descent from the loins of Adam." "By naturall birth," he maintained, "all men are equally and alike borne to like propriety, liberty and freedome."[41] In several documents, the most extensive of which was the 1648 "An Agreement of the People," the Levellers specified rights that they found in fundamental law: among them freedom of religion and freedom from impressment for military service, rights that obviously went beyond those claimed in Magna Charta and the Petition of Right.[42]

Levellers differed also from earlier proponents of rights in their attitude toward Parliament. Critical of its present structure, they called for redistributing seats, creating proportional representation, enlarging the franchise, and limiting its powers, as for example, by denying it the power to imprison a debtor or impress for military service, as just noted. Leveller writings were proscribed after the Restoration of the Stuarts in 1660. Although some of their reform ideas did appear in the late seventeenth century,[43] they fell outside English mainstream rights discourse and had no part in the Revolution of 1688–89. Leveller tracts were read by British radicals in the eighteenth century and were known in the colonies, but there

[40] Morgan, *Inventing the People*, pp. 71–73. The quotation is from William Walwyn, "England's Lamentable Slaverie," in Jack R. McMichael and Barbara Taft, eds., *The Writings of William Walwyn* (Athens, Ga., 1989), p. 147; see p. 143 for attribution to Walwyn.

[41] Haller, ed., *Tracts on Liberty*, 1:113. Clearly, Leveller thought is not monolithic on the Conquest. See R. B. Seaberg, "The Norman Conquest and the Common Law: The Levellers and the Argument from Continuity," *Historical Journal* 24 (1981):791–806.

[42] Morgan, *Inventing the People*, p. 72. See Don M. Wolfe, ed., *Leveller Manifestoes of the Puritan Revolution* (New York, 1967), pp. 223–34, and 311–12 for texts of the 1647 and 1648 "Agreement of the People."

[43] See Richard Ashcraft, *Revolutionary Politics and Locke's Two Treatises of Government* (Princeton, 1986), pp. 164–75, 561, 579.

is no evidence that American leaders appealed directly to them.[44]

In the late seventeenth century, another major component was added to the British Constitution: the Bill of Rights of 1689.[45] Described by an American in 1760 as "that second Magna Charta,"[46] the Bill of Rights was so admired by James Otis that he copied it verbatim into his famous tract *The Rights of the British Colonists Asserted and Proved.* Despite the word *Bill* in its title, the Bill of Rights is a genuine statute of the realm, the only one of the major rights documents to hold that status. The Declaration of Rights, the earlier draft of the Bill of Rights (and a watered-down version of a radical first draft called the Heads of Grievances),[47] was presented to Prince William and Princess Mary of Orange in the ceremony in which they were offerred the crown of England. Eleven months later, after a few modifications, the Declaration in the form of a bill received the assent of the new king and became the law of the land. The nature of the contents of the Bill of Rights is also unique. A political document, the Bill of Rights contains not only a claim to thirteen rights but also the terms of the settlement of the Revolution of 1688–89. This linkage, insisted upon by the Declaration's Whig proponents, gave the claim of rights greater prominence and security than it might otherwise have had.

Like all claims, the Bill of Rights was a response to specific grievances, in this case grievances leveled against Catholic

[44] Caroline Robbins, *The Eighteenth-Century Commonwealthman: Studies in the Transmission, Development, and Circumstance of English Liberal Thought from the Restoration of Charles II until the War with the Thirteen Colonies* (Cambridge, Mass., 1959), pp. 3–4, 15, 19, 379. Clinton Rossiter, *Seedtime of the Republic: The Origin of the American Tradition of Political Liberty* (New York, 1953), p. 357.

[45] See Schwoerer, *Declaration of Rights, 1689.*

[46] "Letter to the People of Pennsylvania" (1760), in Bailyn, ed., *Pamphlets,* p. 266. Compare *Bickerstaff's Boston Almanac* for 1768, which dubbed it the "new Magna Charta" (see Howard, *Road from Runnymede,* p. 124).

[47] Robert J. Frankle, "The Formulation of the Declaration of Rights," *Historical Journal* 17 (1974):265–79.

James II. Drafters connected rights and grievances so closely that the one is the opposite of the other. In essence the Bill restricted the prerogative of the king in five general ways. First, with respect to law, it denied the Crown the power to suspend and dispense with laws, and it protected the subject against excessive bail, excessive fines, cruel and unusual punishments, and from the granting and promising of fines and forfeitures before conviction. Second, with respect to military authority, it prohibited a standing army in time of peace without the consent of Parliament, and it gave a right to some subjects, under certain conditions, to bear arms. Third, with respect to property, it denied the Crown the power to tax without the consent of Parliament. Fourth, with respect to religion, it denied the royal family religious freedom, insisting upon their adherence to the Church of England and absolving the "people" from allegiance to a monarch who defied these restrictions. It said nothing about religious toleration. Fifth, as the prerogative of the king was restricted, the authority of Parliament was affirmed. Further claims for Parliament were the rights of free elections, free speech and debates and proceedings, and frequent meetings. The structure of government the Bill of Rights confirmed was king-in-Parliament, but this settlement prepared the way for ultimate parliamentary supremacy. It is immediately clear that not all these provisions aimed at restraining royal authority in a monarchy were useful a hundred years later to Americans living in a republic who were drafting their own Bill of Rights.

For the decade after the Glorious Revolution, concern over rights continued in much the same terms as before, reflecting anxiety over the royal prerogative and the relationship between monarchy and Parliament and belief that rights were claims that restricted political power. The author of *The Rights and Liberties of Englishmen Asserted* expressed these sentiments in 1701 in terms that might have been used in 1628. Englishmen, he wrote, were "no King's Vassals nor Slaves, but are freeborn Subjects, who have by their own Laws a property in their Goods and Possessions, and a freehold in their Lands, whereof they cannot be deprived but by their own good Wills, or by their Consents delegated to their Representatives in Parliament."[48] Here is the same emphasis on property, the rule of law, propriety, and parliamentary principles that appeared seventy-five years before.

Also during this decade sharp disappointment was expressed in several quarters that the Bill of Rights had not gone further. Although no concerted effort was made to achieve a comprehensive claim of rights that went beyond the Bill of Rights, some of the measures that had been discussed at the time of the Revolution but not included in the claim became law over the next eleven years.[49] Of special interest to the American Bill of Rights is the Toleration Act (1689). Despite the views of John Locke, as expressed in his *Letter on Toleration,* and the efforts of a few men who sincerely believed in freedom of religious conscience, the Toleration Act brought only modest religious toleration to Dissenters and provided no true freedom of religion. It did not cancel the old penal statutes against Catholics and Dissenters; it simply provided that those statutes should not be enforced on persons who fulfilled certain conditions. The right of the individual to worship freely without penalty was not achieved in Great Britain until 1829 and 1832 for Catholics and Dissenters, and not until 1846 for Jews. Freedom of religion is not a right even today for British monarchs. The principle of freedom of religion has to be sought not in the well-known statute, the Toleration Act, but in another strand of the British lineage.

A second act passed at the turn of the eighteenth century of unusual concern to Americans was the Act of Settlement (1701), which contained provisions that no royal pardon may be pleadable to an impeachment and that tenure of judges

[48] Thomas Wagstaffe, *The Rights and Liberties of Englishmen Asserted* (London, 1701), p. 22.

[49] Other acts respecting rights that were passed during the decade were the Triennial Act (1694), which required the king to summon Parliament at least every three years (a limitation on royal prerogative connected with Article 13 of the Bill of Rights, this provision was, in effect, overtaken by the practice of holding annual sessions of Parliament) and the Treason Trials Act (1696), which provided further legal protection to a person charged with treason by laying down that the accused should have a copy of the indictment ten days before the trial and a lawyer to assist him in his defense.

would be for life, not at the pleasure of the king. These clauses enlarged the "rights of Englishmen," as those rights appeared in statutes.The terms of the Act of Settlement, which the Crown had not wanted to apply to the colonies, played a significant role in the coming of the break with Great Britain, the Declaration of Independence charging George III with imposing on colonists judges whose tenure was dependent upon his will.[50]

It may be helpful to summarize the major features of English rights theory as it was transmitted to the eighteenth century. First, a right of the subject was regarded as a legal protection against some danger from the government, not as an entitlement of the individual. This attitude was compatible with the then prevailing belief that the danger to the nation's laws, religion, form of government, and liberties came from a Catholic king exercising in an arbitrary manner the powers of the late Stuart monarchy. The solution laid out in the Bill of Rights was, as we have seen, to proscribe the religion of the ruling monarch, restrict the powers of the kingship, strengthen those of Parliament, and protect the subject's property and person from the power of government. John Somers, one of the Bill's principal authors and later lord chancellor, expressed the ideal well when he declared that the Bill of Rights had secured freedom and liberty by requiring monarchs to act according to the law. "Our happiness . . . consists in this," he wrote, "that our princes are tied up to the law as well as we. . . . Our government not being arbitrary, but legal, not absolute, but political, our princes can never become arbitrary, absolute or tyrants."[51] This assumption about law underlies the American Bill of Rights as well.

[50] Howard, *Road from Runnymede*, p. 210; Wood, *Creation of the American Republic*, pp. 294–95.

[51] John Somers, *Vindication of the Proceedings of the Late Parliament of England, An. Dom., 1689,* in Sir Walter Scott, ed., *A Collection of Scarce and Valuable Tracts . . . Selected from . . . Public As Well As Private Libraries, Particularly That of the Late Lord Somers,* 13 vols. (London, 1809–15), 10:257–58, 261, 263, 267–68. For attribution to Somers, see William L. Sachse, *John, Lord Somers: A Political Portrait* (Manchester, England, 1975), p. 36 n. 41. Lord Delamer expressed the same thought, writing that the greatness and security of kings and the happiness of subjects "depend[s] . . . upon the exact

The legal rights of the individual that were achieved in England are today referred to as "negative" rights to distinguish them from "positive" rights or entitlements.[52] They were of great importance in seventeenth-century England and in eighteenth-century America. (Indeed, their significance in the late twentieth century should not be underestimated.) Some of them—for example, trial by jury and prohibitions against excessive bail—were incorporated in our Bill of Rights and also appeared at about the same time in the French Declaration of the Rights of Man. An American historian has maintained that such points were a matter of *principle* with the Antifederalists, whose interest in a federal Bill of Rights, others have said, reflected only partisan politics.[53] Drafters of the American federal Bill of Rights, to say nothing of the Virginia Declaration of Rights of 1776, for example, copied these clauses providing legal protections verbatim from the 1689 Bill of Rights. Today these old rights, while taken for granted in the Western world, have been overshadowed by concern for other "rights." One has only to consider the 1948 United Nations Universal Declaration of Human Rights: it claims, of course, all the legal protections provided by the English Bill of Rights and the United States Bill of Rights, but the focus of the document is on individual entitlements, such as the right to work, to education, to rest, and to leisure, rights aimed at achieving social and economic justice in a democratic society. The United Nations Declaration provides yet another example of the historicity and time-specificity of claims of rights. It need hardly be said that the notion of entitlement to social and economic rights was not entertained before the twentieth century. The idea of laying a responsibility on society to provide for the rights of subjects

---

observation and maintenance of their Laws, Liberties and Customs" (*The Works of the Right Honourable Henry, Late L. Delamer and Earl of Warrington* [London, 1694], p. 369).

[52] Isaiah Berlin, *Four Essays on Liberty* (London, 1969).

[53] Cecelia Kenyon maintained that the Antifederalists were genuinely alarmed by the absence of traditional procedural rights in law suits. See James H. Hutson, "The Birth of the Bill of Rights: The State of Current Scholarship," *Prologue* 20 (1988):146–47.

was foreign to all early modern English thought on rights. It is one thing that makes that thought appear anachronistic.

Another thing that makes early modern English rights discourse appear anachronistic is that there are certain entitlements, to the surprise of many people today, *not* to be found in any English or British constitutional document: namely, the rights of freedom of religion (as already mentioned), freedom of the press, and freedom of speech. These rights, of course, were secured by Americans a hundred years later, in a step marking a major departure from the British constitution. More will be said about them later in this essay.

Second, although no mainstream English claim of rights hints at a desire to level social distinctions, extend the right of political participation, or redistribute parliamentary seats,[54] none contains language that is class or gender specific. So, if one asks, "Whose rights are protected?" the answer is "everyone's." In the Petition of Right the word *subject* appears without qualifiers and, thus, in terms of language, applies across social, economic, and gender lines.[55] During the Restoration

[54] A handful of tracts supported the last two points in 1688–89. See *Some Remarks upon Government, and Particularly upon the Establishment of the English Monarchy Relating to This Present Juncture* (London, 1689) and John Wildman [?], *A Letter to a Friend, Advising Him, in This Extraordinary Juncture, How to Free the Nation from Slavery Forever* (London, 1689). By "slavery" is meant "arbitrary power" or the opposite of "liberty." See John Phillip Reid, *The Concept of Liberty in the Age of the American Revolution* (Chicago, 1988), esp. chap. 3.

[55] It need hardly be said that no member of Parliament in the seventeenth century was thinking about applying the rights of men to women, but the legal protections that were achieved did serve women as well. It is worth noting that during the Civil Wars, in petitions to Parliament, Leveller women laid claim to their "undoubted right of petitioning" and insisted that they had an "equal interest with the men of this Nation, in those liberties and securities contained in the Petition of Right, and other good Laws of the Land" (quotation in Patricia Higgins, "The Reactions of Women, with Special Reference to Women Petitioners," in Brian Manning, ed., *Politics, Religion, and the English Civil War* [London, 1973], pp. 216–17). In the Restoration, the idea of "rights" for women was the subject of satire (see Susan Staves, *Players' Scepters: Fictions of Authority in the Restoration* [Lincoln, Neb., 1979], pp. 111–89). The topic of women's "rights" in early modern England awaits systematic study.

the idea of the universality of rights for men was expressed. In 1680 a tract writer, Henry Care, averred that the legal rights enshrined in common law applied to everyone: "Each man [has] a fixed Fundamental Right born with him, as to Freedom of his Person and Property in his Estate." Judges swear, he pointed out, "to do equal Law and Right to all the King's Subjects, Rich and Poor."[56] Conformable with such views, the Bill of Rights (with the exception of Article 7)[57] employs no restrictive language. The preamble declares and enacts that the "rights and liberties asserted . . . are the . . . indubitable rights and liberties of the people of this kingdom." The word *people* is nowhere defined. Although the majority of politically conscious persons in 1688–89 (Locke excepting) identified the word *people* with those Protestant, upper-class, property-owning males who had the right to vote and the possibility of election and public service, the document did not say so. Why drafters did not say what they surely believed was probably because they thought that qualifiers would weaken their claim. Asserting rights on behalf of an undefined "people" may well have been a political tactic designed to strengthen the document that was laid before a divine-right monarch in 1628 and presented to a foreign prince in 1689.[58] Whatever the reason, the foundation of the future extension of protected civil rights to all persons, regardless of condition or gender, was embedded in seventeenth-century English documents. There is, of course, no restrictive language in the American Bill of Rights.

Third, rights discourse during the Restoration and Revolution era was richer and more complex than is sometimes understood. On the one hand, reverence for the ancient constitution and Magna Charta as the source of English rights

[56] Henry Care, *English Liberties, or, The Free-Born Subject's Inheritance* (London, 1680), p. 5.

[57] Article 7 limited the right to hold arms according to religion, economic standing, previous law, and, by implication, gender. See Schwoerer, *Declaration of Rights, 1689*, pp. 74–78, 246.

[58] Morgan, *Inventing the People*, pp. 22–25, makes this point with respect to the Petition of Right.

continued into the eighteenth century, notwithstanding some countervailing views.[59] Of many examples, one may take that of Henry Care, who in a 1680 tract printed the texts of Magna Charta and the Petition of Right, and invoked Fortescue and Bracton, in support of his argument that the most important "Birth-right of English-men" was "to be freed [by the law] in Person and Estate, from Arbitrary Oppression and Violence." Protected by the institution of Parliament and trial by jury, the English, Care declared, "are Estated in [their rights] by the Original Constitution of their Government."[60] In 1689 the *majority* of members of the Convention remained committed to the concept of the ancient constitution. One M.P. advised the Convention to "enact no new constitution, but . . . adhere to the ancient constitution."[61] Using time-honored rhetoric, authors of the Bill of Rights wrote that the rights they claimed were theirs by immemorial custom and that they were doing nothing more than their ancestors had done. They were "Vindicating and Asserting their antient Rights and Liberties" just "as their Ancestors in like Case have usually done." Shortly after the Revolution a tract summed up the attitude in its very title, which read *A Vindication of Magna Carta, As the Summary of English Rights and Liberties, in Which . . . the Excellency of the Old English Constitution as the Noblest Commonwealth in the World is Clearly Demonstrated.* A contemporary, commenting with approval on the pamphlet, insisted that "in all the steps the bar-

[59] References to Magna Charta appear in diverse legal and political issues throughout the Restoration era. Examples are gathered in Maurice Ashley, *Magna Carta in the Seventeenth Century* (Charlottesville, Va., 1965).

[60] Care, *English Liberties*, pp. 4–5. See also Sir John Hawles, *The Englishman's Right. A Dialogue between a Barrister at Law, and a Jury-Man: Plainly Setting Forth: I. The Antiquity, II. The Excellent Designed Use, III. The Office, and Just Priviledges, of Juries, by the Law of England* (1680; reprint ed., London, 1844), esp. p. 39, where he urges his readers to turn to Magna Charta, the Petition of Right, and other laws to understand the "true Liberties and Priviledges which every English man is Justly Intituled unto, and Estated in by his Birth-right."

[61] John Somers, "Notes of Debate, January 28, January 29," in Philip Yorke, ed., *Miscellaneous State Papers, from 1501 to 1726*, 2 vols. (London, 1778), 2:415.

ons took [in 1215], we [in 1688–89] followed them."[62] At the
end of the eighteenth century Edmund Burke picked up this
language of the ancient constitution and used it to make his
case that the Revolution of 1688–89 achieved no substantive
change.

Yet also present were views that diluted the strength of the
concept of the ancient constitution. One was a dimunition in
respect for the past. For example, in 1666 during the proceedings against Edward Hyde, the first earl of Clarendon, a
preference for recent precedents was expressed on grounds
that the newness of cases cited "gave them in some sense
greater strength."[63] The radical political theorist Henry Neville candidly admitted that if an ancient precedent could not
be found, then his assertion that a Parliament should be summoned once a year and not dissolved or prorogued until
all grievances had been redressed, "must be so by the fundamental law of this government."[64] In 1689 some Convention
members stressed the difficulties of finding that ancient constitution, one member disparaging the search for precedents
as "tedious and fruitless."[65] The weakening of reverence for
the past was obvious in the decision to omit from the new
Coronation Oath the monarch's traditional promise to uphold
the Laws of Edward the Confessor (which, it will be remembered, had been cited by Coke) on grounds that the oath had
"heretofore been framed . . . with relation to ancient laws and
constitutions at this time unknown."[66]

[62] Quoted in J. P. Kenyon, *Revolution Principles: The Politics of Party, 1689–1720* (Cambridge, 1977), p. 108.

[63] Quoted in Howard Nenner, *By Colour of Law: Legal Culture and Constitutional Politics in England, 1660–1689* (Chicago, 1977), p. 135.

[64] Henry Neville, *Plato Redivivus*, ed. Caroline Robbins (Cambridge, Mass., 1969), p. 124.

[65] Anchitell Grey, *Debates of the House of Commons, from the Year 1667 to the Year 1694*, 10 vols. (London, 1763), 9:32.

[66] E. Neville Williams, ed., *The Eighteenth-Century Constitution, 1688–1815: Documents and Commentary* (Cambridge, 1960), p. 36. See Lois G. Schwoerer, "The Coronation of 1689," in Schwoerer, ed., *The Revolution of 1688–1689: Changing Perspectives* (Cambridge, 1992), pp. 107–30.

Another idea that challenged the concept of the ancient constitution was that of natural law and natural rights. There was no need for historical precedents in the political theory articulated most comprehensively by Locke in his *Two Treatises of Government,* published in the fall of 1689. Locke was not alone. Similar ideas about the contractual origins of government and the sovereignty of the people also appeared in a number of radical tracts during the Restoration and at the time of the Glorious Revolution, when some were written for the occasion and others reprinted.[67] These ephemeral tracts spread more widely in the late seventeenth century than did Locke's book. Among those printed in 1688–89 was *Pro Popolo Adversus Tyrannos,* a reissue of John Milton's tract *The Tenure of Kings and Magistrates,* which presented a radical view of the origins of kingly power with clear implications for a concept of the people's rights. The author asserted that "the power of kings . . . is committed to them in trust from the people . . . in whom the power yet remains fundamentally, and cannot be taken from them without violation of their natural birthright."[68] In somewhat different terms, *Advice Before It Be Too Late* explained that supreme authority in the state had devolved to the people as represented in the Convention, which had a "higher capacity" than a parliament to make "laws for the Constitution."[69] In the House of Commons, Sir Robert Howard spoke of England's government as being "grounded upon pacte and covenant," and declared that if the king breaks that pact, the government is "devolved into the people" to create a new one.

Although in the minority, these views arguably exerted influence on the terms of the Declaration of Rights and Bill of

[67] Ashcraft, *Revolutionary Politics;* Mark Goldie, "The Roots of True Whiggism, 1688–94," *History of Political Thought* 1 (1980):195–236. See also Lois G. Schwoerer, "Lockean Ideas and the Glorious Revolution," *Journal of the History of Ideas* 51 (1990):531–48. My personal file of reprints contains approximately fifty tracts reprinted from earlier times.

[68] *Pro Popolo Adversus Tyrannos, or, The Sovereign Right and Power of the People over Tyrants, Clearly Stated and Plainly Proved. With Some Reflections on the Posture of Affairs* (London, 1689), pp. 8, 10.

[69] [John Humphrey], *Advice before It Be Too Late* (London, 1689), n.p.

Rights. Ignoring the absence of precise precedents (as we saw was the case in 1628 with martial law), authors of the Bill of Rights in 1689 embedded new law in seven Articles, even as they claimed to be doing nothing more than reaffirming "indubitable" rights. The most important new rights were those that denied the king the powers to suspend or dispense with the law and to keep a standing army in time of peace without the consent of Parliament.[70]

The prevalence of the language of the ancient constitution helps to explain what has recently been shown, namely, that when John Locke's *Two Treatises* appeared in 1689 they met with a cool reception and that in the early eighteenth century Whig politicians regarded his ideas, such as those about original contract, the sovereignty of the people, the right of resistance, and freedom of religious conscience, with distaste and found a Lockean interpretation of the Revolution an embarrassment.[71] Yet in the late eighteenth century British reformers revived interest in Lockean ideas and read him as an exponent of the Revolution of 1688–89, whatever the truth of the matter.[72] In like manner, Americans regarded John Locke as the theoretician of the Revolution of 1688–89.[73] English lineages play out in curious ways in eighteenth-century Britain and America!

Finally, another strand of thought pertinent to rights that was articulated during the era was the continuing belief that

[70] Schwoerer, *Declaration of Rights, 1689*, chap. 4 and pp. 283–84. For lawmaking, see Corinne Weston and Janelle Greenberg, *Subjects and Sovereigns: The Grand Controversy over Legal Sovereignty in Stuart England* (Cambridge, 1981); for standing armies, see Schwoerer, *"No Standing Armies!"*

[71] See Kenyon, *Revolution Principles*, and Martyn Thompson, "The Reception of Locke's Two Treatises of Government, 1690–1705," *Political Studies* 24 (1976):184–91.

[72] Isaac Kramnick, "Republican Revisionism Revisited," *American Historical Review* 87 (1982):629–64.

[73] For example, see "The Pennsylvania Convention: Debates," Merrill Jensen, John P. Kaminski, and Gaspare J. Saladino, eds., *The Documentary History of the Ratification of the Constitution*, 10 vols. to date (Madison, Wis., 1976-), 2:343, 354 (Nov. 24, 1787), 555 (Dec. 11, 1787) (hereafter cited as *DHR*).

Parliament was the only institution in society that could protect the nation's rights. As an observer explicitly put it in 1689, "Parliament is the Sovereign and only remedy for publick Distempers."[74] As we have seen, this confidence in Parliament was not new; throughout the century Englishmen regarded Parliament as the institution that protected subjects' rights. For this reason, as already insisted, parliamentary rights were necessary not only to the institution of Parliament but also to the security of the subject. In 1689 there was no thought among members of the Convention of protecting subjects' rights *against* Parliament. The consequences are of uncommon importance. In part because of the presumption that Parliament would protect subjects' rights and because the English government was not, as sometimes mistakenly thought, a government of separated powers, no enabling mechanism to protect the Bill of Rights was provided.

We need not in this essay enter the debate over the question of precisely when parliamentary sovereignty—that is to say, king-in-Parliament—was achieved and acknowledged. It is enough to declare that certainly by the early years of the eighteenth century change in Parliament's role had occurred. Over the seventeenth century the idea of parliamentary sovereignty had been aired as for example by Henry Parker and William Prynne during the Civil War and Cromwellian period and by some Whigs at the time of Exclusion.[75] In the thought of some political writers of the late Stuart era, the immemoriality of Parliament rather then the immemoriality of law became, as J. G. A. Pocock has insisted, the more important feature of the ancient constitution, a view that implies parliamentary sovereignty.[76] Arguably, in 1689 the idea of parlia-

[74] "Some Observations on the Prince of Orange's Declaration, in a Charge to the Grand Jury," in *Works of Warrington*, p. 365.

[75] Margaret Judson, "Henry Parker and the Theory of Parliamentary Sovereignty," in C. Wittke, ed., *Essays in Honor of Charles McIlwain* (New York, 1936), pp. 138–67; Robert J. Frankle, "Parliament's Right to Do Wrong: The Parliamentary Debate on the Bill of Attainder against Sir John Fenwick, 1696," *Parliamentary History* 4 (1985):72–73.

[76] Pocock, *Ancient Constitution*, p. 234.

mentary sovereignty inhered in the steps the Convention took.[77] In 1695, in the debate over the passage of an attainder against Sir John Fenwick, recent work has shown that members of all political persuasions agreed that Parliament possessed sovereign power.[78] In 1716 with the passage of the Septennial Act, scholars have long agreed, parliamentary sovereignty was surely practiced and acknowledged.[79] The theoretical implication for civil rights was that rights could no longer be claimed as immutable; logically they "existed at the pleasure and caprice of the legislature."[80] Only a few people, among them royalists and radicals during the Civil War and Locke and Tories during the Restoration and in the early eighteenth century, had perceived that a powerful danger could come *from* Parliament. It was left, of course, to eighteenth-century radicals in Great Britain and America to appreciate fully the danger implicit in the changed role of Parliament.

In the eighteenth century another strand of thought, known as the country or Commonwealth ideology, was developed by a group of radical thinkers including Bishop Benjamin Hoadly, John Trenchard and Thomas Gordon, and Robert Viscount Molesworth. These men formed a part of the opposition to the government. Drawing upon classical writers, English and European history, and seventeenth-century thinkers, such as Locke, Milton, and Algernon Sidney, they advanced their views in tracts, pamphlets, sermons, and especially in *Cato's Letters* (written by Trenchard and Gordon and published in the *London Journal* in the early 1720s). In such forums, they variously criticized the king and his ministers for, inter alia, maintaining a standing army in peacetime,

[77] Weston and Greenberg, *Subjects and Sovereigns,* and Schwoerer, *Declaration of Rights, 1689.*

[78] Frankle, "Parliament's Right to Do Wrong."

[79] H. T. Dickinson, "The Eighteenth-Century Debate on the Sovereignty of Parliament," *Transactions of the Royal Historical Society,* 5th ser. 26 (1976): 189–210.

[80] Reid, *Constitutional History,* p. 76.

exploiting the Crown's control of a vastly enlarged system of patronage to corrupt Parliament, and ruling Parliament through patronage and bribery to the destruction of English liberties and rights. Cato believed that the basis for laws of a state should be natural law, discoverable by man through his reason. The law that men create is, essentially, "right Reason, commanding things that are good, and forbidding Things that are bad." Thus, laws that do not correspond to natural law are theoretically nil.[81] Deeply distrustful of political power and fearful of the corruption of people and forms of government, Cato urged that restraints be placed on public officials. The people must "put Checks on those who would otherwise put Chains upon them."[82] Particularly alarmed by the growth in power of Parliament and by the corruption of that body, Cato declared that parliaments "should be bounded with many and strong restraints," for "power renders them wanton, insolent to others, and fond of themselves."[83] Concerned not only about the kind of government necessary to secure rights, Commonwealthmen were also intent upon assuring a virtuous people to sustain liberty; without virtue liberty was impossible. Trenchard and Gordon's advocacy of new reforms such as overhaul of rotten boroughs as a part of reform of Parliament, and new rights, such as freedom of the press and freedom of religion (which, as we have seen, had no part in the British Constitution) is another example of the historicity of rights. "Freedom of speech is the great Bulwark of Liberty," wrote Cato. It is "the Right of every Man, as far as by it he does not hurt or controul the Right of Another."[84] Trenchard's defense of religious toleration was impassioned. He wrote, "Every Religion which refuses to tolerate other Religions, charges itself, by so doing, with Tyranny and Imposture. For no Religion can be true that is not merciful, nor merciful if it

[81] Thomas Gordon and John Trenchard, *Cato's Letters, or, Essays on Liberty, Civil and Religious, and Other Important Subjects,* 3d ed., 4 vols. (London, 1733), No. 42, 2:64–65.

[82] Ibid., No. 60, 2:229–30.

[83] Quotation in Frankle, "Parliament's Right to Do Wrong," p. 81.

[84] Gordon and Trenchard, *Cato's Letters,* No. 15, 1:96, 100.

punishes Men for their Faith."[85] In similar terms, Molesworth declared that he looked "upon Bigotry to have always been the very Bane of human Society, and the Offspring of Interest and Ignorance, which has occasion'd most of the great Mischiefs that have afflicted Mankind."[86] Through the efforts of Thomas Hollis and Richard Baron, the ideas of the Commonwealthmen were passed along to successive generations of British theorists and to American Revolutionary leaders.[87] Bernard Bailyn has argued that this group of writers "more than any other single [one] . . . shaped the mind of the American Revolutionary generation."[88] In terms of rights theory and specific rights, they made available to Americans important ideas justifying rights that were not found in the common law tradition or in the documents comprising the British Constitution.

Renewed and heightened interest in rights theory and in adding new rights developed in Great Britain after 1760, and for my purposes the story continues there. At about that time significant changes were under way in political culture and party alignments, changes that were consequent upon such events as the accession of George III, the growing instability in France culminating in the French Revolution, and the dete-

[85] [John Trenchard], *A Collection of All the Political Letters in the London Journal to December 17, Inclusive, 1720* (London, 1721), No. 2, p. 6.

[86] [Robert Molesworth], *Franco-Gallia, or, an Account of the Ancient Free State of France, and Most Other Parts of Europe, before the Loss of Their Liberties, Written Originally in Latin by the Famous Civilian, Francis Hotoman, in the Year 1574. And Translated into English by the Author of the Account of Denmark. The Second Edition, with Additions, and a New Preface by the Translator* (London, 1721), p. xii. Significantly, the Preface was reprinted separately as *The Principles of a Real Whig, Contained in a Preface to the Famous Hotoman's Franco-Gallia . . . and Now Reprinted at the Request of the London Association* (London, 1775).

[87] Robbins, *The Eighteenth-Century Commonwealthman*, pioneered in tracing the transmission of their ideas through eighteenth-century Britain and its colonies.

[88] Ibid., for all of these men; Bailyn, *Ideological Origins*, pp. 35, 40–41, 44–46. See also J. G. A. Pocock, "The Varieties of Whiggism from Exclusion to Reform: A History of Ideology and Discourse," in Pocock, ed., *Virtue, Commerce, and History: Essays on Political Thought and History, Chiefly in the Eighteenth Century* (Cambridge, 1985), part 3, pp. 215–310.

riorating relations with the American colonies leading to the Declaration of Independence, the American Revolution, and the creation of a new and independent nation, the United States.[89] Within this political context, critics of the established government in Britain and of the class that dominated that government developed radical ideas about reform in politics and religion that they deployed in various ways.[90] They appealed to Commonwealth ideology and liberal Whig notions, revived interest in Locke's theories about natural rights and natural law, and at the same time claimed the ancient common law rights of Englishmen. They not only stressed the right to freedom of religion, press, and speech but also insisted upon the new right of a vastly enlarged number of men to vote. As was the case in earlier years, rights that were at issue in the late eighteenth century were designed to meet current needs.

One feature of radical thought was the rediscovery of John Locke's work[91] and the appeal to his ideas in support of contemporary political reforms. The anonymous author of *Reflexions on Representation in Parliament,* published in 1766, called upon Locke's ideas to reinforce his point that the people possess the power to reform the legislature when that body abuses its trust. In a strikingly new departure, he made "equal" representation "a question of right."[92] Ten years later John Cartwright wrote that "mankind universally have in all

---

[89] Compare John Brewer, *Party Ideology and Popular Politics at the Accession of George III* (Cambridge, 1976), chap. 1 for an overview. Also J. G. A. Pocock, "1776: The Revolution against Parliament," in Pocock, ed., *Three British Revolutions: 1641, 1688, 1776* (Princeton, 1980), pp. 265–88.

[90] For an overview, see H. T. Dickinson, *Liberty and Property: Political Ideology in Eighteenth-Century Britain* (New York, 1977), esp. chap. 6.

[91] Recently revisionist scholars have sharply challenged the idea that John Locke dominated political thought throughout the eighteenth century in Great Britain and the colonies. Counterrevisionists grant that Locke's role in the early eighteenth century has been overemphasized, but insist that Lockean ideas were central after 1760. See Kramnick, "Republican Revisionism Revisited"; Peter Laslett, ed., *John Locke's Two Treatises of Government* (London, 1965), pp. 121–29.

[92] Kramnick, "Republican Revisionism Revisited," p. 637.

ages had the same unalienable rights to liberty" and used that proposition to advance his contention that "all the commons have a right to vote in [parliamentary] elections."[93] Similarly, Capel Lofft invoked natural law and the social compact to buttress his campaign to reform Parliament, writing that British liberties are derived "from God, from the nature of man, and the nature and ends of society."[94] Clearly, radicals went beyond Locke in insisting that men had the right to the parliamentary vote.

Radicals also contested the idea of parliamentary sovereignty, seeing in it a threat to subjects' rights. For example, Obadiah Hulme was appalled that Parliament had the power in theory to make anything that they wished law and expressed the fear that Parliament "in the end, may make us slaves, by law." Also rejecting the concept of parliamentary sovereignty, John Wilkes described it as a "false and dangerous doctrine."[95] What these men wanted instead was theoretically popular sovereignty and practically a written constitution and judicial review.[96] Reform of Parliament and the vote was essential.

A rhetorical tactic that radicals used to underline the need for parliamentary reform, the right to petition, and the right to the vote of a wide sector of the male population was to offer brutal criticism of the 1689 Bill of Rights and the Revolution of 1688–89. In the vanguard of such criticism were James Burgh and Catherine Macaulay, both said to have deeply influenced Thomas Jefferson and other American leaders.[97] Committed to the idea of reforming Parliament, both censured the leaders of 1689 for moral turpitude in failing to protect the nation against factions and private interests and

[93] Quotation ibid., p. 639.

[94] Ibid., p. 648.

[95] Quotation in Dickinson, *Liberty and Property*, pp. 217, 222.

[96] Ibid., p. 217.

[97] H. Trevor Colbourn, "Jefferson's Use of the Past," *William and Mary Quarterly*, 3d ser. 15 (1958):65. Carla Hay, "The Making of a Radical: The Case of James Burgh," *Journal of British Studies* 18 (1979):114–16.

to address the corruption of Parliament.[98] Influenced by the Commonwealth ideology of mixed and balanced government, the idea of a mythic past when the balance actually worked, and Locke's ideas, Burgh excoriated Convention members as "unpardonabl[y] negligen[t]" and blamed them for the unbalance in Britain's government, the present "tyranny of ambitious and avaritious ministers." "The danger of all dangers; the evil of all evils," Burgh declared, is when "parliaments through influence and corruption are at the absolute command of the Court."[99] His solution was annual parliaments, redistribution of seats, and extension of the franchise to all but able-bodied males who refused to work. The people were sovereign, and they possessed the right, guaranteed by natural law, to elect their own representatives.[100]

Macaulay's views were similar and were also a combination of Commonwealth principles and Lockean ideology. She felt that as a result of the "wicked system" of 1688–89, Parliament could not serve as a bulwark of "our much boasted constitution."[101] In her view the idea of a "birthright" (as the proponents of the "ancient constitution" would have it) was both arrogant—no other nation claimed such a thing—and beggarly—it depended, Macaulay said, on the "alms" of the prince. The rights of the people could only be justified as "abstract." They were part of nature's laws. Legitimate government rested, she believed, in the will of the people.[102] Burgh and Macaulay did not speak the language of the ancient constitution, but still they wanted to restore the mixed and bal-

[98] Catherine Macaulay, *Observations on a Pamphlet, Entitled, Thoughts on the Cause of the Present Discontents* (London, 1770), pp. 10–11.

[99] James Burgh, *Political Disquisitions, or, An Enquiry into Public Errors, Defects, and Abuses. Illustrated by, and Established upon Facts and Remarks, Extracted from a Variety of Authors, Ancient and Modern*, 2 vols. (London, 1775), 2:365–66, 376, 406–7.

[100] Hay, "Making of a Radical," pp. 94, 96, 103, 105, 109–11.

[101] Macaulay, *Observations on a Pamphlet*, pp. 9–11, 16.

[102] Catherine Macaulay, *Observations on the Reflections of the Right Hon. Edmund Burke, on the Revolution in France, in a Letter to the Right Hon. the Earl of Stanhope* (Boston, 1791), pp. 5–6, 8, 12–13, 39.

anced government that they believed had flourished in the past.

Others, as for example Edward King, seem to have found appeals to England's past rather quaint. Picking up a thread in Commonwealth ideology about virtue and manners, King explained that the "degeneracy" in the government was a result of degeneracy in manners and insisted that civic improvement would occur only when improvements in learning, manners, industry, and commerce occurred. Then liberty would follow. There is no point, he thought, in trying to reconstitute some mythic past. As he put it, "The resemblance between the present constitution and that from which it originally sprung, is not much nearer . . . than that between the most beautiful fly and the abject worm from which it arose."[103]

A second rhetorical tactic the radicals employed was to rehabilitate the Bill of Rights and to evoke it and the Glorious Revolution in support of radical reforms and claims of rights. The centenary of the Revolution in 1788 was widely celebrated and the Revolution itself and the Bill of Rights warmly commended.[104] For example, an anonymous contributor to the *Public Advertiser* praised the 1689 Convention for legalizing the "natural right of resistance" and enjoined his countrymen to keep the memory of the Bill of Rights green: "Write it on your door-ways," he said. "Mark it on your forehead; but, above all, let it be indelibly impressed on your hearts."[105]

This zeal for the Bill of Rights accelerated upon the outbreak of the French Revolution in 1789. The radical Dissenting clergyman Dr. Richard Price in a famous sermon, *A Discourse on the Love of Our Country,* praised the earlier English revolution for asserting the rights of the people and emancipating conscience and inquiry, things which that revolu-

---

[103] Edward King, *An Essay on the English Constitution and Government* (London, 1767), p. 17.

[104] Lois G. Schwoerer, "Celebrating the Glorious Revolution, 1689–1989," *Albion* 19 (1990):1–19; Kathleen Wilson, "Inventing Revolution: 1688 and Eighteenth-Century Popular Politics," *Journal of British Studies* 28 (1989):349–86.

[105] "Letter VI to the People of Great Britain and Ireland," *Public Advertiser* (London), Nov. 1, 1788.

tion had not, in fact, achieved. Describing the Revolution of 1688–89 as "a great work, [but] by no means a perfect work," Price demanded further changes, such as religious toleration, an end to parliamentary corruption, freedom of speech, and freedom of the press.[106] Here was a call for rights that could not be found in the English common law or in the documents of the British Constitution. It was erected upon the ideas of natural law and natural rights.

Conservatives, none more so than Edmund Burke, vehemently rejected Price's radical sentiments. In his *Reflections on the Revolution in France*, Burke dismissed Price's political principles as a "hitherto un-heard of bill of rights" not justified by the Glorious Revolution. Describing the Bill of Rights as the "cornerstone of our constitution," Burke insisted that the document had restored the nation's ancient "indisputable laws and liberties" and argued that those rights were the nation's "entailed inheritance."[107] No further change was needed, he maintained. For generations, it was Burke's reading of the Bill of Rights and his conceptualization of rights that prevailed in Great Britain, although his interpretation was, of course, not popular in the United States. As the French Revolution moved from excess to excess and war with France began, conservatism descended on Great Britain.

The call for rights and reform went unheeded in late eighteenth-century Britain. But interest did not entirely disappear. One example, notable for its exuberant conflation of Commonwealth ideology, Lockean liberalism, and ancient constitutionalism, was the publication in 1793 of the charters of London along with Magna Charta and the 1689 Bill of Rights. The compiler, John Luffman, "Citizen and Goldsmith of London," explained that by 1688–89 the English "Constitution" as established by the "sacred authority of MAGNA CHARTA" had become impaired by the actions of the late Stu-

---

[106] *A Discourse on the Love of Our Country. Delivered on Nov. 4, 1789, at the Meeting-House in the Old Jewry. To the Society for Commemorating the Revolution in Great Britain* (London, 1790), pp. 29–30.

[107] Edmund Burke, *Reflections on the Revolution in France*, ed. J. G. A. Pocock (Indianapolis, 1987), pp. 14–16, 20, 27–29.

art kings. But, he went on, at the "moment" that the Prince of Orange acknowledged the Declaration of Rights as "the supreme law," the "constitution became renovated, the power of the Crown was acknowledged to flow from its only natural force, the people." He concluded, "The offspring of this connexion is the genuine RIGHTS OF MAN."[108]

If the Americans who drafted this nation's federal Bill of Rights had had "at hand" or "in mind" *only* the models provided by the British Constitution, they could not have written our Bill of Rights as they did. But Americans were the heirs of multilayered British lineages respecting rights theory and specific rights. Lists of their libraries prove the availability of books that explicated these lineages, and debates and tracts show by inclusion of references to ideas and particular authors that Americans had read widely.[109] Americans, however, did not passively absorb these lineages; rather they showed a striking inventiveness in weaving them together.

Of primary importance to Americans in drafting our Bill of Rights and selecting the individual rights to be claimed was the heritage of the English common law and the British Constitution. Americans lifted vocabulary and ideas from Magna Charta, the Petition of Right, the Bill of Rights, and other laws such as habeas corpus. They drew upon the work of seventeenth-century lawyers, like Coke, and eighteenth-century legal commentators, like Sir William Blackstone. Our Bill of Rights protects us against billeting of soldiers, provides us the right to a jury trial and due process of law in legal procedures,

---

[108] John Luffman, comp., *The Charters of London Complete; also Magna Charta and the Bill of Rights. With Explanatory Notes and Remarks* (London, 1793), p. 420.

[109] See, for example, Greene, *Intellectual Heritage;* Loren E. Smith, ed., *The Library List of 1783: Being a Catalogue of Books, Composed and Arranged by James Madison, and Others, and Recommended for the Use of Congress on January 24, 1783* (Ann Arbor, Mich., 1985); M. Jennings, *The Library of the College of William and Mary in Virginia, 1693–1793* (Charlottesville, Va., 1968); E. Millicent Sowerby, ed., *Catalogue of the Library of Thomas Jefferson* (Washington, D.C., 1952).

and prohibits excessive bail, excessive fines, and cruel and unusual punishments, just as do English precedents.

But Americans did not limit their rights to those found in those sources alone. Thomas Jefferson identified six rights as essential to the new nation, including freedom of religion, freedom of the press, and restrictions against monopolies as well as the legal rights and the provision against standing armies that were found in the English Bill of Rights.[110] In debates in June 1789 in the House of Representatives on the proposed claim of rights, James Madison pointed out that "the freedom of the press, and the rights of conscience, those choicest flowers in the prerogative of the people, are not guarded by the British Constitution."[111] Americans looked beyond the British Constitution and drew upon another lineage, that of natural law. As early as 1646 the Massachusetts General Court maintained that the foundation of all laws was God's law and right reason.[112] John Dickinson elaborated the point in 1766, declaring that the rights of Americans "are not annexed to us by parchments and seals. They are created in us by the decrees of Providence. They are born with us; . . . In short, they are founded on the immutable maxims of reason and justice." Alexander Hamilton made a similar remark in 1775, saying, "The sacred rights of mankind are not to be rummaged for among old parchments or musty records."[113] These are clear appeals to natural law.

Too much should not be made of a dichotomy between the ancient constitution and natural law, as is sometimes done. It will be remembered that earlier English theorists had said that the ancient constitution was essentially the application of natural law to specific matters, and Blackstone's *Commentaries*

[110] Thomas Jefferson to James Madison, Dec. 20, 1787, Julian P. Boyd et al., eds., *The Papers of Thomas Jefferson*, 28 vols. to date (Princeton, 1950–), 12:440.

[111] Helen E. Veit, Kenneth R. Bowling, and Charlene Bangs Bickford, eds., *Creating the Bill of Rights: The Documentary Record from the First Federal Congress* (Baltimore, 1991), pp. 66, 80.

[112] Wood, *Creation of the American Republic*, p. 295.

[113] Quotation in Bailyn, *Ideological Origins*, pp. 187–88.

contained the same point. Samuel Adams regarded the English Bill of Rights as a "bulwark to the natural rights of subjects."[114]

The appeal to natural law, however, seems to me to be more than simply rhetorical.[115] As early as 1764, as we saw at the beginning of this essay, some people were sensitive to the fact that the British Constitution, alone, was not enough as a basis for American rights. After Independence and even more after the adoption of a new Constitution, Americans invoked the authority of natural law. In 1787 a tract writer declared that the "natural, indefeasible and unalienable rights of mankind form the most eligible ground on which we now stand." In the debate on ratifying the Constitution in the Pennsylvania ratification convention, James Wilson insisted that "the Conduct of [England] in respect to bills of rights cannot furnish an example to the inhabitants of the United States, who by the Revolution have regained all the natural rights."[116] In that debate some spokesmen sought to distance themselves from Great Britain. They described English common law rights as grants from the king, when, as we have seen, in English theory they were regarded as beyond the reach of the king, rooted in immemorial custom. By claiming that English rights *were* grants from the king, Americans distinguished their rights from those of Great Britain. American rights were grounded in the people on the basis of natural rights.[117] Such theoretical underpinnings assisted Americans in adding to their claim the rights of freedom of religion, freedom of speech, and freedom of the press, which had no foundation in English or British law.

[114] Harry Alonzo Cushing, ed., *The Writings of Samuel Adams*, 4 vols. (New York, 1904–8), 1:317.

[115] Reid, *Constitutional History*, pp. 87–92.

[116] "A Democratic Federalist" [Tench Coxe?], *Independent Gazetteer* (Philadelphia), Nov. 26, 1787, *DHR*, 2:298; "The Pennsylvania Convention: Debates," ibid., p. 391 (Nov. 28, 1787), compare p. 430 (Nov. 30, 1787). The speaker at the Pennsylvania ratification convention was James Wilson.

[117] "The Pennsylvania Convention: Debates," ibid., p. 391 (Nov. 28, 1787), compare p. 430 (Nov. 30, 1787).

THE BILL OF RIGHTS

Americans had to break with the prevailing British belief that Parliament was the guardian of rights and liberties and from the British practice of investing in Parliament supreme power. James Wilson, in making the point that supreme power should be vested in the people, underscored the uncontrolled power of the British Parliament: "The British Constitution is just what the British Parliament pleases."[118] Such, too, was the position of William Loughton Smith, member of the House of Representatives from South Carolina. In warning against the power of the legislature, he said flatly that the "constitution of Britain is neither the magna charta of John, nor the Habeas Corpus act, nor all the charters put together; it is what the parliament wills."[119] Noting that the 1689 Bill of Rights only raised a barrier against the power of the Crown, not the Parliament, Madison declared that in the United States men felt it important to limit also the authority of the legislature.[120] Jefferson concurred, writing to Francis Hopkinson that he looked to a bill of rights "to guard liberty against the legislature as well as the executive branches of government."[121] This perception owed a lot to colonial experience, but in the realm of theory, Americans had "at hand" and "in mind" the British Commonwealth heritage and the views of late eighteenth-century British radicals. From such lineages they drew well-developed criticism of Parliament. The experience of Great Britain also well illustrated for Americans that rights embodied in a statute were dependent upon Parliament. For this and other reasons, Americans identified the source of rights as not only common law, but also natural law and the natural rights of the people.

The Commonwealth heritage also supplied Americans with theories about a mixed government of separated powers. Americans maintained that it is the structure of government—mixed and with powers separated—that will ensure

[118] Ibid., pp. 361–62 (Nov. 24, 1787).

[119] Veit, Bowling, and Bickford, eds., *Creating the Bill of Rights*, p. 126.

[120] Ibid., p. 80.

[121] Jefferson to Francis Hopkinson, Mar. 13, 1789, in Boyd et al., eds., *Papers of Jefferson*, 14:650.

the sanctity of rights. It was Jefferson's brilliant insight (which, in turn, was compatible with a reading of Lord Coke's ruling in Bonham's Case) that assisted Americans to recognize that judicial review would help secure rights from Madison's bête noire, the tyranny of the majority. In a letter to Madison in March 1789, Jefferson referred to an argument in favor of a claim of rights "which has a great weight with me, the legal check which it puts into the hands of the judiciary. This is a body, which if rendered independent, & kept strictly to their own department merits great confidence for their learning & integrity."[122] The argument apparently found favor with Madison, who in debate in June 1789 used it in support of a bill of rights, saying that if rights were "incorporated into the constitution, independent tribunals of justice will consider themselves in a peculiar manner the guardians of those rights; they will be an impenetrable bulwark against every assumption of power in the legislative; they will be naturally led to resist every encroachment upon rights expressly stipulated for in the constitution by the declaration of rights."[123] Also following the lead of Commonwealthmen in their concern for virtue, Americans expressed the need of a virtuous people to protect rights and at the same time suggested that a bill of rights would improve the "spirit of the people."[124]

The rights that our Founding Fathers compiled were different in significant details (other than those already mentioned) from those they inherited. Two details merit special attention. The first article of the American Bill of Rights provides an unbounded right of free speech for all persons, subject only to the restraints of the law of slander—and so, too, does the eleventh article of the French Declaration of the Rights of Man. But in early modern England no such right for all people existed or was ever claimed. The claim about free

[122] Jefferson to Madison, Mar. 15, 1789, reprinted in Veit, Bowling, and Bickford, eds., *Creating the Bill of Rights*, p. 219. The point is stressed in an unpublished paper by David N. Mayer, "'Parchment Barriers?' The Jefferson-Madison Dialogue and English Real Whig Influences on the American Bill of Rights."

[123] Veit, Bowling, and Bickford, eds., *Creating the Bill of Rights*, pp. 83–84.

[124] Ralph L. Ketcham, *James Madison: A Biography* (New York, 1971), p. 46.

speech, entered in 1689, was the right of freedom of speech for members of Parliament in parliamentary debates. That claim, as already noted, went back to the reign of Henry VIII. In fact, freedom of speech within Parliament was not always observed by the Crown as protests in 1604, 1621, 1641, 1667, and 1668 illustrate. Finally, by the Bill of Rights, the right became law. At no time in seventeenth-century England did the claim of liberty of speech extend to M.P.s outside of Parliament, much less to ordinary people. The history of parliamentary freedom of speech effectively illustrates how a privilege, or grant from the king, became over time a right for some people.

Freedom of speech for the individual *outside* Parliament was not achieved in seventeenth-century England nor did it advance progressively as the years went by. No British law guarantees it. Faced with war, security of the state, and terrorism, especially from Northern Ireland, successive governments placed restrictions on free expression in the early nineteenth century, again during the wars of the twentieth century, and in the 1980s. For example, the government banned from British radio and television interviews with members of the I.R.A. and other terrorist groups and with Sinn Fein. And the government has sought legislation to forbid any present, past, and future member of the nation's intelligence services to reveal anything about those services without authorization. The right of free speech in Britain is not "inalienable" as it is in the United States. The view of the queen's counsel is that the principle of confidentiality of government secrets takes precedence over the principle of free speech. He is reported as saying, "There is simply no room for saying freedom of speech is important [by comparison]."[125] The difference with the American claim and practice is striking.

The restrictive character of the English concept of individual rights appears also in the closely related issue of freedom of the press. The first clause in the American Bill of Rights and the eleventh article of the French Declaration guarantee

---

[125] Peter Jenkins, "Not-So-Free Speech in Britain," *New York Review of Books*, Dec. 8, 1988, p. 18; Craig R. Whitney, "The Appeal of a British Bill of Rights," *New York Times*, Dec. 11, 1988.

the right to a free press, that is the right of every person to print what he or she wishes, without prepublication censorship, but subject to libel law and laws of decency. No such right appears in the English Bill of Rights, nor was the issue noticed in the debates of the Convention (if the surviving accounts are accurate), or in printed matter published at the time of the Revolution, except for one tract.[126] The leaders of the Glorious Revolution did not inherit a well-developed principle of liberty of the press, nor did they articulate one.[127] On the contrary, although they themselves deliberately and freely violated the government's restrictions on printing during the months of revolution, as soon as they were in a position of power they not only reimposed the same system of prepublication censorship of books, pamphlets, and newspapers that the previous government had used, but they reaffirmed earlier parliamentary orders to prevent the printing of news of Parliament's activities and the free access to its chambers.

It was not the Bill of Rights but new political, international, social, and economic conditions that followed the Revolution of 1689 that made press restraints increasingly unpopular and difficult to enforce. In 1695 Parliament allowed the Licensing Act, which had come up for renewal, to lapse. Freed from the cumbersome procedure of prepublication licensing, authors and printers were made subject to the law of libel and to other different kinds of restrictions. Nothing was done in 1695 about allowing free reporting of debates of Parliament. That was not achieved until the 1770s, and access of the press to both houses was not allowed until the nineteenth century. In 1975 television cameras were placed in the houses, but the earlier restrictions were not repealed. Late twentieth-century observers have charged that Parliament takes more seriously infringements of its prerogatives than threats the executive

[126] Edmund Hickeringill, *A Speech With-out Doors, or, Some Modest Inquiries Humbly Proposed to the Right Honourable the Convention of Estates, Assembled at Westminster, January 22, 1689* (London, 1689).

[127] These points are developed in my "Liberty of the Press and Public Opinion, 1660–1695," in J. R. Jones, ed., *Liberty Secured? Britain before and after 1688* (Stanford, Calif., 1992), 199–230.

offers to freedom of the press.[128] In the 1980s the British government, in the interests of national security and its war against terrorism, sought to restrict what may be printed as well as spoken. The most famous case is that against Peter Wright for his book *Spy Catcher*, which revealed techniques used by MI5 and MI6 against suspected spies and charged that a leader at the highest reaches of MI5 had been converted to Communism and operated as a "mole" for years. Critics of Great Britain's system of British party government (especially critics of former Prime Minister Margaret Thatcher) maintain that the government in power able to command a majority in the House of Commons possesses virtually unlimited power, and thus can, and sometime does, ride roughshod over civil rights. The British do not enjoy the protections that are laid out in the American Bill of Rights.

In sum, Americans in the late eighteenth century adapted to their own needs the rights-theory and specific rights that were part of their British inheritance. In developing an understanding of civil rights and identifying express rights to meet their perceived grievances, Americans used generally the same vocabulary and ideas that English and British critics had employed in the seventeenth and eighteenth centuries. Our Founding Fathers constructed a Bill of Rights that blended British intellectual lineages: they joined the theories of the common law and the specifics of England's great constitutional documents to commonwealth ideology and the doctrine of natural rights. In such fashion they crafted a document that responded to the needs of a different society in a different era, once more illustrating how time-specific rights are. At the same time Americans strove to make their rights permanent; they "constitutionalized" them by appending them to the Constitution as amendments. In a way roughly parallel to the step taken by their English ancestors in 1689 when they linked their claim of rights to the political settlement of the Revolution, Americans attached their Bill of Rights to the Constitution rather than gathering rights in a separate document. The effect was to elevate the importance of rights and to protect them. The Constitution may be

---

[128] Jenkins, "Not-So-Free Speech," p. 17.

amended, of course, but the process is difficult; to remove, change, or add rights requires a constitutional amendment. The choices our Founding Fathers made respecting rights substantially modified the terms of the British lineages that they had inherited. Testimony to their political skill is their success in making the results—our Bill of Rights—permanent.

DONALD S. LUTZ

The Pedigree of the Bill of Rights

WHY SHOULD WE be interested in the lineage from which we derived the Bill of Rights? What difference does it make if we do or do not know its pedigree? Even if we grant that history provides knowledge valuable for its own sake, when it comes to the Bill of Rights do we need to know more than the fact of its existence and its contents to make use of the document today? As it turns out, knowledge about the document's pedigree may make a great deal of difference in how we understand, think about, and use rights today and in the future.

As we seek the pedigree of the Bill of Rights we are examining the evolution of rights consciousness in the Anglo-American world. Seeking this pedigree teaches us how important it is to recognize that the idea of rights did not suddenly emerge full-blown into a widely accepted, unambiguous concept. Equally important, the search teaches us that no list of rights has emerged, including the Bill of Rights, that represents the definitive codification of rights consciousness. The process of an evolving rights consciousness continues to this day and will continue into the indefinite future. It is worth learning anew that the Bill of Rights was not simply handed to future generations for veneration. It is more in the nature of a promise, a promise that if we continue to reflect on the nature of rights we will come to understand them better, and the Bill of Rights will stand as part of the pedigree to our own understanding.

Even though the exercise of seeking a pedigree turns out to be useful and possibly important, it ends up raising more questions than it answers. What causal mechanisms drive the evolution of rights consciousness? Are there psychological processes that undergird liberty, a psychology of hope, possibility, community, redemption, or fulfillment? Are there logical imperatives in social relationships that are unleashed by certain historical conditions, conditions that may be accidental? To what extent does economic need, the search for power, and the tendency of politics to substitute persuasion for force enhance, define, or undergird the evolution of rights consciousness? Who or what part of the population carries this rights consciousness? What conditions hinder or destroy the process?

The search for a pedigree is one way to pursue these questions, but what constitutes a pedigree? How do we construct one? The political theorist answers this question in a manner different from that of the historian. A political theorist is more interested in the meaning of ideas than in the reconstruction of a continuous stream of events. A political scientist might examine rights consciousness in a population through public opinion surveys, but the rights consciousness that we need to tap in order to establish a pedigree nestles invisibly in the brains of many people now long dead and beyond interview. Instead, we examine the public documents in which a people express their accepted, collective understanding of rights so that linked political documents serve as the record of the pedigree as well as the signposts for an evolving rights consciousness. The examination that follows will be limited by the approach used, but the evidence so mustered strongly suggests ways in which we must recapture and rethink our rights tradition.

THE ENGLISH BACKGROUND

As with the Declaration of Independence and the Constitution, the first thing to get clear about the Bill of Rights is that it was neither the sudden, original, spontaneous product of a few minds nor an updated American version of Magna Charta. The Bill of Rights had a long historical pedigree, but that pedigree lay substantially more in documents written on American shores.

One way of demonstrating the relative influence of Magna Charta on the Bill of Rights is a count of overlapping provisions. The Bill of Rights has twenty-six separate rights listed in its ten amendments. As table 1 shows, only four of these

43

Table 1. First statement of rights in Bill of Rights

Bill of Rights guarantee	First document protecting	First American guarantee	First constitutional guarantee
Establishment of religion	Rights of colonists	Same (Boston)	N.J. Constitution Art. XIX
Free exercise of religion	Md. Act Concerning Religion	Same	Va. Declaration of Rights, Sec. 16
Free speech	Mass. Body of Liberties, Sec. 12	Same	Pa. Declaration of Rights, Art. XII
Free press	Address to Inhabitants of Quebec	Same	Va. Declaration of Rights, Sec. 12
Assembly	Declaration & Resolves of Continental Congress	Same	Pa. Declaration of Rights, Art. XVI
Petition	Bill of Rights (England, 1689)	Declaration of Rights and Grievances (1765), Sec. XIII	Pa. Declaration of Rights, Art. XVI
Right to bear arms	Bill of Rights (England, 1689)	Pa. Declaration of Rights, Art. XIII	Same
Quartering soldiers	Petition of Right (England), Sec. VI	N.Y. Charter of Liberties	Del. Declaration of Rights, Sec. 21
Searches	Rights of colonists	Same (Boston)	Va. Declaration of Rights, Sec. 10
Seizures	Magna Charta Chap. 39	Va. Declaration of Rights, Sec. 10	Same
Grand jury	N.Y. Charter of of Liberties	Same	N.C. Declaration of Rights, Art. VIII
Double jeopardy	Mass. Body of Liberties, Sec. 42	Same	N.H. Bill of Rights, Art. XVI
Self-incrimination	Va. Declaration of Rights, Sec. 8	Same	Same

Due process	Magna Charta Chap. 39	Md. Act for Liberty of People	Va. Declaration of Rights, Sec. 8
Just compensation	Mass. Body of Liberties, Sec. 8	Same	Vt. Declaration of Rights, Art. II
Speedy trial	Va. Declaration of Rights, Sec. 8	Same	Same
Jury trial	Magna Charta Chap. 39	Mass. Body of Liberties, Sec. 29	Va. Declaration of Rights, Sec. 8
Cause & nature of accusation	Va. Declaration of Rights, Sec. 8	Same	Same
Witnesses	Pa. Charter of Privileges, Art. V	Same	N.J. Constitution, Art. XVI
Counsel	Mass. Body of Liberties, Sec. 29	Same	N.J. Constitution, Art. XVI
Jury trial (civil)	Mass. Body of Liberties, Sec. 29	Same	Va. Declaration of Rights, Sec. 11
Bail	Mass. Body of Liberties, Sec. 18	Same	Va. Declaration of Rights, Sec. 9
Fines	Magna Charta Chaps. 20–22	Pa. Frame of Government, Sec. XVIII	Va. Declaration of Rights, Sec. 9
Punishment	Mass. Body of Liberties, Secs. 43, 46	Same	Va. Declaration of Rights, Sec. 9
Rights retained by people	Va. Constitution, proposed Amendment 17	Same	Ninth Amendment
Reserved powers	Mass. Declaration of Rights, Art. IV	Same	

SOURCES: Bernard Schwartz, comp., *The Roots of the Bill of Rights*, 5 vols. (New York, 1980), 5:1204. Contrary to Schwartz, this author attributes more to English common law documents. Schwartz attributes the first prohibition on the quartering of troops to the 1683 New York Charter of Liberties instead of the 1628 Petition of Right in England; and he attributes the first prohibition against excessive fines to the 1682 Pennsylvania Frame of Government, whereas it is here attributed to Magna Charta. The difficulty in such attributions lies in the English version always being somewhat different in intent and application, as well as usually being less explicit and sweeping in expression.

twenty-six can be traced to Magna Charta using the most generous interpretation of the language in that famous document. Looking at it from the other direction, only four of the sixty-three provisions in Magna Charta ended up in the Bill of Rights. The lack of overlap is not surprising since Magna Charta and the Bill of Rights had enormously different functions. The former defined the relationship between a king and his barons, whereas the latter placed limits on all branches of a government vis-à-vis an entire citizenry.

Despite the enormous historical importance of Magna Charta, in content, form, and intent it is only a distant forerunner of the Bill of Rights. Nor is the overlap with the rest of English common law, although important, that impressive. In addition to the four rights that can be traced to Magna Charta, another right in the Bill of Rights can be traced to the 1628 English Petition of Right, and two to the 1689 English Bill of Rights.[1] This brings to seven the number of rights among the twenty-six in the Bill of Rights that can be traced to a major English common law document, although the highly respected scholar Bernard Schwartz is only willing to make such a linkage for five of these seven rights.

Furthermore, as writers on the English common law always point out, Magna Charta had to be continually reconfirmed, at least forty-seven times by one count, because the document was ignored for long periods of time, and its contents were at best honored in the breach.[2] Indeed, despite the written guarantees for certain rights contained in major documents of English common law, at the time of the American Revolution these rights were either not protected at all or were not protected to the level that had become the case in America.[3]

Even in those instances where protection of a right in England approached that in America, there was a fundamental difference in whose actions were limited. Partly for this reason

[1] The author has relied upon the texts as found in Richard L. Perry, ed., *Sources of Our Liberties* (New York, 1959), pp. 11–22, 73–75, and 245–50.

[2] See, for example, ibid., pp. 23–24.

[3] See Bernard Schwartz, *The Great Rights of Mankind: A History of the American Bill of Rights* (New York, 1977), p. 197; as well as Irving Brant, *The Bill of Rights: Its Origin and Meaning* (Indianapolis, 1965), esp. chaps. 5 and 6.

James Madison said that there were too many differences between common law and the Bill of Rights to warrant comparison.

> [The] truth is, they [the British] have gone no farther than to raise a barrier against the power of the Crown; the power of the Legislature is left altogether too indefinite. Although I know whenever the great rights, the trial by jury, freedom of the press, or liberty of conscience, come in question [in Parliament] the invasion of them is resisted by able advocates, yet their Magna Charta does not contain any one provision for the security of those rights, respecting which the people of America are most alarmed . . . those choicest privileges of the people are unguarded in the British Constitution. But although . . . it may not be thought necessary to provide limits for the legislative power in that country, yet a different opinion prevails in the United States.[4]

At the very least, then, the attribution of the American Bill of Rights to English common law and its major documents such as Magna Charta must be supplemented, and as table 1 indicates, it is to documents written on American shores that we must turn.

THE IMMEDIATE AMERICAN BACKGROUND

It is natural to assume that James Madison used the amendments proposed by the state ratifying conventions when he produced his own list of proposed amendments for Congress. After all, eight of these ratifying conventions had together proposed ninety-seven distinct amendments, and it was the opposition to the Constitution represented by these proposed amendments that Madison needed to address. However, as table 2 illustrates, the forty-two distinct rights contained in Madison's nine proposed amendments, listed in the order he gave them as numbers 1–42 in the table, bear only slight relation to what was proposed by the ratifying conventions.

Twenty-six of the amendments proposed by the ratifying conventions ended up on Madison's list, but seventy-one did

---

[4] *Annals of Congress,* 1st Cong., 1st sess., p. 436.

Table 2. Amendments proposed by state ratifying conventions compared with Madison's original proposed amendments

	Pa.	Mass.	Md.	S.C.	N.H.	Va.	N.Y.	N.C.	Madison
1. Power derived from people									X
2. Government exercised for common good									X
3. Life, liberty, property, and happiness	X	X	X						X
4. Right of people to change government									X
5. Number of representatives					X	X	X	X	X
6. Congressional raises						X	X	X	X
7. Religious freedom	X		X	X	X				X
8. Right of conscience	X				X				X
9. Free speech	X		X						X
10. Free to write	X		X						X
11. Free press	X		X						X
12. Assembly									X
13. Petition and remonstrance									X
14. Bear arms	X				X				X
15. Pacifists—no arms									X
16. No quartering in peacetime			X		X				X
17. No quartering without warrant									X
18. Double jeopardy			X						X
19. No double punishment									X
20. Self-incrimination	X								X
21. Due process of law			X						X
22. Compensate for property taken									X
23. Excessive bail or fines	X								X
24. Cruel and unusual punishment	X								X

	1	2	3	4	5	6	7
25. Search and seizure trial	X						X
26. Speedy and public trial	X	X					X
27. Told nature of crime	X						X
28. Confronted with accusers	X						X
29. Witnesses for defense		X					X
30. Right to counsel	X						X
31. Rights retained by states or people							X
32. No implied powers for Congress					X		X
33. No state may violate 8, 9, 11, or 26 above						X	X
34. Appeal limited by $ amount	X						X
35. Jury cannot be bypassed							X
36. Impartial jury from vicinity	X						X
37. Jury unanimity							X
38. Right to challenge judicial decision	X	X					X
39. Grand jury			X	X			X
40. Jury trial for civil cases	X	X	X	X			X
41. Separation of powers	X	X	X	X			X
42. Powers reserved to states	X	X	X	X	X	X	X
43. Limit national taxing power	X	X	X	X			X
44. No limit on state taxes	X			X			X
45. No federal election regulation	X	X	X	X	X		X
46. Free elections	X				X	X	X
47. No standing army	X				X	X	X
48. State control of militia	X						X
49. State sovereignty retained	X	X				X	X
50. Limits on judicial power	X				X	X	X
51. Treaties accord w/ state law	X						X
52. National & state courts have concurrent jurisdiction	X						X

49

Table 2. Continued

	Pa.	Mass.	Md.	S.C.	N.H.	Va.	N.Y.	N.C.	Madison
53. No infringing of state constitutions	X		X				X		
54. State courts used as lower federal courts					X		X		
55. Can appeal Supreme Court decisions									
56. Defend oneself in court	X					X	X	X	
57. Civil control of military	X								
58. Liberty to fish, fowl, and hunt	X								
59. Advisory council for president	X								
60. Independent judiciary	X								
61. State courts used if less than x$		X							
62. Trial in state where crime occurs		X							
63. Judges hold no other office		X							
64. 4-year limit on military service					X	X			
65. Limit on martial law			X		X	X			
66. No monopolies		X			X		X		
67. Citizens of two states—no jurisdiction		X					X	X	
68. No titles of nobility		X							
69. Keep a congressional record						X		X	
70. Publish info. on national use of money						X		X	
71. Two-thirds of Senate to ratify commerce treaties						X		X	
72. Two-thirds of both houses for navigation and commerce legislation						X		X	
73. Limit on regulation of D.C.						X	X		
74. Presidential term—8 out of 16 yrs.						X			
75. President limited to two terms						X	X	X	
76. Add state judges to impeach						X	X	X	

77. Senate doesn't impeach senators
78. Limit use of militia out of state
79. Judicial salaries not changed
80. Requirements for being president
81. Two-thirds of both houses to borrow money
82. Two-thirds of Congress to declare war
83. Habeas corpus
84. Congress sessions to be open
85. No consecutive terms—Senate
86. State legislatures fill vacant Senate seats
87. Limit on lower courts
88. No duties to a particular state
89. No interference in paper money
90. No foreign troops
91. State law used on military bases
92. No multiple officeholding
93. Limit on bankruptcy laws
94. No presidential pardon for treason
95. President not field commander
96. Official form for president's acts
97. No poll tax

SOURCES: The first forty-two rights are arranged in the order used by James Madison in his version sent to the House of Representatives. Going from left to right, the states are arranged in the order their ratifying conventions produced a list of recommended amendments, from earliest to latest. The proposed amendments for each state are taken from Merrill Jensen, John P. Kaminski, Gaspare J. Saladino, eds., *The Documentary History of the Ratification of the Constitution*, 10 vols. to date (Madison, Wis., 1976–); and Madison's forty-two proposed rights are based upon an examination of the original document in the National Archives.

not. Sixteen rights proposed by Madison were not suggested by any ratifying convention. Nor was there a very "dense" connection between Madison's list and the amendments proposed by the ratifying conventions as can be illustrated by using a very crude measure of association.

The data on state ratifying conventions in table 2 constitute a matrix that is 8 cells wide and 97 cells from top to bottom. The more cells that have an X in them for the matrix defined by the top forty-two rows (that is, the more state ratifying conventions that proposed one of the amendments that ended up in Madison's list), the denser the relationship between Madison's list and the convention proposals. Eighteen percent of the cells are filled (60 out of 336 cells), which does not suggest a very "dense" relationship between the ratifying conventions' proposals and Madison's list of rights. On the other hand, 24 percent of the cells in the matrix defined by the last fifty-five rows have an X in them (107 out of 440 cells). These proposals, not included in Madison's list, were thus somewhat more likely to be recommended by a state ratifying convention than those he did include. This finding suggests that Madison avoided their more preferred recommendations.

The last conclusion can also be supported by looking at the proposed amendments made by the ratifying conventions that most directly addressed the protection of state sovereignty. Numbers 31, 32, and 42–53 seem to be the best candidates, and only three of these fourteen proposals made it onto Madison's list. The density for these fourteen proposals is 42 percent (47 out of 112 cells), which makes them more than twice as likely to be recommended by a state as those actually picked by Madison, and about twice as likely as the average proposal in the table as a whole (167 out of 776 cells = 21 percent)—which suggests a strong interest in state sovereignty by the state ratifying conventions but a disinterest on Madison's part.

Madison apparently wished to avoid the amendments proposed by the ratifying conventions, but he needed to make some connection with state interests to mollify the Antifederalists. The tactic he fastened upon was to exploit seams in the Antifederalist position on what amendments to make. Americans who argued most vigorously against the proposed Constitution offered three different kinds of amendments that were often intertwined and confused. One type of amendment was aimed at checking the power of the national government by withholding a specific power. Examples included prohibitions on direct taxes, monopolies, and borrowing money on credit. A second type of amendment altered an institution in such a way as to pull its teeth. Examples included making senators ineligible for consecutive terms, giving state and national courts concurrent jurisdiction, and requiring a two-thirds vote in both houses for any bill dealing with navigation or commerce.

A third type of amendment was one suitable for a bill of rights as we now understand it. Examples included protection of the rights to speak, write, publish, assemble, and petition (rights that safeguarded the ability of a people to organize politically), as well as prohibitions on self-incrimination, double punishment, excessive bail, and searches without a warrant (rights that defined an impartial legal system). One can see in Madison's selection process a clear inclination toward the third over the first two kinds of amendments.

In effect, then, Madison avoided any alteration in the institutions defined by the Constitution, largely ignored specific prohibitions on national power, and opted instead for a list of rights that would connect clearly with the preferences of state governments but would not increase state power vis-à-vis the national government defined in the Constitution. The discussion about powers and rights was subtly shifted to one only about rights.

This finesse upset some Antifederalists who argued that he had thrown "a tub to a whale" (that is, had created a distraction to deflect public attention from the real issue), but it worked very well for one critical reason—Madison used the bills of rights attached to the state constitutions as his model. The Antifederalists had difficulty opposing Madison's use of this model. It was a model of their own making, and it was part of what they were demanding. Madison offered the Antifederalists the "parchment barriers" he felt were ineffective in existing state constitutions, and the Antifederalists had to either accept such amendments as useful or admit the truth of Madison's paper barrier argument.

Therefore the immediate background for the Bill of Rights was formed by the state bills of rights written between 1776 and 1787. Madison effectively extracted the least common denominator from these state bills of rights, excepting those rights that might reduce the power of the national government. Almost every one of the twenty-seven rights in the Bill of Rights could be found in two or three state documents, and most of them in five or more.[5]

The state bills of rights typically contained a more extensive listing than did the national version. Maryland's 1776 document listed forty-nine rights in forty-two sections, the Massachusetts document listed forty-nine rights in thirty sections, and New Hampshire listed fifty rights in the thirty-eight sections to its 1784 document.[6] Virginia's (1776) forty-two rights and Pennsylvania's (1776) thirty-five rights came closest to duplicating the length of the national Bill of Rights, although in shared content they were not as close to the national document as the Massachusetts bill of rights.[7]

Table 3 shows clearly the strong connection between the state bills of rights and Madison's proposed amendments. If we look at the matrix formed by the forty-two rights on Madison's list and the seven state bills of rights, 59 percent of the cells in the matrix are filled (173 out of 294 cells) compared to the 18 percent density between Madison's list and the amendments proposed by the state ratifying conventions. If we construct a matrix using the contents of the state bills of rights and the rights on Madison's list that were eventually ratified as the Bill of Rights, we find that the percentage of the matrix filled rises to 71 percent (129 out of 182 cells),

[5] The state constitutions and their respective state bills of rights can be found in Francis Newton Thorpe, comp., *The Federal and State Constitutions, Colonial Charters, and Other Organic Laws . . .* , 7 vols. (Washington, D.C., 1909).

[6] Ibid., 3:1686–91 (Maryland), 1889–93 (Massachusetts), and 4:2453–57 (New Hampshire).

[7] Ibid., 7:3812–14 (Virginia) and 5:3082–84 (Pennsylvania).

compared with a 19 percent filled matrix (40 out of 208 cells) when comparing the state ratifying convention proposals with the rights actually ratified as part of the national Bill of Rights.

A final comparison between tables 2 and 3 indicates another connection between the state and national constitutions. The listing for the two tables is the same for the first forty-two rights since these are, in each case, the rights contained in Madison's proposed amendments in the order in which he proposed them. However, the rights listed after number 42 vary in the two tables depending upon the content of the documents being examined.

In table 3 rights numbers 43–52 have a very high density, and they also happen to be addressed successfully in the body of the Constitution proper, as are 55, 61–65, and 81. In other words, many provisions commonly found in state bills of rights had already been addressed in the Constitution and did not need to be included in the national Bill of Rights. Also, only a few of these provisions from the state bills of rights are directly contradicted by anything in the Constitution. The importance of the state constitutions for the Constitution is thus even stronger than is apparent from an examination of the Bill of Rights alone. On the other hand, if we look at the list of proposals from the ratifying conventions, only eight are addressed in the Constitution proper, while at least twenty of the remaining proposals are directly contradicted by provisions in the Constitution. The state constitutions and their respective bills of rights, not the amendments proposed by state ratifying conventions, are the immediate source from which the Bill of Rights was derived.

THE COLONIAL BACKGROUND TO THE STATE BILLS OF RIGHTS

Where did these state bills of rights come from? They came from bills of rights written by American colonists. Because of English preoccupation with internal political disorder from 1640 to 1688, and then with French competition from 1700 to 1760, the colonists were left with a surprisingly high

Table 3. Madison's list of proposed amendments compared with provisions in the existing state bills of rights

	Va.	Pa.	Del.	Md.	N.C.	Mass.	N.H.	Madison
1. Power derived from people	X	X	X	X	X	X	X	X
2. Government exercised for common good	X	X	X	X		X	X	X
3. Life, liberty, property, and happiness	X	X	X	X		X	X	X
4. Right of people to change government	X	X		X		X	X	X
5. Number of representatives								X
6. Congressional raises								X
7. Free exercise of religion			X	X	X	X	X	X
8. Freedom of conscience	X	X	X	X	X	X	X	X
9. Free speech		X						X
10. Free to write								X
11. Free press	X	X	X	X	X	X	X	X
12. Right to assemble	X			X	X			X
13. Petition and remonstrance	X	X	X	X	X			X
14. Bear arms		X			X	X		X
15. Pacifists—no arms								X
16. No quartering in peacetime			X	X		X	X	X
17. No quartering without warrant			X	X		X	X	X
18. Double jeopardy							X	X
19. No double punishment								X
20. Self-incriminate	X	X	X	X	X	X	X	X
21. Due process of law	X	X	X	X	X	X	X	X

22. Compensate for property taken	X	X	X	X	X			X
23. Excessive bail	X		X	X	X			X
24. Cruel and unusual punishment	X	X	X	X	X	X		X
25. Search and seizure	X	X	X	X	X	X	X	X
26. Speedy and public trial	X	X	X	X	X	X	X	X
27. Told nature of crime	X	X	X	X	X	X	X	X
28. Confronted with accusers	X	X	X	X	X	X	X	X
29. Witnesses for defense	X	X	X	X	X	X	X	
30. Right to counsel	X		X			X		
31. Rights retained by people	X		X					
32. No implied powers for Congress	X							
33. No state may violate 8, 11, or 26, above	X			X				
34. Appeal limited by $ amount	X							
35. Jury cannot be bypassed	X				X	X	X	X
36. Impartial jury from vicinity	X							
37. Jury unanimity	X							
38. Right of challenge	X							
39. Grand jury	X							X
40. Jury trial for lawsuits	X							X
41. Separation of powers	X	X	X	X	X			
42. Powers reserved to states or people	X	X	X	X	X	X	X	X
43. No taxation without consent	X	X	X	X	X	X	X	X
44. Free elections	X	X	X	X	X	X	X	X
45. Frequent elections	X		X					X
46. No standing army	X	X		X				X

Table 3. Continued

	Va.	Pa.	Del.	Md.	N.C.	Mass.	N.H.	Madison
47. Civil control of military	X	X	X	X	X	X	X	
48. No martial law (suspending laws)	X		X	X	X	X		
49. No compulsion to bear arms	X	X					X	
50. No ex post facto laws			X	X	X	X	X	
51. No bills of attainder				X		X		
52. Habeas corpus	X	X	X	X				
53. Justice not sold				X		X	X	
54. Location of trial convenient				X		X	X	
55. Independent judiciary			X	X		X		
56. Recurrence to fundamentals	X	X	X	X	X			
57. Stake in community to vote	X							
58. Equality						X	X	
59. Majority rule	X							
60. Frequent meeting of legislature			X	X		X		
61. Free speech in legislature				X		X		
62. Convenient location of legislature				X				
63. Public office not hereditary	X					X	X	
64. No title of nobility				X				
65. No emoluments or privileges					X			
66. No taxing of paupers				X	X			
67. No monopolies				X	X			

58

68. Collective property right			X		
69. No sanguinary laws	X			X	
70. Right to common law				X	
71. Right to migrate	X				X
72. No poll tax				X	
73. No infringing of state constitutions	X				X
74. No religious test				X	
75. Support of public worship		X	X		
76. Attend religious instruction		X			
77. Uniform support of religion		X	X		
78. Support of public teachers		X			
79. Time to prepare legal defense				X	
80. Rotation in executive office					X
81. No multiple officeholding					X
82. Proportional punishment	X				
83. Qualified jurors	X				

SOURCES: The first forty-two rights are those Madison compiled and sent to the House of Representatives. The order is that used in his list. The rest of the rights are those found in the state bills of rights but not in Madison's proposed amendments. Madison's list is taken from the original document in the National Archives. The rights in the state bills of rights are based on the documents as collected in Francis Newton Thorpe, comp., *The Federal and State Constitutions, Colonial Charters, and Other Organic Laws . . . ,* 7 vols. (Washington, D.C., 1909).

level of political independence. In addition to writing what amounted to functional constitutions between 1620 and 1775, the colonists also wrote many bills of rights, and these colonial documents stood as background to the state bills of rights.[8] Examples are the New York Charter of Liberties and Privileges (1683), the Laws and Liberties of New Hampshire (1682), Penn's Charter of Liberties (1682), the General Laws and Liberties of Connecticut (1672), the Maryland Toleration Act (1649), Laws and Liberties of Massachusetts (1647), and the Massachusetts Body of Liberties (1641).[9]

The Massachusetts Body of Liberties, adopted a century and a half before the American Bill of Rights, and half a century before the English Bill of Rights (1689), which had very little overlap with the later American document, contained sixteen (62 percent) of the twenty-six rights found in the American document. No English document before 1791, nor even the entire English common law, had as much overlap with the Bill of Rights as did the Massachusetts Body of Liberties; although other colonial documents written before the English Bill of Rights, such as William Penn's Charter of Liberties, also had a high degree of overlap. For those who assume that the American notion of rights came from John Locke, it is worth noting that in 1641, when the Massachusetts Body of Liberties was adopted, Locke was nine years old, and by the time Penn's Liberties were adopted forty-one years later, Locke had not yet published any of his political writings.

Where, then, do the rights in the Massachusetts Body of Liberties and later colonial documents come from? It is interesting that these colonial documents frequently cite the Bible to justify their various provisions. However, there is no more a listing of rights in the Bible than there is in the writings of Locke, Hume, or Montesquieu. Basically, American notions of rights developed from their own political experience as colonists, an experience significantly affected by the

[8] These documents are widely scattered, but many can be found in Donald S. Lutz, ed., *Documents of Political Foundation Written by Colonial Americans: From Covenant to Constitution* (Philadelphia, 1986).

[9] See ibid., pp. 435–42, 403–10, 359–62, 309–14, 255–302, and 189–94.

peculiar and historically important conditions in which they found themselves.[10]

First of all, these were a religious people. In attempting to lead exemplary lives, they were acutely sensitive to human relationships and believed these relationships should be based upon God's laws as expressed in the Bible. There is in the Bible a strong sense of fairness and a respect for all individuals that easily lead to community rules that look like what we now call rights. Furthermore, the religion these people professed emphasized certain things supportive of a rights orientation.

All humans were viewed as having been made in the image and likeness of God, and therefore a certain equality in value should be accorded every person. Those in government were thus not of a different order from those they governed and did not have inherent prerogatives or rights different from others. A fundamental equality lay in every person's ability to say yes or no to God's grace on their own. From this came the ability to give or withhold consent for human laws, and in turn the notion that government should rest upon the consent of those governed was a straightforward deduction.

These tendencies were reinforced by the belief in the ability of each individual to read the Bible and have an independent relationship with God. Not only was there no need for priests to interpret the Bible, each person was viewed as having an independent will. Government could not interfere in this fundamental independence. Also, since God's law was accessible to every person's understanding, so should the human law, which was supposed to be in conformity to God's law. There was, by implication, no more need for a class of lawyers to interpret earthly law than there was need for a priestly caste to interpret the divine law in the Bible. The process for making and enforcing human laws was seen as susceptible to codification, a codification that would treat everyone the same and be understandable to all. These codifications were the first American bills of rights.

[10] The argument being made here is fully developed in Donald S. Lutz, *The Origins of American Constitutionalism* (Baton Rouge, La., 1988).

In addition to religion, the desperate situation of colonists isolated in pockets scattered along a thousand-mile coastline put a high premium on cooperation if all were to survive. The earliest colony, in Virginia, initially tried a military style of organization, but this soon gave way to a system of eliciting cooperation by treating people well. Early bills of rights were an effective and efficient means for producing order, stability, cooperative behavior, and economic progress.

Finally, the status of American colonies as economic enterprises, especially as seen from England, tended to emphasize economic output rather than political control as the primary consideration. That a loose political control from England produced the most economic output only enhanced the sense colonists had of running their own lives. A confluence of circumstances led Americans to require, develop, and expect a set of rights not found in England, and this set of rights was characterized by a breadth, detail, equality, fairness, and effectiveness in limiting all branches of government that distinguished it from English common law.

No one represented the disjunction between English and American rights better than William Penn, who, because of his Quaker religion, suffered through a trial in England that shocks us today. When he founded Pennsylvania, Penn granted religious freedom, something lacking in England, as part of a bill of rights grounded in his religion and experiences. He also consulted the existing codes of Massachusetts, Connecticut, Maryland, and Virginia, and possibly because of common religious assumptions his list of rights largely overlapped these earlier ones. His Frame of Government (1682) contained 55 percent (fifteen out of twenty-seven) of the rights listed in the Bill of Rights, whereas the English Bill of Rights seven years later had only one-third as much overlap (five out of twenty-seven). English common law did form part of the background to our bills of rights, but in America the common law breathed in a powerful air of equality and independence that transformed it into a profoundly different American version.

CONTRASTING ENGLISH AND AMERICAN NOTIONS OF LIBERTY

The American view of rights was distinguished from that in Britain by two important conceptual differences. One lay in the respective notions of liberty. In England the concept of liberty had two quite contradictory meanings. One had to do with the general condition of men based upon natural law, or a condition of all Englishmen based upon their common legal and constitutional past. The second meaning had to do with the medieval idea of a hierarchy of liberties that varied according to an individual's or a group's station and purpose in life. Parliament had certain liberties, as did the monarch. The aristocracy had certain liberties, commoners had others. For example, the property rights of aristocratic women were much broader than women not of the aristocracy. Also, certain localities often had special liberties granted by charter. A given town might contain in its charter liberties not found elsewhere, or a shire or locality might retain special liberties as a result of a connection by marriage to the Crown at some time past. A freeman could, by moving to a new locality, alter his liberties.

In this sense liberty was an exemption from normal obligations or punishments. Frequently the distribution of liberties was related to the distribution of property—a holdover from the feudal system of fiefs. In a broader sense this notion viewed liberty as submission to duly constituted authority as opposed to submission to force. It was not, however, submission to government erected by consent. Indeed, under this notion a man was not considered as being deprived of liberty because he was denied self-government. Magna Charta assumed this second notion of liberty, as did much of English common law.

With no aristocracy in America, cut off from the remnants of feudal relationships in England, populated by a people largely holding to Dissenting Protestant theology with the implications noted above, and faced with problems of survival that required cooperation rather than contention over relative rights, the American colonies failed to include this second

63

British notion of liberty in their political development, at least to any significant degree. The governing boards back in England, many of the British-trained lawyers in America, and certainly the Crown-appointed governors of the colonies still had a strong sense of liberty as an exemption from law, but there was no room or prudential basis for it in America. American bills of rights, then, did not include this second notion of liberty, but worked from the first. The Massachusetts Body of Liberties does not look like Magna Charta, and the national Bill of Rights does not look like the English Bill of Rights, and the absence of this conflicting view of liberty is a major reason.

There was another basic difference, and this too stemmed from the religious background and tenuous situation of most colonists. When we look at the earliest colonial documents of political foundation, like the Mayflower Compact (1620), the Pilgrim Code of Law (1636), and the Fundamental Orders of Connecticut (1639), we find that among other things they usually involved the self-creation of a people—in the double sense of forming a new people and then of laying out the common values, interests, and goals that bound them as a people.[11] These self-defining or self-creating people were in the habit of providing in later documents updated versions of their fundamental, shared values, and it is such lists of shared values that evolved into what we now call bills of rights.

It made sense for a religious people to cite the Bible in a bill of rights. Since the Bible was central to what they shared, the values they held could be justified by identifying the place in Scripture where these values were enunciated or implied. As the population became more diverse and less religious, the biblical references might disappear, but not the tendency for bills of rights to use admonitory language rather than legally binding terminology. Consider for example the following typical excerpts from state bills of rights:

> That the freedom of the press is one of the great bulwarks of liberty, and therefore ought never to be restrained (North Carolina, 1776).

[11] These documents can be found in Lutz, ed., *Documents of Political Foundation*, pp. 65–66, 105–12, and 135–42.

64

That the legislative, executive, and judicial powers of government, ought to be forever separate and distinct from each other (Maryland, 1776).

All elections ought to be free; and all the inhabitants of this commonwealth, having such qualifications as they shall establish by their frame of government, have an equal right to elect officers, and to be elected, for public employments (Massachusetts, 1780).

That a frequent recurrence to fundamental principles, and a firm adherence to justice, moderation, temperance, industry, and frugality are absolutely necessary to preserve the blessings of liberty and keep government free (Pennsylvania, 1776).[12]

These may strike some people as peculiar statements for bills of rights, yet they are all from state bills of rights and use language that is typical rather than exceptional. One can see clearly from the use of *ought* and *should* instead of *shall* and *will* that the language is admonitory rather than capable of being legally enforced. One can also easily see how these bills of rights are statements of shared values and fundamental principles. We are here a long way from common law.

CONTENDING VIEWS OF RIGHTS IN 1789

In 1789, on the eve of the writing of America's Bill of Rights, there were several contending positions in the Anglo-Saxon world on the nature of rights. One was associated with the common law view of liberty derived from medieval society and embodied in Magna Charta. In this view the Crown was limited by the rights associated with the aristocracy in the feudal hierarchy, and these rights were attached to property. Even though this was the stronger of two strains in common law, it was not part of the American notion of rights.

A second position on rights was associated with the other common law view of liberty—that all Englishmen possessed from their common legal and constitutional past a set of rights that protected them from an arbitrary Crown, especially in

[12] Thorpe, comp., *Federal and State Constitutions*, 5:2788, 3:1687, 3:1891, 5:3083.

the operation of the court system. This position had been read into Magna Charta even though it was not there, most notably by Sir Edward Coke. In Coke's view the common law protected all Englishmen against royal prerogative. Since this view was used primarily by Parliament in its struggle with the Crown, rights were not seen as limiting Parliament. Since Americans lacked an aristocracy upon which to rest the first version of common law, the second version was dominant in the colonies. However, this view gave them no basis for resisting Parliament in its attempts to tax the colonies, which either left them the older version of common law, which the Glorious Revolution in England had rendered anachronistic, or required them to use a different grounding for rights than that found in the common law.

Fortunately, the colonists had available a view of rights that they had been more or less using for a century and a half, and that was undergirded by both theology and rationalist philosophy. In this third position all human law had to be judged in terms of its conformity with a higher law. By implication all branches of government, including the legislature, were limited by this higher law. A straightforward deduction led to all branches of government being beholden to popular consent and to rights being defined as the set of guarantees that protected the free and effective operation of popular consent.

Bills of rights, according to this view, were lists of common commitments that both protected the operation of popular consent and codified what popular consent had already identified as commonly held commitments. By 1776 the language used to express this position had become thoroughly secular, as exemplified in the following excerpt from a state constitution: "That all power being originally inherent in, and consequently derived from the people: therefore all officers of government, whether legislative or executive, are their trustees and servants, and at all times accountable to them" (Pennsylvania, 1776).[13]

Also, preambles to state constitutions frequently had state-

[13] Ibid., 5:3082.

ments similar to the following from the 1780 Massachusetts document: "The body politic is formed by a voluntary association of individuals; it is a social compact, by which the whole people covenants with each citizen, and each citizen with the whole people, that all shall be governed by certain laws for the common good."[14]

At first blush these last two quotations might appear to be taken from John Locke, but such language was used in America long before Locke's *Second Treatise* was published. The communitarian, popular consent approach to rights was initially derived from Dissenting Protestant theology as it was applied to the design of political institutions in seventeenth- and eighteenth-century North America. This view emphasized the needs of the community rather than the rights of individuals, but it did see all branches of government as limited in their operation by universally shared, unchanging human rights. The use of "covenant" and "common good" here reflect the theological assumption not found in Locke's work.

The similarity in language to that used by John Locke, Algernon Sidney, and other English political theorists is a measure of the extent to which religion and rationalism reached similar political conclusions in late eighteenth-century America. The terms and concepts of Sidney, Locke, Bolingbroke, Milton, and a host of others were efficiently blended with that of Dissenting Protestantism, as illustrated by the opening articles in the bills of rights of two prominent state constitutions.

I. That all men are born equally free and independent, and have certain natural, inherent and inalienable rights, amongst which are, the enjoying and defending life and liberty, acquiring, possessing and protecting property, and pursuing and obtaining happiness and safety.

II. That all men have a natural and unalienable right to worship Almighty God according to the dictates of their own consciences and understanding (Pennsylvania, 1776).[15]

[14] Ibid., 3:1889.

[15] Ibid., 5:3082.

THE BILL OF RIGHTS

Article I. All men are born free and equal, and have certain natural, essential, and unalienable rights; among which may be reckoned the right of enjoying and defending their lives and liberties; that of acquiring, possessing, and protecting property; in fine, that of seeking and obtaining their safety and happiness.

II. It is the right as well as the duty of all men in society, publicly, and at stated seasons, to worship the Supreme Being. . . . And no subject shall be hurt, molested, or restrained, in his person, liberty, or estate, for worshipping God in the manner and season most agreeable to the dictates of his own conscience (Massachusetts, 1780).[16]

The rationalist version of this third position on rights will be termed Lockean, although the language used in the passages just cited is much closer to that used by Algernon Sidney and was probably taken from his *Discourses on Government.* Locke and Sidney saw all branches of government as limited by rights, a position that was roundly ignored in England during the eighteenth century and still is not part of the common law today. What neither the religious nor the rationalist form of rights consciousness envisioned in the eighteenth century was having rights legally enforced by the courts rather than by elections, constitutional revision, or armed rebellion. This important step in the development of American bills of rights was still in the future and to a certain extent would rest upon an accident of history.

DRAFTING THE BILL OF RIGHTS

The American view of rights, derived in part from English common law, undergirded by Dissenting Protestant theology, and reinforced by rationalist political philosophy, was essentially developed in the local political arena and codified at the colony-wide level. Independence in 1776 did not alter the situation in this regard. The articulation, codification, and protection of rights proceeded at the state and local levels. It should not surprise us, then, to learn that it was state and

[16] Ibid., 3:1889.

local leaders, not national political leaders, who insisted upon a national bill of rights.

The United States Constitution, as originally written, contained a number of rights scattered through the document, but it did not have a fully articulated bill of rights. The Federalists, including Madison and Hamilton, felt that a bill of rights at the national level was unnecessary and perhaps dangerous.[17] A national bill of rights was unnecessary for two reasons. First, there were extensive bills of rights already in existence at the state level. Second, the political process defined by the national Constitution was viewed by Federalists as so balanced and limited in powers that it could not impinge upon rights, and if it did the states could always use their own bills of rights to protect their respective citizens. A national bill of rights was potentially dangerous—also for two reasons. First, any listing was bound to leave out rights that would in the future be considered important but by their absence from the bill of rights imply that they were not protected. Second, since bills of rights were statements of commonly held values and commitments, and there were differences in these values and commitments from state to state, a national bill of rights would either have to contain the least common denominator and thus leave out things considered important by many people or else local and state diversity would have to be ignored by the imposition of nationwide standards and values that were in fact not held nationwide. In either case a national bill of rights would be dangerous to rights and liberty in the long run.

These arguments did not convince the opponents to the proposed Constitution, and opposition centered most vociferously upon the lack of a bill of rights. James Madison promised at a critical point in the national debate that if the Constitution was ratified he would personally see that a bill of rights was added. True to his word, Madison did initiate and carry through congressional approval for the Bill of Rights, but it was perhaps the most lukewarm introduction in political history. The *Annals of Congress,* the early version of the

---

[17] See *The Federalist* (Indianapolis, 1970), pp. 555–61.

Congressional Record, show Madison as in effect saying again that a national bill of rights is unnecessary and dangerous, but since he had promised one, here it was.

Madison, mindful of his own words on the dangers of looking to the least common denominator, nevertheless produced a list of nine amendments containing forty-two rights that constituted the core of most state bills of rights. Madison's proposed amendments were given to a select committee in the House of Representatives, with one member from each state on the committee. The House produced a list with seventeen articles that the Senate reduced to twelve. A conference committee worked out the differences, and on October 2, 1789, a proposed bill of rights was sent to the states for ratification.

It was assumed at the beginning of congressional action that the Bill of Rights would either be placed as a list at the beginning of the Constitution, as was the case with state bills of rights, or scattered through the body of the Constitution proper as Madison proposed. However, the Connecticut delegation insisted that the rights be appended at the end of the document as a set of explicit amendments to reflect their true status. Placing them at the beginning or in the body of a document that had been ratified only with great difficulty implied the need to go through the entire ratification process again, whereas treating them as amendments did not require having to change any wording in the Constitution per se.

Roger Sherman's proposal to place the rights at the end, rather than scattering them throughout the document as Madison wanted, turned out to be fateful, since listing the rights together at the end gave them a prominence and combined status over time that would otherwise have been lost. Placing the Bill of Rights at the end, rather than at the beginning as the states preferred, had an unnoted yet historically important effect on the language of the proposed rights.

The lists of rights proposed by the various states almost all used the admonitory *ought* and *should* rather than the legally enforceable *shall* and *will* with which we are now familiar. Madison, on the other hand, intended placing the rights in the body of the Constitution, so he used the constitutionally proper *shall* and *will*. Initially the House of Representatives version used admonitory language, but when the House select committee agreed to go along with Sherman's proposal and place the Bill of Rights at the end as amendments, it was necessary to change everything to legalistically enforceable language since one cannot amend a *shall* with an *ought*.

Without this change in language occasioned by placement at the end rather than the beginning of the Constitution, it is difficult to see how American rights could have developed as they did, or how the Supreme Court could have emerged as the definer and protector of legalistic rights. The change in wording was entirely due to the placement of the Bill of Rights, not to anything in American rights theory as of 1789. Later developments in American theories of rights would be heavily affected and conditioned by what amounts to historical accident.

It took two and a half years for the necessary three-fourths of the states to ratify ten of the twelve proposed amendments to the Constitution, which together are now known as the Bill of Rights. Massachusetts, Connecticut, and Georgia did not ratify these amendments until the Sesquicentennial celebration of the Constitution in 1939. That the process took so long, that it failed to elicit ratification by all of the states, and that two proposed amendments failed to receive the necessary three-fourths support are all indicative of controversy in state legislatures. Much of this controversy stemmed, as Madison had predicted, from different expectations from state to state. Some wanted more or different rights, some wanted fewer. Perhaps we should be surprised that anything coherent passed at all.

THE BILL OF RIGHTS SINCE 1792

Passage of the Bill of Rights did not really change anything at first. The states were still considered the primary protectors of individual rights. It was not until the early twentieth century that the Supreme Court began to use the Bill of Rights to protect individual rights in a systematic fashion.

One major effect the Bill of Rights had during the nineteenth century was to lead drafters of state constitutions to recast the language of their bills of rights into legally binding

Table 4. Madison's proposed amendments compared with later versions

	Madison version	House version	Senate version	Sent to states	Ratified
1. Power derived from people	X				
2. Government exercised for common good	X				
3. Life, liberty, property, and happiness	X				
4. Right of people to change government	X				
5. Number of representatives	X	X		X	
6. Congressional raises	X	X	X	X	
7. Religious freedom	X	X		X	X
8. Right of conscience	X	X			
9. Free speech	X	X		X	X
10. Freedom of written expression	X				
11. Free press	X	X		X	X
12. Assembly	X	X		X	X
13. Petition and remonstrance	X	X		X	X
14. Bear arms	X	X	X	X	X
15. Pacifists—no arms	X	X			
16. No quartering in peacetime	X	X	X	X	X
17. No quartering without warrant	X	X	X	X	X
18. Double jeopardy	X	X	X	X	X
19. No double punishment	X				
20. Self-incrimination	X	X	X	X	X
21. Due process of law	X	X	X	X	X
22. Compensate for property taken	X	X	X	X	X
23. Excessive bail or fines	X	X		X	X
24. Cruel and unusual punishment	X	X		X	X
25. Search and seizure	X	X	X	X	X

26. Speedy and public trial	X		X	X
27. Told nature of crime	X		X	X
28. Confronted with accusers	X		X	X
29. Witnesses for defense	X		X	X
30. Right to counsel	X		X	X
31. Rights retained by people	X		X	X
32. No implied powers for Congress	X	X		
33. No state may violate 8, 9, 11, or 26 above	X			
34. Appeal limited by $ amount	X			
35. Jury cannot be bypassed	X	X	X	X
36. Impartial jury from vicinity	X	X	X	X
37. Jury unanimity	X			
38. Right to challenge judicial decision	X			
39. Grand jury	X	X	X	X
40. Jury trial for civil cases	X	X	X	X
41. Separation of powers	X			
42. Powers reserved to states	X	X	X	X

SOURCES: The rights are arranged in the order used by Madison in his June 8, 1789, version sent to the Committee of Eleven of the House of Representatives (the committee was composed of one member from each of the eleven states that had ratified the Constitution by that date). This table is based upon an examination of the original documents in the National Archives.

language. With their longer lists of rights and strengthened language, most states were ahead of the national government in rights development, although nowhere did the breadth and depth of protection approach what it is now.

Two broad developments have occurred during the twentieth century. The first has been the expansion of national rights, as interpreted by the Supreme Court, to an unprecedented degree. We have come to take these rights so much for granted that we forget how recently they have been expanded. The second development has been the application of the Bill of Rights against the states using the due process clause of the Fourteenth Amendment. Both developments were made possible by the legally enforceable language inserted in the Bill of Rights in 1789.

Scholarship and publicity surrounding the second broad development left the impression that rights at the state level were not well protected and that the national government had forged ahead in rights protection. This was not completely true. The problem was not lagging rights in the states but diversity in rights among the states. Many or most states already protected rights at a level required by the Supreme Court, but ten to fifteen states clearly lagged behind. The net effect of federal action has been to establish what is now considered a "floor" in American rights. That minimum guarantee is still exceeded by many states.

Active expansion of rights by the Supreme Court, as much as it was needed, had the effect of temporarily eclipsing the development of rights in states. That may be changing. In recent years there has been a trend toward "rediscovering" an independent constitutional law at the state level with respect to rights, especially in those states where state bills of rights are stronger and broader in definition than the national Bill of Rights.[18] If this flowering at the state level bears fruit, we may be entering a new era with respect to the Bill of Rights— one that produces a healthy competition in rights protection

[18] For a good introduction to the growing literature on this topic, see John Kincaid, "State Court Protections of Individual Rights under State Constitutions: The New Judicial Federalism," *Journal of State Government* 61 (1988):163–69.

instead of either state or national dominance that has characterized our past.

Taking a historical perspective toward rights in America has a number of implications for how we think about bills of rights, as well as for how we study and teach them. For one thing, the role of the states needs to be more actively considered, as well as the interaction between state and national bills of rights. Changes in the structure, content, and wording of bills of rights reflect changes in how we conceptualize rights, and these theoretical changes need to be more frankly and explicitly faced.

We now rely primarily upon the courts to protect rights, and this is not a bad thing in itself, but it does have the tendency to focus attention upon court cases, and thus upon rights piecemeal, rather than upon bills of rights and the general principles they embody. Certainly we must think deeply about the preferability of using constitutional amendments instead of court interpretation to expand and codify rights. In fact, this is what still tends to happen at the state level, which is one reason why state constitutions so quickly become lengthy and laden with amendments. Many academics view lengthy constitutions as something to be avoided. Another perspective is that long constitutions indicate a people are still taking the constitution seriously enough to amend it through a political process that engages popular consent. Long constitutions may thus be an indication of political health.

There is something to be said for viewing rights as expressions of fundamental commitments by a people, as the grounding for democratic institutions, and thus as an essential part of the total political process in a constitutional order. In short, we may be in need of more frequent public debate as we push our frontiers of freedom forward. These are, after all, our rights, and not simply the conclusions of a priestly caste called judges. Judges may be useful guides to our good conscience as a people, but in the end popular consent, and thus popular support, may be a more secure basis for rights.[19]

---

[19] For further discussion on this point, see Donald S. Lutz, "Protection of Political Participation in Eighteenth-Century America," *Albany Law Review* 53 (1989):1–29.

Finally, the search for a pedigree to the Bill of Rights emphasizes the extent to which rights have been based upon and developed as a result of fundamental commitments shared by politically active Americans. Our rights have not been handed to us by any particular generation, indeed have not been handed to us by anyone, but rather have evolved from a multigenerational political process, a process that continues to this day.

KENNETH R. BOWLING

Overshadowed by States' Rights

Ratification of the Federal Bill of Rights

The seeds of two contending factions appear to be plenti-
fully sown. The names of Federalist and Antifederalist are
no longer expressive of the sentiments which they were so
lately supposed to contain, and I expect soon to hear a cou-
ple of new names, which will designate the respective
friends of the national and particular systems. The people
are very evidently dividing into these two parties.
— John Quincy Adams

AT THE FEDERAL Convention in September 1787 George Mason of Virginia and Elbridge Gerry of Massachusetts proposed that the Constitution include a bill of rights to reassure
the people that the vastly strengthened federal government
would not oppress them. The Convention, voting by states,
refused unanimously. This proved a critical error, almost fatal
to the ratification of the document. The conventions that ratified the Constitution proposed approximately one hundred
different amendments to it, two-thirds of which called for
changes in the structure and powers of the new federal government. Among these, some were concerned with federalism
and aimed to alter the balance of power in the new system
in order to protect the rights of the states; others were sought
by southerners interested in protecting sectional interests in
a Union that they believed to be controlled by the North. Approximately a third of the amendments recommended by the

states sought to provide protection at the federal level for traditional liberties claimed by Americans by virtue of their constitutional ancestry. Among these were freedom of speech, press, and religion, the rights to assemble, petition, and possess arms, and various due process protections.

Federalists generally opposed amendments on the grounds that the Constitution should be allowed a trial period for problems to show themselves. As to a bill of rights, they argued that one was unnecessary because the Constitution provided for a federal government of only delegated powers. Federalists also argued that a bill of rights would be dangerous because those rights not listed would be assumed to be given up to the federal government. Antifederalists believed this argument to be naive at best, since the Constitution made the federal government supreme over the states. They insisted that amendments should be considered in a second convention or be one of the first matters taken up by the First Congress. But Antifederalists fared poorly in the first congressional elections, and the likelihood that Congress would propose amendments dimmed.

Credit for the fact that the First Congress proposed amendments to the states belongs to James Madison, who pushed them through a reluctant House of Representatives. At first as strongly opposed to amendments as fellow Federalists, Madison became a convert because of three factors: the arguments of his friend Thomas Jefferson, the will of the Virginia ratification convention, and the Antifederalism of the district in which he ran for a seat in Congress. By the close of 1788 Madison was persuaded that if Congress recommended to the states some amendments relating to personal liberty but not altering the basic nature of the Constitution, most Antifederalists would be willing to support the new government. This would protect it from fundamental structural change. Madison converted Washington to his view. In his inaugural address, the president recommended that Congress consider amendments that strengthened "the characteristic rights of freemen."

In June 1789 Madison presented to the House several amendments that he believed should be woven into the text of the Constitution. Most of the approximately twenty subjects covered related to civil liberties. Only one related directly to states' rights; it became the Tenth Amendment. Significantly, however, it omitted the words *expressly* or *clearly* in the phrase "The powers not delegated to the United States by the Constitution." The omission of this limiting word gutted the amendment and left interpretation of the Constitution open to the doctrine of implied federal powers, the great enemy of states' rights.

When describing Madison's proposals, both Federalists and Antifederalists turned to the popular ship of state metaphor. They called his proposals "a tub to the whale," an allusion to Jonathan Swift's *Tale of a Tub* (1704). In his satire, Swift described how sailors, encountering a whale that threatened to damage their ship, flung it "an empty tub by way of amusement" to divert it. Madison's contemporaries used the allusion to illuminate the fact that he had proposed mostly rights-related amendments rather than ones designed to alter the structure and balance of the new government. As a result, the Antifederal leviathan would be diverted and the ship of state could sail away intact.

Despite the fact that they held advanced civil libertarian ideas for their times, congressmen were not as willing to consider amendments as Madison expected. Federalists believed that the first congressional elections had demonstrated that Americans were satisfied with the new government and that to consider amendments would consume valuable time that should be devoted to more pressing matters. Several went so far as to ridicule the value of paper declarations of rights. The handful of Antifederalists in Congress also expressed reluctance to consider amendments. They feared that the adoption of rights-related amendments would close the door to consideration of amendments designed to rein in the federal government and strengthen the rights of the states. When the House considered the amendments in August, Antifederalists proposed several structural amendments, but Federalists defeated them one by one. Madison's persistence gradually won support from other Federalists, but both the House and Senate made fundamental changes in his language before sending twelve amendments to the states for ratification in September 1789.[1]

The congressional debate over amendments had been a difficult one, so intense that it produced the first known instance of members challenging each other to duels and caused the Speaker to label it more heated than anything else the First Congress had yet seen.[2] Given the intensity of that debate and all the public interest that the question of amending the Constitution had raised during the campaign to ratify it and during the first congressional elections, one would expect great contention over the ratification of the amendments. Just the opposite occurred. Before looking at the little that is known about the process, I want to suggest three reasons why ratification of what we call the Bill of Rights generated so little interest in the states. These reasons, particularly the third, which I discuss at greater length, go far to explain why, with few exceptions, the existence of the federal Bill of Rights was largely ignored for a century.

First, the political strategy of James Madison in proposing the Bill of Rights proved successful. By gaining congressional approval for amendments guaranteeing certain liberties of the people, he deprived the Antifederal leadership of its most effective weapon against the Constitution. Madison thus won support for the Constitution from the many Antifederalists who were not particularly concerned about structural and states' rights amendments once amendments protecting personal liberties had been promised. To them questions of federalism did not have the popular appeal of amendments guaranteeing them what they considered to be rights won by their English ancestors and reasserted in the American Revo-

[1] Kenneth R. Bowling, "'A Tub to the Whale': The Founding Fathers and the Adoption of the Federal Bill of Rights," *Journal of the Early Republic* 8 (1988):223–51.

[2] Elbridge Gerry to Samuel R. Gerry, June 30, 1790, Frederick A. Muhlenberg to Benjamin Rush, Aug. 18, 1789, Helen E. Veit, Kenneth R. Bowling, and Charlene Bangs Bickford, eds., *Creating the Bill of Rights: The Documentary Record from the First Federal Congress* (Baltimore, 1991), pp. 278–79n, 280. This volume contains all the official and unofficial documents related to the Bill of Rights during its passage through Congress.

lution. It was a brilliant political move by Madison, perhaps the most important and successful in his career, and it certainly made up for the almost fatal error he and others had committed at the federal Convention by omitting a bill of rights. As Thomas Jefferson expressed it to the marquis de Lafayette in April 1790, "The opposition to our new constitution has almost totally disappeared. Some few indeed had gone such lengths in their declarations of hostility that they feel it awkward perhaps to come over, but the amendments proposed by Congress, have brought over almost all their followers."[3]

Second, the issues addressed by the Bill of Rights were carryovers from a Revolution that had been concluded. The First Congress brought it to an end by successfully legislating on fundamental issues that had stymied the Confederation Congress, particularly raising federal revenues, regulating interstate commerce, paying off the Revolutionary war debt, and locating the federal capital. In this context the federal Bill of Rights might even be seen as part of a compromise Revolutionary settlement, similar to that which occurred in England in 1689. Certain rights enunciated by the Revolution such as freedom of the press and freedom of religion were given constitutional protection. Others were not. The First Congress rejected Madison's proposed amendment on separation of powers because the Senate recognized that the Federal Convention had previously rejected the idea in favor of a more sophisticated balance of powers concept. Most prominently, the House gutted Madison's majestic natural law preamble, omitting the right of the people "to reform or change their government, wherever it be found adverse or inadequate to the purposes of its institution"; the statement "that all power is originally vested in, and consequently derived from the people"; and the list of benefits people derive from government: enjoyment of life, liberty, acquiring and using property, pursuing and obtaining happiness and safety. Consider the possibilities for constitutional arguments before the federal

---

[3] Thomas Jefferson to the marquis de Lafayette, Apr. 2, 1790, Julian P. Boyd et al., eds., *The Papers of Thomas Jefferson*, 28 vols. to date (Princeton, 1950-), 16:293.

judiciary had the Bill of Rights stated one of the purposes of government to be the safety and happiness of the citizenry or guaranteed the right of revolution.

The final reason for the absence of interest in the ratification of the Bill of Rights related to federalism, the issue that had been central to American politics for twenty-five years. In implementing the Constitution, the First Congress refocused the debate over federalism in a fundamental way. The coalition that had supported a stronger federal government and secured ratification of the Constitution in 1788 achieved stunning legislative successes in the first session of the First Congress. It provided for federal revenues and regulation of interstate commerce, organized semi-independent executive and judicial branches, and blocked the demand for constitutional amendments limiting federal power over the states. Having achieved its major goals and saved the ship of state from the Antifederal whale, the Federalist consensus split along sectional lines. The southern states in particular raised the issue of states' rights. But, as John Quincy Adams indicated in the quotation printed as epigraph to this essay, the issue concerned northerners as well. The swing away from strengthening the federal government and toward protecting the rights of the states began just at the time that the state legislatures received the Bill of Rights from Congress, and it helped to eclipse their ratification as an issue, most importantly in Virginia.

Even as it was still considering the amendments that we call the Bill of Rights, Congress was torn by the September 1789 debate over where to locate the federal capital. That debate raised for the first time under the Constitution the specter of disunion. Led by James Madison, spokesmen for the South suggested a new concern about the federal equation: it was no longer the federal government that needed to be strengthened, but the states. Madison went so far as to declare that Virginia would not have ratified the Constitution had it been aware of what would occur when Congress debated the location of the capital. More importantly, he admitted some validity to the Antifederal concern that a republic could not survive if the territory it encompassed was too large, the theory that he had argued against so masterfully in *Federalist* No. 10. In some instances local governments, he declared, were better able to protect the rights of citizens than the federal government. This long and widely reported speech marked the public debut of a fundamental shift in his political stance from architect of a strong federal government to defender of the states, and from leader of the Federalists to spokesman for a yet undefined opposition party built on a foundation of decentralism and states' rights.

The sectional tension generated by that legislative battle hardened during the second session as Congress debated Secretary of the Treasury Alexander Hamilton's report on public credit. Indeed, congressional leaders gave serious consideration to an adjournment in hopes that tempers would cool and that threats of disunion on the House floor and of civil war from outraged constituents would disappear. Only a major political compromise in 1790, a compromise of almost constitutional magnitude, restored the fabric of union. By its terms, Congress mollified southerners by locating the federal capital on the Potomac River and satisfied northerners by having the federal government assume the payment of most of the states' Revolutionary war debts, despite questions about the constitutionality of assumption.[4]

President George Washington transmitted the twelve proposed amendments to the states on October 2, 1789. Would they satisfy Antifederalists as Madison hoped, or would there be demands by state legislatures for some or all of the additional amendments that the ratification conventions had proposed in 1788 and Congress had failed to propose in 1789? If there were such demands, they might lead to the convening of a second federal constitutional convention, for which New York and Virginia had already petitioned Congress.

Even before Congress completed its work on the amendments, Antifederalists launched a campaign to stimulate opposition. Samuel Bryan revived his famous Centinel series, numbering the first essay "25" to link it to his nationally important pieces from the ratification campaign. He called the

[4] Kenneth R. Bowling, *The Creation of Washington, D.C.: The Idea and Location of the American Capital* (Fairfax, Va., 1991), pp. 143–44 and chaps. 6 and 7.

proposed amendments inadequate, showy, superficial, and nothing more than an opiate for the people, insisting that they preserved the principal avenues of despotic power for the federal government. Centinel concluded with a call for real amendments. Receiving little support, Bryan soon turned the focus of the Centinel essays elsewhere.[5]

A flurry of newspaper articles in New York and Philadelphia at the end of 1789 suggested that there would be public debate on the amendments. The pieces at first focused on whether a bill of rights made any sense in a society in which the people, not the government, were sovereign. They were followed in January by a brief exchange on the meaning of retained rights in what became the Ninth Amendment.[6] Newspapers elsewhere ignored the discussion, apparently following the lead of an article in the *Gazette of the United States,* which reported that the amendments seemed to meet the approbation of the state legislatures. This widely republished piece reminded readers that if the amendments did not meet all of the Antifederalists' demands, they were a concession by the Federalists to reconcile the opposition and conciliate the doubting. Later newspaper articles mentioning the proposed amendments were either reports of state ratification or tangential comments, such as one from a Georgetown, Maryland, newspaper suggesting that the proposed amendments should have included one granting Congress power to declare where canals should be cut.[7]

[5] "Centinel Revived" appeared in the *Independent Gazetteer* (Philadelphia) from Aug. 27 to Nov. 11, 1789; Nos. 25 and 26, published on Aug. 27 and 29, discussed Congress's proposed amendments.

[6] *New York Morning Post,* Dec. 19, 1789; *Independent Gazetteer* (Philadelphia), Dec. 28, 1789; *Pennsylvania Packet* (Philadelphia), Jan. 6, 1790. For the exchange on the meaning of the Ninth Amendment see the *Gazette of the United States* (Philadelphia), Jan. 11, 1790, and the *Federal Gazette* (Philadelphia), Jan. 15, 1790.

[7] *Gazette of the United States* (Philadelphia), Dec. 23, 1789. Reprints include *Pennsylvania Packet* (Philadelphia), Dec. 29, 1789, *Providence Gazette,* Jan. 2, 1790, *Massachusetts Centinel* (Boston), Jan. 2, 1790, and *Georgetown Weekly Ledger,* Aug. 14, 1790.

By the end of January 1790 four states had acted on the amendments without the question of additional amendments arising. New Jersey was the first. On November 20, 1789, it ratified all except the second (which provided that no law varying the compensation of members of Congress would be effective until an ensuing election). Georgia rejected all twelve on December 1 on the grounds that it was premature to consider amendments when only experience would point out the defective parts of the Constitution. Maryland ratified all twelve on December 19, and New Hampshire approved all but the second on January 25. Three days later Delaware ratified all but the first amendment (which provided for a regular increase in the size of the House of Representatives as population grew), which it postponed.[8]

On the other hand, by the end of January 1790 two states had called for additional amendments. A month after ratifying the Constitution in November 1789, North Carolina ratified the amendments in their entirety; however, the ratification convention also instructed its congressional delegation to obtain eight additional amendments and transmitted certified copies of the resolution to all of the states. The eight amendments limited the power of Congress to regulate federal elections or enlist soldiers for more than four years except in time of war; prevented members of Congress from holding other federal civil office, or Congress from interfering with state money already emitted or the discharging of any of the state securities (for example, assuming responsibility for payment of the state debt); required annual publication of the journals of both houses (except those parts requiring secrecy), and a statement of receipts and expenditures of public money; required a two-thirds vote in both houses for passage

---

[8] The official ratification documents from the nine states that ratified any or all of the proposed twelve amendments during the tenure of the First Congress can be found in Linda Grant DePauw, Charlene Bangs Bickford, and LaVonne Hauptman, eds., *Documentary History of the First Federal Congress*, vol. 3, *House of Representatives Journal* (Baltimore, 1976), pp. 577–97. On Georgia, see John P. Kaminski, "The Making of the Bill of Rights: 1787–1792," in Stephen L. Schechter and Richard B. Bernstein, eds., *Contexts of the Bill of Rights* (Albany, 1990), p. 54.

of commercial legislation; and created some tribunal other than the Senate to try impeachments of senators.[9]

South Carolina ratified all of the amendments on January 19, 1790, but at the same time instructed its delegation to secure adoption of the amendments proposed by the state's ratification convention in 1788. These called for limits on Congress's power to levy direct taxes and regulate federal elections, the insertion of the word *other* into Article VI, Section 3, of the Constitution, so that it would read that "no *other* religious test shall ever be required as a qualification to any office or public trust under the United States" than the oath or affirmation that bound them to support the Constitution, and the reservation to the states of all powers not *expressly* delegated to the federal government.[10]

New York took up the amendments next. Trouble might have been expected from what had been a decidedly Antifederal state. Indeed, had it followed the lead of the Carolinas, the history of ratification of the Bill of Rights might have been more exciting, for Massachusetts was considering the amendments at the same time and two other key states, Pennsylvania and Virginia, had not yet reached a final decision. In the spring of 1789, however, Antifederalists lost control of the state senate and their majority in the assembly dropped. Despite the fact that leading New York Antifederalists privately declared the amendments proposed by Congress to be trivial and equivocal, enough interest in them existed for the press to publish some of the assembly's debate on ratification. As a result, we know that the assembly apparently gave more serious attention to the meaning of freedom of the press than Congress had when it proposed what became the First Amendment. New York adopted all but the second amend-

[9][North Carolina], *In Convention, November 23, 1789* (Edenton, N.C., 1789), in Charles Evans and Clifford K. Shipton, eds., *American Bibliography,* 14 vols. (Chicago and Worcester, Mass., 1903–55), no. 22,039. For the response of North Carolina's representatives in Congress to their instructions, see note 19, below.

[10]Michael E. Stevens and Christine M. Allen, eds., *Journals of the House of Representatives, 1789–1790,* State Records of South Carolina (Columbia, S.C., 1984), pp. 349–51.

ment (on compensation of congressmen), which it defeated 52 to 5, on February 27. Antifederalist Abraham Yates pointed out one reason why the proposed amendments did not generate much excitement in the state. New York's ratification of the Constitution had not been unqualified, at least in its own eyes. It had been modified by the inclusion of a list of twenty-three "rights" that the state held to be unabridged by its act of ratification.[11]

In January 1790 Gov. John Hancock of Massachusetts, a former Antifederalist, transmitted the amendments to the legislature, calling their ratification very important. The senate approved all but the first two (on the size of the House and congressional salaries) and called for a joint committee to consider additional amendments. The house appointed members to the joint committee and agreed to nine of the proposed amendments, rejecting the first two as well as what became the Tenth Amendment on reservation of federal powers to the states, perhaps because it omitted the critical adverb *expressly.* That had been the descriptor included in the first federal constitution, the Articles of Confederation, and in the reservation of powers amendment proposed by the Massachusetts ratification convention in 1788. The senate concurred with the house, and a second joint committee was appointed to bring in a bill. More than a year later Secretary of State Thomas Jefferson wrote one of the state's federal senators requesting an authenticated copy of the state's ratification of the amendments only to learn that the committee had never reported a bill. Massachusetts had failed to complete the ratification process.

When the Massachusetts joint committee on additional amendments made its report, it recommended twelve items: Congress should neither establish commercial monopolies nor interfere in federal elections unless a state failed to provide for an election; republican forms of government should

[11] DeWitt Clinton to Charles Clinton, Feb. 8, 1790, DeWitt Clinton Miscellaneous Manuscripts, New-York Historical Society, New York; Abraham Yates, Miscellaneous Essays, Abraham Yates Papers, Box 3, New York Public Library; assembly debate of Jan. 26, 1790, *Pennsylvania Packet* (Philadelphia), Feb. 10, 1790. For a day-by-day account of New York's ratification, see Kaminski, "Bill of Rights," pp. 51–54.

be guaranteed to the territories of the United States; Congress should use the regular civil authorities—not the military—to enforce compliance to its laws, and the states should have a veto power over peacetime military policy; the federal government should exercise no power that was not "expressly delegated" in the Constitution, and certain tax sources ought to be specifically reserved for the states, except "as war and other extraordinary exigencies may require"; the federal judiciary should "be more explicitly defined," with its jurisdiction specifically distinguished from state courts; the Senate should be divested of executive and judicial powers, and the states should pay the salaries of federal senators and representatives; state legislatures should have the power to recall and replace federal senators; and all senators should be elected at the same time for four-year terms.[12]

The committee stated that its amendments were for the purpose of preserving the forms of a federal republic, thereby preventing the consolidation of the states into one government or the encroachment on them by the federal government. The proposals created a stir among Federalists throughout the United States who saw the effort as an attempt to bolster Antifederalists in Rhode Island, which had not yet ratified the Constitution, and to weaken the federal government, while at the same time launching an opposition to it. The effort failed because the Constitution had much greater support in Massachusetts in 1790 than it had had in 1788. Antifederalists in the senate could do no more than get the report printed, and it soon turned out that the report lacked the support of a majority of the joint committee.[13]

[12] For the joint committee report on additional amendments see [Massachusetts], *In Senate, February 24, 1790 . . . Report* (Boston, 1790), in Evans and Shipton, eds., *American Bibliography,* no. 22,655; the summary here is quoted from Kaminski, "Bill of Rights," pp. 55–56.

[13] In addition to letters cited by Kaminski, see William Ellery to John Adams, March 1790, Adams Family Manuscript Trust, Massachusetts Historical Society, Boston; Henry Jackson to Henry Knox, Mar. 7, 1790, Henry Knox Papers, Mass. Hist. Soc., Boston; Nathaniel Barrell to George Thatcher, Mar. 11, 1790, Thatcher Papers, Boston Public Library; and Fisher Ames to [William Eustis], Mar. 17, 1790, William Eustis Papers, Mass. Hist. Soc., Boston.

On March 10, 1790, Pennsylvania accepted all but the First and Second Amendments. A great irony exists in the fact that the official report came from Speaker of the Assembly Richard Peters, the man who, more than anyone in 1789, sought to dissuade Madison from his support for a bill of rights. In the process, he wrote the "Wise Cooks & Foolish Guests" fable describing how eleven foolish cooks ruined a good soup by adding whatever they pleased to it. This elicited from Madison the phrase "nauseous project" as a descriptor for the process of getting the amendments through the First Congress. He was responding to Peters, and not expressing how he really felt about amendments to the Constitution or the process of getting them recommended to the states.[14]

In May 1790 the Connecticut General Assembly took up the amendments. The assembly adopted all except the First and Second, while the council accepted all twelve, as did the resulting conference committee. The assembly adhered to its original action, and Connecticut, despite the fact that both houses had agreed on ten of the amendments, failed to ratify any of them.[15] In 1939, when the United States celebrated the sesquicentennial of the Bill of Rights, Connecticut joined Georgia and a defensive Massachusetts in belated ratifications.[16]

On June 11, 1790, the Rhode Island General Assembly approved all but the congressional salary amendment. Two weeks earlier, when Rhode Island ratified the Constitution, it proposed twenty-one additional amendments and listed eighteen rights that it, following the language of the New York ratification document verbatim, understood not to be com-

[14] Richard Peters to James Madison, July 20, 1789, and Madison to Peters, Aug. 19, 1789, William T. Hutchinson et al., eds., *The Papers of James Madison*, 22 vols. to date (Chicago and Charlottesville, Va., 1962-), 12:301-3, 346-47.

[15] Bill ratifying certain amendments to the Constitution, May 18, 1790, Civil Officers, ser. 2, vol. 22, doc. 3, Connecticut State Library. This document is courtesy of John P. Kaminski, and corrects an error on page 54 of his "Bill of Rights."

[16] Leverett Saltonstall to Cordell Hull, Mar. 3, 1939, Record Group 11, National Archives, Washington, D.C.

promised by its act of ratification. The additional amendments included several novel ideas, among them a federal guarantee of state sovereignty, a requirement that eleven of the original thirteen states must agree to any amendments after 1793, an all-volunteer army except in cases of invasion, grants of power to Congress to prevent the importation of slaves and to regulate the "inhabitancy or settlement" of the poor throughout the United States, and a requirement of a two-thirds vote in each house to declare war.[17]

Rhode Island's action came near the close of the tumultuous second session of the First Federal Congress, during which the issue of additional amendments to the Constitution had arisen briefly. Representative Fisher Ames of Massachusetts reported concern about the ones that his state senate had ordered printed, and in a speech on the assumption of state debts Representative Theodorick Bland of Virginia observed that he hoped to see the Constitution further amended. As soon as the exhausted House completed its work on the bill funding the federal and state debts, Antifederalist Representative Thomas Tudor Tucker of South Carolina moved that it take up the question of what to do about the additional amendments proposed by the several states. Nothing came of the motion.[18]

Pursuant to instructions from its ratification convention, the North Carolina delegation, under the leadership of Federalist John Steele, had earlier made a serious attempt to force the House to take up the issue. On May 20 Steele moved that a committee of one member from each state be appointed to report on the progress of ratification of the twelve amendments that Congress had recommended to the states and also on what additional amendments the Constitution needed. After some debate the motion lay on the table for a week. Then Federalist Hugh Williamson argued that his state had been unanimous in recommending its eight amendments and that he did not believe they weakened the federal govern-

[17] DePauw, Bickford, and Hauptman, eds., *House Journal*, pp. 571–77.

[18] Ames to [Eustis], Mar. 17, 1790, Eustis Papers; Theodorick Bland speech, Mar. 30, 1790, *Daily Gazette* (New York), Apr. 1, 1790; Thomas Tudor Tucker motion, July 28, 1790, *Daily Gazette* (New York), July 29, 1790.

ment. The motion was divided, and the second part relating to additional amendments lost when only fourteen members voted for it. By July 20 Steele reported that he and Antifederalist Timothy Bloodworth had made an additional attempt, but that it too had been rejected by a large majority.[19]

North Carolina had its final word when, in November 1790, apparently in reaction to the refusal of Congress to consider additional amendments, a member of the state senate moved that a state convention be called to rescind the state's ratification. It was a last gasp, and when the motion lost, Antifederalists abandoned their rearguard attempt to secure constitutional amendments in addition to those proposed by James Madison. Thus ended the debate over the ratification of the Constitution that had begun more than three years earlier.[20] When the question of constitutional amendments arose in the third session of the First Congress, it was in response to concern about how to alter the judicial system created during the first session, not in response to the adoption of the Constitution itself.[21]

By the end of the second session of the First Congress in August 1790, twelve of the thirteen states had acted. Nine had ratified at least ten of the twelve amendments, Georgia had rejected all of them, and Massachusetts and Connecticut

[19] DePauw, Bickford, and Hauptman, eds., *House Journal*, pp. 350, 429; Thomas Lloyd, shorthand notes on debates in the House of Representatives, May 27, 1790, Thomas Lloyd Papers, Library of Congress, translation in Charlene Bangs Bickford, Kenneth R. Bowling, and Helen E. Veit, eds., *Documentary History of the First Federal Congress*, vol. 12, *Debates in the House of Representatives* (Baltimore, 1994); John Steele to Joseph Winston, May 22 and July 20, 1790, Henry M. Wagstaff, ed., *The Papers of John Steele*, 2 vols. (Raleigh, N.C., 1924), 1:61–62, 70–71; Timothy Bloodworth to Gov. Alexander Martin, June 19, 1790, Governor's Papers, North Carolina Department of Archives and History, Raleigh.

[20] Thomas Blount to John Gray Blount, Nov. 27, 1790, Alice B. Keith, ed., *The John Gray Blount Papers*, 2 vols. (Raleigh, N.C., 1959), 2:147.

[21] DePauw, Bickford, and Hauptman, eds., *House Journal*, pp. 768–70. For an analysis of this amendment see Wythe Holt, "'Federal Courts as the Asylum to Federal Interests': Randolph's Report, the Benson Amendment, and the 'Original Understanding' of the Federal Judiciary," *Buffalo Law Review* 36 (1988):341–72.

had each indicated their willingness to adopt ten of the amendments but had failed to complete the ratification process. With ratification by ten states necessary to render the amendments effective, only one more was needed for the amendments to become part of the Constitution. Virginia was the only holdout. More is known about the two-year process of ratification there than about all the other states combined. In the process Virginia set the tone for the debate that would dominate American politics for the next sixty years.

In late September 1789 Virginia's Antifederal senators Richard Henry Lee and William Grayson transmitted copies of the twelve proposed amendments to the governor and the Speaker of the House of Delegates with what proved to be sensational covering letters. Expressing their grief, Lee and Grayson declared that they had done all they could to procure the adoption of the radical amendments proposed by the Virginia ratification convention. They feared the Constitution, if not further amended, would produce a consolidated empire, that is, one in which the states were either abolished or ignored. They predicted that if applications from states desiring further amendment did not succeed, it would not be many years until a sufficient number of state legislatures demanded a second federal convention. Unless, of course, "a dangerous apathy should invade the public mind." Madison considered the letters calculated to keep disaffection with the federal government alive.[22]

The letters were leaked to the press and circulated throughout the United States as a broadside and in newspapers at the end of 1789.[23] The letters, the two senators, and the state itself all quickly came under attack. One of the most

[22] The manuscripts of the Richard Henry Lee and William Grayson letters, dated Sept. 28, 1789, are in the Peter Force Collection, Libr. of Cong. Madison to George Washington, Dec. 5, 1789, Hutchinson et al., eds., *Papers of Madison*, 12:458.

[23] First published in the *Virginia Independent Chronicle* (Richmond) on Dec. 16, 1789, the Lee and Grayson letters were republished in at least a dozen newspapers and as a broadside. Edmund Randolph claimed that the Antifederalists leaked the letter (Randolph to Washington, Nov. 26, 1789, Washington Papers, Libr. of Cong.). For northern reaction to the letters see

widely reprinted newspaper pieces during the First Congress, "A Familiar Epistle," deemed the letters calculated only to create mischief and launched a vicious attack on Richard Henry Lee, whom the author ridiculed for having always considered himself a better man than George Washington. As to "Dicky, we have known him many years. He is a goodnatured fellow when he can have his own way, but as factious as Satan when he is contradicted." Next the anonymous author argued that the two senators found fault with the Union only because it did not give Virginia the controlling power and because the rest of the states were not willing to alter it to its liking. Finally, the author claimed that the spirit of the letters was the same spirit that had led other Virginians in the House of Representatives to raise the issue of the dissolution of the Union during the September 1789 debate over the location of the capital. In one of two newspaper responses, a defender of Virginia agreed that the letters from Lee and Grayson were exceptionable and perhaps should not have been written, stressing that the state had not taken official notice of them.[24]

Not apathy, as Lee and Grayson feared, but satisfaction with Madison's proposals was what had seized the public mind in Virginia. Federalists reported that the letters were not well received, even by some of the men who had voted against the Constitution at the ratification convention. Patrick Henry found little support in the house for an official letter of appreciation to the senators. A movement to postpone consideration of the amendments until 1790, which Henry supported, also failed. Madison found the argument in support of postponement—that it would give the public time to give its opinion on the amendments—untenable because their language

---

Ames to George R. Minot, Jan. 13, 1790, Seth Ames, ed., *Works of Fisher Ames*, 2 vols., (Boston, 1854), 1:72; John Fenno to Joseph Ward, Jan. 31, 1790, Ward Papers, Chicago Historical Society.

[24] "Familiar Epistle," *Connecticut Courant* (Hartford), Jan. 14, 1790 (this piece appeared at least ten times from Vermont to Virginia during the next month alone); "Virginia to New-England, New-York, Pennsylvania, and Carolina," *Virginia Independent Chronicle* (Richmond), Mar. 10, 1790, and "V. to N.E., N.Y., P. and C.," *Times and Potowmack Packet* (Georgetown, Md.), June 23, 1790.

was essentially taken from several of the amendments proposed by the convention. With defeat looming before him, Henry, the most powerful remaining Antifederal voice in the United States, fell back on an old strategy and left Richmond for home. This proved an unfortunate move, for at the end of the session a motion to ask Congress to adopt the rest of the Virginia convention's amendments failed by one vote when the speaker was called on to break a tie.[25]

The most respected Antifederal voice in Virginia, and perhaps in the nation, was that of George Mason, whose call for a bill of rights during the ratification process had been so influential. He had been publicly silenced, for not only was he well known as an advocate of just what Congress had proposed, but the very language of much of it had descended verbatim from his Virginia Declaration of Rights of 1776. Privately, however, he had something to say. "Unless some Material Amendments shall take place," Mason wrote his friend Thomas Jefferson, "I have always apprehended great Danger to the Rights & Liberty of our Country, and to that Cause, in Support of which I have so often had the Honour of acting in Concert with you . . . I fear in vain!" Jefferson responded that he, too, although he approved of the new government on the whole, wished to see additional amendments that would fix the federal government "more surely on a republican basis."[26]

On November 30, 1789, the Virginia House of Delegates voted to ratify all twelve amendments by a good majority and appointed a committee to apply to Congress for additional amendments, expressing particular concern about one limiting Congress's powers of direct taxation. For a while, however, it had looked as if the house might defeat the amend-

---

[25] Kaminski, "Bill of Rights," pp. 57–61, covers ratification of the Bill of Rights in Virginia. Hutchinson et al., eds., *Papers of Madison*, contains many letters relating to its consideration in 1789 (12:440–65). See especially Madison to Washington, Nov. 20, 1789, and Edward Carrington to Madison, Dec. 20, 1789.

[26] George Mason to Jefferson, Mar. 16, 1790, and Jefferson to Mason, June 13, 1790, Robert Allen Rutland, ed., *The Papers of George Mason*, 3 vols. (Chapel Hill, 1970), 3:1189, 1202.

ments. The committee of the whole at first approved only the first ten, defeating the future Ninth and Tenth Amendments, 64 to 58, after a fight led by Edmund Randolph, who considered both, but especially the Ninth, to be ambiguous. His complex argument caused consternation among some supporters of the amendments because they were reluctant to adopt the first ten without the reservation amendments. Madison considered Randolph's concerns altogether fanciful.[27]

The state senate split between those who wanted to adopt and those who feared that adoption would kill any chance for additional amendments, particularly one on direct taxation. Some senators sought postponement until the next session. On December 8 a compromise was reached. The senate agreed to eight of the amendments, postponing until the next session consideration of what became the First, Sixth, Ninth, and Tenth Amendments. The house refused to accept the postponement, each chamber adhered to its position in the conference committee, and consequently none of the amendments were adopted. Both the senate majority and minority felt compelled to enter their reasons on the published senate journal, reflecting a desire for some protection on the changing political sea of the time.

The senate majority's statement was the boldest attempt made by the Antifederalists anywhere in the United States to use the issue of the amendments proposed by the First Congress to stir up opposition to the federal government, but, like the Lee and Grayson letters, it failed. The statement declared that the Constitution had been ratified by Virginia based on the confident hope of "speedily seeing it much more materially altered and amended than it would be by" the inadequate amendments submitted by Congress. While some of the amendments were equivalent to those recommended by the Virginia convention, others were not, in particular the four that had been postponed. These, the senate argued, fell far short of affording the same security to personal rights or "so effectually guarding against the apprehended mischief of the government." Although convinced of the "dangerous ten-

[27] Madison to Washington, Dec. 5, 1789, Hutchinson et al., eds., *Papers of Madison,* 12:459.

dency" of the four postponed articles, the majority declared themselves unwilling to defeat them outright, preferring a postponement so that the people could communicate their opinions to the legislature. The statement included a condemnation of the amendments in general. "These propositions contain all that Congress are disposed to grant . . . and that these are offered in full satisfaction of the whole. . . . Considering therefore that they are far short of what the people of Virginia wish, and have asked, and deeming them by no means sufficient to secure the rights of the people, or to render the government safe and desireable, we think our countrymen ought not to be put off with amendments so inadequate."[28]

Patrick Henry took it upon himself in January 1790 to privately thank Richard Henry Lee for his efforts in the United States Senate on behalf of additional amendments, observing that he saw no ground for good in the amendments proposed by Congress. Nevertheless, by June Lee had reversed himself and come out in favor of Virginia ratifying the amendments. As he told Henry, no prospect of additional amendments existed during the second session of Congress, and the ones proposed were a beginning that alerted the people to their rights. More could be done later. In that regard he proposed that during the second congressional election that summer, each district instruct its representative to procure additional amendments from Congress. Lee's final effort was an official letter in August 1790 to the governor calling for Virginia's ratification of the proposed amendments. Henry, however, was still hopeful for future amendment in January 1791. When this did not materialize, and Madison's strategy proved so successful in defeating the Antifederal whale, Henry later joined the Federalist party rather than cooperate with his old political enemy Madison in a new opposition to it.[29]

[28] *Journal of the Senate of the Commonwealth of Virginia*, [Oct. 19–Dec. 19, 1789] (Richmond, 1790), pp. 61–66.

[29] Patrick Henry to Lee, Jan. 29, 1790, Franklin Collection, Yale University, New Haven; Lee to Henry, June 10, 1790, William Wirt Henry, *Patrick Henry: Life, Correspondence and Speeches*, 3 vols. (New York, 1891), 3:421–22; Lee and John Walker to the governor of Virginia, Aug. 9, 1790, Executive

Arthur Lee, following up on his brother's proposal, raised the issue of additional amendments in his campaign for a seat in the Second Congress. He accused the incumbent of supporting those in the First Congress who had been indisposed to amend the Constitution. The incumbent, his cousin Richard Bland Lee, defended himself and Congress. He stated that as soon as it became evident in 1789 that attempts to destroy the Union and convulse the country would not be made under the guise of amending the Constitution, Congress "without *reluctance* or *hesitation,* agreed to those explicit declarations in favour of 'human liberty and human rights,' which have been recommended to the adoption of the State Legislatures."[30]

Despite Senator Richard Henry Lee's appeal, the Virginia legislature did not take up the amendments in 1790. Instead it devoted its attention to the new issue that dominated southern attention: the funding act of 1790 and particularly its provision for the federal assumption of the state debts. Northerners were content to accept what they had gained by the Compromise of 1790, but many southerners saw assumption, and the doctrine of implied powers that made it possible, as an attack on states' rights. The Virginians, where old political alliances shifted, were the most articulate in their condemnation. Antifederalist Patrick Henry and Federalist Henry Lee joined forces to attack both the policy and constitutionality of assumption. Against this unusual political combination, there was no hope for young John Marshall and the minority of his fellow Federalists who defended assumption.

Long overlooked by historians, the stunning memorial that Virginia sent to the third session of the First Congress in December 1790 illustrates better than anything else the new direction American politics was taking: the Constitution itself

---

Papers, Virginia State Library, Richmond; Henry to James Monroe, Jan. 24, 1791, Monroe Papers, Libr. of Cong.

[30] Richard Bland Lee to Theodorick Lee, June 3, 1790, Richard Bland Lee Papers, Libr. of Cong.; "Richard Bland Lee to the Freeholders of Prince William, Fairfax, Loudoun, Faquier, Stafford, and King Georges Counties," Aug. 21, 1790, Joseph Lyons Miller Collection, Richmond Academy of Medicine.

would not be attacked, but instead the attack would be aimed at its interpretation and its threat to states' rights. By implication it put forth a theory of federalism in which the final power to interpret the constitution lay with the states. Widely reprinted in the press, it marked the first time a state had taken such action and set a precedent for the 1798 Virginia and Kentucky resolutions denying the constitutionality of the Alien and Sedition Acts.

The Federalist newspaper editor Andrew Brown attempted to dismiss Virginia's action, claiming that the legislators who had voted for it must have fallen "asleep in September 1787, (just before the rising of the Federal Convention) and did not awake till a few weeks ago; during which time the Federal Government was adopted and established throughout all the States." Consequently, one of the three resolutions which led to the memorial was "nugatory and ridiculous." For Hamilton the matter was more serious, and he recognized the memorial as symptomatic of a spirit that had to be extinguished if the Constitution was to survive. Soon after the Treasury Department received copies of the first two resolutions, apparently from a federal official in Virginia, Hamilton sought the support of the federal judiciary. Should not "the collective weight of the different parts of the Government . . . be employed in exploding the principles they contain?," he queried John Jay. The chief justice responded cautiously, arguing that such a strong reaction by the federal government would draw more attention to the situation than it deserved.[31]

"Neither policy, Justice, nor the Constitution" warranted

---

[31] Richard Terrell to Garrett Minor, Oct. 27, 1790, Watson Family Papers, University of Virginia, Charlottesville; *Federal Gazette* (Philadelphia), Nov. 20, 1790; Alexander Hamilton to John Jay, Nov. 13, 1790, and Jay to Hamilton, Nov. 28, 1790, Harold A. Syrett and Jacob E. Cooke, eds., *The Papers of Alexander Hamilton,* 27 vols. (New York, 1961–87), 7:149–50, 166–67. The Treasury Department received a draft of the memorial, and probably the resolutions, from John Hopkins, commissioner of loans for Virginia under the funding act; these copies are in the Oliver Wolcott Papers, Connecticut Historical Society, Hartford. The first newspaper publication of the memorial at Richmond is apparently not extant; reprints include *Dunlap's Daily American Advertiser* (Philadelphia), Jan. 18, 1791; *Daily Gazette* (New York), Jan. 20, 1791; *New Hampshire Spy* (Portsmouth), Feb. 2, 1791; and *Augusta Chronicle* (Georgia), Mar. 12, 1791.

the funding act, the memorial argued. The provision in the act that limited to 2 percent the amount of debt principal that the United States could pay off annually was antirepublican. In addition, the act established something in the United States that bore a striking resemblance to the antirepublican system introduced in England after the Glorious Revolution, a system that "has moreover insinuated into the hands of the Executive an unbounded influence, which pervading every branch of the Government bears down all opposition, and daily threatens the destruction of every thing that appertains to English liberty." To create a large monied interest in an agricultural country such as the United States would either prostrate agriculture at the feet of commerce or change the form of the federal government into one fatal to American liberty.

The memorial focused on assumption, giving first the reasons why it was impolitic and unjust and then turning to its "more odious and deformed" implications. No language in the Constitution authorized Congress to assume the state debts. Virginia had been assured during the debate over the ratification of the Constitution that every power not delegated to the federal government was retained by the states: that understanding had made possible its adoption by the state. Virginia refused to acquiesce silently in a measure that violated the hallowed maxim "that every power not granted, was retained." The funding act was unconstitutional, and Congress should revise it in general and, in particular, repeal that part relating to assumption. It did not include the demand that the consent of the state legislatures be obtained before the act took on "a constitutional form," language that had been in the draft version.[32]

Much to the relief of Hamilton and other Federalists, other states in which strong support existed to condemn the funding act as unconstitutional did not react as strongly as Virginia. New Hampshire, whose congressional delegation had been divided on the question of assumption, considered but

---

[32] The memorial is in the Records of the United States Senate, 1A-E1, Record Group 46, Natl. Arch. A copy of a draft of the memorial, apparently sent to the Treasury Department by John Hopkins is in the Wolcott Papers.

did not adopt a resolution declaring the funding act an infringement on the rights of the state. Maryland adopted and then rescinded resolutions that called it a threat to state sovereignty. North Carolina spent days debating the issue but came to no resolution; instead it adopted instructions to its senators to vote against excises on domestically distilled liquor. Hamilton had proposed such an excise in his January 1790 report on public credit, and, when Congress took up an excise bill early in 1791, this legislation, along with the bank bill, would deepen sectional divisions over the interpretation of the Constitution.[33]

A final word came out of Georgia, which had ratified the Constitution unanimously and virtually without debate because it saw a strong federal government as the best way to protect itself from the threats posed by the indigenous Creek Indians and the neighboring Spanish in Florida. Still enamored with the Constitution in 1789, it was the only state to reject all twelve amendments that Congress proposed that year. By late 1790 Georgia had come to perceive the federal government allying itself with the Creeks against the state. This demanded condemnation more than the funding act, and the state legislature adopted resolutions accordingly. In November 1791 a newspaper writer produced a bill of inquest against the First Congress. Among its presentments was "the want of a Bill of Rights, clearly defining the reserved rights of the several states, comprehended in the guarantee of a republican form of government to each state by the constitution of the United States."[34]

Having failed to reach a final decision about ratification of the Bill of Rights in 1789 and having turned its attention to the protection of states' rights in 1790, Virginia again took up

[33] Albert S. Batchellor et al., eds., *New Hampshire State Papers*, 40 vols. (Concord, N.H., 1867–1943), 22:227; *Maryland Journal* (Baltimore), Dec. 31, 1790, and Jan. 4, 11, 1791; Jonathan Hay to James Iredell, Dec. 16, 1790, Griffith J. McRee, *Life and Correspondence of James Iredell*, 2 vols. (New York, 1857–58), 2:303.

[34] *Augusta Chronicle* (Georgia), Sept. 18, 1790–Jan. 15, 1791; *Baltimore Daily Respository*, Nov. 24, 1791.

consideration of the Bill in the fall of 1791. Debate proceeded without the rancor of two years earlier. As a response to the census of 1790 and the congressional debate over reapportionment in the third session of the First Congress early in 1791, Virginia adopted the first of the twelve proposed amendments on November 3, 1791, the one on the size of the House that so many of the states had rejected. On December 14, 1791, the state senate adopted the remaining eleven amendments. The house followed suit the next day.

Because of Virginia's vote, December 15 is celebrated as Bill of Rights day. Nevertheless, to complete the story of the ratification of the Bill of Rights, a few later significant dates must be mentioned. On December 30 Washington informed Congress that Virginia, the long awaited tenth state, had ratified. By the time Virginia acted, however, the number of states required to give the amendments constitutional status had risen to eleven because Vermont had entered the Union. Congress learned on January 14, 1792, that it had ratified all of the amendments on November 3, 1791, more than a month before Virginia. Jefferson informed the states on March 1, 1792, that the ten amendments that we call the Bill of Rights had become part of the Constitution.[35] Ironically, perhaps, considering the number and nature of the structural amendments that the states had called for during the process of considering the Constitution and the subsequent twelve amendments, the two congressionally proposed amendments most clearly structural, the ones on the size of the House and congressional salaries, were not adopted by the states at the time. The latter became the Twenty-seventh Amendment in 1992.

Significantly, the state that gave constitutional status to the Bill of Rights was Virginia, the home of George Mason, whose language in the Virginia Declaration of Rights of 1776 so influenced the federal Bill of Rights; the home of James Madison, whose persistence in the First Congress resulted in its adoption; and the home of Thomas Jefferson, whose forward-looking perspective recognized that the true importance of a bill of rights was "the legal check which it puts into the hands

[35] Kaminski, "Bill of Rights," pp. 60–61.

of the judiciary."[36] The judiciary would wait for more than a century to use that check, preoccupied as it was with questions of federalism. The reemergence of that issue in the form of states' rights during the First Congress had overshadowed interest in the ratification of the Bill of Rights.

In 1789 Madison had championed the cause of amending the Constitution to protect the liberties of individual citizens and led the fight to block any amendments that enhanced the states at the expense of the federal government. Having failed to achieve amendments protecting states' rights, its advocates turned to their legislatures to express concerns about, and disapproval of, federal decisions impacting the states. Madison, who in 1789 had blocked amendments designed to protect states' rights, quickly assumed for himself leadership of their cause in the post-Revolutionary era that lay ahead. Historians have long recognized that, but usually think in terms of the Virginia and Kentucky Resolutions of 1798. They have not only ignored the constitutional importance of the stunning memorial that Virginia sent to Congress in December 1790, but they have also missed the fact that it was James Madison who chose to present it to the House of Representatives on behalf of his state. James Monroe presented it to the Senate. Both houses tabled it without debate. Thomas Jefferson believed that the memorial epitomized "a vast mass of discontent gathered in the South, and how and when it will break god knows. I look forward to it with some anxiety."[37]

[36] Jefferson to Madison, Mar. 15, 1789, Hutchinson et al., eds., *Papers of Madison*, 12:13.

[37] *Gazette of the United States* (Philadelphia), Jan. 15, 1791; Linda Grant DePauw, Charlene Bangs Bickford, and LaVonne Hauptman, eds., *Documentary History of the First Federal Congress*, vol. 1, *Senate Legislative Journal* (Baltimore, 1972), p. 531; Jefferson to Robert R. Livingston, Feb. 4, 1791, Boyd et al., eds., *Papers of Jefferson*, 19:241.

PAUL FINKELMAN

Between Scylla and Charybdis

Anarchy, Tyranny, and the Debate over a Bill of Rights

THE DEBATES OF 1787–89 illustrate how Americans of the Founding period feared tyranny and anarchy and hoped to prevent both through their constitutional structures.[1] Federalists and Antifederalists were deeply concerned with the problem of how to launch a national government that could preserve individual liberty, establish justice, and retain its republican political structure while at the same time creating political and economic stability, ensuring domestic tranquility,

I wish to thank my research assistants Degna Levister, Elayna Nacci, Philip Presby, Marni Schlissel, and Jordan Tamagni for their help and the Brooklyn Law School for its financial support.

[1] During the Revolution a similar debate occurred between loyalists and patriots. "Loyalists, fearful of anarchy, called American whigs 'the violent sons of licentiousness' and charged that, far from preserving liberty, they were introducing 'the worst species of tyranny, and the most dangerous kind of slavery that any country had ever experienced.'" On the other hand, "whigs comprehended and occasionally expressed respect for the tory fear of anarchy through licentiousness." But the patriots "feared unchecked government more than potential anarchy and agreed with Richard Price that between licentiousness and tyranny, licentiousness was 'the least to be dreaded, and has done the least mischief . . . that if licentiousness has destroyed its thousands, despotism has destroyed its millions'" (John Phillip Reid, *The Concept of Liberty in the Age of the American Revolution* [Chicago, 1988], pp. 36–37). Significantly, in the debate over ratification, the Antifederalists often accused their opponents of being tories.

and providing for the common defense. Both Federalists and Antifederalists used the concepts of tyranny and anarchy to bolster their respective positions when debating the need for a bill of rights.

THE FEDERALIST GOAL:
LIBERTY THROUGH STRENGTH

A few months before the Philadelphia Convention began, Alexander Hamilton clearly laid out what would be a mainstay of Federalist thinking: "It might be said that too little power is as dangerous as too much, that it leads to anarchy, and from anarchy to despotism."[2] At the Philadelphia Convention Hamilton argued that a proper governmental structure would prevent anarchy and tyranny: "If government [is] in the hands of the few, they will tyrannize over the many," but if the government is in "the hands of the many, they will tyrannize over the few." The solution was that the government should "be in the hands of both; and they should be separated." Hamilton believed the Constitution's separation of powers would prevent aristocracy, tyranny, and anarchy.[3] In this regard Hamilton had simply expanded on concepts from the Revolutionary period that "free government . . . was balanced government, under which branches of the legislature were mutually independent."[4]

Connecticut's delegation reported to the governor that "the Convention endeavored to provide for the energy of government on the one hand and suitable checks on the other hand to secure the rights of the particular states, and the liberties and properties of the citizens." The Constitution was a means

[2] Speech of Alexander Hamilton in the New York Assembly, Jan. 19, 1787, Harold C. Syrett and Jacob E. Cooke, eds., *The Papers of Alexander Hamilton*, 27 vols. (New York, 1961–87), 4:706.

[3] Max Farrand, ed., *The Records of the Federal Convention of 1787*, rev. ed., 4 vols. (New Haven, 1966), 1:308–9.

[4] John Phillip Reid, *Constitutional History of the American Revolution: The Authority of Rights* (Madison, Wis., 1986), p. 20.

"of securing" the rights of the states "and lengthening their tranquility."[5]

Federalists thought the Constitution contained the right combination of checks and balances to prevent anarchy without imposing tyranny on the nation. They believed that liberty and stability through a strong central government was the accomplishment of the Convention.

Federalists also believed that security from foreign powers and domestic stability were prerequisites to ensuring liberty. George Washington told Lafayette that the Constitution would "guard against . . . calamities of domestic discourd or foreign interposition to secure our liberties, with all the benefits of an efficient Government."[6] Citizens in Delaware believed the Constitution would bring about "peace, stability, efficacy, and prosperity in all the confederate states, respect and confidence to foreign nations, and meet the applause and cordial approbation of all the true votaries of LIBERTY whatever country they inhabit."[7] The "Tradesmen of the Town of Boston" similarly thought that "the proposed frame of government, is well calculated to secure the liberties, protect the property, and guard the rights of the citizens of America" while at the same time "revive and increase" the nation's "trade and navigation" and "promote industry and morality."[8]

James Madison was less concerned about international trade and foreign affairs than about successful government at home. He urged his friends in Virginia to support ratification because the Constitution "blend[ed] a proper stability & en-

[5] Roger Sherman and Oliver Ellsworth to Gov. Samuel Huntington, Sept. 26, 1787, Merrill Jensen, John P. Kaminski, and Gaspare J. Saladino, eds., *The Documentary History of the Ratification of the Constitution*, 10 vols. to date (Madison, Wis., 1976-), 3:351 (hereafter cited as *DHR*).

[6] George Washington to the marquis de Lafayette, Jan. 10, 1788, ibid., 15:331.

[7] "Petition of New Castle County Inhabitants," ibid., 3:54–55.

[8] "Resolutions of the Tradesmen of the Town of Boston," Jan. 7, 1787, ibid., 15:293.

ergy in the Government with the essential characters of the republican Form" while retaining "a proper line of demarcation between the national and State authorities."[9] James Wilson believed the Constitution provided for a government that would combine the "vigor" of a "wide-spreading monarchy" and the "freedom and beneficence of a contracted republic."[10]

The major reservation Federalists had about the Constitution was that the new national government might not be strong enough to secure stability. Madison was initially ambivalent about the Constitution because it did not create a powerful, consolidated government. "Madison was not convinced that the proposed plan went far enough to control the democratic excesses of the state governments."[11] Indeed, "the Constitution Madison expounded and defended as 'Publius' was a pale version of the plan he had carefully worked out before the Philadelphia meeting."[12] He thought the proposed plan was a vast improvement over the Confederation, but privately admitted that the new government might be too weak and would "neither effectually answer its national object nor prevent the local mischiefs which every where excite disgusts agst. the state governments."[13] He regretted that the Conven-

[9] James Madison to Edmund Pendleton, Sept. 20, 1787, William T. Hutchinson et al., eds., *The Papers of James Madison,* 22 vols. to date (Chicago and Charlottesville, Va., 1962-), 10:171.

[10] Jonathan Elliot, ed., *The Debates in the Several State Conventions, on the Adoption of the Federal Constitution,* 2d ed., 5 vols. (1888; reprint ed., New York, 1968), 2:428 (speech of James Wilson at the Pennsylvania ratifying convention, Nov. 26, 1787).

[11] Peter S. Onuf, "James Madison's Extended Republic," *Texas Tech Law Review* 21 (1990):2375–76. On Madison's unhappiness with the Constitution, see generally Jack N. Rakove, *Original Meanings: Politics and Ideas in the Making of the Constitution* (New York, 1996).

[12] Charles F. Hobson, "The Negative on State Laws: James Madison, the Constitution, and the Crisis of Republican Government," *William and Mary Quarterly,* 3d ser. 36 (1979):217.

[13] Madison to Thomas Jefferson, Sept. 6, 1787, Hutchinson et al., eds., *Papers of Madison,* 10:163–64.

tion had rejected his proposal to give Congress a "constitutional negative on the laws of the States."[14]

Madison feared that a weak national government would lead to tyranny at the state level, anarchy at the national level, and instability everywhere. Other Federalists agreed with this analysis. Throughout the debates of 1787–89 Federalists returned again and again to the argument that the new government needed to be strong to defend successfully against foreign powers and to prevent domestic anarchy, which the Federalists believed were the two greatest threats to liberty. These Federalists opposed the addition of a bill of rights because they understood that amendments would be a limitation on government.

THE ANTIFEDERALIST GOAL: LIBERTY THROUGH DEMOCRACY AND GUARANTEES OF RIGHTS

Where Federalists thought the Constitution created a government that was barely capable of staving off anarchy, Antifederalists saw a dangerously strong central government with no bill of rights, a powerful executive, a standing army, an aristocratic Senate, and a judiciary with seemingly limitless jurisdiction. They believed that under this Constitution tyranny was just around the corner.

Even before the Constitution was written some future Antifederalists anticipated the arguments of the Federalists against a bill of rights, while at the same time pointing out the dangers to liberty that could come from a strong government. In 1784 Thomas Tudor Tucker, writing as Philodemus, accused those favoring a stronger government (who might be called proto-Federalists) of using the threat of "anarchy and confusion" to promote antidemocratic institutions. Such men argued that "the capricious humour of the people" led them to "run riot with too much liberty" and made them "always unreasonable in their demands." Accordingly, the people were "never satisfied but when ruled with a rod of iron." Tucker

[14] Madison to Jefferson, Oct. 24, 1787, ibid., p. 212.

dismissed such an analysis as "the pleas of ambition to introduce Aristocracy, Monarchy, and every species of tyranny and oppression."[15]

Tucker also anticipated Federalist arguments that anarchy was the greatest menace to society and that a bill of rights would create too much liberty and lead to instability. Tucker conceded that "a government approaching to Democracy, is apt to be disorderly." But was this so terrible? He argued that, in a democracy, "the people have a right to complain."[16] Tucker, who became an Antifederalist in 1787, thought the threat of aristocracy and tyranny from a strong central government far outweighed the "disorder" that might be caused by liberties.

Ideas like Tucker's were in circulation in 1787. Thus, when the Constitution was presented to the American people, the opposition immediately coalesced around the threat to democracy, the lack of a bill of rights, and the potential of tyranny.

When Patrick Henry looked at the Constitution, he did not see the "beautiful features" Madison saw. "When I come to examine these features," Henry told Virginia's ratifying convention, "they appear to me horridly frightful: Among other deformities, it has an awful squinting; it squints towards monarchy. . . . Your President may easily become King."[17] Members of the Society of Western Gentlemen in Washington County, Virginia, who claimed to reflect the "sentiment of the great body of the Yeomanry of America, especially in the Southern States," simply believed that the Constitution "seems to have too many of the features of despotism." To

---

[15] Philodemus [Thomas Tudor Tucker], "Conciliatory Hints, Attempting, by a Fair State of Matters, to Remove Party Prejudice" (1784), Charles S. Hyneman and Donald S. Lutz, eds., *American Political Writing during the Founding Era, 1760–1805*, 2 vols. (Indianapolis, 1983), 1:616.

[16] Ibid., p. 617.

[17] "Speeches of Patrick Henry in the Virginia State Ratifying Convention," June 5, 1788, Herbert J. Storing, ed., *The Complete Anti-Federalist*, 7 vols. (Chicago, 1981), 5:224 (hereafter cited as *CAF*).

prevent this despotism, they proposed a "Declaration of Rights."[18]

Some Antifederalists, especially Henry, wanted nothing at all to do with the new Constitution; others believed that with amendments the Constitution might be palatable. The majority of Antifederalists wanted some guarantee that the new government would not become a tyranny or a monarchy. Antifederalists proposed numerous structural changes, but their most common demand was a bill of rights.

THE COMMON FEAR

While Federalists and Antifederalists disagreed about the potential benefits or dangers of the Constitution, they were in striking agreement about what might happen if their worst nightmares came true. Both sides discussed the threat of tyranny and anarchy in the debates over ratification and the Bill of Rights. Ironically, both Federalists and Antifederalists envisioned similar outcomes if their formula for success failed; they genuinely believed that the liberty they struggled for during the Revolution hung in the balance of the debate over the Constitution.

Simply put, Federalists feared the nation would collapse into anarchy if they failed to secure the adoption of the Constitution as written and if they then failed to prevent the addition of amendments that might alter the structure of the new government and weaken its power. Conversely, Antifederalists feared that the nation would slip into tyranny if the Constitution were adopted without amendments explicitly protecting liberty.

The Federalist Nightmare

Federalists believed a strong central government would create prosperity *and* preserve liberty through stability and strength.

---

[18] Arthur Campbell to Francis Bailey, Mar. 8, 1788, and Campbell to Adam Orth, Mar. 9, 1788, *DHR*, 16:352–53.

Even before the Convention finished its deliberations John Marshall, who was not a delegate, succinctly stated the emerging Federalist position: "Nothing but the adoption of some efficient plan from the Convention can prevent Anarchy first, & civil Convulsions afterwards."[19] After the Convention, Oliver Ellsworth, who would precede Marshall as chief justice, summed up this position: "Anarchy, or a want of such government as can protect the interests of the subjects against foreign and domestic injustice, is the worst of all conditions."[20]

Although until May 1789 they were nearly unanimous in opposing the addition of a bill of rights to the Constitution, most Federalists were not hostile to individual liberty.[21] Tench Coxe would "readily admit that the most serious Convulsions of our Empire should not induce us to sacrifice the essential requisites of Liberty & Happiness." But, he warned, "we have more than *the fear* of Anarchy before us."[22] Coxe, like most Federalists, thought the Constitution did not "sacrifice . . . Liberty & Happiness," but that it would stave off anarchy.

From 1787 to 1789 Federalists simply doubted that liberty could be secured through a bill of rights. Federalists believed instability, chaos, and eventually anarchy were the greatest threats to liberty. The Federalists' motto might have been "liberty through stability." For Federalists the proper method of protecting fundamental rights was a strong central govern-

---

[19] James McClurg to Madison, Aug. 5, 1787, James H. Hutson, ed., *Supplement to Max Farrand's The Records of the Federal Convention of 1787* (New Haven, 1987), pp. 205–6.

[20] "A Landholder" [Oliver Ellsworth] (IX), *Connecticut Courant* (Hartford), Dec. 31, 1787, *DHR*, 3:515.

[21] Madison assured Jefferson that he had "always been in favor of a bill of rights" (Madison to Jefferson, Oct. 17, 1788, Hutchinson et al., eds., *Papers of Madison*, 11:297–98). Whether Madison really had "always" favored a bill of rights seems questionable. In this letter Madison also offered a litany of Federalist arguments against a bill of rights. See, generally, Paul Finkelman, "James Madison and the Adoption of the Bill of Rights: A Reluctant Paternity," *Supreme Court Review* (1990):301–47.

[22] "An American" [Tenche Coxe] to Richard Henry Lee (II), *DHR*, 15:175.

ment, not the adoption of what Madison derisively called "parchment barriers." [23] As Gov. Samuel Huntington of Connecticut argued, the main cause of tyranny among a free people "has been their not supporting government." [24] Strong and stable government, not a declaration of rights, was the way Federalists would protect liberty. Alexander Hamilton argued that "a Firm Union will be the utmost moment to the peace and liberty of the States" and would prevent "domestic faction and insurrection." The alternative was a society "kept in a state of perpetual vibration, between the extremes of tyranny and anarchy." Only the Constitution could prevent the recurring "tempestuous waves of sedition and party-rage." [25]

The Federalists believed that a bill of rights would not prevent tyranny. Rather they feared that any amendments might so weaken the national government that it could not function. A weak government would lead to anarchy, and the only way to stop anarchy was with military force. Hence, the Federalist nightmare was that a bill of rights would lead to a weak government, which in turn would lead to anarchy, tyranny, or both.

The Antifederalist Nightmare

Antifederalists feared that without a bill of rights the national government would destroy fundamental liberties. The people would eventually oppose this oppression, which would lead to civil war, and in turn lead to either anarchy or tyranny.

Just as most Federalists were not against liberty per se, many Antifederalists did not totally oppose a stronger national union. However, to pass Antifederalist muster such a compact had to prevent tyranny and preserve liberty. Richard Henry Lee, like his Federalist opponents, preferred "a

[23] Madison to Jefferson, Oct. 17, 1788, Hutchinson et al., eds., *Papers of Madison,* 11:297–98.

[24] Samuel Huntington, Oliver Wolcott, Sr., and Richard Law, "Speeches in the Connecticut Convention," Jan. 9, 1788, *DHR,* 15:313.

[25] *Federalist* No. 9, Garry Wills, ed., *The Federalist Papers* (New York, 1982), pp. 37–38.

bad Government to Anarchy."[26] Lee believed "our greater strength, safety, and happiness, depends on our union." But Lee was adamant that "this union had infinitely better be on principles that give security to the just rights and liberties of mankind" and not on "principles as permit rulers to destroy them."[27] Similarly, Melancton Smith was "strongly impressed with the necessity of a union as any one could be" and said he would willingly "sacrifice every thing for a union, except the liberties of his country." Smith thought this "dreadful" alternative—between liberty and union—could be avoided by amendments, including a bill of rights, or a new convention. Smith agreed with the staunchest Federalists that "the defects of the old Confederation needed as little proof as the necessity of a union." He agreed the old Confederation was "defective" but thought the Federalist cure—the new Constitution— would only make things worse. He doubted that the proposed Constitution "was a good one."[28]

The anonymous "Federal Farmer" at times seemed almost as enthusiastic about the Constitution as any Federalist might be.[29] He acknowledged his generation was "making a consti-

[26.] Richard Henry Lee, paraphrased in "An American" [Coxe] to Lee (II), *DHR*, 15:174.

[27] Lee to James Gordon, Jr., Feb. 26, 1788, ibid., 16:211.

[28] Elliot, ed., *Debates*, 2:221–22 (speech of Melancton Smith at the New York ratifying convention, June 20, 1788).

[29] Traditionally the "Letters from the Federal Farmer to the Republican" were attributed to Richard Henry Lee. William Winslow Crosskey, Herbert Storing, Gordon S. Wood, and J. R. Pole all conclude that this is not the case (see Crosskey, *Politics and the Constitution in the History of the United States*, 2 vols. [Chicago, 1953], 2:1299–1300n; *CAF*, 2:215; Wood, "The Authorship of the *Letters from the Federal Farmer*," *William and Mary Quarterly*, 3d ser. 31 [1974]: 299–308; and Pole, *The Constitution—For and Against: The Federalist and the Anti-Federalist Papers* [New York, 1987], p. 28). Steven R. Boyd, "Impact of the Constitution on State Politics: New York as Test Case," in James Kirby Martin, ed., *The Human Dimensions of Nation Making: Essays on Colonial and Revolutionary America* (Madison, Wis., 1976), p. 276n, argues on the basis of overwhelming contemporary evidence that Lee was the "Federal Farmer." Short of the unlikely discovery of some "smoking gun" document, this riddle is unlikely to be fully resolved. Perhaps the final comment on who the "Federal Farmer" was is best left to a contemporary Antifederal-

tution, it is to be hoped, for ages and millions yet unborn."[30] Precisely because of this expected longevity, the "Federal Farmer" thought a bill of rights was absolutely necessary to preserve liberty. For example, with surprising prescience, the "Federal Farmer" noted that while most Americans of 1787 did not have insurmountable disagreements about religion, in the future a written guarantee of "free exercise of religion" would be useful. This was just one example why Antifederalists concluded it was necessary to formally protect liberty through written guarantees.

A constitution "for ages and millions yet unborn" had to guarantee stability and security. Antifederalists were not opposed to either but doubted if these goals could be achieved without protections of liberty. Like the Federalists, Samuel Osgood conceded "the extreme Necessity of a more efficient federal Government than the present." But he was unwilling to achieve stability through "Despotism."[31] Richard Henry Lee agreed with his Federalist opponents that securing financial credit in Europe was vital to the success of the nation and that "credit abroad depends much upon union and happiness at home." But he argued that such union and happiness could only be achieved through "that industry and real strength which grows out of the possession of civil liberty."[32]

In the same vein Philadelphiensis agreed that a capable common defense was important but believed that "for a new country to become strong and energetic, so as to be able to repel a foreign foe, the government must be *free* and *patriotic*." Philadelphiensis argued that the failure to protect basic liberties, including freedom of the press and the right of the people to maintain a militia—liberties that would be secured

---

ist, who anticipated the modern debate: "It is not material whether the federal farmer belongs to Virginia or Kamtschatka—whether he owns five hundred negroes, or is a man of no property at all—if his arguments are cogent—his reasonings conclusive" ("Essays by Helvidius Priscus," Jan. 22, 1788, *CAF*, 4:158).

[30] "Letters from the Federal Farmer" (IV), *CAF*, 2:249.

[31] Samuel Osgood to Samuel Adams, Jan. 5, 1788, *DHR*, 15:263.

[32] Lee to Gordon, Feb. 26, 1788, ibid., 16:211.

in the First and Second Amendments—seriously weakened the new nation. Philadelphiensis was certain that under the proposed constitution the "government will neither be *free* nor *patriotic;* but on the contrary, *despotic* and *oppressive;* and the people will be *abject slaves,* toiling to support a government, which they curse in their hearts; a government composed only of an *emperor and a few lordlings,* surrounded by thousands of blood-suckers, and cringing sycophants."[33]

THE FEAR OF ANARCHY AND TYRANNY AT THE CONSTITUTIONAL CONVENTION

The fear of tyranny and anarchy did not emerge full blown during the ratification debates. When the Philadelphia Convention began most of the delegates thought that the nation faced anarchy if the national government was not strengthened. They understood that if they were not careful they might avoid anarchy only to find they had created a tyranny. These themes, which would come to dominate the debates over the bill of rights, first emerged during the creation of the Constitution.

The Scylla of Anarchy at the Constitutional Convention

While introducing the Virginia Plan, Edmund Randolph, who would later express his fears of tyranny, raised the specter of anarchy. Randolph discussed "the difficulty of the crisis, and the necessity of preventing the fulfillment of the prophecies of the American downfal." He argued that "the danger of our situation" included the inability of the national government to guard "against dissentions between members of the Union, or seditions in particular states." Randolph asserted that one of "the defects of the confederation" was "that the foederal government could not check the quarrals between states, nor a rebellion in any[,] not having constitutional power Nor means to interpose." Reminding delegates of the

---

[33] "Essays of Philadelphiensis" (III), *CAF,* 3:111. Philadelphiensis is believed to have been Benjamin Workman, a University of Pennsylvania mathematics tutor.

recent "rebellion . . . in Massts." he warned of "the prospect of anarchy from the laxity of government every where."[34]

For the rest of the Convention the emerging Federalists used the threat of anarchy to argue for a stronger national government. Weakness, they consistently asserted, would lead first to anarchy and would result in tyranny. For example, during the debate over what became Article II of the Constitution, Randolph, anticipating later Antifederalist fears of tyranny, argued that a single executive would be "the foetus of monarchy."[35] James Wilson responded that "Unity in the Executive instead of being the fetus of Monarchy would be the best safeguard against tyranny." Wilson asserted that the uncertainty and chaos of a "plurality in the Executive of Government would probably produce a tyranny as bad as the thirty Tyrants of Athens, or as the Decemvirs of Rome."[36] A three-man executive, designed to prevent a dictatorship, would lead to "anarchy and confusion."[37]

Madison made a similar point, asserting that a strong central government was preferable to a weak alliance of the states: "All the examples of other confederacies prove the greater tendency in such systems to anarchy than to tyranny; to a disobedience of the members than to usurpations of the federal head."[38] Charles Pinckney argued that a strong national government was necessary to create "a real military force." He noted that "the United States had been making an experiment without" a strong military "and we see the consequence in their rapid approaches toward anarchy."[39] James Wilson believed the nation had to worry about "anarchy & tyranny within" but also needed to be strong to avoid "wars" and to make "treaties."[40]

[34] Farrand, ed., *Records of the Convention*, 1:18–19.

[35] Ibid., p. 66.

[36] Ibid., pp. 66, 74.

[37] Ibid., p. 105.

[38] Ibid., p. 356.

[39] Ibid., 2:332.

[40] Ibid., 1:426.

Hamilton similarly thought that the greatest threat to liberty came from government instability. He believed the Convention was "now to decide for ever the fate of Republican Government; and that if we did not give to that form due stability and wisdom, it would be disgraced & lost among ourselves, disgraced & lost to mankind for ever." Hamilton "professed himself to be as zealous an advocate for liberty as any man whatever, and trusted he should be as willing a martyr to it though he differed as to the form in which it was most eligible."[41] He believed a powerful central government, not a bill of rights, was the key to liberty. Similarly, Wilson argued that a weak government would be "liable to anarchy & tyranny."[42] Hugh Williamson feared that "the probable consequences of anarchy in the U.S." would be military force against the states, which in turn would lead to tyranny.[43]

During a debate over representation, Gouverneur Morris equated liberty with the lack of government and property with stability in government. The protection of the latter, he thought, was the goal of civil society. Morris noted that "life and liberty were generally said to be of more value, than property. An accurate view of the matter would nevertheless prove that property was the main object of Society. The savage State was more favorable to liberty than the Civilized; and sufficiently so to life. It was preferred by all men who had not acquired a taste for property; it was only renounced for the sake of property which could only be secured by the restraints of regular Government."[44]

For Morris and many other delegates, property could only be protected by a sacrifice of at least some individual liberty; in other words, some tyranny was necessary to protect property and prevent anarchy.[45] This position reflected a conserva-

[41] Ibid., p. 324.

[42] Ibid., p. 426.

[43] Ibid., p. 532.

[44] Ibid.; John Rutledge of South Carolina immediately endorsed these sentiments (ibid., p. 533).

[45] Ibid., p. 552. In discussing the makeup of the Congress, Gouverneur Morris expressed concern that the small states would exploit "the necessity

tive tradition of the Revolutionary period,[46] aptly expressed by John Dickinson that people "cannot be happy, without Freedom, nor free, without Security of Property."[47]

The possibility of instability and insurrection made Nathaniel Gorham of Massachusetts anxious to see a stronger central government, even if it threatened liberty. Reminding the Convention of Shays's Rebellion, Gorham argued that only a strong national government could prevent some "enterprising Citizen" from erecting "the standard of Monarchy in a particular State" and then "extend[ing] his views from State to State, and threaten to establish a tyranny over the whole & the Genl. Govt."[48] While couched as an opposition to tyranny, Gorham's main concern was the threat of rebellion, violence, and anarchy.

In the end supporters of the Constitution made it clear that they favored stability over liberty and, forced to choose, they would accept some tyranny to avoid any anarchy. Most Federalists accepted the argument that anarchy or a popular demagogic tyranny was the only alternative to supporting the Constitution. In urging all the delegates to sign the Constitution, Morris admitted that he had some reservations about the proposed government. But, he asserted, "the moment this plan goes forth all other considerations will be laid aside— and the great question will be, shall there be a national Government or not? and this must take place or a general anarchy will be the alternative."[49] Hamilton declared that "no man's

---

of preventing anarchy, and taking advantage of the moment" would "extort" political equality from the large states. This at least suggests that the fear of anarchy might have driven Federalists from large states to make concessions to delegates from smaller states.

[46] During the Revolution, Lee and others who eventually became Antifederalists were at odds with Morris, John Jay, and other conservatives (see Gordon S. Wood, *The Creation of the American Republic, 1776–1787* [Chapel Hill, 1969], p. 420). Part of the debate over the Constitution and the Bill of Rights was a continuation of these earlier disagreements over the nature of government in America.

[47] John Dickinson, quoted in Reid, *Constitutional History*, p. 36.

[48] Farrand, ed., *Records of the Convention*, 2:48.

[49] Ibid., p. 645.

ideas were more remote from the plan than his own were known to be; but is it possible to deliberate between anarchy and Convulsion on one side, and the chance of good to be expected from the plan on the other."[50]

Wilson contemptuously dismissed his opponents' fears. "Bad Governts. are of two sorts. 1. that which does too little. 2. that which does too much: that which fails thro' weakness; and that which destroys thro' oppression. Under which of these evils do the U. States at present groan? under the weakness and inefficiency of its Governt. To remedy this weakness we have been sent to this Convention."[51]

The Charybdis of Tyranny at the Convention

Most Convention delegates believed that under the Articles of Confederation the country was collapsing and something needed to be done to prevent anarchy. Nevertheless, even the delegates most concerned about chaos also worried about tyranny. But for a few delegates who would eventually become Antifederalists, the fear of tyranny outweighed their fear of anarchy. Ultimately, however, there was a crucial distinction in the way supporters and opponents of the Constitution viewed the problem of tyranny.

Initially some future Federalists were nervous that a strong national executive would become a tyrant. In early June, Charles Pinckney warned that "the Executive" might become "a Monarchy, of the worst kind, towit an elective one."[52] At first Roger Sherman wanted the executive appointed "by the Legislature" and was "for making him absolutely dependent on that body, as it was the will of that which was to be executed." "An independence of the Executive on the supreme Legislative," Sherman believed, was "the very essence of tyranny if there was any such thing."[53]

By the end of the Convention, however, most Federalists

[50] Ibid., pp. 645–46.

[51] Ibid., 1:483–84.

[52] Ibid., pp. 64–65.

[53] Ibid., p. 68.

no longer feared the executive. Rather, they favored a strong executive, who would not be limited by an overpowerful Congress or a bill of rights. Wilson argued that the "prejudices agst the Executive resulted from a misapplication of the adage that the parliament was the palladium of liberty. Where the Executive was really formidable, King and Tyrant, were naturally associated in the minds of people; not legislature and tyranny. But where the Executive was not formidable, the two last were most properly associated. After the destruction of the King in Great Britain, a more pure and unmixed tyranny sprang up in the parliament than had been exercised by the monarch." Wilson "insisted" that the Constitution really needed a "self-defensive power either to the Executive or Judiciary department" to prevent a legislative tyranny.[54] Morris similarly feared a "legislative tyranny" which he "consider[ed] . . . the great danger to be apprehended."[55]

The emerging Antifederalists were also concerned about the power of the legislature. But this was only a superficial point of agreement. The Federalists, hoping for a strong executive, feared that the legislature would limit the flexibility of the president. The Antifederalists, fearful of too much power in national government, feared the Congress would trample on the liberties of the people. Federalists would have weakened the Congress to strengthen the president; Antifederalists would have weakened both to prevent tyranny.

At the end of the Convention, Randolph explained that he could not sign the Constitution because he could not "promote the establishment of a plan which he verily believed would end in Tyranny."[56] Among his many fears was the "necessary and proper clause." During the ratification contest Antifederalists would focus on this clause, along with the lack of a bill of rights, to explain why the Constitution endangered liberty.

Similarly, Elbridge Gerry refused to sign the Constitution because he feared the prospect of a national legislature that

[54] Ibid., 2:300–301.

[55] Ibid., pp. 403–4, 551.

[56] Ibid., p. 564.

could pass whatever it deemed was "necessary and proper," unrestrained by a bill of rights but aided and supported by a powerful executive. Gerry thought that the failure to have annual elections destroyed "the only defence of the people agst. tyranny." He thought the lack of annual elections was as dangerous as "a hereditary Executive."[57] Federalists told Gerry and other skeptics that they had nothing to fear from the legislature of a republic elected by Americans. Gerry succinctly responded: "Confidence is the road to tyranny."[58]

Besides fearing an omnipotent legislature, the emerging Antifederalists also expressed their fear of the president, who would be commander-in-chief of the army and, like the Congress, be unrestrained by a bill of rights. Gerry reminded the Convention that "our fellow citizens" were virtually unanimous in their opposition to "Monarchy." He warned that they would never "agree to a plan which seems to make such an approach" toward monarchy, and thus the "Convention ought to be extremely cautious in what they hold out to the people." If the people should believe the Constitution would lead to monarchy it might "rouse a violent opposition" that could lead to "discord & confusion."[59] Randolph argued for a three-man executive to prevent the "Danger of Monarchy, or Tyranny."[60]

Near the end of the Convention Randolph proposed a second convention to consider amendments that would come from the states. Randolph expressed concern for the "indefinite and dangerous power given by the Constitution to Congress." George Mason seconded Randolph's motion, arguing that the "power and structure of the Government" would "end either in monarchy, or a tyrannical aristocracy."[61] Gerry would not sign the Constitution because he believed it would

[57] Ibid., 1:215.

[58] Ibid., 2:285.

[59] Ibid., 1:425–26.

[60] Ibid., p. 71.

[61] Ibid., 2:631–32.

lead to "a Star-chamber as to Civil cases," a standing army, and other dangers to liberty.[62] Two days later Gerry predicted "with painful feelings" that "a Civil war may result from the present crisis of the U.S."[63]

By the end of the Convention, George Mason determined that under the necessary and proper clause "the Congress may grant Monopolies in Trade & Commerce, constitute new Crimes, inflict unusual and severe Punishments, and extend their Power as far as they shall think proper; so that the State Legislatures have no Security for the Powers now presumed to remain to them, or the People for their Rights." He further noted, "There is no Declaration of any kind, for preserving the Liberty of the Press, or the Tryal by jury in civil Causes; nor against the Danger of standing Armys in time of Peace." Sadly, Mason concluded, "This Government will commence in a moderate Aristocracy: it is at present impossible to foresee whether it will, in it's Operation, produce a Monarchy, or a corrupt oppressive Aristocracy; it will most probably vibrate some years between the two, and then terminate in the one or the other."[64]

The Convention's end marked the beginning of an argument, popular among most Antifederalists, that without a bill of rights the new constitution would lead to tyranny and oppression. As Richard Henry Lee predicted during the early stages of the ratification process, if the Constitution were ratified as written "either a tyranny will result from it, or it will be prevented by a Civil war."[65]

This theme—the fear of tyranny that might lead to violence and civil war—would dominate Antifederalist thought throughout the struggle for a bill of rights. In opposition to this argument, Federalists would assert that a bill of rights was

[62] Ibid., p. 633.

[63] Ibid., p. 647.

[64] There is some dispute as to whether George Mason actually gave this speech in the convention or merely wrote it out while in Philadelphia and published it later (ibid., p. 640).

[65] Lee to Mason, Oct. 1, 1787, *DHR*, 8:28–29.

unnecessary and perhaps even dangerous to the liberties of the people and that those who supported it were simply trying to undermine the Constitution itself.

THE FEAR OF ANARCHY: FEDERALIST OPPOSITION TO A BILL OF RIGHTS

The ink was hardly dry on the printed copies of the Constitution when citizens in Berkeley County, Virginia, declared that the new form of government would "secure peace, liberty and safety to the citizens of the United States."[66] A few days later a Fairfax County meeting asserted that "the Peace, Security, and Prosperity of the State of Virginia and the United States in general do depend on the speedy Adoption of the System of Government."[67] Thus began a Federalist propaganda campaign that focused on the threat of anarchy and the necessity of a speedy ratification without any amendments.

Federalists feared the persistent complaints about the lack of a bill of rights would prevent ratification and this would lead to anarchy. Even after ratification, they did not want the Constitution amended. They feared that any amendments, including a bill of rights, would weaken the national government and create instability. With the nation at a crossroads between anarchy and stable government, Federalists believed that only the Constitution could defeat the former and secure the latter.

Federalist opposition to amendments was based on a complicated analysis that included some or all of three related arguments. First, Federalists rejected the notion that a bill of rights was really necessary to protect liberty under the Constitution. Second, Federalists argued that the very demand for a bill of rights undermined the nation and threatened to create anarchy or demagogic tyranny. Third, most Federalists believed that those people who called for a bill of rights were insincere in their demands for protections of liberty.

Federalists thought the call for a bill of rights was a smoke screen for a different agenda: to prevent the adoption of the

[66] Resolution of the Berkeley County meeting, Sept. 28, 1787, ibid., p. 22.

[67] Ibid., pp. 23–24.

Constitution altogether. This led to ad hominem attacks on proponents of a bill of rights; Federalists assumed they were either stupid men who did not understand the workings of the proposed Constitution or evil people willing to sacrifice stability and risk anarchy to further their own very narrow self-interest. The most Federalists would concede was that after ratification there would be time enough for amendments, if they were truly necessary. Thus Hamilton concluded *Federalist* No. 85: "The zeal for attempts to amend, prior to the establishment of the constitution must abate in . . . all sincere lovers of the union, and ought to put them upon their guard against hazarding anarchy, civil war, a perpetual alienation of the states from each other, and perhaps the military despotism of a victorious demagogue, in the pursuit of what they are not likely to obtain, but from TIME and EXPERIENCE."[68]

The Unnecessary Bill of Rights

Federalists made six general arguments against the necessity of a bill of rights. Most of these, as historian J. R. Pole has put it, were "rather lame."[69] In opposing a bill of rights Federalists argued that: (1) rights were fully protected by the state constitutions; (2) under a constitution with enumerated and limited powers the national government could never abridge individual liberties; (3) a bill of rights might endanger liberty because it would be incomplete, and any rights not protected would be permanently lost; (4) under a republican form of government a bill of rights was unnecessary; (5) the Constitution as written already protected individual rights and thus a bill of rights was redundant; and (6) a bill of rights would be a useless addition to the Constitution, because a parchment barrier could never protect individual liberties.

An analysis of these arguments illustrates that Federalists honestly could not see why anyone would demand a bill of rights, and, therefore, they could easily believe that all demands for a bill of rights were simply designed to undermine the Constitution for narrow and partisan reasons.

[68] *Federalist* No. 85, Wills, ed., *Federalist Papers*, p. 449.

[69] Pole, *Constitution—For and Against*, p. 17.

Basic rights were protected by the state constitutions. Throughout the Convention, soon-to-be Federalists argued that a bill of rights was unnecessary because the state constitutions would protect individual liberties. James Wilson declared the states existed "to preserve the rights of individuals." Oliver Ellsworth explained that he looked to the state governments "for the preservation of his rights." Roger Sherman argued that "the State Declarations of Rights are not repealed by this Constitution; and being in force are sufficient."[70]

Most Federalists believed that the state constitutions would not only protect liberty, but that under the new Constitution the states would probably be *too* powerful. Federalists feared the national government would not be sufficiently strong to prevent the states from undermining national power. At the Convention, Madison argued that "guards were more necessary agst. encroachments of the State Govts.—on the Genl. Govt. than of the latter on the former."[71] During the ratification debates Oliver Ellsworth argued that explicit protections of liberty were unnecessary: "It is enough that Congress have no power to prohibit either and can have no temptation. This objection is answered in that the states have all the power originally, and Congress have only what the states grant them."[72]

In other words, a bill of rights that would restrain the national government was not only unnecessary to the Constitution but actually dangerous. Since Federalists equated the success of the Constitution with stability and peace, they quite naturally believed that those who opposed the Constitution, for whatever reason, would willingly lead the country to anarchy and chaos.

The Constitution created a limited government and the national government had no power over individual liberties. Late in the Convention, Elbridge Gerry and Charles Pinckney proposed "that

[70] Farrand, ed., *Records of the Convention*, 1:354, 492; 2:588.

[71] Ibid., 1:357.

[72] "A Landholder" [Oliver Ellsworth] (VI), *Connecticut Courant* (Hartford), Dec. 10, 1787, *DHR*, 3:490.

the liberty of the Press should be inviolably observed."[73] Roger Sherman answered that under a government of limited powers specific protections of liberty were unnecessary because "the power of Congress does not extend to the Press."[74] By a one-vote majority the state delegations sided with Sherman, defeating the motion to protect "the liberty of the Press."[75] This analysis was soon applied to other protections of individual liberty that the Antifederalists demanded.

James Wilson told Philadelphians that under the Constitution "every thing which is not given, is reserved." Thus, "it would have been superfluous and absurd to have stipulated with a foederal body of our own creation, that we should enjoy those privileges, of which we are not divested either by the intention or the act, that has brought that body into existence."[76]

Sherman declared that "the liberty of the Press can be in no danger, because that is not put under the direction of the new government."[77] In *Federalist* No. 84 Hamilton argued that a bill of rights was unnecessary because "in strictness, the people surrender nothing, and as they retain every thing, they have no need of particular reservations." He argued that the preamble, which began "WE THE PEOPLE" was "a better recognition of popular rights than volumes of those aphorisms which make the principal figure in several of our state bills of rights."[78]

Responding to Antifederalist arguments of "A Georgian"

---

[73] Farrand, ed., *Records of the Convention*, 2:5.

[74] Madison recorded the vote as four in favor and seven states opposed. Both the official records and James McHenry's notes recorded five states in favor and six opposed (ibid., pp. 611, 618, 620).

[75] Ibid., pp. 617–18.

[76] James Wilson, "Speech in the State House Yard, Philadelphia," Oct. 6, 1787, *DHR*, 2:168–69; also reprinted as James Wilson, "Speech at a Public Meeting in Philadelphia," ibid., 13:339–40.

[77] "A Citizen of New Haven" [Roger Sherman], "Observations on the New Federal Constitution," *Connecticut Courant* (Hartford), Jan. 7, 1788, ibid., 15:282.

[78] *Federalist* No. 84, Wills, ed., *Federalist Papers*, p. 437.

that the Constitution needed an amendment protecting a free press, the anonymous Demosthenes Minor asked "what control has the federal government upon that sacred palladium of national freedom?" Indeed, to even declare that the government could not regulate the press would have been "an implication that some degree of power was given." Echoing better known Federalist commentators, Demosthenes Minor asserted, "In short, everything is reserved that is not given."[79] Gen. Charles Cotesworth Pinckney made a similar argument to the South Carolina House of Representatives: "With regard to the liberty of the press . . . It was fully debated, and the impropriety of saying any thing about it in the Constitution clearly evinced. The general government has no powers but what are expressly granted to it; it therefore has no power to take away the liberty of the press."[80]

After ratification but well before the adoption of a bill of rights, Madison argued that "the rights in question are reserved by the manner in which the federal powers are granted."[81] In the House of Representatives James Jackson of Georgia opposed a bill of rights, claiming the national government could never threaten liberty unless its powers were "improperly exercised."[82]

A bill of rights might be dangerous to liberty because it would be incomplete, and any rights not protected would be permanently lost. This was probably the argument that was the least "lame" in the federal arsenal. It was based on the commonly accepted eighteenth-century legal theory that when listing rights or

[79] Demosthenes Minor, *Gazette of the State of Georgia* (Savannah), Nov. 22, 1787, *DHR*, 3:247.

[80] Charles Cotesworth Pinckney, "Speech in South Carolina House of Representatives," Jan. 18, 1788, Farrand, ed., *Records of the Convention*, 3:256.

[81] Madison to Jefferson, Oct. 17, 1788, Hutchinson et al., eds., *Papers of Madison*, 11:295–300, quotation p. 297.

[82] Bernard Schwartz, comp., *Roots of the Bill of Rights*, 5 vols. (New York, 1980), 5:1018; Helen E. Veit, Kenneth R. Bowling, and Charlene Bangs Bickford, eds., *Creating the Bill of Rights: The Documentary Record from the First Federal Congress* (Baltimore, 1991), p. 71.

obligations anything not enumerated would be lost.[83] In explaining why the Constitution did not guarantee freedom of the press, James Wilson argued it was unnecessary because the "proposed system possesses no influence whatever upon the press." In fact, any explicit protection of the press "might have been construed to imply that some degree of power was given, since we undertook to define its extent."[84] At the Pennsylvania ratifying convention Wilson elaborated on this position, tying it to the concept of a limited government:

> In a government consisting of enumerated powers, such as is proposed for the United States, a bill of rights would not only be unnecessary, but, in my humble judgment, highly imprudent. In all societies, there are many powers and rights, which cannot be particularly enumerated. A bill of rights annexed to a constitution is an enumeration of the powers reserved. If we attempt an enumeration, everything that is not enumerated is presumed to be given. The consequence is, that an imperfect enumeration would throw all implied power into the scale of the government and the rights of the people would be rendered incomplete. On the other hand, an imperfect enumeration of the powers of government reserves all implied power to the people . . . of the two it is much safer to run the risk on the side of the constitution; for an omission in the enumeration of the powers of government is neither so dangerous, nor important, as an omission in the enumeration of the rights of the people.[85]

Similarly, Hamilton asserted that a bill of rights was "not only unnecessary in the proposed Constitution, but would even be dangerous. They would contain various exceptions to powers not granted; and, on this very account, would afford a colorable pretext to claim more than were granted."[86] Alexander Contee Hanson thought a bill of rights "might not be this innocent quieting instrument." He commended the Con-

[83] Suzanna Sherry, "The Founders' Unwritten Constitution," *University of Chicago Law Review* 54 (1987):1162–64.

[84] Wilson, "Speech in the State House Yard," *DHR*, 2:168–69.

[85] Debates in the Pennsylvania convention, Nov. 28, 1787, ibid., p. 388.

[86] *Federalist* No. 84, Syrett, ed., *Papers of Hamilton*, 4:706.

vention for not writing a bill of rights because "an omission of a single article would have caused more discontent, than is either felt, or pretended" by the failure to have a bill of rights at all.[87] Charles Cotesworth Pinckney took the same position: "We had no bill of rights inserted in our Constitution; for, as we might perhaps have omitted the enumeration of some of our rights, it might hereafter be said we had delegated to the general government a power to take away such of our rights as we has had not enumerated; but by delegating express powers, we certainly reserve to ourselves every power not mentioned in the Constitution."[88]

The public arguments of Hamilton, Wilson, and others mirrored the private analysis. Samuel Holden Parsons, for example, told William Cushing that the Constitution was "grounded on the idea that the people are the fountain of all power, that no dominion can be exercised against them without their consent, and that every officer of the government is amenable to them in the exercise of the authorities granted." Thus, a "bill of rights would be dangerous, as it would at least imply that nothing more was left with the people that the rights defined and secured in such a bill of rights."[89]

Madison expanded on the potential dangers of a bill of rights. He thought it better that the Constitution did not have a bill of rights because "a positive declaration of some of the most essential rights could not be obtained." Madison assumed, for example, that New Englanders would have weakened any attempt to require a separation of church and state and thus feared that the "rights of Conscience" would be "narrowed much more" by a bill of rights than any government would dare do through legislation.[90] An incomplete or

[87] Aristides [Alexander Contee Hanson], "Remarks on the Proposed Plan of a Federal Government," Jan. 31, 1788, *DHR*, 15:537.

[88] Pinckney, "Speech in South Carolina House of Representatives," Farrand, ed., *Records of the Convention*, 3:256.

[89] Samuel Holden Parsons to William Cushing, Jan. 11, 1788, *DHR*, 3:569. Parsons, a Connecticut lawyer, was appointed by Congress as a judge of the Northwest Territory. Cushing later became a Supreme Court justice.

[90] Madison to Jefferson, Oct. 17, 1788, Hutchinson et al., eds., *Papers of Madison*, 11:297.

limited protection of conscience was, in Madison's mind, worse than none at all.

Under a republican form of government a bill of rights was unnecessary. Federalists argued that a bill of rights was needed to limit a king and was not something the people needed to secure from themselves. At the Convention, Roger Sherman argued that the national legislature, which would be elected by the people, might "be safely trusted" not to interfere with the liberties of the people.[91] James Iredell, writing as Marcus, noted that the need for a bill of rights "was originally . . . in consequence of usurpations of the Crown, contrary, as was conceived, to the principles of" English government. But such conditions did not exist in the United States because the new government "cannot act beyond the warrant of that authority" granted by the people through the Constitution. Tying the concept of republicanism to the limitations on power granted by the Constitution, Marcus concluded: "As well might they [the government] attempt to impose a King upon America, as go one step in any other respect beyond the terms of their institution."[92]

Connecticut Lt.-Gov. Oliver Wolcott, Jr., after examining "whether it be a dangerous system; whether it secures the liberties of the people, or whether its tendency be unfavourable to the rights of the people," concluded that the Constitution's democratic elements would preserve liberty. Because the government was "founded upon the election of the people," Wolcott believed "that love of liberty which prevails among the people of this country" would "prevent such a direful calamity" as the destruction of fundamental rights.[93]

John Jay told the New York ratifying convention that

> in days and countries, where Monarchs and their subjects were frequently disputing about prerogative and privileges, the latter often found it necessary, as it were to run out the line between them, and oblige the former to admit by solemn acts, called bills

[91] Farrand, ed., *Records of the Convention*, 2:588.

[92] Marcus (I), *Norfolk and Portsmouth Journal*, Feb. 20, 1788, *DHR*, 16:163–64.

[93] Huntington, Wolcott, and Law, "Speeches," ibid., 15:315.

of rights, that certain enumerated rights belonged to the people, and were not comprehended in the royal prerogative. But thank God we have no such disputes—we have no Monarchs to contend with, or demand admission from—the proposed Government is to be the government of the people—all its officers are to be their officers, and to exercise no rights but such as the people commit to them.[94]

The future chief justice believed that liberty would be safe after ratification because "this plan or constitution will always be in the hands and power of the people, and that if on experiment, it should be found defective or incompetent, they may either remedy its defects, or substitute another in its room."[95]

In *Federalist* No. 84 Hamilton argued that the origin of a bill of rights was in "stipulations between kings and their subjects, abridgement of prerogative in favor of privilege, reservations of rights not surrendered to the prince." But under the federal constitution such declarations were unnecessary because this was a government "professedly founded upon the power of the people, and executed by their immediate representatives and servants."[96]

More dramatically, Noah Webster, the patriotic lexicographer, asked, "But what is tyranny? Or how can a free people be deprived of their liberties?" Webster defined tyranny as "the exercise of some power over a man, which is not warranted by law, or necessary for the public safety." He argued that the "people can never be deprived of their liberties, while they retain in their own hands, a power sufficient to any other power in the state." As long as the people elected the government, Webster saw no reason to fear tyranny.[97]

---

[94] John Jay, "An Address to the People of the State of New-York on the Subject of the Constitution Agreed upon at Philadelphia, the 17th of September, 1787" (1788), Paul Leicester Ford, ed., *Pamphlets on the Constitution of the United States, Published during Its Discussion by the People, 1787–1788* (Brooklyn, 1888), p. 77.

[95] Ibid., p. 85.

[96] *Federalist* No. 84, Wills, *Federalist Papers*, p. 436.

[97] "A Citizen of America" [Noah Webster], "An Examination into the Leading Principles of the Federal Constitution Proposed by the Law Con-

James Wilson told the Pennsylvania ratifying convention that under the Constitution "liberty shall reign triumphant" because of "the principles and dispositions of their citizens."[98] The anonymous Civis Rusticus noted the Constitution created a "thoroughly popular" government and thus was "in need of no bill of rights." Rusticus believed that under the Constitution "the liberties of the people never can be lost, until they are lost to themselves, in a vicious disregard of their dearest interest, a sottish indolence, a wild licentiousness, a dissoluteness of morals and a contempt of all virtue."[99] The Constitution, combined with republican virtue, would create stability and preserve liberty. As Civis Rusticus implied, if the only threat to liberty came from the failure of public virtue and popular support for republican values, then a stronger national government, not a bill of rights, would preserve liberty.

In New Jersey an unknown writer argued that the people did not need a "written bill of rights to prove their authority, being the only human source of power known in the empire." Indeed, "the good sense of the people would universally have revolted" if the Framers had placed a bill of rights in the Constitution because such an action would have implied the government had powers it did not have.[100]

Philadelphia's Benjamin Rush offered the most extreme example of this sort of analysis. He argued that the Constitution would have "been disgraced with a bill of rights." Rush thought that from the arguments in favor of a bill of rights "one would imagine . . . that this government was immediately to be administered by foreigners—strangers to our

---

vention Held at Philadelphia. With Answers to the Principal Objections That Have Been Raised against the System" (1787), Ford, ed., *Pamphlets on the Constitution*, quotation p. 55. Webster's willingness to suspend liberties when "necessary for the public safety" was precisely the sort of open-ended power that Antifederalists feared.

[98] Elliot, ed., *Debates*, 2:428 (speech of Wilson).

[99] Civis Rusticus, *Virginia Independent Chronicle* (Richmond), Jan. 30, 1788, quoted in *CAF*, 2:13n.

[100] "Reply to George Mason's Objections to the Constitution," *New-Jersey Journal* (Elizabethtown), Dec. 19, 26, 1787, *DHR*, 3:154–55.

habits and opinions, and unconnected with our interest and prosperity."[101] His hyperbole aside, Rush expressed what most Federalists believed: that republican values and a republican form of government would be sufficient to guard individual liberty.

The Constitution actually protected basic liberties, and thus a bill of rights was a redundant addition to the Constitution. While arguing that a bill of rights was either dangerous or unnecessary, Federalists inconsistently claimed that the Constitution already protected liberty. While asserting that the Constitution did not need a bill of rights per se, Federalists were quick to note the document already contained many clauses protecting individual liberties and rights.

Roger Sherman argued there was nothing "in the Constitution to deprive" Americans "of trial by jury in cases where that mode of trial has been heretofore used." Because "every department and officer of the federal government" would be "subject to the regulation and control of the law," the "people" would "have all possible security against oppression." The Constitution was "well framed to secure the rights and liberties of the people and for preserving the governments of the individual states," to "restore and secure public and private credit, and to give respectability to the states both abroad and at home." The Constitution secured liberty and made prosperity likely.[102]

How did the Constitution protect liberty? In response to the Antifederalist arguments that the "constitution contains *no declaration of rights,*" Pelitiah Webster, a Philadelphia merchant, wrote, "I answer this is not true,—the constitution contains a declaration of many rights, and very important ones, e.g. that people shall be obliged to fulfil their contracts, and not avoid them by tenders of any thing less than the value stipulated; that no *ex-post facto* laws shall be made &c."[103]

---

[101] Benjamin Rush, quoted in *CAF,* 3:213 n. 6.

[102] "A Citizen of New Haven" [Sherman], *DHR,* 3:527.

[103] "A Citizen of Philadelphia" [Pelatiah Webster], "Remarks on the Address of Sixteen Members," Oct. 18, 1787, ibid., 13:302.

Other Federalists pointed out that the Constitution prohibited any "religious test" for officeholding, prohibited government officials from simultaneously holding more than one office, and prohibited the suspension of the writ of habeas corpus except in time of actual invasion or rebellion. In *Federalist* No. 44 Madison noted the Constitution prohibited the states from passing bills of attainder, ex post facto laws, or laws impairing the obligations of contracts, even though such laws were also prohibited in the "declarations prefixed to some of the state constitutions." [104] In *Federalist* No. 84 Hamilton discussed "a number of such provisions" that protected liberty. Hamilton listed the provisions of Article I, Section 9 of the Constitution, including the ban on titles of nobility, and provisions in Article III guaranteeing a jury trial in all criminal cases and eliminating old English concepts of treason and constructive treason. He argued these were "greater securities to liberty and republicanism than" found in the New York state constitution. [105]

Other constitutional provisions protected basic liberties and rights. One Madison biographer found "twenty-four elements of a Bill of Rights in a Constitution that is said to contain none." [106] Federalists did not make such a careful count, but they extolled the protections of liberty in the document. They of course never confronted the obvious inconsistency between saying that a bill of rights would be dangerous because it might omit, and therefore destroy, certain liberties, and the argument that the Constitution already protected many liberties.

A bill of rights would be a useless addition to the Constitution. Federalists were masters of arguing in duplicity. As already demonstrated, they argued that the state constitutions protected liberty, that the federal government could not harm liberty, that the federal constitution already protected fundamental rights, and that it was impossible to fully protect rights in any

[104] *Federalist* No. 44, Hutchinson et al., eds., *Papers of Madison*, 10:421.

[105] *Federalist* No. 84, Wills, ed., *Federalist Papers*, pp. 434–35.

[106] Irving Brandt, *The Bill of Rights: Its Origin and Meaning* (Indianapolis, 1965), p. 12.

constitution. Finally, in an argument that could hardly have comforted their opponents, Federalists claimed a bill of rights was useless in protecting liberty.

During a debate in the Convention over ex post facto laws, Daniel Carroll and James Wilson argued that the prohibitions of such laws "in the State Constitutions have no effect" and thus it was "useless to insert them" in the national constitution.[107] Echoing this view, but in a more positive light, a correspondent in the *New Jersey Journal* argued that under the Constitution the people were sovereign and thus could not "be affected by any such declaration of rights, they being the source of all power in the government; whatever they have not given away still remains inherent in them." Thus, a bill of rights was both unnecessary and useless.[108]

"The only real security that you can have for all your important rights," Roger Sherman told citizens of Connecticut, "must be in the nature of your government." He believed "no bill of rights ever yet bound the supreme power longer than the *honeymoon* of a new married couple, unless the *rulers were interested* in preserving the rights." If Americans had to trust their "liberties with people whom it is necessary to bind by stipulation . . . your stipulation is not worth even the trouble of writing." The protections of liberty that the Antifederalists wanted were "much too important to depend on mere paper protection."[109] In the New York convention Hamilton made virtually the same point: it was useless to "depend on regulations on paper for safety"; only "the Genius of our country" could protect liberty.[110]

In his private correspondence Madison made a similar point. More than a year after the Convention, Madison told Thomas Jefferson that "experience proves the inefficacy of a bill of rights on those occasions when its controul is most

[107] Farrand, ed., *Records of the Convention*, 2:376.

[108] "Reply to George Mason's Objections," *DHR*, 3:154.

[109] "A Countryman" [Roger Sherman] (II), *New Haven Gazette*, Nov. 22, 1787, ibid., 3:471–72.

[110] "New York Ratifying Convention: Third Speech of July 19 [1788]," Syrett, ed., *Papers of Hamilton*, 5:180.

needed. Repeated violations of these parchment barriers have been committed by overbearing majorities in every state." He noted that in Virginia he had "seen the bill of rights violated in every instance where it has been opposed to a popular current." He warned that "restrictions however strongly marked on paper will never be regarded when opposed to the decided sense of the public; and after repeated violations in extraordinary cases, they will lose even their ordinary efficacy."[111]

Madison's view on the inefficacy of "parchment barriers" reflected the fundamental distrust of most Federalists for democratic majorities. In the Virginia legislature Madison had encountered men who "seemed so parochial, so illiberal, so small-minded," who "seemed to have only 'a particular interest to serve.' They had no regard for public honor or honesty" and were "reluctant to do anything that might appear unpopular."[112] Such "clods," as historian Gordon S. Wood has characterized them,[113] could not be expected to obey the restrictions of a bill of rights. Madison thought that the greatest threat to liberty "was not the conspiracy of the few against the many" but "rather of the many against the few."[114] Madison did not believe that a bill of rights could prevent what Alexis de Tocqueville would later describe as the tyranny of the majority. In *Federalist* No. 10 Madison argued that diversity within the population, and not a parchment barrier, was the only way of preventing the majority from trampling on the liberties of the minority.[115] This analysis led Madison and other Federalists to conclude that a bill of rights would be a

[111] Madison to Jefferson, Oct. 17, 1788, Hutchinson et al., eds., *Papers of Madison*, 11:297–99. For similar views by Federalists, see "Letters of Cassius" (VIII), Paul Leicester Ford, ed., *Essays on the Constitution of the United States* (Brooklyn, 1892), p. 28, and Elliot, ed., *Debates*, 2:174.

[112] Gordon S. Wood, "Interests and Disinterestedness in the Making of the Constitution," in Richard Beeman, Stephen Botein, and Edward C. Carter, eds., *Beyond Confederation: Origins of the Constitution and American National Identity* (Chapel Hill, 1987), p. 74.

[113] Ibid.

[114] Onuf, "Madison's Extended Republic," p. 2380.

[115] Finkelman, "Madison and the Adoption of the Bill of Rights," pp. 301–47.

futile gesture, or worse yet, a dangerous addition that would in the end delude the people into believing the Constitution protected their rights.

The Threat of a Collapsing Nation and the Bill of Rights

Late in his life Madison recalled that as early as 1784 "the rapid growth of anarchy in the Fedl. System" threatened the new nation.[116] By 1787 most soon-to-be Federalists believed the government under the Articles of Confederation was in a state of total collapse and the nation was at a crossroads between anarchy and stable government. Only the Constitution could defeat the former and secure the latter. As Henry Knox, who was not a delegate, wrote just as the Convention began to get down to business, "We are verging fast to anarchy and . . . the present convention is the only means to avoid the most flagitious evils that ever afflicted three millions of freemen."[117]

Because they believed that only adoption of the Constitution could stop this drift, Federalists thought the call for a bill of rights, which might slow ratification or stop it altogether, was tantamount to a call for anarchy. Knox argued ratification "must be done speedily." He thought the government under the Articles had "run down" and that "the machine cannot be wound up again." Speedy ratification was the only alternative to "the horrors of anarchy."[118]

Hamilton agreed. He told New Yorkers that "something is necessary to be done to rescue us from impending anarchy." America was in "almost the last state of national humiliation"; the "imbecility of our Government" was apparent to the whole world; the United States was "destitute of energy." Thus, Hamilton was convinced that any delay of ratification would be dangerous.[119] He would admit that some parts of the Constitution might not be perfect but asked, "Where is

---

[116] James Madison, "Preface to Debates in the Convention of 1787," Farrand, ed., *Records of the Convention*, 3:544.

[117] Henry Knox to John Sullivan, May 21, 1787, ibid., p. 13.

[118] Knox to Sullivan, Jan. 19, 1788, *DHR*, 15:417.

[119] *Federalist* No. 15, Wills, ed., *Federalist Papers*, pp. 68–69.

the standard of perfection to be found?" If the nation refused to adopt a government "until every part of it had been adjusted to the most exact standard of perfection, society would soon become a general scene of anarchy, and the world a desert."[120]

Federalist opposition to a bill of rights was rooted in their vision of a successful national government. They believed in stability through strength. Hamilton wanted a strong executive, unencumbered by a bill of rights, because "energy in the executive is a leading character in the definition of a good government. It is essential to the protection of the community against foreign attacks: It is not less essential to the steady administration of the laws, to the protection of property against those irregular and high handed combinations, which sometimes interrupt the ordinary course of justice to the security of liberty against the enterprises and assaults of ambition, of faction and of anarchy."[121] For Hamilton a strong executive was more likely to protect liberty and property than any bill of rights.

Madison worried that the national government would be as "impotent" as had existed under the Articles of Confederation.[122] Gouverneur Morris feared a Congress that would be "a mere whisp of straw."[123] In debating the powers of Congress, Morris noted that Elbridge Gerry had said that "the new Governt. would be partly national, partly federal; that it ought in the first quality to protect individuals; in the second the States." Morris, however, wondered "what quality was it to protect the aggregate interest of the whole."[124]

Once the Constitution was written, Federalists argued that the strength of the national government was the key to protecting liberty. Madison compared the government under the Articles to a failed system in ancient Greece where "weakness,

[120] *Federalist* No. 65, Syrett, ed., *Papers of Hamilton,* 4:575.

[121] *Federalist* No. 70, ibid., p. 599.

[122] Farrand, ed., *Records of the Convention,* 1:551.

[123] Ibid.

[124] Ibid., pp. 551–52.

the disorders, and finally the destruction of the confederacy"
led the more powerful states to "tyrannize" the others. This
in turn destroyed "the last of antient liberty," and the Greek
republics fought among themselves, until they were easily
taken over by Rome. The moral of the story, for Madison, was
that a weak federation, such as the United States had under
the Articles, would eventually degenerate to "rather anarchy
among the members, than to tyranny in the head." Such a
calamity, Madison implied, would soon befall America if the
Constitution were not ratified, or the new government were
weakened by amendments.[125]

Tench Coxe asserted that the argument for the Constitution went beyond "*the fear* of Anarchy." He felt liberty had
already been destroyed by the weakness of the Articles. The
"emissions of paper money" had undermined commerce; the
"rights of property [had] been violated & religion & morality
trampled under foot"; the economy was in shambles because
of "laws to discharge specific & pecuniary contracts."[126] Hugh
Williamson was certain the country was "in a sea of troubles,
without sails, oars, or pilot; ready to be dashed into pieces by
every flaw of wind." Only the Constitution could rescue the
nation.[127] Any amendments to the Constitution would weaken
the new government. A weak national government was, in
Hamilton's view, "the parent of anarchy."[128] Such a system
would lead to a repetition of the "feudal anarchy" of an earlier
era.[129] Hamilton was annoyed with the demands for a bill of
rights because such demands threatened ratification. He
complained of "the pretended defects" of the Constitution,
which included "the omission of a formal bill of rights, the
omission of a provision respecting the liberty of the press."[130]

---

[125] *Federalist* No. 18, Wills, ed., *Federalist Papers*, pp. 85, 89.

[126] "An American" [Coxe] to Lee (II), *DHR*, 15:174.

[127] Hugh Williamson, "Speech at Edenton, N.C.," *New York Daily Advertiser,*
Feb. 25–27, 1788, ibid., 16:201–9.

[128] *Federalist* No. 16, Wills, ed., *Federalist Papers*, p. 75.

[129] *Federalist* No. 17, ibid., p. 82.

[130] *Federalist* No. 85.

John Jay drew the analogy between human health and political health. Rejecting Antifederalist fears that the new government would lead to tyranny, he asked, "Who on a sick bed would refuse medicines from a physician, merely because it is as much in his power to administer deadly poisons, as salutary remedies."[131] For Jay, the very survival of the nation was at issue. He believed "the cause of freedom greatly depends on the use we make of the singular opportunities we enjoy governing ourselves wisely." He wondered "who will hereafter be the advocates for systems" based on republican values and liberty if "the people of this country either cannot or will not govern themselves." America's choice was whether "licentiousness, disorder, and confusion reign" and thus "the minds of men every where, will insensibly become alienated from republican forms." If this happened Americans and all other people would in the future "prefer and acquiesce in Governments, which, though less friendly to liberty, afford more peace and security."[132]

The Perfect Constitution

Tied to the argument that the nation was in a crisis was the Federalist belief that the Constitution was either perfect, or as nearly perfect as anyone could hope for.[133] The cost of improvement and the risks of delay were simply too great.

Tench Coxe argued that the Constitution, "taken in Connexion with & as it is supported by the State constitutions, is the best that human Wisdom has ever devised, or that providence has given to mankind."[134] Roger Sherman had no

---

[131] Jay, "Address to the People," Ford, ed., *Pamphlets on the Constitution*, p. 85. The answer, of course, is someone who simultaneously believed they could probably get well, in time, without medicine, and who also feared that the physician did not know the difference between medicine and poison.

[132] Ibid., p. 86.

[133] Some Federalists, including Madison, thought the Constitution did not create a government that was sufficiently strong, but, in the context of the ratification debate, this was not an issue for public discussion.

[134] "An American" [Coxe] to Lee (II), *DHR*, 15:174.

doubts about the perfection of the Constitution, or that it would protect individual liberty:

> Every department and officer of the federal government will be subject to the regulation and controul of the laws, and therefore the people will have all possible security against oppression. Upon the whole the constitution appears to be well framed to secure the rights and liberties of the people and for preserving the governments of the individual states, and if well administered, to restore and secure public and private credit, and give respectability to the states both abroad and at home.—Perhaps a more perfect one could not be formed on mere speculation; and if upon experience it shall be found deficient, it provides an easy and peaceable mode to make amendments.[135]

North Carolina's Hugh Williamson thought that supporters of a bill of rights were people who wished "for troubled times and fluctuating measures." Williamson argued for a government "that gives the fairest promise of being firm and honorable; safe from Foreign Invasion or Domestic Sedition. A Government by which our commerce must be protected and enlarged; the value of our produce and of our lands must be increased; the labourer and the mechanic must be encouraged and supported. It is a form of Government that is perfectly fitted for protecting Liberty and Property, and for cherishing the good Citizen and the Honest Man."[136] A New Hampshire writer had celestial visions when he read the Constitution: "The federal plan, like the globe of the moon, will appear perfect from a true observation—though both may seem covered with inferior spots."[137] For Federalists a crater here or there was no reason to reject such a heavenly document; if the Constitution was nearly perfect as written, then there was no reason for amending it.

John Jay was willing to admit that the Constitution might not be absolutely perfect. There might be craters on this moon. But he wondered who could be certain of "a better

[135] "Citizen of New Haven," ibid., p. 283.

[136] Williamson, "Speech at Edenton, N.C.," ibid., 16:201–9.

[137] "Political Scraps," *New Hampshire Spy,* Jan. 1, 1788, ibid., 15:210.

plan." Even if the Constitution could be slightly improved by a second convention or a bill of rights, Jay thought the cost of waiting was far too high. Delay would "give further opportunities to discord to alienate the hearts of our citizens from one another, and thereby encourage new Cromwells to bold exploits." With America's "distresses . . . accumulating like compound interest," Jay believed any delay might be fatal. The choice was to accept a nearly perfect document as written, or face "our present humiliated condition" and risk anarchy or dictatorship in the hope that the Constitution might be improved.[138]

Most Federalists of course doubted another convention or amendments could improve the Constitution. Jay predicted that a "new Convention, instead of producing a better plan, should give us only a history of their disputes, or should offer us one still less pleasing than the present." The "old Confederation" had "done its best" and was now "feeble."[139] The new Constitution offered a better plan than could ever be hoped for again.

Even a speedy ratification of the Constitution and a subsequent addition of a few amendments presented dangers. Many Federalists feared that a "bill of rights might actually weaken the federal government and thus impair the very protections which it had the power to bestow."[140] During the Congressional debate over what became the Bill of Rights some Federalists continued to oppose amendments for this reason.

Georgia's James Jackson argued the Constitution was "like a vessel just launched, lying at the wharf; she is untried, you can hardly discover any one of her properties." He opposed any amendments until this ship of state could be tested and the Congress "guided by the experiment."[141] While debating what became the Eighth Amendment, New Hampshire's Sam-

[138] Jay, "Address to the People," Ford, ed., *Pamphlets on the Constitution,* p. 83.

[139] Ibid, p. 84.

[140] Pole, *Constitution—For and Against,* p. 18.

[141] Schwartz, comp., *Roots of the Bill of Rights,* 5:1017–18.

uel Livermore articulated a similar fear. He admitted the proposed amendment expressed "a great deal of humanity," which he claimed to admire, but worried about its open-ended phrasing. Livermore wondered what was "meant by the terms excessive bail" and who would decide when bail was excessive. He noted that "it is sometimes necessary to hang a man, villains often deserve whipping and perhaps having their ears cut off." He asked, "Are we in future to be prevented from inflicting these punishments because they are cruel?"[142] Federalists like Livermore and Jackson wanted to avoid limiting the power of the national government to suppress crime and prevent anarchy. Of course Antifederalists demanded a bill of rights precisely because of such sentiments.

Federalists believed anything that might undermine the power of the new national government—and ruin the seemingly perfect Constitution—was to be avoided. A bill of rights would limit the power of the government to act and in that respect undermine its ability to govern successfully. Only a strong national government, one that could prevent anarchy, could preserve liberty. "Parchment barriers" would be useless in the face of determined majorities or during a period of chaos and civil war. Stability was the key to liberty. As early as 1784 Madison believed that only dramatic measures, such as the Constitution he helped draft three years later, could bring about "a rescue of the Union and the blessings of liberty staked on it, from an impending catastrophe."[143]

The Insincere, Foolish, or Evil Opposition

If the Constitution was nearly perfect, then only a fool or a knave would want to amend it. No honest and intelligent patriot, so the Federalist argument went, could want amendments. Federalists were thus contemptuous of those Americans who asked for a bill of rights. Since most Antifederalist leaders were not fools, Federalists quickly assumed they were

[142] *Annals of Congress,* 1st Cong., 1st sess., 1:782–83.

[143] Madison, "Preface to Debates," Farrand, ed., *Records of the Convention,* 3:543.

knaves "governed by narrow views and local prejudices,"[144] or worse yet, men under "the influence of foreign gold, or, if possible, the still baser intention of betraying their country into anarchy, that they may either retain their present unmerited stations or rise upon her ruins." These seemed to be the only possible motivations for "that abominable falsehood . . . which charges the Federal Constitution with abolishing the liberty of the press."[145]

Calls for a bill of rights, the Federalists believed, came from self-interested politicians—"impertinent politicasters, assiduous seekers of their own interest, office hunters, makers of paper money and test laws"[146]—who would rather see anarchy than good government. The campaign for a bill of rights, Federalists thought, was just a ploy to get "the ignorant and jealous"[147] to follow these knaves.

Federalists believed that proponents of a bill of rights were narrow-minded localists, "Men of Little Faith" as historians once called them.[148] Shortly after the Convention, James Wilson set the tone, telling Philadelphians that opposition to the Constitution would come from "every person . . . who either enjoys, or expects to enjoy, a place of profit under the present establishment . . . not, in truth, because it is injurious to the liberties of this country, but because it affects his schemes of wealth and consequence."[149]

Reflecting this view, Hugh Williamson extolled "the honest patriot who guards with a jealous eye the liberties of his country, and apprehends danger under every form." Such patriots,

144 "Landholder" [Ellsworth] (VI), *DHR*, 3:491.

145 "Avenging Justice," *Pennsylvania Gazette* (Philadelphia), Oct. 17, 1787, ibid., 2:192.

146 [Benjamin Rush], "The Arraignment of Centinel," *Pennsylvania Mercury* (Philadelphia), Feb. 28, 1788, ibid., 16:258–59.

147 "Landholder" [Ellsworth] (IX), ibid., 3:516.

148 Cecelia M. Kenyon, "Men of Little Faith: The Antifederalists on the Nature of Representative Government," reprinted in Kermit L. Hall, *The Formation and Ratification of the Constitution* (New York, 1987), pp. 348–88.

149 Wilson, "Speech in the State House Yard," *DHR*, 2:168–69.

Williamson implied, understood that the Constitution would lead to liberty because of the "particular benefits" it would bring to the nation. The only people who could oppose such a document were the "placeman in every State, who fears lest his office should pass into other hands" as well as the "idle, the factious, and the dishonest." [150] A widely reprinted New Hampshire writer expressed these sentiments in one simple sentence: "Never expect to proselite an antifederal officer who is afraid of a new arrangement." [151]

Federalists held their opponents in such contempt that they could not seriously evaluate the demands for a bill of rights. Oliver Ellsworth had no patience for their arguments. In answer to the complaint that freedom of the press was not protected, he sarcastically observed "nor is liberty of conscience, or of matrimony, or of burial of the dead." [152] Pelitiah Webster noted that "the *liberty of the press is not asserted* in the constitution" but sarcastically pointed out that "neither are any of the ten commandments." [153]

Federalists assumed that anyone who could oppose the Constitution must be venal or evil. Henry Knox called Antifederalists "demagogues and vicious characters." New England Federalists described their opponents as "wicked," "malignant, ignorant, and short-sighted triflers." A North Carolina Federalist referred to his opponents as "a blind stupid set, that wish Damnation to their Country," who were "fools and knaves" opposed to "any man of abilities and virtue." A New Hampshire Federalist thought "none but *fools, blockheads,* and *mad men*" opposed the Constitution. In New York, Caesar thought that the demands for a bill of rights were made by "designing croakers" in order "to frighten the people with ideal bugbears." [154]

---

[150] Williamson, "Speech at Edenton, N.C.," ibid., 16:201–9.

[151] "Political Scraps," ibid., 15:210.

[152] "Landholder" [Ellsworth] (VI), ibid., 3:490.

[153] "Citizen of Philadelphia," ibid., 13:302.

[154] Robert Allen Rutland, *Ordeal of the Constitution: The Antifederalists and the Ratification Struggle of 1787–1788* (Norman, Okla., 1966), pp. 34, 73, 269, 216. "Letters of Caesar" (II), Ford, ed., *Essays on the Constitution,* p. 289.

Federalists doubted the sincerity of their opponents. "They talk of amendments" implying that once adopted "they will heartily join in a safe plan of federal government." But Oliver Ellsworth asked, "When we look on their past conduct, can we think them sincere. Doubtless their design is to procrastinate." Ellsworth argued that the Antifederalists were "the same who have been unfederal from the beginning" and have always advocated measures "destructive" of the national good.[155]

Benjamin Rush outdid all others in denouncing his opponents. His "indictment" of the anonymous Antifederalist Centinel was the ne plus ultra of Federalist venom. The "indictment" charged Centinel with being a "false traitor" with no "fear of God in his heart," who had been "moved and seduced by the instigation of Satan, Belzebub, Lucifer, Belial, and the whole herd of Devils." According to Rush, Centinel wanted to "disturb the peace and common tranquillity" of the United States and "stir up and move opposition, faction, riot, sedition, insurrection, civil wars, rebellion and murder." Centinel was "diabolically" plotting crimes of all magnitude; distributing "false, factious, opprobrious, disgraceful, shameful, vile, defamatory, scandalous, libellous, traiterous, malicious, infamous and stinkabuss pieces . . . filled with lies, false quotations, trifling tales, fears, suggestions, prognostications, broken-hearted signs, enthusiastic rhapsodies, tautological repetitions, and the whole palladium of nonsense and absurdities, liberally and spontaneously embellished, with the words, miscreants, infernal wretches, conclave, aristocrats, well-born, accursed villains, conspirators, and other Billingsgate expressions" designed "to raise and stir up riot, opposition, civil wars, and rebellion." This article accused Centinel of corresponding with "a detestable triumviri, disturbers of the peace of society, insignificant babblers, noisy, ignorant . . . seceders, protestors, promoters of riot, faction, sedition, discord, civil wars and rebellion; and at the same time impudently, ungraciously, burlesquically and ironically, together (with a very

---

Ford incorrectly identifies the author of this letter as Hamilton (see Syrett, ed., *Papers of Hamilton*, 4:278–79).

[155] "Landholder" [Ellsworth] (IX), *DHR*, 3:516.

small number of other low, trifling slubberdegullions of an inferior class) calling themselves Patriots!" Furthermore, "in order to fulfil his most horrid and diabolical treasons" Centinel collaborated with "certain wheel-barrow men, convicts and criminals" as well as "sneakups, timeserving pickthanks, sycophants and traitors."[156] With attitudes such as this, it is no wonder that the Federalists did not seriously consider the validity of the opposition arguments.

THE FEAR OF TYRANNY AND THE LACK OF A BILL OF RIGHTS: THE ANTIFEDERALIST ARGUMENT

Antifederalists feared much in the Constitution that did not immediately concern the lack of a bill of rights. Some thought tyranny would result even if a bill of rights was added to the Constitution.[157] But, as one Federalist succinctly put it, "all the objections which are made against it are reducible to this single one: that it is dangerous to liberty."[158]

Just as Federalists argued that a bill of rights was unnecessary, Antifederalists argued that it was essential to protect liberty in the new nation. The argument stemmed from four propositions: that a bill of rights was obviously necessary to avoid tyranny; that only people who wanted to impose a tyranny on the nation would oppose a bill of rights; that the ac-

---

[156] [Rush], "Arraignment of Centinel," ibid., 16:258–60.

[157] The New York Antifederalists Robert Yates and John Lansing believed that the national "government, however guarded by declarations of rights, or cautionary provisions, must unavoidably, in a short time, be productive of the destruction of civil liberty" because of the size of the nation (Yates and Lansing, "Reasons of Dissent," Dec. 21, 1787, *CAF,* 2:17). Samuel Chase believed that "a declaration of rights alone will be of no essential service. Some of the powers must be abridged, or public liberty will be endangered, and in time, destroyed" (Chase to John Lamb, June 13, 1788, ibid., p. 14n). This is particularly ironic, because during the Sedition Act crisis, while attending to his circuit court duties as a member of the United States Supreme Court, Chase was unrelenting in his assaults on liberty in his attempts to ensure the conviction of Jeffersonians.

[158] "The Republican," "To the People," *Connecticut Courant* (Hartford), Jan. 7, 1788, *DHR,* 3:528.

tions of the Federalists showed their proclivity to tyranny; and that the Federalist arguments against a bill of rights were wrong.

The Necessary Bill of Rights

Many Antifederalists reflected the politics of an older age based on consensus and a strong commitment to natural rights.[159] Even before the Revolution they had supported written protections of liberty. "The rights of *America* have often been declared to the public," one whig said on the eve of Independence, but "related strokes on the anvil, tempers the metal: They cannot be too often mentioned."[160] For such men the need for a bill of rights in 1787 was "self-evident," just as the right to life, liberty, and the pursuit of happiness had been in 1776.

George Mason refused to sign the Constitution for many reasons. He disliked the commerce power, the treaty-making provisions, the continuation of the African slave trade for *at least* twenty more years,[161] and the power of the president to grant pardons, especially to "those whom he had secretly instigated to commit" crimes and "thereby prevent a discovery of his own guilt."[162] These complaints about the Constitution were magnified by the lack of a bill of rights. Mason feared that the Senate and the president would combine "to accomplish what usurpations they pleased upon the rights and liberties of the people," while the federal judiciary would "absorb and destroy the judiciaries of the several States." He thought the expansive powers of Congress threatened the "security" of "the people for their rights." Without a bill of rights all this was possible. All dangers flowed from this deficiency.

Thus, Mason began his explanation for his refusal to sign,

[159] Pauline Maier, *The Old Revolutionaries: Political Lives in the Age of Samuel Adams* (New York, 1980).

[160] John Mackenzie, quoted in Reid, *Constitutional History*, p. 3.

[161] For a discussion of the continuation of the slave trade for at least twenty years, see Paul Finkelman, *Slavery and the Founders: Race and Liberty in the Age of Jefferson* (Armonk, N.Y., 1996), pp. 27–30.

[162] Farrand, ed., *Records of the Convention*, 2:637–38.

"There is no Declaration of Rights; and the Laws of the general Government being paramount to the Laws & Constitutions of the several States, the Declaration of Rights in the separate States are no Security."[163] Mason noted that under this Constitution "the people" were not "secured even the enjoyment of the benefit of the common law."[164] He continued: "There is no declaration of any kind, for preserving the liberty of the press, or the trial by jury in civil causes; nor against the danger of standing armies in time of peace."[165] Mason's other major objections to the Constitution flowed from this deficiency.

Elbridge Gerry similarly explained his decision not to sign: "It was painful to me, on a subject of such national importance, to differ from the respectable members who signed the constitution: But conceiving as I did, that the liberties of America were not secured by the system, it was my duty to oppose it."[166] Gerry had grave reservations about the entire structure of the government, but his foremost objection was "that the system is without the security of a bill of rights."[167]

Edmund Randolph realized that not signing the Constitution was "a step which might be the most awful of his life." But it was a matter of "conscience" with him. He believed "that the holding out this plan with a final alternative to the people, of accepting or rejecting it in toto, would really produce the anarchy & civil convulsions which were apprehended from the refusal of individuals to sign it."[168]

Mason, Gerry, and Randolph did not feel the need to develop their position. It was self-evident that a bill of rights was necessary for the security of a free people. The minority in the Pennsylvania ratifying convention elaborated on the need

[163] "George Mason's Objections to the Constitution of Government Formed by the Convention," *DHR*, 8:43.

[164] Farrand, ed., *Records of the Convention*, 2:637–38.

[165] Ibid., pp. 639–40.

[166] "Hon. Mr. Gerry's Objections to Signing the National Constitution," *CAF*, 2:6.

[167] Ibid., pp. 6–7.

[168] Farrand, ed., *Records of the Convention*, 2:645.

for "a declaration of RIGHTS to which the people may appeal for the vindication of their wrongs in the court of justice." Without such a declaration the people must "obey the most arbitrary laws, as the worst of them will be pursuant to the principles and form of the constitution."[169]

Jefferson, although not clearly an Antifederalist, succinctly expressed this idea in his famous December 20, 1787, letter to Madison. Jefferson complained about "the omission of a bill of rights providing clearly and without the aid of sophisms for freedom of religion, freedom of the press, protection against standing armies, restriction against monopolies, the eternal and unremitting force of the habeas corpus laws, and trials by jury in all matters of fact triable by the laws of the land."[170] Jefferson argued that "a bill of rights is what the people are entitled to against every government on earth, general or particular, and what no just government should refuse, or rest on inference."[171]

Jefferson's point, which he made privately, seemed intuitively obvious to the Antifederalists. Well before Jefferson wrote this letter, supporters of a bill of rights in America were making similar points. The comments of Mason, Gerry, and others set the tone. For opponents of the Constitution the need for a bill of rights was self-evident; therefore anyone opposed to their goal must be secretly interested in creating a tyranny.

Federalists Want Tyranny

Shortly after receiving his copy of the Constitution, Congressman Richard Henry Lee prepared a series of amendments for the new document. His list included many proposals that would be later incorporated into the Bill of Rights. Lee feared

[169] "The Address and Reasons of Dissent of the Minority of the Convention of the State of Pennsylvania to Their Constituents," *Pennsylvania Packet* (Philadelphia), Dec. 18, 1787, *DHR*, 2:636.

[170] Jefferson to Madison, Dec. 20, 1787, Julian P. Boyd et al., eds., *The Papers of Thomas Jefferson*, 28 vols. to date (Princeton, 1950-), 12:440.

[171] Madison to Jefferson, Oct. 24, 1787, ibid., pp. 270–86; Jefferson to Madison, Dec. 20, 1787, ibid., pp. 438, 440.

that without "some such alterations & provisions . . . for the security of those essential rights of Mankind, without which liberty can not exist, we shall soon find that the New plan of Government will be far more inconvenient than any thing sustained under the present Government." The Virginian feared that in order "to avoid [the] Scilla" of a weak national government, America had "fallen upon [the] Caribdis" of tyranny.[172]

The Confederation Congress defeated Lee's proposals, with Madison and other Federalists arguing it would be "inexpedient" to alter the work of the Convention.[173] Lee blamed this defeat on a "coalition of Monarchy men, Military Men, Aristocrats, and Drones" who cared little "for such changes and securities as Reason and Experience prove to be necessary against the encroachments of power upon the indispensable rights of human nature." Lee predicted that if the Constitution were ratified as written "either a tyranny will result from it, or it will be prevented by a Civil war."[174] He feared the "adoption" of the Constitution would leave "Civil Liberty and the happiness of the people at the mercy of Rulers who may possess the great unguarded powers given." Lee thought the Constitution generally useful and believed amendments to protect civil liberties would "by no means interfere with the general nature of the plan" but would "restrain from oppression the wicked & Tyrannic."[175] A group of Pennsylvanians similarly feared the Constitution would "rivet the fetters of slavery" on to the people and usher in an age of tyranny. They thought the American people "understand their rights better than . . . to sacrifice their liberty at the shrine of aristocracy or arbitrary government."[176]

[172] Lee to Elbridge Gerry, Sept. 29, [1787], *DHR*, 8:25.

[173] Madison to Washington, Sept. 30, 1787, Hutchinson et al., eds., *Papers of Madison*, 10:179–81.

[174] Lee to Mason, Oct. 1, 1787, *DHR*, 8:28–29.

[175] Lee to William Shippen, Jr., Oct. 2, 1787, ibid., pp. 32–33. For similar sentiments, see Lee to Adams, Oct. 5, 1787, ibid., pp. 36–39.

[176] "An Address to the Minority of the Pennsylvania Convention," *Carlisle Gazette*, Jan. 2, 1788, ibid., 15:229.

The lack of a bill of rights emerged as the most potent weapon in the Antifederalist arsenal because it was the most plausible. The Federalists foolishly denied that a bill of rights was needed and their "lame" excuses for not having a bill of rights were unconvincing.[177] In Pennsylvania "A Federal Republican" asked, "If the people are jealous of their rights, where will be the harm in declaring them? If they be meant, as they certainly are, to be reserved to the people, what injury can arise from a positive declaration of it?"[178] By vehemently opposing the addition of a bill of rights, even after the Constitution was ratified, Federalists seemed to confirm in the minds of many that the supporters of the Constitution did in fact want to establish a tyranny. Thus, Arthur Lee, Richard Henry's brother, thought the Constitution "too Aristocratic" and believed "an Oligarchy" would "spring from it." For Lee the omission of a declaration of rights was not an error but was "designed" by the Framers.[179]

The Tyrannical Tactics of the Federalists

In addition to their adamant opposition to a bill of rights, the Federalists' tactics did little to alleviate Antifederalist concerns. The events in Pennsylvania immediately after the Convention ended put the emerging Antifederalists on notice that the struggle over the Constitution would be rough, perhaps violent, and indicative of the tyranny that might follow ratification.

On the penultimate day of the legislative session supporters of the Constitution in the Pennsylvania assembly "enjoying a temporary majority . . . pressed for immediate action."[180] Those skeptical about the Constitution believed the decision to call a ratifying convention should be made by the new legis-

---

[177] Pole, *Constitution—For and Against*, p. 17.

[178] "A Federal Republican," "A Review of the Constitution Proposed by the Late Convention Held at Philadelphia . . . ," Nov. 28, 1787, *DHR*, 2:304.

[179] Arthur Lee to John Adams, Oct. 3, 1787, ibid., 8:34.

[180] Steven R. Boyd, *The Politics of Opposition: Antifederalists and the Acceptance of the Constitution* (Millwood, N.Y., 1979), pp. 23–24.

lature, which would be elected the following month. This would allow voters to read the proposed Constitution and choose assembly members on the basis of that document. The Antifederalists also complained that many assemblymen who opposed the Constitution had already left Philadelphia because they lived in the remote western part of the state and, not anticipating any more important business, wanted to get started on their long journey home. When the temporary Federalist majority rejected these arguments, the remaining Antifederalist members of the assembly boycotted the last session in order to prevent a quorum. The next day a mob forced two Antifederalist assemblymen back to the chamber in order to establish a quorum. The assembly then approved the call for a convention.[181]

If this behavior on the part of the Federalists reflected the tenor of politics to be expected under the new Constitution, it is understandable that many people feared an impending end to liberty. Philadelphiensis wondered:

> If the proposed plan be a good one upon the whole, why should its friends endeavour to prevent investigating its merits or defects? Why should they hurry it on us before we have even read it? Does not this look suspicious like? Is it not a proof that it is the works of darkness, and cannot bear the light? Why should they summon a Convention in Pennsylvania, before the tenth part of the people had time to judge for themselves, or to know whether it was a free or a tyrannical system of government? Why employ bullies to drag some members of the Assembly per force to the House to make a quorum, in order to call a Convention?[182]

Another Philadelphian, "An Old Whig," noted that in Boston

> no man is permitted to publish a doubt of the infallibility of the late convention, without giving up his name to the people, that he may be delivered over to speedy destruction; and it is but a

[181] Ibid., p. 24; Jackson Turner Main, *The Antifederalists: Critics of the Constitution, 1781–1788* (Chapel Hill, 1961), pp. 187–88.

[182] "Essays of Philadelphiensis" (X), *CAF,* 3:131.

short time since the case was little better in this city [Philadelphia]. Now this is a portion of the very same spirit, which has so often kindled the fires of the inquisition: and the same Zealot who would hunt a man down for a difference of opinion upon a political question which is the subject of public enquiry, if he should happen to be fired with zeal for a particular species of religion, would be equally intolerant.[183]

Noting that the proposed Constitution contained no bill of rights, protections of speech, or "Liberty of Conscience,"[184] the "Old Whig" expressed concern about the implications of force in the ratification process. "Suppose that an act of the continental legislature should be passed to restrain the liberty of the press;—to appoint licensers of the press in every town in America;—to limit the number of printers;—and to compel them to give security for their good behaviour."[185] Without a bill of rights, what would prevent such legislation? The "Old Whig" warned: "They are idiots who trust their future security to the whim of the present hour."[186] He would not support the Constitution without a guarantee of his rights.

Like the "Old Whig," most Antifederalists understood that even a legislature in a republic might overstep its bounds, the majority might oppress the minority, and a president who was also commander-in-chief might collude with others in the government to seize power. This fear was more realistic if one believed, as many Antifederalists did, that most Federalists could not be trusted to protect liberty. The proof of this was that the Federalists so adamantly opposed a bill of rights. As J. R. Pole has observed, "The deliberate omission of a bill of rights seemed to many Anti-Federalists to represent a damaging admission of the ulterior motives of their opponents."[187]

---

[183] "Essays of an Old Whig" (V), ibid., p. 35.

[184] Ibid., p. 34.

[185] "Essays of an Old Whig" (III), ibid., p. 27.

[186] "Essays of an Old Whig" (V), ibid., p. 35.

[187] Pole, *Constitution—For and Against,* p. 28.

The Lameness of the Federalist Arguments

Advocates of explicit protections of liberty were not much impressed with the Federalist arguments against a bill of rights. They saw them as self-serving and intellectually dishonest. More importantly, they thought such arguments underscored the Federalist propensity toward tyranny. Federalists thought that their opponents must want anarchy, or why would they so adamantly oppose the Constitution? Antifederalists thought Federalists must truly want a tyranny, or why would they both behave as they did and so adamantly oppose a bill of rights?

An examination of the responses to the Federalist arguments against a bill of rights illustrates the common ground and language of the two sides, even as it shows how much they disagreed. These debates also reveal that on balance, the Antifederalists had much the better argument. If there was a foolish or misguided opposition in the years 1787–91, it was the Federalists who opposed a bill of rights.

The state constitutions are no answer. Federalists argued that liberty was fully protected by the state bills of rights; Antifederalists laughed, or cried, at the proposition. The whole purpose of the Constitution was to strengthen the national government at the expense of the states. Nothing was more clear to Antifederalists than the likelihood that the states would be unable to prevent the national government from trampling on their liberties. With no need for analysis, Antifederalists in rural Pennsylvania simply asserted that "the bill of rights contained in the constitutions of the several states are no security, nor are the people secured in the privileges of the common law."[188]

When George Mason proposed that the entire Constitution be "prefaced with a Bill of Rights," Roger Sherman replied that this was unnecessary because the Constitution did not repeal the state bills of rights. Mason replied that federal laws would be "paramount to State Bills of Rights." This argument, however correct, had little effect on the Convention, which

---

[188]"Cumberland County Petition to the Pennsylvania Convention," Dec. 5, 1787, *DHR*, 2:310.

defeated Mason's motion with all states voting no.[189] In explaining why he would not sign the Constitution Mason reiterated this point: "There is no Declaration of Rights, and the
laws of the general government being paramount to the laws
and Constitutions of the several States, the Declaration of
Rights in the separate States are no security." Under this Constitution "the people" were not "secured even the enjoyment
of the benefit of the common law."[190]

Connecticut Antifederalists thought the "Constitution
would institute and erect an aristocracy which . . . would end
in despotism and tyranny and extinguish or nearly absorb our
ancient charter privileges ever sacred to us . . . and finally
prove destructive to our most valuable liberties and privileges."[191] Rather than the state charter protecting the people
from the national government, these Connecticut citizens
believed the federal charter would destroy their state-
protected liberties.

In the Pennsylvania ratifying convention William Findley
argued that the new government "will swallow up eventually
all state governments" and, of course, destroy the utility of the
state bills of rights.[192] In the Maryland ratifying convention
Samuel Chase made a similar argument, noting the Constitution created "a general or *national* government" and thus the
states were "melted down and consolidated into one *National*
Government." Chase believed that the Constitution "swallows
up the state governments and state legislatures—it alters our
[Maryland] Constitution and annuls our [Maryland] Bill of
Rights in many of its most essential parts."[193] This meant that
a federal bill of rights was absolutely essential to preserve lib-

[189] Farrand, ed., *Records of the Convention*, 2:587–88.

[190] Ibid., pp. 637–38. Recent evidence suggests that this speech, while
written during the Convention, may not have actually been given there
(*CAF*, 2:9–11; *DHR*, 8:43).

[191] Records of the town meeting of Simsbury, Conn., Nov. 12, 1787,
DHR, 3:442–43.

[192] Debates in the Pennsylvania convention, Dec. 1, 1787, ibid., 2:447.

[193] Samuel Chase, "Notes of Speeches Delivered to the Maryland Ratifying Convention," *CAF*, 5:80. Ironically, as a member of the United States

erty. In Virginia an "Impartial Examiner" noted that under the Articles of Confederation of a national bill of rights was unnecessary because "the authority of Congress cannot extend so afar as to interfere with, or exercise any kind of coercion on, the power of legislation in the different states; but the internal police of each is left free, sovereign and independent; so that the liberties of the people being secured as well as the nature of their constitutions will admit; and the declaration of rights, which they have laid down as the *basis* of government, having their full force and energy, any farther stipulation on that head might be unnecessary." But this doctrine could not be applied to "the *proposed* foederal constitution, which is framed with such large and extensive powers, as to transfer the individual sovereignty from each state to the *aggregate body*." The state bills of rights were meaningless because the Constitution gave the new Congress "supreme powers of legislation throughout all the states—annihilates the separate independency of each; and in short—swallows up and involves in the plentitude of its jurisdiction all other powers whatsoever."[194]

"A Farmer," writing in Maryland, pointed out that a citizen of his state could have "no benefit of his own bill of rights in the confederal courts" because a state bill of rights would not be binding on the national government. Because there was "no bill of rights of the United States," the "Farmer" wondered how a citizen could "take advantage of a natural right founded in reason." Rhetorically, he asked if a citizen might "plead" a natural right in a federal court "and produce Locke, Sydney, or Montesquieu as authority?"[195] In Virginia, Denatus predicted the federal constitution "will easily overleap our state constitutions with impunity." The federal constitution would be "sovereign in all things" and thus "we ought to have a bill of rights; to save us from oppression."[196]

Supreme Court, Chase would enforce the Sedition Act of 1798 as though neither the state nor the federal bills of rights mattered.

[194] "Essays by the Impartial Examiner" (I), ibid., p. 179.

[195] "Essays by a Farmer" (I), ibid., p. 13.

[196] "Address by Denatus," ibid., p. 261.

The Antifederalists were accused by their contemporaries—and by modern historians—of being narrow-minded localists. Their localism was partially due to the lack of a bill of rights. If the state bills of rights were to be the main guarantors of American liberty, the states had to be more powerful than the national government. Otherwise, as the New York Antifederal Committee predicted, the states would be "at the mercy of the general government." Under such circumstances, the state constitutions would be of little value in protecting liberty.[197]

The "limited" government has almost limitless powers. Antifederalists were unimpressed with the notion that the limitations on Congress written into the Constitution guaranteed that the national government could never pass laws, or implement policies, that would touch the liberty of the people. They saw a new government with virtually limitless powers trampling on individual rights with impunity. They looked at the necessary and proper clause, the war powers clauses, and the supremacy clause and saw a government with virtually unlimited powers. In this aspect of the debate they were far more realistic than their opponents. They understood that the national government under the Constitution would have awesome powers, and thus they correctly saw that a bill of rights was absolutely necessary to protect liberty by limiting that government.

Elbridge Gerry saw dangers to liberty in the aristocratic nature of the Senate, the centralizing tendencies of the commerce power, and the necessary and proper clause. He would have been able to "get over all these" defects "if the rights of the Citizens were not rendered insecure" by the virtually unlimited power of Congress.[198]

In his December 20, 1787, letter to Madison, Jefferson dis-

---

[197] "Address of the Albany Antifederal Committee," Apr. 26, 1788, ibid., 6:124.

[198] Farrand, ed., *Records of the Convention,* 2:632–33; "Hon. Mr. Gerry's Objections," *CAF,* 2:6–7. A month later Gerry would inform the Massachusetts legislature that "the liberties of America were not secured" by the Constitution because "the system is without the security of a bill of rights."

puted James Wilson's arguments "that a bill of rights was not necessary because all is reserved in the case of the general government which is not given." Jefferson thought Wilson's argument was "gratis dictum" which was "opposed by strong inferences from the body" of the Constitution.[199]

Jefferson's private views were well represented among the public views of the Antifederalists. "A Democratic Federalist" challenged Wilson's assertions that in the federal Constitution "every power which is not *given* is *reserved*." If this was true, this author thought, "it ought at least to have been clearly expressed in the plan of government."[200] With a telling reference to the trial of John Peter Zenger, the "Democratic Federalist" argued that "there is no knowing what corrupt and wicked judges may do in process of time, when they are not restrained by express law."[201]

In Maryland "A Farmer" wondered what would happen if "an officer of the United States should force the house, the asylum of a citizen, by virtue of a general warrant." He asked, "Are general warrants illegal by the constitution of the United States?"[202] Clearly, he thought they would not be illegal.

Similar complaints were a mainstay of Antifederalist literature. Antifederalists did not believe the Constitution granted only limited powers to the national government. They saw the creation of a government unrestrained by a bill of rights that could quickly usurp all power. They saw no protection from their states, which they believed were to be swallowed up by the national government. The federal Constitution, according to one Virginian, "has fairly annihilated the Constitution of each individual state." The Convention "has proposed to you a high prerogative government, which, like *Aaron's* serpent, is

[199] Jefferson to Madison, Dec. 20, 1787, Boyd, ed., *Papers of Jefferson*, 12:440. For further discussion of this letter, see note 171, above. See also Madison to Jefferson, Oct. 24, 1787, ibid., pp. 270–86.

[200] "A Democratic Federalist," *Pennsylvania Herald* (Philadelphia), Oct. 17, 1787, *DHR*, 2:193; also ibid., 13:387.

[201] Ibid., 2:194. On Zenger, see Paul Finkelman, ed., *A Brief Narrative of the Tryal of John Peter Zenger* (St. James, N.Y., 1997), pp. 1–60.

[202] "Essays by a Farmer" (I), *CAF*, 5:14.

to swallow up the rest." Americans had supported the Convention because of the inadequacy of the Articles. But the result was to go "from one extreme to the other; from anarchy to tyranny; from the inconvenient laxity of thirteen separate Governments to the too sharp and grinding one" that threatened the power of the states to protect the liberty of their people.[203]

In New York "A Countryman," probably DeWitt Clinton,[204] offered an analysis of the Constitution that stood the limited government theory on its head. "Countryman" noted that the Constitution specifically prohibited the granting of titles of nobility. Following the logic of Wilson and other Federalists, "Countryman," noted that "if there was not power given to this government to grant titles of nobility . . . then there was no occasion to say that they should not do it, because it would be very foolish to say, that they should not do a thing which they could not do."[205] But because there was no specific clause that might be construed to allow the creation of a nobility, the logical conclusion was that some clauses of the Constitution had "a very broad meaning" which might have allowed for the creation of a nobility, and in fact, these clauses could "give them [the new government] power to do every thing" not specifically prohibited.[206] In other words, the government was not one of limited powers but rather one of unlimited powers except where the limitations were explicit.

Protections of some liberties in the Constitution requires a bill of rights protecting all liberties. The analysis of "Countryman" also undercut the strong Federalist argument that an incomplete bill of rights would, by inference, cede unenumerated rights to the national government. After all, if some protections of liberty, such as the prohibitions on titles of nobility, were in the Con-

---

[203] "Address by Cato Uticensis," ibid., p. 121.

[204] This author should not be confused with the Federalist essays of a "A Countryman," written by Roger Sherman and published in the *New Haven Gazette.*

[205] "Letters from a Countryman" [DeWitt Clinton] (III), *CAF,* 6:80.

[206] Ibid.

stitution, then, according to the logic of Wilson, Hamilton, Madison, and others, that meant that in accepting the Constitution the people were giving up all other fundamental rights. As "An Old Whig" noted, "The same argument which proves the necessity of securing one of them shews also the necessity of securing others."[207]

"A Federal Republican" thought Wilson's argument on the danger of enumerating rights might impress "the votaries of scholastic philosophy" but it had no place "in the political world, where reason is not cultivated independently of action and experience." The experiences of the political world proved the value of enumerating rights. But if the Federalists were unwilling to enumerate the rights the people "already possess," this author was willing to accept an amendment declaring "that whatever is not decreed to Congress is reserved to the several states for their own disposal."[208] The adamant refusal of Federalists to support such an amendment led Antifederalists to conclude that their opponents in fact did not want to limit the powers of Congress. Unlimited power, as most eighteenth-century political theorists understood, was the first step to tyranny.

The persistent demand for a guarantee of jury trials in civil cases illustrates why Antifederalists believed that the Wilson-Hamilton-Madison position on the dangers of enumerating rights was both disingenuous and dangerous. The Constitution guaranteed a jury trial for all federal criminal cases. By omitting such a guarantee for civil trials, the Convention was clearly leaving it up to Congress to decide under what circumstances juries should hear civil cases. James Wilson in fact defended the Constitution on this point, arguing that "it is not in all cases that the trial by jury is adopted in civil questions," and thus the issue should be left for the Congress or the Supreme Court to decide.[209]

[207] "An Old Whig" (V), *Independent Gazetteer* (Philadelphia), Nov. 1, 1787, *DHR*, 13:541.

[208] "A Federal Republican," "Review of the Constitution," ibid., 2:304.

[209] Wilson, "Speech in the State House Yard," ibid., 169–70; also reprinted as Wilson, "Speech at a Public Meeting," ibid., 13:340–41.

Wilson's position frightened Antifederalists. Writing in New York, Timoleon thought that the failure to protect the civil jury was part of a plot against liberty: "*Some* who framed this new system, saw with Dr. Blackstone, how operative jury trial was in preventing tyranny of the great ones, and therefore frowned upon it, as this new Constitution does."[210] "A Democratic Federalist," following Wilson's logic, concluded that because the criminal jury was explicitly protected, the "*trial by jury in civil cases, is, by the proposed constitution entirely done away, and effectually abolished.*" This was an "enormous innovation, and daring encroachment, on the liberties of the citizens." This deliberate decision not to protect a civil jury trial, especially when tied to the failure to protect against unreasonable searches, was a prelude to the worst sorts of tyranny:

> Suppose therefore, that the military officers of congress, by a wanton abuse of power, imprison the free citizens of America, suppose the excise or revenue officers . . . [act as an English constable once did, who] having a warrant to search for stolen goods, pulled down the clothes of a bed in which there was a woman, and searched under her shift,—suppose, I say, that they [the revenue officers] commit similar, or greater indignities, in such cases a trial by jury would be our safest resource, heavy damages would at once punish the offender, and deter others from committing the same: but what satisfaction can we expect from a lordly court of justice, always ready to protect the officers of government against the weak and helpless citizen?

With the federal courts sitting hundreds of miles from where the aggrieved citizen lived, "A Democratic Federalist" asked, "What refuge shall we then have to shelter us from the iron hand of arbitrary power?" He exclaimed: "O! my fellow citizens, think of this while it is yet time, and never consent to part with the glorious privilege of trial by jury, but with your lives."[211]

The arguments about the lack of a protection for a civil jury trial illustrate the way in which Antifederalists saw a tyranny

[210]"Timoleon," *New York Journal, Extraordinary*, Nov. 1, 1787, ibid., pp. 537–38.

[211]"Democratic Federalist," ibid., pp. 389–90.

being created by a Constitution that protected just a few rights. Brutus noted that wisely the state constitutions had "either formal bills of rights, which set bounds to the power of the legislature, or have restrictions for the same purpose in the body of the constitutions." Logically, Brutus thought, the same should hold true for the national constitution. Brutus noted that "some of our new political Doctors" rejected the idea of a bill of rights. But he pointed out that the Framers at Philadelphia "were of a contrary opinion, because they have prohibited the general government, the exercise of some powers, and restricted them in that of others."[212] The obvious point here was that if some rights were protected in the main body of the Constitution, it was dangerous not to protect all rights.

The "crisis" isn't such a crisis. The Federalists predicated their opposition to a bill of rights on the assumption that the nation was in a state of crisis and that any delay in ratification would lead to a collapse of the nation and would in turn lead to anarchy. They also argued that anarchy would flow from too much liberty, and thus a bill of rights would upset the stability of the new government. To use very modern terminology, these arguments just didn't wash with the proponents of a bill of rights.

William Findley thought the Federalist arguments about a crisis were "like persuading a man in health that [he] is sick." Americans were "enjoying liberty and happiness to a great extent." Findley did not see a crisis and thus saw no reason to be "hastened" by claims of "necessity."[213] The "Federal Farmer" saw no crisis. He thought if "we remain cool and temperate, we are in no immediate danger of any commotions; we are in a state of perfect peace, and in no danger of invasions; the state governments are in the full exercise of their powers." The "Federal Farmer" acknowledged there were problems with the "regulation of trade, securing credit," and paying public debts, but he asserted "whether we adopt a change, three or nine months hence" did not matter. The nation was

---

[212] Brutus (IX), *New York Journal*, Jan. 17, 1788, ibid., 15:394.

[213] Debates in the Pennsylvania convention, ibid., 2:445.

only just recovering from "a long and distressing war." The "Farmer" thought the nation should finish its postwar recovery and "reform our federal system" but not by hastily adopting a new government that might "totally destroy the liberties of this country."[214]

The anonymous Brutus, Jr.,[215] came right to the point: "I deny that we are in immediate danger of anarchy and commotions. Nothing but the passions of wicked and ambitious men, will put us in the least danger on this head: those who are anxious to precipitate a measure, will always tell us that the present is the critical moment; now is the time, the crisis is arrived, and the present minute must be seized. Tyrants have always made use of this plea; but nothing in our circumstances can justify it."[216]

Brutus, Jr., also responded to the Federalists who suggested that supporters of a bill of rights were willing to lead the country into violence, civil war, and anarchy. "If any tumults arise," Brutus, Jr., declared, "they will be justly chargeable on those artful and ambitious men, who are determined to cram this government down the throats of the people."[217]

The Albany Antifederal Committee noted that the most common argument in favor of the Constitution was "that the present confederation is defective and will tend to anarchy and confusion." But to these men it was "the weakest of all weak reasons, to adopt a bad constitution because the present one is defective." By this logic "a person of a sickly habit or constitution might as well put an end to his existence, for fear that his sickness or infirmity would be the cause of his death."[218] The Albany Antifederalists preferred to risk anar-

---

[214] "Letters from the Federal Farmer" (I), *CAF,* 2:225–26.

[215] See Gaspare J. Saladino, "Pseudonyms Used in the Newspaper Debate over the Ratification of the United States Constitution in the State of New York, September 1787–July 1788," in Stephen L. Schechter and Richard B. Bernstein, eds., *New York and the Union: Contributions to the American Constitutional Experience* (Albany, 1990), p. 303.

[216] "Essay by Brutus, Jr.," *CAF,* 6:39.

[217] Ibid.

[218] "Address of the Albany Antifederal Committee," ibid., p. 125.

chy (which they doubted was likely) than risk losing their liberty. They reminded readers that "the free men of America have fought and bled to oppose the oppression and usurpation of Great-Britain; and shall they now resign these rights and privileges, to a government which, if possible, may be still more arbitrary and despotic?"[219]

Antifederalists are not venal—but the Federalists might be. Federalists implied or asserted that the Antifederalists had a pecuniary interest in the status quo and opposed the Constitution, "not in truth, because it is injurious to the liberties of his country, but because it affects his schemes of wealth and consequence."[220] Arthur Lee, writing as Cincinnatus, thought this argument was "the shibboleth" of the Federalists that "reaches every man who will not worship the new idol." Such an argument "imputed" the opinion of every Antifederalist by implying that he was "actually a placeman under the present establishment" or "an expectant."[221]

Cincinnatus also pointed out this was "a two-edged argument, and might cut its inventor." He suggested that "these very violent gentlemen for the new establishment" might "be actuated by the same undue motives" and that some of the Framers of the Constitution "might have had its honours and emoluments in view." Cincinnatus accused James Wilson of hoping to become a "chief justice."[222] This was not far from the mark, as Wilson would in fact become an associate justice of the Supreme Court.[223] Philadelphiensis believed that the

---

[219] Ibid., p. 126.

[220] James Wilson's language quoted in [Arthur Lee], "Essays by Cincinnatus" (VI), ibid., p. 30.

[221] Ibid., p. 30. Although a Virginian, Arthur Lee published his Cincinnatus essays attacking Wilson in the *New York Journal* (see Saladino, "Pseudonyms Used," p. 306).

[222] [Lee], "Essays by Cincinnatus" (VI), *CAF,* 6:30.

[223] Federalists also knew this to be true. In Philadelphia, William Jackson, who had been the secretary at the Constitutional Convention, was "looking out for some lucrative place under the new Constitution, despairing of suc-

proposed constitution would create "a government composed only of an *emperor and a few lordlings,* surrounded by thousands of blood-suckers, and cringing sycophants."[224] Despite his hyperbole, the point was clear—a new government would have many new offices, and the Federalists undoubtedly expected to fill them.

Important for the fears of tyranny and anarchy is the language Arthur Lee used in his Cincinnatus essays. References to the Constitution as "the new idol" and to its supporters as "very violent gentlemen" suggest the Antifederalists feared that their opponents would resort to force verging on religious fanaticism to secure the Constitution. Naturally such men would oppose a bill of rights.

A long-range plot for tyranny will overcome republican virtue. That Antifederalists saw the Constitution as a plot against liberty seems clear. Their arguments focused on the tyranny that could emerge from the lack of a bill of rights. Federalists responded to these complaints with sarcasm, contempt, and sincere disbelief. Antifederalists, on the other hand, "stood amazed at the Federalists' affrontery" to the rights of the people.[225]

How, the Federalists constantly asked, could tyranny emerge in America where the people were free and ever vigilant of their liberties? Some Antifederalists were simply "unable to grasp the sweeping significance the Federalists were attributing to the sovereignty of the people."[226] Madison argued in *Federalist* Nos. 10, 51, and 57 that the political process, governmental structures, and America's social and demographic diversity would protect liberty. Ever attuned to turning private interest to the public good, he believed that members of Congress would never betray the liberties of

---

cess at the bar" (William Shippen, Jr., to Thomas Lee Shippen, Nov. 18, 22, 1787, *DHR,* 2:288).

[224] "Essays of Philadelphiensis" (III), *CAF,* 3:111, emphasis in original.

[225] Wood, *Creation of the American Republic,* pp. 540–41.

[226] Ibid.

the people because, if they did, they would not be reelected. He thought the "vigilant and manly spirit which actuates the people of America" would prevent the legislature from usurping power.[227]

This was a powerful argument that Antifederalists could not ignore or, in the end, overcome. The fact that the Constitution was ratified *without* amendments suggests that a substantial number of Americans (although probably not a numerical majority of even the free adult male population) thought their liberties were safe, at least for the immediate short term, under the Constitution. These Federalists doubtless believed that Americans would not vote for tyrants, and that the elected officials would not readily become tyrants.

Some Antifederalists clearly did not see the "sweeping significance" of Federalist concepts of popular sovereignty. Thus, Patrick Henry continued to view "government as a delegation of express powers."[228] But other Antifederalists seem to have understood what the Federalists were saying—they simply rejected the notion that liberty could be secure even if the people were theoretically sovereign.

Cato agreed with Madison that the voters should place "a reasonable confidence" in those they elected to office. But he warned that "such an unbounded" confidence "as the advocates and framers of this new system advise . . . would be dangerous to your liberties." Cato warned that "unlimited confidence in governors as well as individuals is frequently the parent of deception." In answer to Madison's trust for Republican institutions, Cato argued that "rulers in all governments will erect an interest separate from the ruled, which will have a tendency to enslave them." Without a bill of rights Congress could "at one stroke . . . do away your liberties for ever."[229]

How could legislators in a republic "erect an interest separate from the ruled"? Antifederalists feared that the lack of a bill of rights combined with the structure of the government

---

[227] *Federalist* No. 57, Hutchinson et al., eds., *Papers of Madison*, 10:523.

[228] Wood, *Creation of the American Republic*, pp. 540–41.

[229] Cato (VII), *New York Journal*, Jan. 3, 1788, *DHR*, 15:242.

could lead to precisely this result.[230] For Antifederalists the tiny number of representatives in Congress was one threat to liberty. The Congress would be so small that Madison's notions of representation would be meaningless. In this context it is worth remembering that one of the unratified amendments Congress proposed in 1789 would have led to one representative for every fifty thousand Americans.[231] The unrepresentativeness of Congress was a common theme for Antifederalists. "A Georgian" argued the Constitution would create "an ARISTOCRATICAL government, whereby about 70 nabobs would lord over three millions of people as slaves."[232] Some Antifederalists tied this structural defect directly to the lack of a bill of rights.

The minority of the Pennsylvania convention complained that there was no "declaration of RIGHTS" in the Constitution, but at the same time "that strongest of all checks upon the conduct of administration, *responsibility to the people,* will not exist in this government." Because Congress could control the manner of elections, lawmakers would be "independent of the sentiments and resentment of the people," and there would "be no consideration to restrain them from oppression and tyranny."[233]

Sydney articulated another danger of the system—the long terms of legislators. Sydney noted that New York lacked a bill of rights, and the Federalists made much of this to prove that a bill of rights was unnecessary in the national constitution. But Sydney pointed out significant differences between New York state and the national government. Especially important was the fact that "state officers" were "elected by the people

[230] For a discussion of the structure of the Constitution and its relationship to the Bill of Rights, see Akhil Reed Amar, "The Bill of Rights as a Constitution," this volume. For criticism of this analysis, see Paul Finkelman, "The Ten Amendments as a Declaration of Rights," *Southern Illinois University Law Journal* 16 (1992):351–96.

[231] For the text of this amendment see Veit, Bowling, and Bickford, eds., *Creating the Bill of Rights,* p. 3.

[232] "A Georgian," *Gazette of the State of Georgia* (Savannah), Nov. 15, 1789, *DHR,* 3:236.

[233] "Address and Reasons of Dissent," ibid., 2:636.

at short periods, and thereby rendered from time to time liable to be displaced in case of malconduct."[234] This touched on another common Antifederalist theme—that the federal government would be so remote from the people, and federal officeholders would serve such long terms, that tyranny could easily result.

In New York "A Plebeian" argued that "the common people, the yeomanry," would be the "principal losers, if the constitution should prove oppressive." While not spelling out the details, he implied that the rich would eventually take over the nation, and they would be better able to do this, and be more oppressive once they did so, if the Constitution lacked a bill of rights. "When a tyranny is established," the "Plebeian" warned, "there are always masters as well as slaves; the great and the well-born are generally the former, and the middling class the latter."[235]

Samuel Osgood, a Massachusetts Antifederalist, had an even more concrete theory of how tyrants could take power, even in a republic. He spelled this out in a detailed letter to the old revolutionary Samuel Adams. Like the Federalists, Osgood conceded "the extreme Necessity of a more efficient federal Government than the present." He was initially tempted to believe that it was better to approve the Constitution without amendments than risk "the Delay" of not adopting the new plan of government. He noted many supporters of the Constitution were motivated not by their enthusiasm for the document but rather by the "extreme Necessity" of the time. But for Osgood the "Plain Meaning" of this conclusion was "that Despotism is better for us, than to remain as we are."[236] Osgood, however, was not so fearful of the potential anarchy of the present that he was willing to risk a despotism in the future.

Osgood quoted "Mr. Wilsons Observation, so often repeated. . . 'That what ever is not given is reserved,'" but went

[234] [Abraham Yates], "Address by Sydney," *CAF,* 6:109.

[235] "Address by a Plebeian," ibid., p. 142.

[236] Samuel Osgood to Samuel Adams, Jan. 5, 1788, *DHR,* 15:263.

on to note that "the great Question upon this is what is there of Consequence to the People that is not given." Osgood in fact found little that had not been surrendered. He noted that "the extent of the Judicial Power is therefore, as indefinite & unlimited as Words can make it." This led back to the problem of state bills of rights. Osgood asked, "What Use then for a State Judicial? of what Consequence will be the State Bill of Rights.—The continental [national] Judicial are not bound by it." Under the Constitution the people would be "conclaved out of a Bill of Rights." Without a bill of rights, Osgood saw tyranny emerging from two sources. First, the national government would limit the electorate, regulating presidential and senatorial elections. This would be especially easy because the large electoral districts created by the Constitution would undermine the voice of the people in their own government.[237]

Most dangerous of all would be the national capital—the area "not exceeding ten Miles Square" where "unlimited Power of exclusive Legislation is expressly given to Congress." Here, where no state bills of rights could interfere, Osgood predicted a government based on tyranny would grow. The government would "be shut up in the ten Miles Square" and the people would have "very little Knowledge of its Operations," while through "Bribery and Corruption, & and an undue Use of the public Monies, Nabobs are created in each State." In this federal city "capable of holding two Millions of People—Here will the Wealth and Riches of every State center—And shall there be in the Bowels of the united States such a Number of People, brot up under the Hand of Despotism." Osgood did not object to a federal city, but he demanded "let the People settled there, have a Bill of Rights. Let them know that they are Freemen—Let them have the Liberty of Speech, of the Press, of Religion, &ca." Otherwise tyranny could arise, even in a republic.[238]

A strong central government, large electoral districts, re-

---

[237] Ibid., pp. 263–67.

[238] Ibid.

mote legislators with long terms, an isolated capital, and no bill of rights—these were the components that could so easily lead to tyranny.

STRENGTH THROUGH LIBERTY: TOWARD A BILL OF RIGHTS

A key component of the Federalist opposition to a bill of rights stemmed from the fear that any amendments would weaken the new national government. That would lead to the same instability caused by the Articles of Confederation. Many Antifederalists agreed with their opponents that a stronger national government was necessary. But they believed this strength had to be based on liberty. The "Old Whig" argued that when "the liberty of the subject is secured, the government is really strengthened; because wherever the subject is convinced that nothing more is required from him than what is necessary of the good of the community, he yields a cheerful obedience, which is more useful than the constrained service of slaves."[239]

In the end the supporters of a bill of rights sounded much like the opponents. Their position was simple. If a bill of rights was not added the nation would suffer from anarchy and civil war. Most Federalists never accepted this argument, but by 1789 some of the Federalists, most notably Madison, were willing to allow some amendments.

In June 1789 Madison proposed a series of amendments in the new Congress.[240] Until this time he had openly opposed amendments. His change now was hardly a conversion; rather it reflected his understanding that a bill of rights would not harm the Constitution and would help diminish Antifederalist opposition.[241] Tench Coxe, a stalwart Federalist, praised Madison for proposing amendments. Coxe saw the amend-

---

[239] "An Old Whig" (IV), ibid., 13:501 (also in *CAF,* 3:33).

[240] The fullest documentation of the Congressional debates over the amendments is Veit, Bowling, and Bickford, eds., *Creating the Bill of Rights.*

[241] See, generally, Finkelman, "Madison and the Adoption of the Bill of Rights."

ments as a way of ending the partisan arguments that threatened to lead to civil war and then anarchy. Coxe thought the amendments would "greatly tend to promote harmony among the late contending parties and a general confidence in the patriotism of Congress."[242] Madison took much the same position in Congress. He did not argue with passion or even much conviction for his proposal. He admitted that he had "never considered this provision so essential to the federal constitution" that it should have been allowed to impede ratification. But with the Constitution ratified Madison was willing to concede "that in a certain form and to a certain extent, such a provision was neither improper nor altogether useless."[243]

By the time the issue was debated in Congress a number of former Federalists accepted Madison's analysis that a bill of rights was not necessary to preserve liberty, but "if we continue to postpone from time to time, and refuse to let the subject [of amendments] come into view, it may occasion suspicions, which, though not well founded, may tend to inflame or prejudice the public mind against our decisions." Congressional consideration of amendments would "quiet that anxiety which prevails in the public mind."[244] Alexander White of Virginia thought a bill of rights "would tend to tranquillize the public mind," while John Page of Virginia warned that if Congress did not quickly consider a bill of rights "you will not have power to deliberate. The people will clamor for a new convention; they will not trust the House any longer." John Vining of Delaware thought a bill of rights would "quiet the perturbation of the public mind" and "give permanency and stability to constitutional regulations."[245] In the end the desire for national harmony overcame most Federalist opposition to amendments. The antithesis of harmony, after all, was chaos. Once again the issue was avoiding anarchy.

---

[242] Tench Coxe to Madison, June 18, 1789, Hutchinson et al., eds., *Papers of Madison*, 12:239–41.

[243] *Annals of Congress,* 1st Cong., 1st sess., 1:453.

[244] Schwartz, comp., *Roots of the Bill of Rights,* 5:1019–20.

[245] Ibid., pp. 1021–22.

CONCLUSION

The willingness of the Antifederalists to accept the Constitution with only the promise of a bill of rights suggests that they were, in the end, not "Men of Little Faith" as historians once argued.[246] Quite the opposite, they were men of great faith. In the end they accepted the risks of an unprecedented experiment in government with only the promise that their opponents would support amendments guaranteeing a free press, jury trials, due process, bans on arbitrary and cruel justice, and the continuation of state militias that would be able to strike back against any president or general who might attempt to seize power.

In another sense they were also the great realists of the period. Most scholars point to the *Federalist Papers* to illustrate that Madison and Hamilton understood the dangers of the majority. The great beauty of the American system, we are told, is that the rights of the minority were protected through the diffusion of power and limited government. This was certainly Madison's understanding of how the system would work, and partially because he thought this would be a sufficient protection of liberty he opposed a bill of rights.

It was the Antifederalists who saw that without a bill of rights there would be few limits on the government. They understood just how corrupting power could be. Had it been left to Hamilton and Wilson, the republic might not have survived to celebrate its two hundredth birthday. Some imperial president, acting as commander-in-chief and aided by a pliant Congress utilizing the necessary and proper clause, might long ago have created his own empire. Americans kept their republic in part because of the faith of the Antifederalists like Centinel who understood that "if the liberty of the press" were "rendered *sacred* . . . despotism would fly before it."[247]

Paradoxically, both Federalists and Antifederalists of the

---

[246] Kenyon, "Men of Little Faith," pp. 3–43, and James H. Hutson, "Country, Court, and the Constitution: Anti-Federalism and the Historians," *William and Mary Quarterly*, 3d ser. 38 (1981):337–68, both reprinted in Hall, *Formation and Ratification of the Constitution*, pp. 348–88, 249–80.

[247] "Letters of Centinel" (I), *CAF,* 2:143, emphasis in original.

founding generation feared the same result if their opponents achieved their goals. Ironically, in the end both sides more or less won.

The Federalists saw their Constitution ratified and with it the creation of a stable national government with rather remarkable powers. They quickly, although only briefly, came to control this new government.

The Antifederalists saw a bill of rights ratified that limited the power of the national government to overtly undermine fundamental liberties. Certainly some Antifederalists, such as Patrick Henry, had wanted to dismantle the new Constitution as soon as it was written. They thought the bill of rights was a "tub to the whale," designed to undermine the opposition to the Constitution without actually getting rid of its evils.[248] But other Antifederalists were more accommodating. James Monroe, one of Henry's Antifederalist allies in Virginia, wanted "to form a government that shall shield you from dangers from abroad, promote your general and local interests, protect in safety the life, liberty, and property, of the peaceful, the virtuous and the weak, against the encroachments of the disorderly and licentious."[249] The Bill of Rights, when added to the Constitution, allowed this to happen.

The Bill of Rights also enabled many Antifederalists to become active participants in the new government. Elbridge Gerry, who refused to sign the Constitution, twice became vice-president under it. Jefferson, who disliked the Constitution's lack of a bill of rights, became secretary of state, vice-president, and president. Monroe, who voted against the Constitution in the Virginia ratifying convention, also became secretary of state and president. If the Antifederalists at first thought the bill of rights was but a "tub to the whale," they eventually came to like that tub. Indeed, it was that tub which enabled them to take control of the whale itself and effectively govern the nation.

In the end, the Bill of Rights worked. The result was that

[248] Kenneth R. Bowling, "'A Tub to the Whale': The Founding Fathers and the Adoption of the Federal Bill of Rights," *Journal of the Early Republic* 8 (1988):223.

[249] James Monroe, "Some Observations on the Constitution," *CAF,* 5:307.

neither tyranny nor anarchy emerged, although at times the nation would flirt with both. Eventually, of course, the nation faced civil war over the most fundamental of liberties: human freedom. This would not have surprised some Antifederalists, who predicted that the Constitution's compromises over slavery would lead to disastrous results.[250] It might be argued that the Civil War resulted from the failure of the Federalists to produce a national government that was strong enough to deal with the nation's greatest problem,[251] or conversely, that the war resulted from the creation of too strong a government. Similarly, of course, we might argue that the failure of the Antifederalists to understand that freedom was indivisible simply set the stage for the horrors of 1861–65. That, however, is the subject of a different paper for a different forum.

[250] On Antifederalist criticism of the compromises over slavery in the Constitution, see Paul Finkelman, "Antifederalists: The Loyal Opposition and the American Constitution," *Cornell Law Review* 70 (1984):182–207; on the evolution of the proslavery constitution, see Finkelman, *Slavery and the Founders*, pp. 1–33.

[251] Some Federalists opposed a bill of rights precisely because it might have undermined slavery. Charles Cotesworth Pinckney told the South Carolina House of Representatives: "Such bills generally begin with declaring that all men are by nature born free. Now, we should make that declaration with a very bad grace, when a large part of our property consists in men who are actually born slaves" (Charles Cotesworth Pinckney, "Speech in South Carolina House of Representatives," Farrand, ed., *Records of the Convention*, 3:256).

SAUL CORNELL

Mere Parchment Barriers?

Antifederalists, the Bill of Rights, and the Question of Rights Consciousness

ONE OF THE most puzzling features of the original debate over the Bill of Rights is the seemingly contradictory position of the Antifederalists. The opponents of the Constitution had attacked the new frame of government for failing to include a bill of rights. Yet when the First Congress addressed the question of alterations to the new Constitution, a number of prominent Antifederalists opposed the amendments under consideration. How can we account for the apparent inconsistency between the Antifederalists' initial enthusiasm for amendments and their opposition to the final form of the Bill of Rights adopted by the First Congress? The most influential historical interpretation of the Antifederalists suggests that their support for the Bill was a cynical political maneuver designed to block adoption of the Constitution and protect a narrow states' rights position.[1] Legal scholars have not con-

[1] For an overview of this literature, see James H. Hutson, "The Birth of the Bill of Rights: The State of Current Scholarship," *Prologue* 20 (1988):150. Leonard W. Levy's views on the origins of the Bill of Rights are developed in *Freedom of Speech and Press in Early American History: Legacy of Suppression* (New York, 1963), *Emergence of a Free Press* (New York, 1985), *Essays on the Making of the Constitution*, 2d ed. (New York, 1987), and *Original Intent and the Framers' Constitution* (New York, 1988). For a more useful framework for understanding the nature of Antifederalist involvement in the origins of the Bill of Rights, see Kenneth R. Bowling, "'A Tub to the

cerned themselves with the political motivations of the Antifederalists and have therefore not considered what appears to
be an inconsistency in the Antifederalist position. For these
scholars, questions about the subjective intent of historical
actors seem insignificant. It is the professed values of the Antifederalists, not their actual beliefs, that concerns lawyers.[2]

The existing historical and legal scholarship on the origins
and meaning of the Bill of Rights has failed to set the debate
over the amendments within the context of the ideological struggles of post-Revolutionary American political life. In
particular the current scholarship fails to explore the nature
of rights consciousness, the diverse ways Americans from
different social groups have conceptualized law and politics
in terms of rights.[3] Focusing on the varieties of rights consciousness within late eighteenth-century American constitutionalism makes it possible to appreciate the full range of
Antifederalist attitudes toward the Bill of Rights.

WHIGS AND ANTIWHIGS

Scholarship on the origins of the Constitution runs the gamut
from Beardian materialism to Derridian deconstructionism.[4]

Whale': The Founding Fathers and the Adoption of the Federal Bill of
Rights," *Journal of the Early Republic* 8 (1988):223–51.

[2] The law review literature on original intent is voluminous. For one effort to chart some of the more notable examples of this genre of legal history, see Richard B. Bernstein, "Charting the Bicentennial," *Columbia Law
Review* 87 (1987):1565–1624, and Jack N. Rakove, ed., *Interpreting the Constitution: The Debate over Original Intent* (Boston, 1990).

[3] See Hendrik Hartog, "The Constitution of Aspiration and 'The Rights
That Belong to Us All,'" *Journal of American History* 74 (1987):1013–34. On
writing constitutional history from the bottom up, see William E. Forbath,
Hendrik Hartog, and Martha Minow, "Legal Histories from Below," *Wiscon-
sin Law Review* 4 (1985).

[4] The classic progressive account is Charles A. Beard, *An Economic Inter-
pretation of the Constitution of the United States* (New York, 1913); for a prob-
lematic poststructural reading of the Constitution, see Michael Warner, *The
Letters of the Republic: Publication and the Public Sphere in Eighteenth-Century
America* (Cambridge, Mass., 1990); for historiographic overviews, see James
H. Hutson, "Country, Court, and Constitution: Anti-Federalism and the

By comparison the literature on the origins of the Bill of Rights seems somewhat bland. Most studies of the origins of the Bill have worked within a narrow range of conventional interpretive strategies.[5] Defenses of the Federalist and Anti-federalist points of view exist, and accounts of the origins of the amendments are also readily available.[6] There are myriad studies of particular provisions of the Bill of Rights, many of which can trace the genesis of individual amendments back to their ancient roots within the English common law.[7] Narrative accounts of the Bill of Rights, like the various studies of their individual provisions, have been cast in the mold of "law office history" and are essentially Whig in character.[8] In his classic study *The Whig Interpretation of History,* Herbert Butterfield noted that Whig history glorifies the principle of progress and presents a story in which history appears to flow inevitably toward the present.[9] For the Bill of Rights, Whiggish accounts have focused on the expanding tradition of liberty in American constitutional life, a tradition, so the argument goes, that

Historians," *William and Mary Quarterly,* 3d ser. 38 (1981):337–68, and Saul A. Cornell, "The Changing Historical Fortunes of the Anti-Federalists," *Northwestern University Law Review* 84 (1989):39–73.

[5] For an overview of this literature, see Hutson, "Birth of the Bill of Rights," p. 150.

[6] For the most recent in a long series of efforts to defend the Federalist position, see Hadley Arkes, "On the Dangers of a Bill of Rights: A Restatement of the Federalist Argument," in Sarah Baumgartner Thurow, ed., *To Secure the Blessings of Liberty: First Principles of the Constitution* (Lanham, Md., 1988), pp. 120–45. For a discussion of modern defenses of the Anti-federalist position, see the essay by David Broyles, "Federalism and Political Life," in Charles R. Kesler, ed., *Saving the Revolution: The Federalist Papers and the American Founding* (New York, 1987), p. 220.

[7] Bernard Schwartz, *The Great Rights of Mankind: A History of the American Bill of Rights* (New York, 1977); Robert Allen Rutland, *The Birth of the Bill of Rights, 1776–1791* (Chapel Hill, 1955).

[8] Alfred H. Kelly, "Clio and the Court: An Illicit Love Affair," in Philip B. Kurland, ed., *Supreme Court Review* (1965): 449–517.

[9] Herbert Butterfield, *The Whig Interpretation of History* (London, 1931); and, more generally, David Hackett Fischer, *Historians' Fallacies: Toward a Logic of Historical Thought* (New York, 1970), p. 139.

was established by the Bill of Rights. Robert Allen Rutland, one of the most distinguished political historians of the constitutional era, closed his account of *The Birth of the Bill of Rights* with this observation: "The great men of the Revolution . . . risked their lives for the principle that individual freedom was the sine qua non of good government." [10] A similar point of view informs the work of Bernard Schwartz, a noted legal scholar, whose narrative account of the origins of the Bill of Rights, *The Great Rights of Mankind,* closes with a paean to the evolving constitutional tradition of individual freedom and liberty. It is interesting that Schwartz chooses to counterpose this ever-expanding sphere of liberty with the views of modern legal theorist John Rawls. For Schwartz, Rawls's contractarian doctrines and distributive theory of social justice mark a departure from mainstream constitutional thought. The dominant theme in American constitutionalism, Schwartz argues, is an inexorable growth of individual rights. As Schwartz observes, Rawls's theory "tends toward a bloc view of life rather than an individual one; it reverses the historic movement toward respect for the individual." [11]

There is a convergence between the interpretive positions of Rutland and Schwartz: each scholar assumes that liberty was the defining feature of American political thought in the era of the Constitution. While it would be hard to deny that the concept of liberty figured prominently in the rhetoric of the American Revolution and the discourse of American constitutionalism in the late eighteenth century, there are serious problems with trying to characterize American political theory in terms of a dominant ideological tradition. Rather than seeking a single voice, it makes far more sense for scholars to acknowledge the plurality of competing discourses available to American citizens in the late eighteenth century.[12] One

[10] Rutland, *Birth of the Bill of Rights,* p. 232.

[11] Schwartz, *Great Rights of Mankind,* p. 230.

[12] Daniel Walker Howe, "European Sources of Political Ideas in Jeffersonian America," *Reviews in American History* 10 (1982):28–45; Isaac Kramnick, "'The Great National Discussion': The Discourse of Politics in 1787," *William and Mary Quarterly,* 3d ser. 45 (1988):3–32.

of the most important countervailing forces arrayed against the libertarian tradition was the constellation of ideas that historians have grouped together under the rubric of civic republicanism.[13] While liberalism stressed the centrality of liberty, civic republicanism stressed the good of the commonweal.[14] In the preface to *The Great Rights of Mankind,* Bernard Schwartz evokes Bernard Bailyn's analysis of the ideological sources of Revolutionary political ideas. While liberty unquestionably played an important role in Bailyn's pioneering study, it is also true that he described a dialectical tension between liberty and authority. Part of the power of Bailyn's analytical framework resided in his effort to balance the libertarian dimensions of American political thought with an opposing civic republican tradition. Together with J. G. A. Pocock and Gordon S. Wood, Bailyn and the other writers associated with the "republican synthesis" have provided a useful corrective to the idea that American political culture in the eighteenth century was dominated by a libertarian ethos.[15] Liberty was only one of several important concepts that played a crucial role in American political thought in this period.[16] Americans in the eighteenth century understood constitutionalism in terms of a dialectic of liberty and power.

[13] Bernard Bailyn, *The Ideological Origins of the American Revolution* (Cambridge, Mass., 1967); J. G. A. Pocock, *The Machiavellian Moment: Florentine Political Thought and the Atlantic Republican Tradition* (Princeton, 1975); Gordon S. Wood, *The Creation of the American Republic, 1776–1787* (Chapel Hill, 1969).

[14] On liberalism, see Joyce Appleby, *Capitalism and a New Social Order: The Republican Vision of the 1790s* (New York, 1984), and John Patrick Diggins, *The Lost Soul of American Politics: Virtue, Self-Interest, and the Foundations of Liberalism* (New York, 1984).

[15] On the notion of a republican synthesis, see Robert E. Shalhope, "Toward a Republican Synthesis: The Emergence of an Understanding of Republicanism in American Historiography," *William and Mary Quarterly,* 3d ser. 29 (1972):49–80; idem, "Republicanism and Early American Historiography," *William and Mary Quarterly,* 3d ser. 39 (1982):334–56.

[16] For a concise discussion of the divergent intellectual traditions shaping American political thought in this period, see Forrest McDonald, *Novus Ordo Seclorum: The Intellectual Origins of the Constitution* (Lawrence, Kans., 1985).

Invoking liberty as the sine qua non of Revolutionary principles also ignores the degree to which liberty was itself an essentially contested concept.[17] While it is probably true that few if any Americans of the Revolutionary generation would have disputed the claim that the Revolution was fought to preserve liberty, it is also true that they disagreed bitterly over what liberty actually meant in both theory and practice. Nor can these disagreements be viewed as narrow instrumental questions about the best way to secure a common libertarian ideal. Within the ranks of American society there were distinctly different views of what sort of social order would best promote liberty. Conflicts over public funding for religion and paper money acts were only two of the most notable instances in which radically different conceptions of liberty were articulated by different groups within Revolutionary America.[18]

Like narrative accounts of the Bill of Rights, most legal scholarship casts constitutional issues in terms of a single uninterrupted and ever-expanding idea of liberty. The character of "law office history" is readily discernible in the vast literature on the history of the free speech clause of the First Amendment. The terms of the modern legal debate over the meaning of the First Amendment were set by Zechariah Chafee, Jr., whose pioneering study of freedom of speech argued that the Bill of Rights challenged the doctrine of seditious libel.[19] Since Chafee wrote his influential study, innumerable attempts have been made to buttress his claim. In his essay "The Checking Value in First Amendment Theory," Vincent Blasi, a distinguished First Amendment scholar, sought to demonstrate that the Framers accorded the press a

<hr>

[17] On the relevance of the notion of "essentially contested concepts," see Terence Ball and J. G. A. Pocock, eds., *Conceptual Change and the Constitution* (Lawrence, Kans., 1988). For one not entirely successful effort to distinguish between diverse libertarian traditions in America, see David Hackett Fischer, *Albion's Seed: Four British Folkways in America* (New York, 1989).

[18] For useful narrative accounts of this period, see Richard B. Morris, *The Forging of the Union, 1781–1789* (New York, 1987), and Edward Countryman, *The American Revolution* (New York, 1985).

[19] Zechariah Chafee, Jr., *Free Speech in the United States* (Cambridge, Mass., 1941).

privileged position in the American constitutional order. To sustain his interpretation, Blasi avoids those glaring instances in which members of the Revolutionary generation trampled on the rights of oppositional political voices. He ignores the suppression of loyalists during the Revolution, preferring to focus on James Madison's response to the Sedition Act. The numerous attempts to justify the act receive scant attention.

While Blasi may well be correct in his analysis of the libertarian dimensions of Madison's opposition to the Sedition Act, he ignores the fact that a number of Madison's former Federalist allies believed that the act was not only perfectly compatible with the First Amendment but an essential safeguard necessary for the preservation of republican government. If anything, the debate over the Sedition Act challenges the idea of a libertarian consensus and instead demonstrates the dissension within the early American constitutional tradition.[20]

The problem of how to account for the Sedition Act and still validate a libertarian interpretation of early American constitutional thought has been taken up more directly by David Anderson in his article "The Origins of the Press Clause."[21] Rather than avoiding the arguments of Madison's opponents, Anderson seeks to drive a wedge between the thinking of the Federalists of 1798 and the Federalists of 1788.[22] To support his thesis, he notes that a number of dramatic events had transformed American politics in the years between 1787 and 1798. The split between Madison and Hamilton on issues like the Bank of the United States fractured the Federalist alliance of 1787–88. The outbreak of the French Revolution further polarized American politics. It would be hard to dispute Anderson's claim about the distance separating 1787–88 and 1798. Still, problems exist with his account, particularly with his reliance on Madison as the true spokesman for Federalist ideals in 1788. Of course, one might

[20] Vincent Blasi, "The Checking Value in First Amendment Theory," *American Bar Foundation Research Journal* 3 (1977):521–649.

[21] David A. Anderson, "The Origins of the Press Clause," *UCLA Law Review* 30 (1983):455–537, esp. p. 521.

[22] Ibid., p. 521.

argue that Madison's role as the chief architect of the Bill of Rights in the First Congress confers special authority on his views. Yet, as Anderson notes, at least ten members of the First Congress who voted for the Bill of Rights also voted in favor of the Sedition Act. Rather than dismissing such evidence, it makes far more sense to acknowledge that an influential core of Federalist jurists and a significant minority of the original supporters of the Bill of Rights did not view the Sedition Act as incompatible with the First Amendment. Anderson, like Blasi, accepts the libertarian reading of the First Amendment. In essence, each scholar opts to play the Madisonian card, using Madison's voice as a proxy for all of the many diverse constituencies who supported the Constitution during ratification and the congressional battle over adoption of the Bill of Rights. The result of such an interpretive strategy is that Anderson and Blasi effectively mute the many discordant voices present during this phase of our constitutional history.

The point of calling attention to the weakness of Whiggish accounts of the Bill of Rights is not to deny that there was a libertarian heritage in eighteenth-century America. Questioning the existence of a uniformly libertarian heritage ought not lead us to the equally dubious idea that the Framers bequeathed us an authoritarian legacy of suppression. Rather, the goal of this critique is to restore some balance to our understanding of the origins of the Bill of Rights. The problem with the libertarian thesis is not that it is untrue but that it is at best a half-truth.

Given the conventions governing modern historical interpretation, it is easy to see why excessively Whiggish scholarship would invariably call forth an aggressively revisionist anti-Whig position.[23] The most notable attempt to mount an anti-Whig counteroffensive is evidenced in the writings of Leonard W. Levy, who argues that there is a noticeable divergence between modern jurisprudence's libertarian impulses and the original understanding of various constitutional pro-

---

[23] On the tropes of historical writing, see Hayden White, *Metahistory: The Historical Imagination of Nineteenth-Century Europe* (Baltimore, 1973).

visions of the Bill of Rights.[24] At one level, Levy's analysis appears to employ a straightforward critique of the anachronistic character of much conventional legal scholarship. Upon closer examination, however, his work displays a less obvious, but no less anachronistic, view of history.[25]

Contrary to scholars like Chafee, Blasi, and Anderson, Levy argues that the existence of a broad consensus on the legality of seditious libel for Americans in the post-Revolutionary period undermines any argument that the Framers articulated a libertarian ethos. There is much in Levy's work to appeal to historians, particularly his broad knowledge of legal sources. Still, the anti-Whig character of Levy's scholarship leads him to seriously overstate his challenge to the libertarian case. Employing the acceptance of the doctrine of seditious libel as a litmus test to evaluate the presence of true libertarian beliefs is simply anachronistic. Although belief in the doctrine of seditious libel is incompatible with modern views of freedom of the press, it need not necessarily have been incompatible with many eighteenth-century conceptions of liberty. Levy's work ignores the important contributions of writers associated with the "republican synthesis." The concept of liberty, for both Federalists and Antifederalists, cannot be easily separated from civic republican ideals. Rather than adopting Levy's view that Federalists and Antifederalists were both insincere, it makes far more sense to acknowledge that each side genu-

[24] On the influence of Leonard Levy in contemporary scholarship, see Hutson, "Birth of the Bill of Rights," p. 150. For Levy's views, see his *Freedom of Speech and Press, Emergence of a Free Press,* and *Original Intent and the Framers' Constitution.*

[25] Levy's interpretation has been subjected to a number of withering attacks: Fischer, *Historians' Fallacies,* pp. 132–33; Robert C. Palmer, "Liberties as Constitutional Provisions, 1776–1791," in William E. Nelson and Robert C. Palmer, *Liberty and Community: Constitution and Rights in the Early American Republic* (New York, 1987), pp. 55–148; David Rabban, "The Ahistorical Historian: Leonard Levy on Freedom of Expression in Early American History," *Stanford Law Review* 37 (1985):795–856; and Richard Buel, Jr., "Freedom of the Press in Revolutionary America: The Evolution of Libertarianism, 1760–1820," in Bernard Bailyn and John Hench, eds., *The Press and the American Revolution* (Boston, 1981), pp. 59–97.

inely sought to protect its own distinctively republican conceptions of liberty. The structure of the various state bills of rights makes this point clear. Unlike freedom of conscience, freedom of the press was not an inalienable right. Liberty of the press was an alienable right, a qualifiable right that had to be balanced against other competing social goods.[26] In most cases, the language of the relevant clauses pertaining to freedom of the press employed the recommendatory "ought" and not the more forceful "shall not" construction that was adopted in the federal Bill of Rights. Leading Antifederalists and Federalists were reluctant to abandon the idea of seditious libel because they accepted the civic republican belief that a licentious press threatened virtue.[27] The press in this particular scheme was designed to serve as a check on government corruption. Seditious libel would in turn provide a check on a licentious press.

To disparage Federalists and Antifederalists because they do no live up to the ACLU's view of the Bill of Rights is essentially ahistorical. Although Levy often chides lawyers for practicing "law office history," his own work hardly seems more contextualist than the work he so often criticizes. The mere fact that so many Americans were quite capable of believing in both seditious libel and a free press demonstrates how different modern notions of liberty are from those espoused by Americans of the Revolutionary era.

The significance of Levy's work extends beyond his involvement in the debate over the meaning of the First Amendment. His work has also played an important role in shaping scholarly discussion of the relationship between Federalists, Antifederalists, and the origins of the Bill of Rights. Essentially, Levy's thesis about the origins of the Bill of Rights contains two interrelated suppositions. First, he argues that Federalists did not seriously believe their own arguments against the ne-

[26] For a useful discussion of freedom of the press in this context, see Palmer, "Liberties as Constitutional Provisions."

[27] Norman L. Rosenberg, *Protecting the Best Men: An Interpretive History of the Law of Libel* (Chapel Hill, 1986).

cessity of a bill of rights. Antifederalists, in his view, were similarly disingenuous in their demands for a bill of rights. In Levy's view, the Antifederalists cleverly manipulated the issue of a bill of rights to further their own narrow states' rights political agenda.

Levy finds it hard to believe "that the Framers of the Constitution actually believed their own arguments to justify the omission of a bill of rights."[28] Part of Levy's misreading of Federalist intentions derives from his failure to grapple with the implications of Gordon Wood's analysis of Federalist views of popular sovereignty. The Federalist claim that bills of rights were unnecessary in the American context was, in Levy's view, "patently absurd . . . and unhistorical." Of course, this was precisely the point made by Wood: Federalist ideas about the locus of sovereignty represented a conscious break with traditional constitutional theory. Federalists deliberately abandoned traditional Whig republican notions in favor of a new theory of constitutionalism. Rather than accept the justifications provided by Federalists, Levy attributes their opposition to a bill of rights to "their single-minded purpose of creating an effective national government," a task that Levy believes had "exhausted their energies and good sense."[29] Even granting that the Philadelphia Convention's failure to include a bill of rights was a function of the delegates' physical exhaustion, this fact would hardly explain the tenacity with which leading Federalists adhered to their position throughout the struggle over ratification. Levy seeks to position himself as a realist who is not taken in by the rhetoric of the ratifiers. The contrast between rhetoric and reality evidenced in Levy's analysis fails to comprehend the process by which even the most exaggerated rhetoric functions in the arena of ideological conflict. Rhetoric reveals deeply felt cultural assumptions and values. The reasoning supplied by the participants themselves does not mask reality—it in part constitutes social reality.

Levy's revisionist account has been even more influential

[28] Levy, *Original Intent and the Framers' Constitution,* p. 156.

[29] Ibid., pp. 156–57.

in shaping contemporary views of the Antifederalists.[30] He argues that the Antifederalists "sought to prevent ratification and exaggerated the bill of rights issue because it was one with which they could enlist public support. Their prime loyalty belonged to states' rights, not civil rights."[31] In effect, Levy dismisses the innumerable Antifederalist politicians and authors who clamored for a bill of rights as shrewd manipulators who showed no genuine concern with individual liberty. To match his view that Federalist opposition to a bill of rights was insincere, Levy adds the equally dubious proposition that the Antifederalists were not really committed to individual rights or liberty.

To buttress his claim that Antifederalists were concerned with states' rights, not civil rights, Levy relies quite heavily on the actions of the two Virginia Antifederalists who served in the First Congress, Richard Henry Lee and William Grayson. For Levy "the private correspondence of Senators Lee and Grayson of Virginia reveals the explanation for the attitude of their party toward a bill of rights."[32] Grayson confided to Patrick Henry that amendments being considered in Congress "shall effect personal liberty alone, leaving the great points of the Judiciary, direct taxation, &c, to stand as they are." Grayson later observed that the proposed amendments "are good for nothing, and I believe, as many others do, that they will do more harm than benefit."[33]

There are several problems with Levy's evidence and argument. To begin with, the claim that the Antifederalists constituted a coherent party with a single intellectual and political agenda seems highly problematic. Like the Whig historians he derides, Levy never articulates a coherent explanation to justify his choice of which Antifederalist voices are to be taken as representative of Antifederalism. He never explains why

[30] James Hutson has described Levy's discussion of the Antifederalists as "the best account in print of their involvement with the bill of rights" (Hutson, "Birth of the Bill of Rights," p. 150).

[31] Levy, *Emergence of a Free Press*, p. 221.

[32] Leonard W. Levy, "Bill of Rights," in his *Essays on the Constitution*, p. 285.

[33] Ibid.

William Grayson's views can be taken as a full and fair representation of Antifederalist ideas in other states. In fact, there
is good reason to wonder if Grayson's views are entirely representative of the full spectrum of Antifederalist attitudes even
within the Old Dominion. After all, it was Grayson's fellow Virginian and Antifederalist George Mason who wrote the Virginia Declaration of Rights. Mason had even gone so far as
to offer his services at the end of the Federal Convention, arguing that a draft of a bill of rights could easily be produced
in a short interval. If any figure within eighteenth-century
America deserves the appellation "libertarian," then surely
the title belongs to Mason.[34] Yet Levy never explains why
Grayson's view of a bill of rights is more representative than
Mason's.

A close examination of Levy's evidence about Grayson's
views also casts doubt on the charge that Antifederalist
thought was hostile to individual liberty. Consider Grayson's
dismissal of the version of the Bill of Rights being debated in
Congress. He explicitly faulted Congress for failing to address
Antifederalist concerns about the "great points of the Judiciary, direct taxation, &c." It is a bit puzzling how Levy could
argue that the issue of taxation and the structure of the judiciary would not impinge upon basic liberties. Both of these
issues were crucial to the constitutional arguments that Revolutionary leaders enunciated in the struggle against Britain. If
there was any liberty interest at stake during the Revolution, it
was the question of taxation and access to an impartial administration of justice. In this sense, Antifederalists continued to
adhere to a view of liberty and rights that was closely akin to
the one patriot leaders espoused in 1776.[35]

[34] For an argument along these lines, see Jack P. Greene, "Character, Per-
sona, and Authority: A Study of Alternative Styles of Political Leadership
in Revolutionary Virginia," in W. Robert Higgins, ed., *The Revolutionary War
in the South: Power, Conflict, and Leadership* (Durham, N.C., 1979), pp. 3–42.

[35] Here the work of legal scholar John Phillip Reid is crucial, especially
his *Constitutional History of the American Revolution: The Authority of Rights*
(Madison, Wis., 1986), and *The Concept of Liberty in the Age of the American
Revolution* (Chicago, 1988). For an analysis stressing the libertarian dimensions of Antifederalism, see Gary J. Schmitt and Robert H. Webking, "Revo-

Ultimately, Levy's distinction between states' rights and individual rights must be faulted for its deeply anachronistic character.[36] Counterposing civil rights and states' rights makes sense if one is interested in constitutional discourse in the post–World War II era.[37] This sort of distinction makes little sense if one is interested in understanding the eighteenth century. Federalists and Antifederalists articulated different views of liberty and envisioned different methods for guarding their particular version of libertarianism. Indeed, even within the ranks of Federalists and Antifederalists there could be significant differences regarding the meaning of liberty and the best way to protect it. By abandoning the homogenized version of the past characteristic of both Whig and anti-Whig studies of this period we can begin to see the complex range of ideas articulated by the participants in this debate.[38]

Part of the problem with Whiggish and anti-Whiggish accounts is that they do not attempt to adequately contextualize concepts like liberty. Liberal and republican ideals were blended together in the thought of Federalists and Antifederalists.[39] Both sides in the ratification controversy sought to preserve liberty and republicanism. Another problem with most traditional scholarly accounts of the origins of the Bill of Rights is their marked elitist bias. Consider Levy's dismissal of Antifederalist appeals to the people as mere rhetorical hy-

lutionaries, Antifederalists, and Federalists: Comments on Gordon Wood's Understanding of the American Founding," *Political Science Reviewer* 9 (1979):195–229.

[36] On the anachronistic character of Levy's scholarship, see Fischer, *Historians' Fallacies*, pp. 133–34, and Rabban, "Ahistorical Historian."

[37] Kermit L. Hall and James W. Ely, Jr., "The South and the American Constitution," in Hall and Ely, eds., *An Uncertain Tradition: Constitutionalism and the History of the South* (Athens, Ga., 1989), pp. 3–16.

[38] Cornell, "Changing Historical Fortunes," pp. 63–65.

[39] Saul Cornell, "Reflections on the Late Remarkable Revolution in Government: Aedanus Burke and Samuel Bryan's History of the Ratification of the Federal Constitution in Pennsylvania," *Pennsylvania Magazine of History and Biography* 112 (1988):103–30; idem, "The Political Thought and Culture of the Anti-Federalists," Ph.D. diss., University of Pennsylvania, 1989.

perbole. "The history of the framing and ratification of the Bill of Rights indicates slight passion on the part of anyone," Levy writes, "except perhaps 'the people,' to enshrine personal liberties in the fundamental law of the land."[40] It was precisely these sorts of fictive appeals that provided the legitimacy for so many ideas and institutions within Anglo-American political culture. This dismissal of the invocation of the people as a mere rhetorical ploy seems misguided. Every appeal to the people did signal a popular mandate. Yet Patrick Henry's claim that he spoke the language of thousands cannot be so easily dismissed. Given that nearly all justifications for originalist jurisprudence derive from the argument that the Constitution was popularly ratified, the intent of the people is a very serious issue worthy of scholarly attention.[41] Levy's variant of constitutional history effectively banishes the people from any active role in shaping their constitutional and legal culture.

Neither Whig nor anti-Whig interpretations have been willing to acknowledge the diversity within the ranks of both the Federalists and the Antifederalists. Both approaches have sought a monolithic original intent for each side in this debate. To escape the tyranny of the Whig-anti-Whig dialectic, we need to recast our understanding of the Federalists and the Antifederalists in different terms. Another conceptual scheme is required if we are to move beyond the limits of traditional constitutional history. Here methodological insights derived from other avenues of historical inquiry can be extremely useful. Traditional legal and constitutional history closely resemble the impressionistic intellectual history of an earlier generation. More recent work in intellectual history has abandoned the idea of a single American mind and has increasingly been concerned with exploring communities of discourse. More and more, intellectual historians have en-

---

[40] Levy, *Emergence of a Free Press*, p. 266.

[41] On this point, see Edmund S. Morgan, *Inventing the People: The Rise of Popular Sovereignty in England and America* (New York, 1988), pp. 209–39. On the importance of a democratic theory to original intent jurisprudence, see Daniel A. Farber, "The Originalism Debate: A Guide for the Perplexed," *Ohio State Law Journal* 49 (1988–89):1085–1106.

deavored to expand the range of ideas, individuals, and groups included in standard accounts of events like the American Revolution. By contrast, scholars working on the Bill of Rights have remained interested in a fairly narrow range of thinkers who espoused "serious" legal and constitutional ideas.[42]

The effort of intellectual historians to study communities of discourse closely resembles the effort of some legal scholars to elucidate the nature of "rights consciousness." Hendrik Hartog, a leading proponent of this approach, advises scholars to eschew the "search for the single meaning of the law." A focus on rights consciousness forces us to address the distinctive social and legal visions of subordinate groups in American society. The study of rights consciousness can disclose a range of voices that have been "banished from the domain of constitutional history" because these voices were not accorded the status of "official interpreters." Finally, the analysis of rights consciousness requires a recognition that the meaning of legal rules and texts for elites "could differ significantly from the meaning constructed by a group of people having different class status, race, or gender."[43] In short, an

[42] Laurance Veysey, "Intellectual History and the New Social History," in John Higham and Paul K. Conkin, eds., *New Directions in American Intellectual History* (Baltimore, 1979); David A. Hollinger, *In the American Province: Studies in the History and Historiography of Ideas* (Bloomington, Ind., 1985); Stanley Fish, *Is There a Text in This Class? The Authority of Interpretive Communities* (Cambridge, Mass., 1980); and Janice Radway, "American Studies, Reader Theory, and the Literary Text: From the Study of Material Objects to the Study of Social Processes," in David E. Nye and Christen Kold Thomsen, eds., *American Studies in Transition: Essays* (Odense, Denmark, 1985). On the need to apply insights from the new social history to the subject matter of constitutional history, see Cornell, "Changing Historical Fortunes," p. 63, and, more generally, his "Moving beyond the Canon of Traditional Constitutional History: Anti-Federalists, the Bill of Rights, and the Promise of Post-Modern Constitutional Historiography," *Law and History Review* 12 (1994):1–28.

[43] Forbath, Hartog, and Minow, "Legal Histories from Below," p. 764. Artisan republicanism is treated by Sean Wilentz in *Chants Democratic: New York City and the Rise of the American Working Class, 1788–1850* (New York, 1984); gendered meanings of republicanism are treated in Linda K.

examination of rights consciousness promises to open up the prospect of writing a constitutional history from the bottom up. Such an account can allow us to see that the thinking of a formally trained jurist like James Wilson existed on a continuum with the legal and constitutional thought of farmers and artisans.[44]

ANTIFEDERALIST RIGHTS CONSCIOUSNESS

Few issues provoked the ire of the opponents of the Constitution more than the omission of a bill of rights. Patrick Dollard, a South Carolina Antifederalist, noted that his constituents "are nearly all, to a man, opposed to this new Constitution, because, they say, they have omitted to insert a bill of rights therein, ascertaining and fundamentally establishing, the unalienable rights of men, without a full, free, and secure enjoyment of which there can be no liberty, and over which it is not necessary that a good government should have the control."[45] The Antifederalist author who assumed the name Brutus reminded New Yorkers that "the Constitution proposed to your acceptance, is designed not for yourselves alone, but for generations yet unborn." It was for precisely this reason that Brutus felt it essential that "the most express and full declarations of rights" should be included in the Constitution.[46] Antifederalists mounted a vigorous campaign to expose the threat to liberty posed by the absence of a bill of rights. The widely reprinted objections of Antifederalist George Mason began by

---

Kerber, *Women of the Republic: Intellect and Ideology in Revolutionary America* (Chapel Hill, 1980).

[44] Within Federalist constitutional thought one could find several distinctive types of rights consciousness. It is, however, beyond the scope of this essay to explore how each of these variants of rights consciousness was articulated within Federalist thought.

[45] Jonathan Elliot, ed., *The Debates in the Several State Conventions, on the Adoption of the Federal Constitution*, 2d ed., 5 vols. (New York, 1888), 4:337.

[46] Herbert J. Storing, ed., *The Complete Anti-Federalist*, 7 vols. (Chicago, 1981), 2:372 (hereafter cited as *CAF*).

noting that "there is no Declaration of Rights."[47] Other Antifederalist authors hammered away at this defect in the structure of the Constitution in similar terms. This theme figured prominently in a number of the most influential Antifederalist publications including the "Letters of Centinel" and the "Letters from the Federal Farmer."[48] Antifederalists invoked four basic arguments to support their claim that a bill of rights was necessary.[49] Among the reasons they most often cited were:

1. The inclusion of certain basic rights like trial by jury in criminal cases, bans on religious tests, prohibitions on ex post facto laws and bills of attainder, and the provision for habeas corpus in the body of the text of the Constitution necessitated the inclusion of other basic rights. Failure to enumerate these rights might be taken to mean that these rights were not reserved to the people and the states.[50]

2. The breadth of the necessary and proper clause provided the new government with extensive undefined powers. To make the government one of delegated authority alone required including some sort of clause restricting that government to those powers *expressly* granted by the text of the Constitution.[51]

3. The extensive powers of taxation, coupled with the fact that the new government was to be the supreme law of the land, could provide the pretext for limiting other basic liberties like speech and religion.[52]

4. The necessity of restating the first principles of the social

---

[47] For useful background information on Mason's published statement of opposition, see Merrill Jensen, John P. Kaminski, and Gaspare J. Saladino, eds., *The Documentary History of the Ratification of the Constitution,* 10 vols. to date (Madison, Wis., 1976-), 13:346–51, 147–58, 332 (hereafter cited as *DHR*).

[48] For information on the publication of these items, see ibid., p. 593; 14:14–18, 531; 15:156.

[49] A list of some of the most important Antifederalist writings that deal with the omission of a bill of rights may be found in *CAF,* 7:12–13.

[50] [Samuel Bryan], "Letters of Centinel" (II), *CAF,* 2:152.

[51] Ibid. (V), pp. 168–69; (VIII), p. 177.

[52] Ibid. (II), pp. 146–47; (IV), p. 161.

contract and instilling republican principles in the body of the people required the inclusion of a formal bill of rights.[53]

The absence of a bill of rights became one of the most powerful weapons in the Antifederalist arsenal. Federalists were well aware of the rhetorical power of their opponents' criticism. In the view of Massachusetts Federalist Henry Knox, one of the greatest sources of Antifederalist support came from "honest men . . . whose minds are apprehensive of danger to their liberties."[54] Although Federalists like Knox might concur with Antifederalists like Dollard about the weight attached to this issue by those who opposed the Constitution, the two parted company when it came to assessing the legitimacy of this complaint. For Knox, the majority of Antifederalist supporters were comparable to "people in the dark" who "possess no principles to ascertain the quality, degree or nearness of the danger."[55]

Most commentators have simply accepted that Antifederalist ideas about the appropriateness of a bill of rights reflected notions that were simply truisms of republican thought. It is necessary to move beyond the catalog of reasons provided by the Antifederalists to justify their argument for amendments and consider the underlying conceptions of rights that animated Antifederalism. By exploring the varieties of Antifederalist rights consciousness it is possible to see why some Antifederalists came to believe that the Bill of Rights finally adopted by the First Congress was actually inimical to liberty. To sort out the contradictory claims that have been made about Antifederalist attitudes toward the Bill of Rights, we must acknowledge that there were at least three distinctive variants of Antifederalist rights consciousness: The protection of rights depended on federalism, textualism, and localism. While in some cases individual Antifederalist spokesmen might combine one or more of these approaches, for purposes of preserving analytical clarity, this essay will treat the differ-

[53] Ibid. (I), pp. 143, 139.

[54] Henry Knox to George Washington, Feb. 14, 1788, Washington Papers, Library of Congress.

[55] Ibid.

ent types of Antifederalist rights consciousness as distinctive. It is also true that these different types of rights consciousness could be articulated in different ways depending on one's social class.[56]

FEDERALISM

The preservation of rights was closely connected to questions of federalism, particularly the way the power relations were structured between the states and the new federal government. This form of structuralist rights consciousness was vitally important to Antifederalism. For most Antifederalists the problem of rights had to be understood within the context of federalism. Montesquieu's theory of the small republic provided the intellectual rationale for many Antifederalists who depended on state governments for their base of political support.[57] In the minds of most Antifederalists, the existing model of federalism, one in which the bulk of authority rested with the states, was the only viable system capable of protecting liberty. For most Antifederalists it was only natural to view the individual states as the most effective instruments for protecting liberty. The states were, in the minds of most Antifederalists, the seats of government least liable to corruption and most responsive to the popular will. Luther Martin reminded readers of his *Genuine Information* that it was "the *State governments* which are to watch over and protect the *rights* of the *individual*." He went on to remark that "a *number* of

[56] A similar typology might be applied to Federalists. Among supporters of the Constitution one could find structuralists who favored shifting power to the national government, antitextualists who placed no great faith in mere parchment barriers, and civic republicans who placed considerable faith in the continuing virtue of a legal elite and the corresponding deference of the citizenry. Within the ranks of Federalist artisans it is possible to discern evidence of a dissenting strain of plebeian-populist rights consciousness that interpreted republicanism in a more radical fashion.

[57] Cecelia M. Kenyon, "Men of Little Faith: The Antifederalists on the Nature of Representative Government," *William and Mary Quarterly*, 3d ser. 12 (1955):3–43; Herbert J. Storing, "What the Anti-Federalists Were *For*," *CAF*, 1:1–76; on the problem of size, see Rosemarie Zagarri, *The Politics of Size: Representation in the United States, 1776–1850* (Ithaca, N.Y., 1987).

strong and *energetic State governments*" were essential "for securing and protecting the rights of individuals."[58] Antifederalists showed little concern with the threat posed by state government because they viewed the states as champions, not opponents of liberty.[59]

The particular solution to the problem of protecting rights envisioned by Antifederalists like Luther Martin, Richard Henry Lee, and William Grayson shared more with the Federalist vision than is readily apparent at first glance. Both displayed a form of rights consciousness that looked to the organization of the federal system to protect liberty. Where Federalists like Madison saw the states as the grave enemy of liberty, Antifederalists saw the individual states as the champions of liberty. It is easier to understand the attitudes of leading Antifederalist spokesmen who dismissed the final form of the Bill of Rights adopted by the First Congress if we acknowledge the assumptions embedded in this type of rights consciousness. Much like those Federalists who dismissed parchment barriers as ineffective safeguards of rights, Antifederalist structuralists believed that only powerful state governments could effectively guard rights. Patrick Henry offered this advice to Virginians: "Tell me not of checks on paper; but tell of checks founded on self love. . . . Fair disinterested patriotism, and professed attachment to rectitude have never been solely trusted to by an enlightened free people."[60] Richard Henry Lee reiterated this skepticism when he wrote that "it must never be forgotten, however, that the liberties of the people are not so safe under the gracious manner of government, as by the limitation of power."[61] Only in a properly balanced federal system in which structural safe-

[58] [Luther Martin], "The Genuine Information Delivered to the Legislature of the State of Maryland Relative to the Proceedings of the General Convention Lately Held at Philadelphia," *CAF,* 2:44, 48.

[59] Palmer, "Liberties as Constitutional Provisions."

[60] "Speeches of Patrick Henry in the Virginia State Ratifying Convention," June 9, 1788, *CAF,* 5:233.

[61] Richard Henry Lee to Patrick Henry, May 28, 1789, William Wirt Henry, *Patrick Henry: Life, Correspondence, and Speeches,* 3 vols. (1891; reprint ed., New York, 1969), 3:388.

guards were in place to protect the power of the states could liberty be maintained. William Grayson's concerns about the judiciary and taxation can only be understood within the context of this ideological concern. From Grayson's perspective, written guarantees of individual liberty were meaningless if the new government contained large unrestricted grants of authority, especially in the area of taxation. Because the only legal recourse to challenge federal authority would be through the federal courts, one can readily understand the fears of individuals like Grayson. Lee voiced similar concerns when he noted that "the idea of subsequent amendments, was little better than putting oneself to death first, in expectation that the doctor, who wished our destruction, would afterwards restore us to life. . . . The great points of free election, jury trial in criminal cases, and the unlimited rights of taxation, and standing armies, remain as they were."[62] Antifederalists like Henry, Grayson, and Lee based their views on what was a republican commonplace, that free republics could not survive over an extended territory. This particular assumption about the nature of republicanism shaped Antifederalist attacks on consolidation. Lee made this clear when he explained his own concerns about the Bill of Rights to Henry.

> The most essential danger from the present system arises, in my opinion, from its tendency to a consolidated government, instead of a union of confederated states. The history of the world and reason concur in proving, that so extensive a territory as the United States comprehend, never was, or can be, governed in freedom under the former idea; under the latter it is abundantly more practicable, because extended representation, knowledge of characters . . . secure the good opinion of rulers. . . . I take this reasoning to be irrefutable, and therefore it becomes the friends of liberty to guard with perfect vigilance every right that belongs to the states, and to protest against every invasion of them.[63]

Thus, a form of structuralist rights consciousness united many Antifederalists who continued to think that the theory

---

[62] Richard Henry Lee to Patrick Henry, Sept. 14, 1789, ibid., pp. 399–400.

[63] Ibid.

of the small republic provided the best way of protecting liberty. The key to implementing this strategy was the insertion of the word *expressly* in what would eventually become the Tenth Amendment and securing other structural changes in the body of the Constitution. Without these changes, a bill of rights was little more than a piece of parchment.

One advantage of the concept of rights consciousness is that it allows scholars to consider the possibility that the same language and set of arguments might be used in distinctively different ways by different social groups. If we look closely at the language of popular constitutional discourse we can discern a number of subtle but important differences in the way rights consciousness was articulated within elite and popular ideology. Abandoning the search for a monolithic and univocal Antifederalist approach to rights can allow us to see how issues like social class informed the debate over the Bill of Rights. For Antifederalists committed to a more radical egalitarian political agenda, federalism could be cast in populist terms. Maintaining the traditional conception of federalism in which the bulk of authority remained in the individual states furthered this populist agenda. In the view of Centinel, Pennsylvanians enjoyed the "peculiar felicity of living under the most perfect system of local government in the world." Centinel feared that the "ambitious . . . have been united in a constant conspiracy to destroy . . . [this] great palladium of equal liberty." While history provided countless examples of republics in which "the few generally prevail over the many . . . in Pennsylvania the reverse has happened; here the *well born* have been baffled in all their efforts to prostrate the altar of liberty."[64] The democratic character of the states made them better guardians of popular liberty.

TEXTUALISM

The Antifederalists' faith in written bills of rights depended on a specific attitude toward constitutional texts. The distinctive character of this approach to constitutionalism can be more easily grasped if it is contrasted with the approach of

[64] "Letters of Centinel" (IX), *CAF,* 2:179–80.

leading Federalists such as Madison. Writing as Publius, Madison commented that "all new laws, though penned with the greatest technical skill, and passed on the fullest and most mature deliberation, are considered as more or less obscure and equivocal, until their meaning be liquidated and ascertained by a series of particular discussions and adjudications."[65] Words were endowed with force by social convention and were therefore subject to different political constructions. For Madison, mere parchment barriers were a feeble means of protecting liberty. Constitutional texts had never been effective when overbearing majorities or corrupt governments threatened liberty. The reverence for the textuality of written bills of rights that James Madison labored to dismiss in *Federalist* No. 37 formed an important part of a type of Antifederalist rights consciousness that is best described as a form of textualism.

Opponents of the Constitution repeatedly charged that the general and imprecise language of the Constitution would allow designing politicians to manipulate and twist the words of the new document. Mercy Otis Warren described this characteristic of Antifederalism in her *History of the Rise, Progress, and Termination of the American Revolution,* noting that the opponents of the Constitution were "solicitous that every thing should be clearly defined; they were jealous of each ambiguity in law or government, or the smallest circumstance that might have a tendency to curtail the republican system, or render ineffectual the sacrifices they have made, for the security of civil and religious liberty. . . . They were of opinion, that every article that admitted of doubtful construction, should be amended. . . . They held up the ideas . . . of pure and genuine republicanism."[66]

This variant of rights consciousness can best be described

---

[65] *Federalist* No. 37, Jacob E. Cooke, ed., *The Federalist* (Middletown, Conn., 1961), pp. 236–37. For a suggestive discussion of Madison's views of the relationship between language and politics see Terence Ball, "A Republic If You Can Keep It," in Ball and Pocock, eds., *Conceptual Change,* pp. 154–60.

[66] Mercy Otis Warren, "History of the Rise, Progress, and Termination of the American Revolution," *CAF,* 6:209.

as a form of textual literalism. Repeatedly, Antifederalists demanded that explicit safeguards for basic rights be included and that vague and extensive grants of authority to the new government be replaced by more concrete and specific language. At the root of this desire was a pronounced antihermeneutic impulse, a fear that ambiguous and vague language would be exploited by those in power to further their own self-aggrandizing schemes.[67] One important source for this antihermeneutic impulse was Protestant theology, with its emphasis on plain style and simple language and hostility to a priestly caste sanctioned to provide authoritative interpretations. It is hardly surprising that the somewhat technical and legalistic character of Federalist arguments failed to quell popular apprehensions. No figure within the established Antifederalist elite proved to be more attuned to the depth of popular concern on this issue than Patrick Henry. In particular, Henry captured the fears of the many evangelical dissenters who were extremely fearful about the failure of the Constitution to include an explicit statement protecting religious freedom. Henry warned the Virginia ratification convention that "there is many a religious man who knows nothing of argumentative reasoning;—there are many of our most worthy citizens, who cannot go through all the labyrinths of syllogistic argumentative deductions."[68] It was precisely because such abstract and legalistic arguments were not likely to convince the people at large that Henry argued that protection of basic rights and liberties "ought not to depend on constructive logical reasoning." Only explicit written guarantees backed up by structural safeguards could meet the objections of Antifederalists like Henry and his supporters. It is easy to see this influence in the writing of the Antifederalist who chose to describe himself as a spokesman for the "Sentiments of Many": "It is known that the bulk of the people do not understand abstruse, or lengthy political disquisitions. The fundamental laws of a nation, might be expressed in a few articles, and those in a few words, yet plain, and pithy,

[67] H. Jefferson Powell, "The Original Understanding of Original Intent," *Harvard Law Review* 98 (1985):885–948.

[68] "Speeches of Henry," June 12, 1788, *CAF*, 5:240.

to which the people would pay a similar deference, as to the decalogue."[69]

In addition to the religious sources for this position, civic republicanism provided an important foundation for this antihermeneutic posture. Written constitutions with explicit bills of rights provided an important safeguard against government officials who would be tempted to exploit the ambiguity of constitutional language to further their own corrupt designs. In the view of one Antifederalist, it was an axiom of politics that "language is so easy of explanation, and so difficult is it by words to convey exact ideas, that the party to be governed cannot be too explicit. The line cannot be drawn with too much precision."[70] The idea that a bill of rights was unnecessary because all rights not delegated by the parties were reserved did little to allay the fears of this particular Antifederalist. For the author who chose the venerable republican pen name of John DeWitt, the history of all republics and the immutable character of human nature seemed more compelling evidence in favor of a bill of rights than did the Federalists' logical syllogisms demonstrating its superfluity. John DeWitt showed himself to be a good student of traditional republican precepts when he advised his readers, "That insatiable thirst for unconditional controul over our fellow-creatures, and the facility of sounds to convey essentially different ideas, produced the first Bill of Rights ever prefixed to a Frame of Government. The people, altho' fully sensible that they reserved every title of power they did not expressly grant away, yet afraid that the words made use of, to express those rights so granted might convey more than they originally intended, they chose at the same moment to express in different language those rights which the agreement did not include, and which they never designed to part with."[71] The textual literalism that informed so much Antifederalist thought led many to claim that Federalists were exploiting the ambiguity of the Constitution to their own advantage. Mere parchment

[69] "Sentiments of Many," *CAF,* 5:275.

[70] "Essays of John DeWitt" (II), *CAF,* 4:21.

[71] Ibid., p. 22.

barriers could in the view of textualists serve as an important check on government corruption and tyranny.

The antihermeneutic impulse gave rise to a pronounced fear about the role of judicial review under the new Constitution. The Antifederalist author who adopted the republican penname of the "Federal Farmer" provided one of the most sustained Antifederalist attacks on the judiciary. The "Federal Farmer" believed that the judiciary contained "a very extensive influence for preserving or destroying liberty, and for changing the nature of the government." In particular he feared that Americans were insufficiently attentive to the dangers posed by the judicial branch. Americans schooled in republican precepts were apt to be "jealous of the legislature, and especially the executive; but not always the judiciary." The "Federal Farmer" concluded that "our inattention to limiting properly the judicial powers" left Americans "more in danger of sowing the seeds of arbitrary government."[72] While he acknowledged that the legislature might overstep its bounds occasionally, he framed his criticism of the legislature in terms that echoed the democratic ethos characteristic of so many Antifederalist writings. "The measures of popular legislatures naturally settle down in time, and gradually approach a mild and just medium," he wrote, "while the rigid system of the law courts naturally become more severe and arbitrary."[73]

Antitextualism could be rendered in a more markedly class-conscious fashion. The textual literalism of middling radicals or plebeian populists reflected the more egalitarian and democratic sentiments of these groups.[74]

---

[72] "Letters from the Federal Farmer" (XV), ibid., 2:315–16. On this aspect of Antifederalist thought see Gary McDowell, "Were the Anti-Federalists Right? Judicial Activism and the Problem of Consolidated Government," *Publius* 12 (Summer 1982): 99–108.

[73] "Letters from the Federal Farmer," *CAF*, 2:316.

[74] Saul Cornell, "Aristocracy Assailed: The Ideology of Backcountry Anti-Federalism," *Journal of American History* 76 (1990):1148–72. On the ideological character of middling Antifederalist radicalism, see Saul Cornell, "Politics of the Middling Sort: The Anti-Federalism of Abraham Yates, Melancton Smith and the New York Anti-Federalists," in Paul Gilje and William Pencak, eds., *New York in the Age of the Constitution, 1775–1800* (Rutherford, N.J., 1992).

One aspect of the "Federal Farmer's" critique that historians have ignored was its class-consciousness. Antifederalist radicals like the "Federal Farmer" fashioned themselves as spokesmen for the interests of the middling sort. For such men, the realities of politics in American society, questions of political sociology, were essential to understanding the true impact of the new Constitution.[75] The question the "Federal Farmer" asked his readers was simple: What impact would the new Constitution have on various groups within American society, particularly the broad range of individuals within the middling ranks of society?

The "Federal Farmer" felt that the structure of the judiciary would favor the rich and diminish the rights of the middling and lower sorts. Judges would be able to exploit the vast jurisdiction accorded federal courts and use their interpretive powers to construe the vague language of the Constitution in such a way that justice would be beyond the reach of humbler citizens. According to the "Federal Farmer," the structure of the new frame of government would not "give a chance of justice to the poor and midling class."[76] Part of the problem derived from the costly character of bringing suits in the new federal court. "We have just reason to suppose, that the costs in the supreme general court will exceed either of our courts; the officers of the general court will be more dignified than those of the states. . . . The trouble and expence of attending them will be greater. From all these considerations, it appears, that the expence attending suits in the supreme court will be so great, as to put it out of the power of the poor and midling class of citizens to contest a suit in it."[77] The "Federal Farmer" sought to expose the baneful consequences that would result from the establishment of a national judiciary. The potentially vast powers of judicial review ceded to the new national judiciary might be used to curb the authority of the various state legislatures. In the view of Antifederalists like the "Federal Farmer," the power of judicial review was yet another example

[75] Cornell, "Politics of the Middling Sort."

[76] "Essays of Brutus" (XIV), *CAF,* 2:434.

[77] Ibid., p. 435.

of Federalist efforts to scale back the democratic achievements of the Revolution.

The antihermeneutic textualism that inspired the Antifederalist hostility to judicial review could be cast in more stridently populist terms. The Antifederalist author who appropriated the name "A True Friend," for example, showed a pronounced hostility to lawyers and judges. "A True Friend" reminded his readers that "the rights of the people should never be left subject to problematical discussion: They should be clear, precise and authenticated." Constitutional interpretation could itself become corrupt and the judicial process degenerate into one of the most dangerous forms of arbitrary government. Aristocratic cabal by members of the judiciary worried many Antifederalists of the middling and lower sort. "A True Friend" warned Antifederalists about this threat to republican government when he remarked that the text of a properly drafted constitution did not "stand in need of the comments or explanations of lawyers or political writers, too apt, we know, to entangle the plainest rights in their net of sophistry."[78] For this Antifederalist, the textualist antihermeneutic impulse was rendered in class-conscious terms.

One often-neglected aspect of Antifederalist political discourse was its plebeian populism. The most radical wing of the Antifederalist coalition displayed a marked hostility to traditional republican ideology's emphasis on the need for a virtuous class of mediating elites like lawyers. In the place of mediating elites, populists championed a more egalitarian legal system in which a learned caste of officially licensed interpreters would not be necessary. No group within society possessed a monopoly on virtue and hence no group was more qualified than any other group to decide matters of law.[79]

---

[78] "A True Friend," Dec. 6, 1787, *DHR*, 14:377.

[79] Cornell, "Aristocracy Assailed." For an interesting discussion of how lawyers used the notions of civic republicanism to solidify their power in eighteenth-century America, see A. G. Roeber, *Faithful Magistrates and Republican Lawyers: Creators of Virginia Legal Culture, 1680–1810* (Chapel Hill, 1981).

LOCALISM

One variant of rights consciousness was distinctly localist in conception and looked to local institutions such as the jury as a means of protecting rights.[80] Arthur Lee, a Virginian, developed a variant of this type of rights consciousness in his Cincinnatus essays. Published in the New York press during the height of the ratification controversy, these essays highlighted the Zenger trial, a rhetorical move intended to appeal to New Yorkers. In his discussion of the freedom of the press, Cincinnatus wrote that "it was the jury only, that saved Zenger. . . . it can only be a jury that will save any future printer from the fangs of power."[81] For Lee, the institution of trial by jury in cases of seditious libel served as a fundamental check on arbitrary government. Like many Antifederalists, he was unwilling to abandon the concept of seditious libel entirely. To do so would have removed an important structural check on the possible licentiousness of the press. Admittedly, Lee's position would not satisfy modern libertarians. Antifederalists like Lee, however, were interested in protecting an eighteenth-century republican conception of liberty, not a modern libertarian ethos. The concept of liberty that Lee sought to protect more closely resembles our modern idea of ordered liberty.[82] Cincinnatus displayed his commitment to republican ideals by placing his faith in the virtue of the people and the institution of trial by jury as a structural safeguard for liberty. The jury was the embodiment of the will of the local community.

In much the same way that Cincinnatus looked to local institutions like juries as the most effective safeguard for the people's rights, plebeians also championed these institutions. What distinguished the plebeian version of rights conscious-

---

[80] Wood, *Creation of the American Republic*, pp. 46–125. On the jury, see Shannon C. Stimson, *The American Revolution in the Law: Anglo-American Jurisprudence before John Marshall* (Princeton, 1990). For a useful overview of the Zenger case and the relationship between libertarian thought and civic republican ideals in America, see Rosenberg, *Protecting the Best Men*.

[81] [Arthur Lee], "Essays by Cincinnatus" (I), *CAF,* 6:9.

[82] On this point see *Palko* v. *Connecticut*, 302 U.S. 319 (1937).

ness from the more elite conception espoused by Antifederalists like Lee was the clear egalitarian and populist tone of the critique they voiced.

Some sense of this popular ideology can be obtained from a parody of Federalist views written by William Petrikin, an Antifederalist from Carlisle, Pennsylvania. Assuming the name Aristocrotis, Petrikin managed to capture the essence of this populist view of rights.

> Another privilege which the people possess at present, and which the new congress will find it their interest to deprive them of is, trial by jury—for of all of the powers which the people have wrested from government, this is the most absurd; it is even a gross violation of common sense. . . . In the first place it is absurd, that twelve ignorant plebians, should be constituted judges of a law, which passed through so many learned hands;— first a learned legislature. . . . Second, learned writers have explained and commented on it—Third, learned lawyers twisted, turned and new modeled it—and lastly, a learned judge. . . . Yet after all these learned discussions, an illiterate jury . . . must determine whether it applies to the fact or not.[83]

Aristocrotis pointed out that empowering juries to determine both the facts and the law in most situations would create a situation where an "insignificant cottager" might successfully challenge a "learned gentlemen." Populists were eager to create the type of social equality that Aristocrotis described. Insuring that juries would have the power to determine both matters of fact and law would, he believed, serve as a counterweight to the power of society's existing elite. Under such a scheme it would be possible for a simple cottager to challenge the authority of a rich merchant. Petrikin, whose own social status corresponded to that of an insignificant cottager, articulated a clear class-conscious critique of the existing legal order. What emerges from Aristocrotis's pen is a populist assault on Federalist legal and constitutional theory. The Constitu-

---

[83] Aristocrotis [William Petrikin], "The Government of Nature Delineated," *CAF,* 3:204.

tion, he argued, favored the class interests of a natural aristocracy.[84]

One point worth stressing about populist localism is that this particular legal and constitutional vision could be distinctly hostile to the rights of minorities. When Federalists in Carlisle, Pennsylvania, sought to celebrate their victory in the state ratification convention with a parade, Antifederalists, a majority in Carlisle, warned them that "their conduct was contrary to the minds of three-fourths of the inhabitants, and must therefore produce bad consequences if they persisted."[85] When Federalists disregarded the Antifederalist warnings, the opponents of the Constitution sought to enforce the will of the community with extralegal crowd action. Interestingly, Antifederalists viewed themselves as "friends of liberty," linking their actions to the traditions of crowd activity associated with the Revolution.[86] From the perspective of modern civil libertarians, the actions of the Carlisle rioters seem anything but liberty-enhancing. Yet from the viewpoint of plebeian populists there was no contradiction. In the minds of these Antifederalists their denial of liberty to their Federalist opponents and their own affirmation of liberty were perfectly reasonable when understood in republican terms. For radical localists, the good of the community and the protection of the commonwealth provided a reasonable justification for the Antifederalist suppression of their opponents.

While the views of populists on the question of liberty may seem incomprehensible to us, the existence of what we might view as a glaring contradiction in the way so-called "friends of liberty" could trample on the liberties of those they disagreed with is itself a sign of how little we really share with many of the men who first proposed the Bill of Rights. It should also provide a warning against simplistic efforts to discern a monolithic original intent attributable to the Founders.

[84] For more on Petrikin and the importance of the Carlisle riot, see Cornell, "Aristocracy Assailed."

[85] "One of the People," *Carlisle Gazette*, Jan. 9, 1788, *DHR*, 2:675.

[86] "The Scourge," *Carlisle Gazette*, Jan. 23, 1788, ibid., p. 685.

While Federalist rights consciousness contained several distinctive approaches to the problem of rights, most leading Federalists agreed that written bills of rights, mere parchment barriers, were relatively ineffectual means for protecting liberty. There was a far greater range of views on the usefulness of written bills of rights within the Antifederalist camp. The concept of rights consciousness provides one way for historians to conceptualize the range of beliefs present among Antifederalists about the usefulness of written bills of rights as safeguards for liberty. The notion of rights consciousness also provides one way of understanding why Antifederalists were not of a single mind on the question of adopting a bill of rights. One of the most important tensions within Antifederalism resulted from the distinctive class consciousness of plebeians and middling sorts.

Antifederalists were united behind the goal of seeking substantial amendments to the Constitution. Yet this broad area of agreement regarding the desirability of a bill of rights masked deeper ideological cleavages. Recognizing that there were several distinctive varieties of Antifederalist rights consciousness makes it possible to see how the Antifederalist coalition would be easily splintered over the Bill of Rights proposed by the First Congress. As was so often the case with Antifederalist ideology, a shared rhetoric and critique effectively disguised deeper divisions within their ranks. The sincerity of the Antifederalist demand for a bill of rights is beyond reproach, as is the dissatisfaction of many within their ranks over the final form of the Bill of Rights. Antifederalist hostility to the final form of the Bill of Rights reflected the distinctive approaches to rights that had initially led many to oppose the Constitution for threatening liberty.

The Bill of Rights failed to meet the demands of those who believed that structural changes were necessary to restore power to the states and localities. The ideal of states' rights and localism championed by these opponents of the Constitution was not a cynical political maneuver, but reflected a particular view of how liberty could be maintained in a republic as large and heterogeneous as America. This vision was not antistatist but anticentralizing. Antifederalists continued to have tremendous faith in state and local governments as the appropriate guardians of popular liberty.

Although the Bill of Rights did include protections for individual liberty and other safeguards to insure the continued viability of republican government, it did not completely allay the concerns of textual literalists who continued to fear the ambiguity and vague language of the Constitution. In particular, amendments had not provided a means to prevent corrupt politicians and judges from exploiting the elastic clauses of the Constitution to further their own agendas.

Antifederalist rights consciousness provided a foundation for the emergence of a distinctive language of dissent that would shape the evolution of constitutional discourse in the new republic. Many of the apprehensions articulated by Antifederalists were later taken up by Democratic-Republicans. The emergence of a theory of states' rights and strict construction owed much to Antifederalist rights consciousness. Jury rights and localism would also continue to play an important part in dissenting constitutional theory. Finally, the tensions and divisions between elite and popular constitutional theory would continue to influence the character of dissent in the early republic. Antifederalist rights consciousness laid the foundation for many of the most important elements of Jeffersonian and Jacksonian constitutional theory. Indeed, the legacy of Antifederalist rights consciousness continues to shape the contours of American constitutional life as later generations have turned their attention to the ideas of the Antifederalists, other Founders of the American constitutional tradition.

WHITMAN H. RIDGWAY

Popular Sentiment and the Bill of Rights Controversy

THE SCHOLARSHIP ON the ratification of the Constitution and the adoption of the Bill of Rights relies heavily on the partisan debate between Federalists and Antifederalists, or upon legal and constitutional traditions, but only infrequently considers the issues from a popular perspective.[1] What has been missing is a broader examination of the popular roots of the debate over a bill of rights. This essay will attempt to understand how various groups reacted to the debate about a bill of rights and how they interacted with the political process.

RIGHTS CONSCIOUSNESS IN THE CONSTITUTIONAL ERA

The people of Prince Frederick's Parish . . . are nearly all, to a man, opposed to this new Constitution, because, they say, they have omitted to insert a bill of rights therein, ascer-

---

[1] These include Robert Allen Rutland, *The Birth of the Bill of Rights, 1776–1791* (1955; reprint ed., London, 1969); Edward Dumbauld, *The Bill of Rights and What It Means Today* (Norman, Okla., 1957); Bernard Schwartz, *The Great Rights of Mankind: A History of the American Bill of Rights,* expanded ed. (Madison, Wis., 1992); and Donald S. Lutz, "Religious Dimensions in the Development of American Constitutionalism," *Emory Law Journal* 39 (1990):21–40. For a convenient collection of historical sources on the Bill of Rights, see Philip B. Kurland and Ralph Lerner, eds., *The Founders' Constitution,* 5 vols. (Chicago, 1987), 5:Amendments I–XII; and for a collection of essays on their derivation, see Jon Kukla, ed., *The Bill of Rights: A Lively Heritage* (Richmond, 1987).

taining and fundamentally establishing, the unalienable
rights of men, without a full, free, and secure enjoyment of
which there can be no liberty, and over which it is not neces-
sary that a good government should have the control.
— Patrick Dollard
South Carolina Ratification Convention

Individual liberty could be traced to several sources in the
constitutional era. Tradition, the sacred rights of Englishmen
that colonists brought with them to America, the colonial
charters and other foundation documents, the declarations of
rights that began most Revolutionary state constitutions or
were adopted by state statute, and the constitutional provisions to maintain English common law in some states after
Independence, all defined the rights of individuals in their
society. As the debate over the ratification of the Constitution
revealed, however, there was ample reason to question the security of these traditional barriers to encroachment by the
new national government because of provisions within the
Constitution itself. The Antifederalists attracted significant
popular support by claiming that the Constitution undermined liberty; the Federalists responded with less effect that
the Constitution posed no danger to individual liberty in the
least.

Americans in the constitutional era looked to their state
constitutions for the delineation of individual rights. Eleven
of the thirteen former colonies wrote new constitutions during the Revolutionary period. Six included specific comprehensive declarations of rights (seven if New Hampshire's 1784
revision of its 1776 constitution is included), four protected
specific rights in the body of their constitutions, and two states
enacted statutory bills of rights before the Constitution was
ever ratified. And those states that adhered to the English
common law had even greater protections because other individual rights, such as habeas corpus, were incorporated into
their legal systems by tradition. Whatever variations existed
in the definition of individual rights among the several states,
few Americans in the constitutional era failed to appreciate
that whatever rights and liberties they enjoyed were part of

their Revolutionary heritage and were linked directly to the integrity of their state constitutions.[2]

Because of the nature of the federal union under the Articles of Confederation, individual liberties guaranteed by state constitutions were never threatened, but the proposed Constitution established an entirely new federal system, one where state guarantees were less secure. The Articles created a true federal republic by granting only limited powers to the central government and explicitly reserving to the states all powers not "expressly delegated." Because the states were supreme, and the federal government possessed only carefully delineated powers, there was no need for a separate national bill of rights. Indeed, the only mention of individual rights in the Articles related to the guarantee that "free citizens" of one state would enjoy equal privileges and immunities to travel and trade as were enjoyed by citizens of other states.

The Constitution, on the other hand, created a federal system where the states lost significant power to the national government, and their ability to protect individual liberties against federal encroachment seemed to be at risk. While the Antifederalist protest against the Constitution highlighted many issues having to do with this erosion of state sovereignty, the threat to individual liberties was often discussed in the context of two specific clauses: the supremacy clause and the necessary and proper clause.

The supremacy clause posed the greatest problem. It directly threatened provisions in existing state constitutions that might be in conflict with the Constitution, federal law, or national treaties. The necessary and proper clause was also suspect because it could be used to expand powers given to

[2] The general comparisons were compiled from the state constitutions listed in Francis Newton Thorpe, comp., *The Federal and State Constitutions* . . . , 7 vols. (Washington, D.C., 1909), and William F. Swindler, ed., *Sources and Documents of the United States Constitutions,* 10 vols. (Dobbs Ferry, N.Y., 1973). The best single source on the importance of the state constitutions is Willi P. Adams, *The First American Constitutions* (Chapel Hill, 1980). The two states that adopted statutory bills of rights were Connecticut and New York. The above observations do not extend to slaves, Indians, aliens, or women, whose rights and liberties were severely limited by law and custom.

Congress beyond the limits of their enumeration. Critics of the Constitution quickly demanded a federal bill of rights to protect individual liberties.

There were two efforts to add a bill of rights to the Constitution before it was sent to the people for ratification. In the waning days of the Philadelphia Convention, George Mason unsuccessfully proposed consideration of a bill of rights.[3] When the Constitution was sent to the Confederation Congress, Richard Henry Lee tried to attach a fully framed bill of rights to the Constitution before it was sent to the people for ratification. This effort also failed, and he complained that "the rights of conscience, the freedom of the press, and the trial by jury are at mercy."[4]

Federalists argued that this concern about individual liberty fundamentally misconstrued governmental powers under the Constitution. James Wilson, an early and widely quoted Federalist spokesman, asserted that the Constitution gave Congress only specifically enumerated powers and queried Antifederalists in the Pennsylvania ratification convention, "What part of this system puts it in the power of

---

[3] Max Farrand, ed., *The Records of the Federal Convention of 1787*, rev. ed., 4 vols. (New Haven, 1966), 2:587–88; "George Mason's Objections to the Constitution of Government Formed by the Convention" began with the lament "There is no Declaration of Rights" and, after dissecting the structural failures of the Constitution, continued, "There is no Declaration of any kind for preserving the Liberty of the Press, the Tryal by jury in civil Causes; nor against the Danger of standing Armys in time of Peace" (Merrill Jensen, John P. Kaminski, and Gaspare J. Saladino, eds., *The Documentary History of the Ratification of the Constitution*, 10 vols. to date [Madison, Wis., 1976-], 8:43–46) (hereafter cited as *DHR*).

[4] Richard Henry Lee to Gov. Edmund Randolph, Oct. 16, 1787, *DHR*, 14:368, 370–72. In this letter Lee also included his proposed amendments, which were patterned after the Virginia Declaration of Rights (1776), written by George Mason. This protest was picked up by popular writers in the press, such as Benjamin Workman, a recent Irish immigrant writing as Philadelphiensis, who insisted that the Constitution "does not protect the people in those liberties and privileges that all freemen should hold sacred. The *liberty of conscience*, the *liberty of the press*, the *liberty of trial by jury*, &c are all unprotected" (Philadelphiensis [III], *Freeman's Journal* (Philadelphia), Dec. 5, 1787, ibid., 14:351.

Congress to attack those rights? When there is no power to attack, it is idle to prepare the means of defense."[5]

Antifederalist writers asserted that Wilson's arguments were inconsistent with the Constitution itself. Not only did a literal reading of the necessary and proper clause expand the enumerated powers, but other parts of the Constitution assumed powers not enumerated. Arthur Lee pointed out that the Constitution included a provision against religious tests, and concluded that "this exception implies, and necessarily implies, that in all other cases whatever liberty of conscience may be regulated."[6] If, as Wilson argued, Congress only possessed express powers, what was the justification for Article I, Section 9, which limited those powers? What gave Congress authority to restrict habeas corpus, or ex post facto laws? As John Smilie commented in the Pennsylvania ratification convention: "Does it not rather appear from the reservation of these two articles that everything else, which is not specified, is included in the powers delegated to the government? This . . . must prove the necessity of a full and explicit declaration of rights."[7] Even advocates of a stronger national government,

---

[5] James Wilson defended the Constitution in his "Speech at a Public Meeting in Philadelphia," Oct. 6, 1787, ibid., 13:339–44; for his comment at the Pennsylvania ratification convention (Dec. 4, 1787), see ibid., 2:471. Another Federalist writer, Tench Coxe, writing as "A Freeman," made much the same point: "Every regulation relating to religion, or the property of religious bodies, must be made by the state governments, since no power affecting those points are contained in the constitution" ([II], *Pennsylvania Gazette* [Philadelphia], Jan. 30, 1788, ibid., 15:508). See also Cassius (II), *Virginia Independent Chronicle* (Richmond), Apr. 9, 1788, ibid., 9:714–15, and the comments of Randolph at the Virginia ratification convention (ibid., 9:1085, 10:1350–51).

[6] Cincinnatus [Arthur Lee] (III), to James Wilson, *New York Journal*, Nov. 15, 1787, ibid., 14:125. For a comprehensive elaboration of this theme, see also "Letters from the Federal Farmer" (XVI), Herbert J. Storing, ed., *The Complete Anti-Federalist*, 7 vols. (Chicago, 1981), 2:323–30 (hereafter cited as *CAF*).

[7] Nov. 28, 1787, *DHR*, 2:392. Antifederalist Robert Whitehill reinforced this two days later: "We have called upon them [the Federalists], in vain, to reconcile this reservation [habeas corpus and the right to a jury trial in criminal cases] with the tenor of their favorite proposition. For, if there was

such as Thomas Jefferson and John Adams, felt that Wilson was being disingenuous and privately argued that a bill of rights was appropriate.[8]

The question of whether the adoption of a bill of rights was necessary to preserve American liberties remained before the public through the meeting of the First Congress in the late spring of 1789.

THE RELIGIOUS ROOTS OF THE DEBATE FOR A BILL OF RIGHTS

If the rights of conscience, for instance, are not sacredly reserved to the people, what security will there be, in case the government should have in their heads a predilection for any one *sect in religion? What will hinder the civil power from erecting a national system of religion?*

—"Z"

Boston Independent Chronicle

The ratification debate revealed a widespread concern that the proposed Constitution might be used to establish a national religion and that it might impair the free exercise of religion guaranteed by several state constitutions, a concern reflected by amendments proposed by state ratification conventions.[9] While Antifederalists quickly capitalized on the

---

danger in the attempt to enumerate the liberties of the people, lest it should prove imperfect and defective, how happens it, that in the instances I have mentioned, that the danger has been incurred? Have the people no other rights worth their attention, or is it to be inferred . . . that every other right is abandoned?" (ibid., p. 427). See also Patrick Henry in the Virginia ratification convention (ibid., 10:1212–14).

[8] Thomas Jefferson observed that the people were entitled to a bill of rights "against every government on earth" (Jefferson to James Madison, Dec. 20, 1787, Julian P. Boyd et al., eds., *The Papers of Thomas Jefferson*, 28 vols. to date [Princeton, 1950-], 12:440). John Adams commented: A "Declaration of Rights I wish to see with all my Heart. . . . The Press, Conscience & Juries I wish better Secured" (Adams to Cotton Tufts, Feb. 12, 1788, *DHR*, 14:463 n. 4).

[9] Of the five ratifying conventions that proposed amendments, three specifically called for the protection of the rights of conscience. The widely

popular apprehension, it is not always clear how specific religious groups reacted to this issue. To understand whether religious groups were genuinely concerned about the Constitution, or whether this was a phantom issue exaggerated by Antifederalists, it is instructive to examine the opinion of Baptists in Virginia and Massachusetts and Quakers in Pennsylvania.[10]

The formation of a more powerful national government generated a variety of reactions among religious groups. Federalists publicly and privately noted that the New England clergy favored the Constitution, while their counterparts in the southern states opposed it.[11] Friends of religion and an orderly society, as they characterized themselves, welcomed the salutary influence of a strong central government on the disorganizing social influences evident in the mid-1780s.

The Baptists, however, appeared to be divided. The Philadelphia Association of Baptist Churches meeting in October 1787 advocated the ratification of the Constitution and sent a circular letter endorsing it to other Baptist churches. Prominent Baptist leaders, such as James Manning and Isaac

---

published minority dissents of the Pennsylvania and Maryland ratifying conventions also addressed this issue. The amendments proposed by the various state ratifying conventions are conveniently listed in Helen E. Veit, Kenneth R. Bowling, and Charlene Bangs Bickford, eds., *Creating the Bill of Rights: The Documentary Record from the First Federal Congress* (Baltimore, 1991), pp. 14–28. For "The Address and Reasons of Dissent of the Minority of the Convention of the State of Pennsylvania to Their Constituents," *Pennsylvania Packet* (Philadelphia), Dec. 18, 1787, see *DHR*, 2:617–39, and for the "Address of a Minority of the Maryland Ratifying Convention," see *CAF*, 5:97.

[10] Stephen A. Marini wrote an insightful essay on the religious background of the delegates to the state ratification conventions in which he argues that evangelicals strongly associated with the Antifederalists and liberal faiths with the Federalists. See "Religion, Politics, and Ratification," in Ronald Hoffman and Peter J. Albert, eds., *Religion in a Revolutionary Age* (Charlottesville, Va., 1994), pp. 184–217.

[11] See "A Meeting of New Haven County Congregational Clergy," Sept. 25, 1787, David Humphreys to George Washington, Sept. 28, 1787, Madison to Randolph, Oct. 21, 1787, and Benjamin Lincoln to Washington, Feb. 9, 1788, *DHR*, 3:351, 354, 13:430, 16:464.

Backus, were identified with ratification. Simultaneously, Baptists in rural areas of Massachusetts and Virginia expressed fear that the new Constitution jeopardized the rights of conscience and religious freedom. Rural Baptists continued to express concern through the spring of 1789 when the new government was formed.

The Baptist response to the Constitution was complex and sometimes inconsistent. Cosmopolitan Baptist leaders, such as James Manning, who was president of Rhode Island College and a former Rhode Island congressman (1785–86), or Samuel Stillman, minister of Boston's First Baptist Church and a Federalist delegate to the Massachusetts ratification convention, enthusiastically endorsed ratification because it promised to restore order and prosperity to a badly divided nation, yet did so without any expressed concern that the rights of conscience would be endangered. Other Baptist leaders, such as Virginia's John Leland and Massachusetts' Isaac Backus, who was also a delegate to the Massachusetts ratifying convention, initially opposed ratification because they feared for religious liberty, although each ultimately came to support ratification with amendments.

Lesser Baptist leaders and the faithful often looked upon the Constitution with suspicion and dread. To them it threatened freedom of conscience, and it promised the end to republican government and the beginning of a new aristocracy. They were responsive to those who demanded amendments, either through a second constitutional convention or through the amendment process of Article 5.

The cosmopolitan Baptist leaders acted quickly to encourage acceptance of the Constitution by the faithful. Soon after it was sent to the states for ratification, the Philadelphia Association of Baptist Churches held a meeting in New York City, with James Manning as moderator. In a highly unusual foray into secular politics, the meeting advocated ratification of the Constitution to rescue the country from anarchy and ruin and hinted that any deficiencies could be corrected by future amendment. Manning was also instrumental in distributing a report of this meeting to Baptists in New England, hoping thereby to assuage their reservations about the Constitution.[12] The appearance of the report in public prints generated unfavorable responses from Baptists who felt that the church should not be engaged in secular affairs.[13]

Manning's concern about Baptist reaction to the Constitution throughout New England was well founded. New England Baptists were unsettled in the 1780s. Not only had they participated in the endemic debtor-creditor crisis that affected the region, some had joined Shays's Rebellion, and many had been caught up in the religious enthusiasm that swept the rural areas after the Revolution. Notwithstanding the fact that increasing numbers of people called themselves Baptists, which was reflected in the growth of churches and associations, church organization was divided and disorganized and would remain so until the early decades of the nineteenth century. This was due in part to doctrinal controversies and the jarring influences of unprecedented and uncontrolled growth.[14]

[12] See *Minutes of the Philadelphia Baptist Association, Held in New York, Oct. 1787* (New York, 1787). The circular letter advocated the Constitution, "which promises, on its adoption, to rescue our dear country from that national dishonour, injustice, anarchy, confusion, and bloodshed, which have already resulted from the weakness and inefficiency of the present form; and which we have the greatest reason to fear is but the beginning of sorrows, unless the people lay hold of this favorable opportunity offered to establish an efficient government, which, we hope, may, under God, secure our invaluable rights, both civil and religious; which it will be in the power of the great body of the people, if thereafter found necessary, to controul and amend" (*DHR*, 13:374–75). For the effect of this letter, see "Extract of a Letter from Rhode-Island," *Pennsylvania Gazette* (Philadelphia), Nov. 21, 1787, ibid., 14:164. James Manning sent copies of this letter to New England Baptists with instructions that it be read in an effort to show unanimity (see William G. McLoughlin, ed., *The Diary of Isaac Backus*, 3 vols. [Providence, 1979], 3:1208).

[13] See "A Baptist," *Freeman's Journal* (Philadelphia), Jan. 23, 1788; "A Real Baptist" attacked the above as a fraud and argued that Baptists favored the Constitution (ibid., Jan. 30, 1788). There is some evidence that Virginia Presbyterians were also concerned (Richard Terrill to Garret Minor, Dec. 6, 1787, *DHR*, 8:208).

[14] My interpretation of religion in New England relies heavily on Stephen A. Marini, *Radical Sects of Revolutionary New England* (Cambridge, Mass., 1982), and his excellent article "The Religious World of Daniel Shays," in

In Massachusetts specifically, the situation was even more complex because of a long-term controversy between Baptists and Congregationalists over state support for religion. Isaac Backus, who had led the dissenter's protest against their treatment by the established church and government since before the Revolution, petitioned the Continental Congress to intercede on their behalf because of the continued oppression Baptists faced in Massachusetts during the Revolution.[15] He was an outspoken critic of Article 3 of the Massachusetts constitution of 1780 authorizing public support for religious teachers. Although Backus did not favor a complete wall of separation between church and state, and was primarily unhappy with the Congregationalist monopoly of state religious support under Article 3, he was initially concerned that the proposed federal Constitution created a threat to the rights of conscience. He was identified as an Antifederalist when he was elected to the Massachusetts ratifying convention. Although his commitment to the broader tenets of Antifederalism is unclear, he wrote that he decided to attend the convention "as religious liberty is concerned in the affair."[16]

Robert A. Gross, ed., *In Debt to Shays: The Bicentennial of an Agrarian Rebellion* (Charlottesville, Va., 1993), pp. 239–77. For a different view of this period, which asserts that religion was less important, see John L. Brooke, "A Deacon's Orthodoxy: Religion, Class, and the Moral Economy of Shays's Rebellion," in Gross, ed., *In Debt to Shays*, pp. 205–38. Baptists, who were organized into eight associations before 1776, expanded through 1790 into thirty-five associations, incorporating some 668 churches with an approximate membership of 64,975. See John Asplund, *The Annual Register of the Baptist Denomination* (Richmond, 1792).

[15] See McLoughlin, ed., *Diary of Backus*, 2:915–16. For the response of the Continental Congress (President John Hancock), see Isaac Backus, *Truth Is Great, and Will Prevail* (Boston, 1781), Appendix. It is interesting to note that they worked with prominent Philadelphia Quakers, Israel and James Pemberton, to organize this effort.

[16] Isaac Backus, *An Appeal to the People of the Massachusetts State, against Arbitrary Power . . .* (Boston, 1780), pp. 1–8; David Weston, *A History of New England*, 2d ed., 2 vols. (Newton, Mass., 1871), 2:335. See also William G. McLoughlin, "Isaac Backus and the Separation of Church and State in America," *American Historical Review* 73 (1968):1392–1413. Baptist dissatisfaction with established churches in Connecticut is evidenced in "Baptistos

The internal tensions among the Massachusetts Baptists were evident when the ratification convention met in Boston. James Manning, who "considered Massachusetts as the hinge upon which the whole must turn," attended so that he could wield his influence among the Baptists in favor of ratification.[17] Samuel Stillman was a member of that city's delegation to the convention. A Federalist privately described his election: "He is a high Federal Man & charmed with the proposed plan.—he being at the head of the *Baptists* in this State and of great influence among them. it is thought policy to choose him one of the Delegates by which means we shall gain the whole *Sect* in favor of it."[18] Such expectations, however, were only partially realized. Isaac Backus was convinced by the convention debates that the safety of the nation required ratification and that the rights of conscience could be protected by subsequent amendment. Backus reported, with unintended irony, that he and Stillman subsequently voted for ratification along with twelve Congregational ministers, while two-thirds of the twenty Baptists who attended the convention voted against the Constitution.[19]

Virginia Baptists were also sensitive to any threat to the

Address to Baptists, Separates, Quakers, Rogerites, and All Other Denominations of Christians in Connecticut" and Catholicus, *Connecticut Courant* (Hartford), Apr. 20 and June 22, 1789.

[17] Manning to Hezekiah Smith, Feb. 11, 1788, James Manning Papers, John Hay Library, Brown University Archives, Providence; see also William G. Goddard, "Memoir of the Rev. James Manning, D.D., First President of Brown University," *American Quarterly* 11 (1838–39):349–50.

[18] Henry Jackson to Henry Knox, Nov. 11, 1787, Henry Knox Papers, Massachusetts Historical Society, Boston.

[19] McLoughlin, ed., *Diary of Backus*, 3:1212, 1215–21n. McLoughlin described William Hooper, a Baptist leader who attended the New Hampshire ratification convention, with the words "like most rural Baptists he opposed ratification" (ibid., 2:967). He hypothesized that Baptists did not make an issue of the freedom of conscience at the convention because they believed that the federal government did not have power over it and the states would continue their dominion. This may have been true for Backus, but it does not explain why rural Baptists continued to oppose the Constitution (William G. McLoughlin, *New England Dissent*, 2 vols. [Cambridge, Mass., 1971], 2:780–83).

rights of religious conscience in the 1780s. During the colonial period they had suffered at the hands of the Anglican establishment and were disappointed with the reality of religious toleration under the Virginia constitution of 1776. The issue came to a head in the mid-1780s when Anglicans, under the leadership of Patrick Henry, attempted to enact a state tax to support religious instruction. Virginia Baptists, who, along with Presbyterians, rejected all state involvement with religion, mounted a petition campaign that added momentum to James Madison's effort to pass the Virginia Statute for Religious Freedom in 1786.[20] Even the passage of that bill did not guarantee the separation of church and state in Virginia, although it did guarantee liberty of conscience. Baptists still had to deal with established religions in other southern states as well, notably South Carolina, and efforts in 1783 by Maryland Anglicans to implement state support may have reinforced their sensitivity to the issue.[21]

From its initial appearance through the meeting of the First Congress, Virginia Baptists questioned the wisdom of adopting the Constitution without amendments. A general convention of Baptists met at Goochland in March 1788 and discussed "whether the new Federal Constitution . . . made sufficient provision for the secure enjoyment of religious liberty; . . . it was agreed unanimously that . . . it did not."[22]

---

[20] For an excellent collection of essays on this issue, see Merrill D. Peterson and Robert C. Vaughan, eds., *The Virginia Statute for Religious Freedom: Its Evolution and Consequences in American History* (Cambridge, 1988), especially Rhys Isaac, "'The Rage of Malice of the Old Serpent Devil': The Dissenters and the Making and Remaking of the Virginia Statute of Religious Freedom," pp. 139–70.

[21] Under Article XXXIII of the Maryland Declaration of Rights (1776), the legislature "may, in their discretion" lay a tax for the support of religion. The Rev. William Smith and Samuel Chase attempted to implement this section, and there was a firestorm of opposition. For a short discussion of this event, see Whitman H. Ridgway, *Community Leadership in Maryland, 1790–1840* (Chapel Hill, 1979), pp. 9–10 (esp. notes 20–22).

[22] See *DHR*, 8:426 n. 2. Considering the active involvement of Baptists and other dissenting groups, it is surprising that Methodists were silent on the issue of ratification. They are not mentioned in the political correspondence or in the press, and they made no comment on political matters in

Whatever affinity they may have had for Madison because of his efforts on behalf of religious liberty in the mid-1780s was undermined by his public stand against amendments during the ratification debate. Ironically, it was Patrick Henry who voiced the greatest concern for liberty of conscience.

There were persistent reports, especially at election time, of Baptists who opposed the new Constitution because of its threat to their religious independence.[23] Much has been made of Madison's apparent success in winning over Baptist leaders, such as John Leland, and inducing them to work for the adoption of the Constitution thereafter.[24] Even if Madison had converted Pastor Leland, other Baptists continued to denounce Madison for favoring the adoption of the Constitution without amendments, which still dogged him when he ran for Congress in January 1789.[25] Their concern was best expressed by an address of Virginia Baptists to President Washington: "When the Constitution first made its appearance in

---

their meeting reports. See *Minutes of the Methodist Conferences, Annually Held in America, from 1773 to 1794, Inclusive* (Philadelphia, 1795).

[23] See James Gordon, Jr., to Madison, Feb. 17, 1788, and James Madison, Sr., to James Madison, Jan. 30, 1788, William T. Hutchinson et al., eds., *The Papers of James Madison,* 22 vols. to date (Chicago and Charlottesville, Va., 1962–), 10:515–16, 446–47; Joseph Spencer to James Madison, Feb. 28, 1788, and Randolph to James Madison, Feb. 29, 1788, *DHR,* 8:424–27, 436–37.

[24] Pastor John Leland was an influential Baptist preacher in Virginia. His influence is suggested in correspondence (see George Nicholas to James Madison, Jan. 2, 1789, Hutchinson et al., eds., *Papers of Madison,* 11:406–9), in documents (*DHR,* 8:472 n. 4), and in a classic article by Lyman H. Butterfield ("Elder John Leland, Jeffersonian Itinerant," *Proceedings of the American Antiquarian Society* 62 [1952]:155–242). Leland initially opposed the Constitution on the basis that "Religious Liberty" was not sufficiently secured. See Spencer to James Madison, Feb. 28, 1788, *DHR,* 8:425–26. For Leland's regard for James Madison, see Leland to Madison, ca. Feb. 15, 1789, Hutchinson et al., eds., *Papers of Madison,* 11:442–43.

[25] For this issue, see Benjamin Johnson to James Madison, Jan. 19, 1789, Hutchinson et al., eds., *Papers of Madison,* 11:423–24. For his efforts to defuse this Baptist concern in his congressional campaign, see James Madison to George Eve, Jan. 2, 1789, to Thomas Mann Randolph, Jan. 13, 1789, and "To a Resident of Spotsylvania County," Jan. 27, 1789, ibid., pp. 404–5, 415–17, 428–29.

Virginia, we, as a society, had unusual strugglings of mind, fearing that the liberty of conscience, dearer to us than property or life, was not sufficiently secured."[26]

In sum, notwithstanding the fact that several prominent Baptist leaders supported ratification, rural Baptists in Virginia and Massachusetts continued to be troubled by the insecurity of the rights of conscience from the appearance of the Constitution through the formation of the new federal government in the spring of 1789.

Quakers were another religious group that drew political attention during the ratification debate, especially in Pennsylvania after the publication of the Constitution in September 1787. Early reports stated that Quakers had joined Republicans and Constitutionalists to petition the legislature to call a convention, although some questioned if they really understood the issues.[27] Federalist Benjamin Rush wrote confidently after Pennsylvania ratified the Constitution, "I am very happy in being able to inform you that they are all (with an exception of three or four persons only) highly foederal.— There was a respectable representation of that Society in our Convention, all of whom voted in favor of the New Constitution."[28]

Antifederalists challenged the impression of Quaker unanimity and argued that there was good reason for the Society of Friends to oppose the Constitution.[29] Samuel Bryan, writ-

[26]"Address of the Committee of the United Baptist Churches of Virginia . . . ," in L. F. Greene, ed., The Writings of the Late Elder John Leland . . . (New York, 1845), p. 53.

[27]For reports of Quakers signing petitions, see the Pennsylvania Gazette (Philadelphia), Sept. 26, 1787, cited in DHR, 2:137–38, and F. Murray to John Nicholson, Nov. 1, 1787, ibid., pp. 207–8. Some questioned their understanding. See David Redich to William Irvine, Sept. 24, 1787, ibid., p. 135.

[28]Benjamin Rush to Jeremy Belknap, Feb. 28, 1788, ibid., 16:250.

[29]"A New-Yorker" observed: "The people called Quakers, are generally opposed to this system;—that is, the men of any weight among them;—to be sure, it strikes at the very foundation of their society, above all others" (Independent Gazetteer [Philadelphia], Dec. 31, 1787, ibid., 2:microform supplement, document number 298); see also an unsigned comment in the same paper, Jan. 11, 1788 (ibid., doc. no. 324).

ing as Centinel, asserted that the "sacred rights of conscience" guaranteed by the Pennsylvania constitution would be jeopardized by the ratification of the proposed federal Constitution.[30] Antifederalist leaders from western Pennsylvania such as William Findley and Robert Whitehill argued that a federal military would compel conscientious objectors to bear arms without regard for their religious convictions.[31] But the strongest exhortation concerned the Constitution's slavery provisions. According to William Findley, "The importation of slaves is not to be prohibited until the year 1808, and SLAVERY will probably resume its empire in Pennsylvania."[32] Similar appeals would be made in Virginia.[33]

Notwithstanding such Antifederalist entreaties, Pennsylvania Quakers probably supported the adoption of the Constitution more than they opposed it. They were responsive to the promise of greater economic stability under the Constitution and endorsed federal restraint over state governments through Article I, Section 10. Federalists questioned the sincerity of Antifederalists by pointing out that these were the same politicians who voted for the "Test Act," which had rendered Quakers second-class citizens after the Revolution.[34]

[30] Centinel (III), *Independent Gazetteer* (Philadelphia), Nov. 8, 1787, ibid., 14:61. Samuel Bryan, writing as Centinel Revived (XXXV), made similar appeals to Quakers to oppose efforts to revise the state constitution (*Independent Gazetteer* [Philadelphia], Oct. 12, 1789).

[31] William Findley wrote "An Officer in the Late Continental Army," *Independent Gazetteer* (Philadelphia), Nov. 6, 1787, *DHR*, 2:212. Robert Whitehill proposed in the Pennsylvania ratifying convention that the militia would be formed according to the rules of the state to protect conscientious objectors, Dec. 12, 1787 (ibid., p. 598). This position was continued in the "Address and Reasons of Dissent" (ibid., p. 624). See also Philadelphiensis (II), *Freeman's Journal* (Philadelphia), Nov. 28, 1787, ibid., 14:252.

[32] Findley, "Officer of the Late Continental Army," ibid., 2:212.

[33] See "A Virginian," *Virginia Independent Chronicle* (Richmond), Feb. 13, 1788, *DHR*, 8:367–68. For an answer to this item, see "One of the People Called Quakers in the State of Virginia," *Virginia Independent Chronicle* (Richmond), Mar. 12, 1788, ibid., pp. 482–83.

[34] Pelatiah Webster, writing as "A Citizen of Philadelphia," pointed out that six members of the minority in the ratification convention were the

Benjamin Rush even argued that the Constitution's slavery provisions were acceptable since it would "put it in the power of Congress twenty years hence to restrain it altogether."[35] Baptists, like Quakers, questioned the Constitution's endorsement of slavery, but their primary concern was its threat to religious liberty.[36]

Although Quakers may have favored the ratification of the Constitution over its rejection, Quaker leaders recognized the importance of possible amendments and quick political action. While historians argue that Quakers did not take a more active stand on the Constitution because they eschewed politics on principle, they did not show such restraint on the state level.[37] Between October 1787 and October 1788 five states either passed laws prohibiting the slave trade or strengthening existing laws, and Quakers petitioned the Rhode Island legislature protesting its legal tender law.[38] Quakers in Massa-

---

same politicians who voted for the "Test Act" and observed, "Their conduct contradicts all their speeches and publications" (*Pennsylvania Gazette* [Philadelphia], Jan. 23, 1788, ibid., 2:658). Portius made the same point in his answer to Centinel (III), *Independent Gazetteer* (Philadelphia), Nov. 12, 1787 (ibid., 2:microform supp., doc. no. 220). See also "Undeniable Facts," *Independent Gazetteer* (Philadelphia), Jan. 15, 1788 (ibid., doc. no. 333), and "A True Whig," *Pennsylvania Mercury* (Philadelphia), Jan. 15, 1788 (ibid., doc. no. 334), which answer the assertions by "A New-Yorker" cited above.

[35] Rush to Belknap, Feb. 28, 1787, ibid., doc. no. 461.

[36] As early as September 1787 the Warren Association expressed its concern with the renewal of the slave trade by several states. The Chelsford meeting disbanded before the publication of the Constitution and the next meeting made no reference to the Constitution (Warren Association, *Minutes of the Yearly Meeting* [Boston, 1787], pp. 5–6).

[37] The editors of the *Documentary History of Ratification* observed in an Appendix devoted to the Quakers: "Despite these provisions [in the Constitution], Quakers generally favored adoption of the Constitution. But Quakers were not active in the politics of ratification, partly because of the slavery provision, but more importantly because of their general policy not to engage in politics" (*DHR*, 14:504).

[38] The states were Rhode Island, New York, Massachusetts, Pennsylvania, and Connecticut (ibid). James Pemberton, a Philadelphia Quaker antislavery advocate, wrote: "It is generally agreed, that the conclusion of the Convention on this Subject [the ratifying convention], will not restrain the

chusetts argued that the fugitive slave clause violated the state constitution and questioned if the Constitution could be ratified there.[39] Quakers were also preparing to submit a memorial to the First Congress promoting the abolition of slavery.[40] Some expressed a growing awareness that the new Constitution had imperfections and believed that there would be "pressing Solicitations" for amendments when the government was formed.[41]

The complaints of the Quakers and the Baptists kept popular concerns about the inadequacies of the proposed Constitution before the public during the ratification process. Their reservations reinforced the momentum that had been building since the call for amendments by the Massachusetts ratification convention and convinced James Madison and some other Federalists that the people expected a bill of rights.

URBAN MECHANICS, RURAL YEOMEN, AND LIBERTY ENDANGERED

Urban mechanics and rural yeomen perceived several apparent contradictions when they considered the Constitution. If it reversed the economic problems of the 1780s, stimulated prosperity, protected the nation's borders, and guaranteed access to the Mississippi River, it would be welcomed by both groups. But if it did so at the cost of traditional liberties,

---

Assemblies of the Separate States from passing any prohibitory laws which they may judge expedient to abolish that infamous traffic" (James Pemberton to John Pemberton, May 3, 1788, ibid., 2:microform supp., doc. no. 667). For the February 1788 Rhode Island petition, see ibid., 16:403 n. 3.

[39] Moses Brown to James Pemberton, Oct. 17, 1788, ibid., 14:506–8.

[40] The Quaker memorial, which was not presented to the Philadelphia Convention to avoid offending the southern delegates, was discussed by "J. H.," in the *Pennsylvania Gazette* (Philadelphia), Mar. 5, 1788 (ibid., 2: microform supp., doc. no. 489), and in Robert Wahn to Richard Wahn, Oct. 3, 1787 (ibid., 14:505–6). See also the correspondence of James Pemberton to John Pemberton, Sept. 20, 1787, and Apr. 20, 1788, ibid., 2: microform supp., doc. nos. 133, 644.

[41] James Pemberton to James Phillips, May 4, 1788, ibid., 2:microform supp., doc. no. 668.

which were secured by custom and the state constitutions, or if it raised a new aristocracy, which would fatten itself through public officeholding and entrench itself in a standing army, leading to despotic government, the cost would be too high. The Antifederalists cleverly appealed to these concerns by warning of such dangers and advocating the preservation of state sovereignty. If an aroused electorate would elect Antifederalists to ratification conventions where they could demand amendments, to state legislatures that would draw the election boundaries for the new congressional districts and choose federal senators in the fall of 1788, and to the new Congress where they could participate in the establishment of the new federal government, then the Antifederalist cause could be saved. This process, which would span almost eighteen months between 1787 and 1789, may be observed in Baltimore City and in rural areas, notably western Pennsylvania.

In Baltimore City urban politics after the Revolution was identified with factions that formed along religious, ethnic, and economic lines.[42] These divisions, however, were sublimated in the late 1780s by the general expectation that the adoption of the Constitution would restore prosperity. The highlight of urban unanimity was a gala parade held after the ratification of the Constitution by the Annapolis Convention, much like those that would take place in Philadelphia and New York City. Mechanics, marching by craft, celebrated the event with civic leaders and merchants.[43]

This united front began to unravel following Maryland's controversial ratification convention, where the minority charged that the Federalist majority had rushed to ratify the Constitution without discussion, which reinforced the con-

---

[42] My understanding of its politics has benefited greatly from the work of Tina H. Sheller, "Artisans and the Evolution of Baltimore Town, 1765–1790," Ph.D. diss., University of Maryland, College Park, 1990, esp. chap. 5. A more comprehensive examination, which is in progress, will extend to the major cities of Boston, Philadelphia, and New York.

[43] See L. Marx Renzulli, Jr., *Maryland: The Federalist Years* (Rutherford, N.J., 1972), pp. 93–95, and Charles G. Steffens, *The Mechanics of Baltimore* (Urbana, Ill., 1984), pp. 92–94.

cern that individual liberties were at risk. While many merchants and mechanics never deviated in their support for a more energetic central government and continued to oppose any alteration to the Constitution, others responded to the Antifederalist appeal that individual rights were endangered. This was especially evident in election campaigns in the fall of 1788.

Elections, which were held over several days, were ideal opportunities for popular demonstrations. The Antifederalists hoped to attract voters at the election by ordering a number of caps—"inscribed with the word *Liberty*, . . . and intended to be carried about the streets on long polls"—and they "engaged some fifes and drums" for street parades.[44] Federalist merchants, mindful that mechanics depended upon them for work and hoping to influence their vote, paraded in support of the Constitution in Fells Point, the workers' section of Baltimore.[45]

One of the more remarkable things to happen during the fall elections in Baltimore was the advocacy of a bill of rights by Federalist candidates.[46] Although this belated conversion

[44] Caveto, "A Caution to the Federalists," *Maryland Journal* (Baltimore), Oct. 4, 1788 (Extra).

[45] See "An Irishman to the Mechanics, Tradesmen, and Poor Citizens of Baltimoretown," *Maryland Journal* (Baltimore), Oct. 4, 1788 (Extra). One commentator observed critically, "The Baltimoreans in the late election—to their shame be it written, adopted the English method of polling in bodies—with cockades and standards, bearing inscriptions designative of the causes they were engaged in" (*Massachusetts Centinel* [Boston], Dec. 24, 1788).

[46] This surprising situation was reported by "An Irishman," who described a meeting in Old Town, where James McHenry (the Federalist candidate) threw off his disguise "and told you (voters), what every man from New Hampshire to Georgia knew, that the constitution wanted amendments: Good God, thought I, can this be the Doctor? Is this the man who so lately entered the lists against Mr. Sterett and Mr. McMechen, for using similar words, tho not so strong? Less words from the latter gentlemen sent the doctor's party raving about the town, with the cry of danger, fire, Antifederalists, and what not that could inflame the passions, bias the judgments, and strengthen their party. But Mr. McHenry has now changed

was undoubtedly due in part to the fact that the Constitution had been ratified by the time the fall elections were held, it also represented an effort to attract voters who were attuned to the issue. What was surprising was that these were the same men who, as candidates for the ratification convention only a few months earlier, opposed any alteration of the Constitution and attacked Antifederalist candidates for arguing that the Constitution required amendments.

The motivations of rural yeomen were more varied. Those to the west of the Allegheny Mountains, who were dependent upon the river system to carry their goods to market, were especially concerned with the free navigation of the Mississippi.[47] Reports of their meetings say little about endangered liberty. Others, who were threatened by Indians or by the presence of British troops on the American frontier, sought a strong national government at almost any cost.

In the rural areas of western Pennsylvania there was considerable dissatisfaction with the Constitution and the society it appeared to create. It was perceived as part of a conspiracy to create a new aristocracy at the cost of honest yeomen. If such a government were created, it would consolidate power into the hands of a self-created elite, reduce the states to mere dependencies, and trample liberties guaranteed by state con-

---

sides, and become, according to his first principle, the Antifederalist Doctor. His first creed (to obtain the popular cry) was, no amendments; his oration at Old Town was, 'The right of trial by jury, the inviolable liberty of the press, and liberty of conscience wanted to be secured,' but it seems that was a new discovery by him, and that he had changed in opinion concerning those very important objects" ("An Address to the Mechanics of Baltimore-Town by a Tradesman," *Maryland Journal* [Baltimore], Sept. 30, 1788). Samuel Sterett, the Antifederalist congressional candidate, made much the same appeal several months later; see his "Circular Letter and Address to the Public," *Maryland Journal* (Baltimore), Jan. 2, 1789.

[47] For the controversy surrounding the Mississippi navigation question, see Henry Innes to John Brown, Dec. 7, 1787, John Blair Smith to James Madison, June 12, 1788, and Nicholas Gilman to John Sullivan, Apr. 19, 1788, *DHR*, 8:221–23; 9:608, 742–43. See also the report of a Pittsburgh meeting, Nov. 9, 1787, ibid., 2:286–87; "G," *Pittsburgh Gazette*, Nov. 10, 1787, and Alex Fowler to John Nicholson, Feb. 9, 1788, ibid., 2:microform supp., docs. nos. 217 and 414.

stitutions. Without a federal bill of rights to restrain such potential abuse, the future looked bleak indeed.[48]

The "Address and Reasons of Dissent of the Minority of the Convention of the State of Pennsylvania to their Constituents" reflects this popular orientation and demonstrates how particular liberties concerned different groups. In addition to its conspiratorial tone, with constant attention to the dangers of despotism, it is one of the few calls by a ratification convention endorsing an armed citizenry and specifically protecting rural popular rights.[49] Article 7 of the dissent, closely following the wording of the Pennsylvania constitution, which justified arms for the defense of the self and state, expanded the right to include "the purpose of killing game."[50] The next article preserved the people's control over public lands: "The inhab-

[48] This sentiment is aptly stated in a resolution of a meeting in Westmoreland Co., Pa., calling for a second convention to add a bill of rights: (Resolution #6) "They [the committee] conceive that by so imperfect a bill or declaration of rights as the new plan of general government contains, whereby the trial by jury in criminal cases, the *habeas corpus*, &c. only, is secured; trial by jury in civil cases, and every other essential right of freemen is implicitly given up to the arbitrary will of future men. They therefore wish that such a declaration of rights may be added to the general frame of government as may secure to posterity those privileges which are essential to the proper limiting the extent of sovereign power and securing those rights which are essential to freemen. And that Congress may not have power to pass any laws which in their effect may infringe on, or tend to subvert the constitution of any state, except in such cases as are mentioned in the first clause to be of a general nature, and properly belong to Congress" (*Freeman's Journal* [Philadelphia], Sept. 24, 1788).

[49] The New Hampshire and New York conventions also called for the right to bear arms. See reports of the New Hampshire ratification convention: "Congress shall never disarm any citizen, unless such as are or have been in actual rebellion" (*Massachusetts Centinel* [Boston], June 23, 1788), and the New York ratification convention: "That the People have a right to keep and bear Arms; that a well regulated Militia, including the body of the People *capable of bearing Arms*, is the proper, natural and safe defense of a free State" (Linda Grant DePauw, *The Eleventh Pillar: New York State and the Federal Constitution* [Ithaca, N.Y., 1966], p. 294).

[50] Compare Article XIII of the Pennsylvania Declaration of Rights, "That the people have a right to bear arms for the defense of themselves and the state; and as standing armies in the time of peace are dangerous to liberty, they ought not to be kept up; and that the military should be kept under

itants of the several states shall have liberty to fowl and hunt in seasonable times, on the lands they hold, and on all other lands in the United States not enclosed, and in the like manner to fish in all navigable waters, and others not private property, without being restrained therein by any laws to be passed by the legislature of the United States."[51] The minority wanted to make certain that people in unsettled areas should have full access to traditional rural rights over the land.

Deepening dissatisfaction with the manner in which the Constitution had been ratified in Pennsylvania culminated in a call in early July for a second convention that would consider amending it and nominate candidates for the congressional election.[52] Preconvention meetings were called in rural

---

strict subordination to, and governed by, the civil power" (Thorpe, ed., *Federal and State Constitutions*, 5:3083), with Article VII of the Dissent, "That the people have a right to bear arms for the defense of themselves and their own state, or the United States, *or for the purpose of killing game;* and no law shall be passed for disarming the people, or any of them, unless for crimes committed, or real danger of public injury from individuals; and as standing armies in the time of peace are dangerous to liberty, they ought not to be kept up; and that the military shall be kept under strict subordination to and be governed by the civil powers" (emphasis added; *DHR*, 2:623–24).

[51] *DHR*, 2:624.

[52] There were several confrontations between Federalists and Antifederalists in rural Pennsylvania following the ratification convention that indicate deepening opposition to the Constitution. The most important was the Carlisle riot, which is examined in Saul Cornell, "Aristocracy Assailed: The Ideology of Backcountry Anti-Federalism," *Journal of American History* 76 (1990):1148–72, and *DHR*, 15:225–26n and 2:670–708. Veritas, characterizing the rioters as "men of infamous character and bankrupt fortunes, who have nothing to lose themselves, ardently wish for a civil war in this State, that they may come in for a share of the plunder," argued that this was a perfect example of the need for an "energetic and coercive foederal government" (reprinted in the *Providence Gazette*, Apr. 19, 1788). There was also a delicate situation in Luzerne Co. when Col. Timothy Pickering was captured by the Wild Boys in July 1788 (see *New York Journal*, July 17, 18, 1788; *Boston Gazette*, Aug. 25, 1788). There was a report from Franklin Co. in the spring of 1788 that committees of observation and correspondence were appointed in every township and that there were twenty thousand armed men in Western Pennsylvania "determined to secure their liberties" (see extract of a letter from Franklin Co., Apr. 24, 1788, reprinted in the *Providence Gazette*, May 17, 1788).

areas to elect delegates in August, and the convention itself met in Harrisburg in early September 1788.[53]

The Harrisburg convention epitomized the dilemma facing many Antifederalists in the fall of 1788. Rural dissatisfaction with the Constitution remained intense, but it was obvious that the document would be ratified. Concerned Federalists feared that the convention would "devise and adopt, in concert with the Antis throughout the continent, some Plan for subverting the Federal Government."[54]

Actually, the Antifederalists, many of whom were members of the minority at the ratification convention, had more modest goals. In a series of resolutions they affirmed the need for a central government, questioned the allocation of power vested by the Constitution, and proposed the adoption of a bill of rights recommended by the minority.[55] An anonymous Federalist derided the convention by observing that "the whole squad of Malcontents was dull and dissatisfied, as there appeared to be no chance of kindling a Civil War in the United States."[56] Antifederalist William Shippen was more

[53] For the circular letter, signed by Benjamin Blyth, see *Pennsylvania Gazette* (Philadelphia), Sept. 10, 1788. For a report of the Greensburg, Westmoreland Co., meeting (Aug. 5, 1788), see the *Freeman's Journal* (Philadelphia), Sept. 24, 1788. The resolutions began affirming the need for a stronger central government but continued with specific objections to the concentration of power to the federal government at the cost of the states. See also "To the Inhabitants of the Western Counties of Pennsylvania from a Friend of Society and Liberty," *Maryland Journal* (Baltimore), Aug. 12, 1788. There is also a protest from Philadelphia that the preconvention circulars were not sent to townships near Philadelphia (*Pennsylvania Gazette* [Philadelphia], Aug. 20, 1788) and a report of a Bucks Co. meeting of Federalists who planned to send delegates to the Harrisburg convention (*Independent Gazetteer* [Philadelphia], Sept. 3, 1788).

[54] See a letter from Carlisle, Aug. 28, 1788, in the *Virginia Independent Chronicle* (Richmond), Sept. 10, 1788.

[55] For a report of the Harrisburg convention, see *Pennsylvania Gazette* (Philadelphia), Sept. 17, 1788.

[56] Anonymous "Report from a Gentleman who passed through Harrisburg a few days ago," *Pennsylvania Gazette* (Philadelphia), Sept. 10, 1788. For other Federalist assessments of the Harrisburg convention, see "A Doubter," *Pennsylvania Gazette* (Philadelphia), Sept. 24, 1788.

hopeful: "There is so respectable a minority in every state that I think one of the first acts of the new Government will be to propose a general convention of the people to make these necessary alterations—till then the minds of a great part of the U. States will not be easy."[57]

Not all rural demonstrations threatened violence. During the election for Maryland ratification convention delegates from Anne Arundel County, a purported safe haven for Federalists, Antifederalists circulated the following handbill:

Bill of Rights
Liberty of Conscience
Trial by Jury
No Excise
No Poll Tax
No Standing Army in Time of Peace,
Without Limitation.
No Whipping Militia
Nor Marching them out of
The State, Without Consent
of the General Assembly.
No Direct Taxation,
Without Previous
Requisition

The handbill had a remarkable effect on the voters. According to a Federalist observer: "The people were alarm'd at their positive assertions, and I am afraid when they attended the polls, a wildness appear'd in which many show'd they were realy frightened by what they had just heard."[58] While it is not entirely clear what the voters feared most—being taxed, whipped, or having their liberties undermined—the effect of this handbill demonstrates a popular concern that the adop-

[57] William Shippen to Thomas Lee Shippen, Aug. 21, 1788, Shippen Family Papers, Library of Congress.

[58] A copy of the handbill is held by the Maryland State Archives and is reprinted in *Documentary History of the Constitution of the United States of America, 1787–1870*, 5 vols. (Washington, D.C., 1894–1905), 4:641–42. For the letter, see Daniel Carroll to James Madison, May 28, 1788, Hutchinson et al., eds., *Papers of Madison*, 11:63.

tion of the proposed Constitution would result in a significant shift in authority without any protection against its abuse.

Urban mechanics and rural yeomen were justifiably concerned about the safety of their liberties under the Constitution. While Antifederalist politicians may have wanted to use such discontent to reduce the power of the new government by calling a second convention, much of the discourse focused on questions of individual rights and liberties. In an attempt to counteract this Antifederalist appeal, some Federalist leaders promised the possibility that amendments might be adopted after ratification.

The questions facing the nation when Congress convened in New York City were whether the First Congress would address the issue of individual liberties, or, if it did not, could Antifederalist leaders use the issue to generate support to call a second constitutional convention?

PROMISES TO KEEP: JAMES MADISON AND A FEDERAL BILL OF RIGHTS

> *Gentlemen say this section [Article 1, Section 8] is as clear as the sun, and that all power is retained which is not given. But where is the bill of rights which shall check the power of this Congress; which shall say,* Thus far shall ye come, and no farther. *The safety of the people depends on a bill of rights. If we build on a sandy foundation, is it likely we shall stand?*
>
> —S. Thompson
> Massachusetts Ratification Convention

James Madison's dominant role in framing and advocating the Bill of Rights in the First Congress has been well-documented.[59] It is important, however, to assess why he abandoned his long–held aversion to parchment barriers to become the champion of a national bill of rights and to under-

---

[59] The most insightful treatment of the adoption of the Bill of Rights is Kenneth R. Bowling, "'A Tub to the Whale': The Founding Fathers and the Adoption of the Federal Bill of Rights," *Journal of the Early Republic* 8 (1988):223–51.

stand his vision of what liberties should be protected in a federal system from the state and national governments.

Madison shared the general Federalist antipathy to engrafting a bill of rights onto the new Constitution.[60] Unlike Thomas Jefferson,who believed that "a bill of rights is what the people are entitled to against every government on earth," Madison felt that the demand for a bill of rights was predicated on constitutionally unsound principles.[61] He argued that the creation of a stable national government under the Constitution would secure republican government, under which the states would be the natural guarantors of individual liberties, and he agreed with James Wilson that the specific enumeration of powers in the Constitution precluded any federal threat to fundamental liberties, such as freedom of the press or trial by jury.[62] At the same time, he shared a prevailing

[60] A good example of the Federalist opposition to a bill of rights is provided by "Foreign Spectator," "Remarks on the Amendments to the Federal Constitution Proposed by the Conventions of Massachusetts, New Hampshire, New York, Virginia, South and North Carolina, and the Minorities of Pennsylvania and Maryland," in the *Federal Gazette* (Philadelphia), Oct. 21, 1788 through Feb. 16, 1789. See also editorial, ibid., Mar. 10, 1789; Gehenapolis commented on this evaluation: "So many absurdities and contradictions have been pointed out in the supposed amendments, that if they should be brought forward on the floor of Congress, it will not be necessary to oppose them. They will immediately, like Swift's books, give battle to each other, and soon destroy themselves" (ibid., Feb. 18, 1789).

[61] Jefferson to James Madison, Dec. 20, 1787, Boyd et al., eds., *Papers of Jefferson*, 12:440. Madison responded to this letter with his fullest discussion of the question, and observed: "My own opinion has always been in favor of a bill of rights; provided it be so framed as not to imply powers not meant to be included in the enumeration. At the same time I have never thought the omission a material defect, not been anxious to supply it even by subsequent amendment, for any other reason than it is anxiously desired by others" (James Madison to Jefferson, Oct. 17, 1788, ibid., 14:18).

[62] For Madison's observation that the state would protect liberty in a federal system, see *Federalist* No. 45, Jacob E. Cooke, ed., *The Federalist* (Middletown, Conn., 1961), p. 313. For his belief that an energetic national government would assure stability, see *Federalist* No. 39, ibid., pp. 250–57; and that pluralism would naturally resist majority oppression, see *Federalist* No. 51, ibid., pp. 351–53. During the debate over Richard Henry Lee's proposals to add a bill of rights to the Constitution (Sept. 27, 1787), Mel-

Federalist skepticism about the efficacy of parchment barriers protecting unpopular minorities against legislative majorities.[63] Along with other Federalists, he believed that Antifederalists exaggerated the Constitution's threat to individual liberty for political advantage in order to eviscerate the power of the new government.[64] His public opposition to amending the Constitution, which he reaffirmed at the Virginia ratification convention, would not change until his congressional campaign in January 1789.[65]

Madison's private correspondence, however, reveals that he recognized during the previous fall that the adoption of a bill

---

ancton Smith recorded Madison as saying: "A bill of rights [is] unnecessary because the powers are enumerated and only extend to certain cases" (*DHR*, 1:335).

[63] As Benjamin Rush remarked at the Pennsylvania ratification convention, Nov. 30, 1787, "As it has happened with treaties, so . . . has it happened with bills of rights, for never yet has one been made which has not, at some period or another, been broken" (*DHR*, 2:433). Madison commented privately: "Experience proves the inefficacy of a bill of rights on those occasions when its controul is most needed. Repeated violations of these parchment barriers have been committed by overbearing majorities in every State" (James Madison to Jefferson, Oct. 17, 1788, Hutchinson et al., eds., *Papers of Madison*, 11:297).

[64] For a full discussion between James Madison and his correspondents about the real objectives of the Antifederalists, see, with respect to the danger to the government's taxation power, Coxe to James Madison, July 23, 1788, Gordon to James Madison, Aug. 31, 1788, Miles King to James Madison, Mar. 3, 1789, and Edmund Randolph to James Madison, Aug. 18, 1789, Hutchinson et al., eds., *Papers of Madison*, 11:194–96, 245–46, 12:1–2, 345, and, concerning the prospects for a second convention, Gordon to James Madison, cited above, James Madison to Washington, Sept. 14, 1788, James Madison to Edmund Pendleton, Oct. 20, 1788, and James Madison to George Lee Turberville, Nov. 2, 1788, ibid., 11:254–55, 306–7, 330–32.

[65] For James Madison's change of heart, see his letters to George Eve, Jan. 2, 1789, and to Thomas Mann Randolph, Jan. 13, 1789, ibid., 11:404–5, 415–17. The Randolph letter was reprinted widely in the press. For a discussion of the need for Madison to make such an announcement, see James Madison to Turberville, Nov. 2, 1788, and two letters from Edward Carrington to James Madison, Nov. 14 and 18, 1788, ibid., pp. 330–32, 345–46, 351–53.

of rights was necessary to quiet political opposition and to blunt the momentum for a second convention. He observed that amendments were better suited to be introduced in the First Congress than by a general convention and that they "may be employed to quiet the fears of many by supplying those further guards for private rights which can do no harm to the system in the judgments even of its most partial friends, and will even be approved by others who have steadily supported it."[66] During the congressional campaign he propounded "all those essential rights, which have been thought in danger, such as the rights of conscience, the freedom of the press, trials by jury, exemption from general warrants, &c."[67] The challenge was how to structure such a bill without impairing the powers of the new government.

The solution to this dilemma was to craft a bill of rights that would both satisfy the popular concern for individual liberty and could be adopted by a Federalist dominated Congress when it formed in New York City. As Madison would later describe his proposed bill of rights: "It is limited to points which are important in the eyes of many and can be objectionable in those of none. The structure & stamina of the Govt. are as little touched as possible. Nothing of a controvertible nature can be expected to make its way thro' the caprice & discord of opinions which would encounter it in Congs. when 2/3 must concur in each House, & in the State Legislatures, 3/4 of which will be requisite to its final success."[68]

[66] James Madison to Edmund Pendleton, Oct. 20, 1788, ibid., p. 307. See also his letter to Jefferson, Oct. 17, 1788, cited above.

[67] James Madison to Thomas Mann Randolph, Jan. 13, 1789, ibid., p. 416. Jefferson agreed with most of this list of essential rights. He wrote: "By a declaration of rights I mean one which shall stipulate the freedom of religion, freedom of the press, freedom of commerce against monopolies, trial by juries in all cases, no suspensions of habeas corpus, no standing armies. These are fetters against doing evil which no honest government should decline" (Jefferson to Alexander Donald, Feb. 7, 1788, Boyd et al., eds., *Papers of Jefferson*, 12:571).

[68] James Madison to Edmund Randolph, Jan. 15, 1789, Hutchinson et al., eds., *Papers of Madison*, 12:219.

When the First Congress met in March it was uncertain whether a bill of rights would even be considered.[69] Notwithstanding Madison's belief that the Federalists were obligated to consider a bill of rights, both by a popular mandate and by the promises some had made during the previous election campaigns, many Federalists believed that the people had repudiated the entire Antifederalist agenda in the recent state and federal elections, and they did not want to be distracted from the important and controversial business of organizing the new government. There was also strong sentiment to put the national government into operation before repairing imagined structural defects.[70]

Such Federalist intransigence ignored the increasing public expectation that a bill of rights would be considered by the Congress. Newspapers had reported Madison's conversion and George Washington's endorsement of a bill of rights be-

---

[69]There was also a recognition that a second convention could not be held before the first session of Congress and that amendments would be introduced there (*United States Chronicle* [Providence], Apr. 2, 1789; "Extract of letter from New York to a gentleman in Providence," *Providence Gazette,* Mar. 14, 1789). Antifederalists argued that the First Congress was obligated immediately to call for a second convention ("The New Era," *Freeman's Journal* [Philadelphia], Mar. 4, 1789). James Madison, noting that the Antifederalists were a minority in Congress, observed: "Notwithstanding this character of the Body, I hope and expect that some conciliatory sacrifices will be made, in order to extinguish opposition to the system, or at least break the force of it, by detaching the deluded opponents from their designing leaders" (Madison to Jefferson, Mar. 29, 1789, Boyd et al., eds., *Papers of Jefferson,* 15:5–7). Jefferson wrote from abroad: "It is tolerably certain that Congress will propose amendments to the assemblies, as even the friends of the constitution are willing to make amendments, some from a conviction they are necessary, others from a spirit of conciliation. The addition of a bill of rights will probably be the most essential change" (Jefferson to William Short, Feb. 9, 1789, ibid., 14:52; see also Congressman Paine Wingate to the president of New Hampshire, Apr. 27, 1789, Gratz Collection, Historical Society of Pennsylvania, Philadelphia).

[70]As a sampling of Federalist opinion, consider: David Humphreys to Jefferson, Nov. 29, 1788, ibid., 14:302; Amator Justitiae [Theodore Sedgwick], *Massachusetts Centinel* (Boston), May 30, 1789; and Andrew Ellicott to the *Pennsylvania Gazette* (Philadelphia), Apr. 30, 1789.

fore the new government was formed.[71] President Washington publicly lent his prestige by supporting the consideration of a bill of rights in his inaugural address.[72]

Madison proposed a nine-part bill of rights to Congress on June 8, 1789. As state constitutions were often prefaced with declarations of rights, he wanted to begin the Constitution with a declaration that power was vested in the people and that the goal of government should be to benefit the people in their "enjoyment of life and liberty, with the right of acquiring and using property, and generally pursuing and obtaining happiness and safety." The people also retained the right to reform or change their government "whenever it be found adverse or inadequate to the purposes of its institution."[73]

In one of the more controversial proposals, Madison sought to write amendments into the body of the Constitution itself. The fourth proposal expanded the protection of individual rights by adding a number of clauses to Article I, Section 9, which restricted congressional power. These included all of the elements regarding personal liberty that would become the final bill of rights (with condensed wording). They specifically prohibited the establishment of "any national reli-

---

[71] It was reported that "His Excellency General GEORGE WASHINGTON has recently declared himself in favor of the proposed amendments to the new Constitution" (*Independent Gazetteer* [Philadelphia], Jan. 21, 1789). Another correspondent reported that the passions in Virginia had subsided, "it being agreed, on all hands, that a *bill of rights*, declaratory of the *freedom of the press, trial by jury*, &c. ought to be annexed, and those *essential* points explained and defined, so as to fix the liberties of the people on the most safe and permanent foundation" (ibid., Jan. 23, 1789). James Madison's letter to Thomas Mann Randolph, announcing his support for a bill of rights, was also reprinted widely before Congress convened (ibid., Feb. 10, 1789; *Massachusetts Centinel* [Boston], Mar. 4, 1789).

[72] For the president's address, see Hutchinson et al., eds., *Papers of Madison*, 12:123; for James Madison's role in preparing this address, see ibid., pp. 120–21; for Washington's earlier opinion favoring a bill of rights, see his letter to Jefferson, Aug. 31, 1788, Boyd et al., eds., *Papers of Jefferson*, 13:556.

[73] The quotations in the following discussion are taken from the text of James Madison's resolution, June 8, 1789, in Veit, Bowling, and Bickford, eds., *Creating the Bill of Rights*, pp. 11–14.

gion," guaranteed that "the right of the people to keep and bear arms shall not be infringed," and ended with the general admonition: "The exceptions here or elsewhere in the constitution, made in favor of particular rights, shall not be so construed as to diminish the just importance of other rights retained by the people; or as to enlarge the powers delegated by the constitution; but either as actual limitations of such powers, or as inserted merely for caution."

The breadth of Madison's vision for the maximum protection of individual liberties in a federal system was revealed in his fifth section. Just as he had deprecated state declarations of rights because they often were inadequate to restrain a legislative majority from violating minority rights, a phenomenon he had witnessed in Revolutionary Virginia, he sought to establish a federal guarantee against such abuse by expanding Article I, Section 10. The following rights would be protected against state action: "No state shall violate the equal rights of conscience, or the freedom of the press, or the trial by jury in criminal cases."

The sixth and seventh sections were to be inserted in Article III of the Constitution to preserve and define the right to jury trials and to draw such juries from the vicinage. The eighth and final article expressly prohibited any one branch of government from exercising the powers of the other two and ended with the prohibition: "The powers not delegated by this constitution, nor prohibited by it to the states, are reserved to the states respectively."

Madison's proposed amendments reflected his knowledge of the various state constitutions, his familiarity with the amendments proposed by the state ratifying conventions, and his desire to preserve an energetic federal government. His amendments purposely omitted the majority of the Antifederalist proposals, which would have diminished the powers of the national government. Madison, like other Federalists, continued to believe that a strong and energetic central government was necessary to the preservation of the Union and that it would not endanger the sovereignty and integrity of the several states. Those amendments guaranteeing personal liberty would not restrict the operation of the federal government.

Madison's proposed amendments reflected his commitment to the principles of republican government, federalism, and balanced sovereignty. He wanted to limit a federal bill of rights to "an enumeration of simple and acknowledged principles. Such rights ought to be expressly secured as were certain and fixed."[74] The prohibition against a national religion avoided the problems of an unpopular established church while recognizing the right of some states to support religion as their constitutions allowed.[75] The limitations on the power of the federal government to infringe upon individual liberty, which emulated the strongest prohibitions in any state declaration of rights, did not encroach upon the relationship between a citizen and his state government. Such liberties continued to be defined and enforced by the individual states as they had since the Revolution.

Madison believed, however, that there were certain fundamental rights that neither the federal government nor the sovereign states could violate and still maintain a republican government. Responding to a motion to delete this section, which guaranteed the freedom of the press, the right to a jury trial, and freedom of conscience against state action, Madison argued "that it was the most valuable amendment on the whole list; if there was any reason to restrain the government of the United States from infringing upon these essential rights, it was equally necessary that they should be secured against the state governments."[76] It was no accident that eleven state constitutions protected the free exercise of religion (twelve, with New Hampshire's 1784 revision of its 1776 constitution); eight the freedom of the press (nine with New Hampshire's 1784 revision); and nine states guaranteed the

[74] Report of congressional debate, Aug. 15, 1789, ibid., p. 152.

[75] Three state constitutions created established religions (Massachusetts, New Hampshire [1784], and South Carolina), attempts were made to use public funds to support religion in the 1780s (Maryland and Virginia), and four states explicitly forbade established religion (Delaware, New Jersey, North Carolina, and Pennsylvania).

[76] *Congressional Register*, Aug. 17, 1789, in Veit, Bowling, and Bickford, eds., *Creating the Bill of Rights*, pp. 188–89.

right to a jury trial in criminal prosecutions (ten with New Hampshire's 1784 revision).

Congressional response to Madison's proposals was less than enthusiastic. Acknowledging that he had fulfilled his obligation to bring the matter forward, Federalists rejected his plan on the grounds that there were more pressing concerns facing Congress.[77] Antifederalist congressmen were dissatisfied with his proposals because they did little to restrain the national government's power or sovereignty.

The popular response was harder to gauge. Isaac Backus noted that he attended Congress the day Madison presented his proposals but failed to record his reaction to Madison's speech.[78] Madison's bill of rights was printed nationally in the public press, most often without comment. Federalist Tench Coxe published a comprehensive commentary on Madison's proposals under the pseudonym "A Pennsylvanian." It was effusive in praise of the underlying spirit of accommodation and the thoroughness with which individual rights were protected. Surprisingly, it was not reprinted widely in other newspapers.[79]

---

[77] Robert Morris commented: "The House of Representatives . . . are now playing with Amendments, but if they make *one* truly *so* I'll hang. poor Madison got so Cursedly frightened in Virginia, that I believe he has dreamed of amendments ever since" (Morris to Francis Hopkinson, Aug. 15, 1789, Veit, Bowling, and Bickford, eds., *Creating the Bill of Rights*, p. 278). Theodore Sedgwick observed: "We are still engaged about the uncompromising subject of amendments. The introduction of it at this period, of the existence of our government was in my opinion unwise and will not produce those beneficial effects which its advocates predicted. Before we could be said to have a government to attempt to amend the constitution argues a frivolity of character very inconsistent with national dignity" (Theodore Sedgwick to Pamela Sedgwick, Aug. 20, 1789, ibid., p. 283).

[78] McLoughlin, ed., *Diary of Backus*, 3:1273.

[79] The editorial statements accompanying the announcement of James Madison's initial proposal were mild (*Massachusetts Centinel* [Boston], June 17, 1789). For the two-part series, see "A Pennsylvanian," "Remarks on . . . the Amendments to the FEDERAL CONSTITUTION . . . ," *Federal Gazette* (Philadelphia), June 18, 30, 1789. See also Coxe to James Madison, June 18, 1789, Hutchinson et al., eds., *Papers of Madison*, 12:239–41.

THE BILL OF RIGHTS

A bill of rights would not be adopted by Congress for over three months. Delayed because of more pressing legislation, Madison's proposals were referred to a select committee, the Vining Committee, which made its report at the end of July. After a protracted debate that took place in August, the House sent a seventeen-part bill to the Senate. The debate showed a remarkable veneration for the work of the Founding Fathers. The House refused to amend the body of the Constitution as Madison wanted and decided to attach amendments to it. Most of Madison's ideas survived and the House added "freedom of speech" to the restrictions against the states. The Senate, however, dropped this whole section for reasons that were not recorded and accepted a twelve-part Bill of Rights that was sent to the states for ratification on September 14, 1789.[80]

THE BILL OF RIGHTS:
WERE LIBERTIES SECURE?

The ten amendments ratified by the states in 1791 as the Bill of Rights satisfied Madison's purpose to respond to a popular concern that certain individual liberties needed protection against the national government and that amendments could be accomplished without weakening the Constitution. The Antifederalist plan to make basic structural changes, or to redefine the national taxing authority, or to reintroduce the "express" provisions from Article II of the Articles of Confederation into an amendment reserving powers to the states, had all been defeated. Many Antifederalists expressed serious disappointment in the final Bill of Rights. Congressman Thomas Tudor Tucker commented: "You will find our Amendments to the Constitution calculated merely to amuse, or rather to deceive."[81] Senator Richard Henry Lee forwarded the amendments to the governor of Virginia with this pessimistic comment: "It is with grief that we now send forward propositions inadequate to the purpose of real and sub-

---

[80] Veit, Bowling, and Bickford, eds., *Creating the Bill of Rights,* pp. 57–213.

[81] Thomas Tudor Tucker to St. George Tucker, Oct. 2, 1789, ibid., p. 300.

stantial Amendments, and so short of the wishes of our Country."[82]

There was also a renewed call for a second convention to remedy these defects.[83] Such disenchantment recalled Centinel's cynical observation on a bill of rights a year earlier: "Like a barrel thrown to a whale, the people were to be amused with fancied amendments, until the harpoon of power should secure its prey and render resistance ineffectual."[84] But others, such as Sam Adams, seemed less apprehensive that the Constitution would consolidate all power or extinguish the sovereign states, and they expressed satisfaction with the amendments being considered by Congress.[85]

The Federalist response to the Bill of Rights was equally complex. As one congressman expressed it: "We have agreed in recommending some conciliatory amendments, about trial by jury, liberty of the press, all powers not given reserved etc. which will not hurt and may give ground to antifeds. to wheel

[82] Senators Richard Henry Lee and William Grayson to the governor of Virginia, Sept. 28, 1789, *Virginia Independent Chronicle* (Richmond). It was general knowledge that Lee wrote this joint letter. For other Antifederalist expressions of disappointment, see Elbridge Gerry to John Wendell, July 10, 1789, Gratz Collection, and Mason to Jefferson, Mar. 16, 1790, Boyd et al., eds., *Papers of Jefferson*, 16:232–34.

[83] Moderatus (V) commented bitterly about the proposed amendments: "But among them all, is there none, except the second, but what the warm and zealous supporters of the constitution told us were either unnecessary or superfluous, as being either expressly or implicitly contained in the constitution itself" (*Boston Gazette*, Jan. 25, 1790).

[84] Centinel (XIX), *Independent Gazetteer* (Philadelphia), Oct. 7, 1788.

[85] Samuel Adams wrote Richard Henry Lee, Aug. 24, 1789: "I mean, my friend to let you know how deeply I am impressed with a sense of the Importance of Amendments; that the good People can clearly see the distinction, for there is a distinction, between the *federal* Powers vested in Congress, and the *sovereign* Authority belonging to the several States, which is the palladium of the private and personal rights of the citizens. I freely protest to you, that I earnestly wish some Amendments may be judiciously, and deliberately made without partial or local considerations—that there may be no uncomfortable Jarrings among the several Powers; that the whole People may in every State contemplate their own safety on solid-grounds, and the Union of States be perpetual" (Veit, Bowling, and Bickford, eds., *Creating the Bill of Rights*, p. 286).

about with a salve to their pride."[86] There was even hope that the adoption of the Bill of Rights would encourage North Carolina to ratify the Constitution and to induce Rhode Island to reconsider its protracted inaction.

Writing President Washington, Madison was sanguine that the adoption of the Bill of Rights quieted the opposition to the federal government: "A far as I can gather, the great bulk of the late opponents are entirely at rest, and more likely to censure a further opposition to the Govt. as now Administered than the Government itself. One of the principal leaders of the Baptists lately sent me word that the amendments had entirely satisfied the disaffected of his Sect, and that it would appear in their subsequent conduct."[87] A persistent popular demand for protection of individual liberty against the federal government played a large role in convincing James Madison to incorporate a bill of rights into the Constitution. The many sources from which this popular concern emanated revealed America to be a fractured society in the 1780s. Madison's vision that an extended republic could contain such diversity under the government created by the Constitution was as enlightened as it was controversial. His appreciation that a bill of rights would assuage popular resistance to the Constitution was equally prescient. The Antifederalists accurately despaired their political future. As the political divisions of the 1790s show, popular concern about a federal threat to individual liberties evaporated.

[86]Abraham Baldwin to Joel Barlow, Sept. 29, 1789, Abraham Baldwin Collection, Yale University Library, New Haven.

[87]James Madison to Washington, Nov. 20, 1789, Hutchinson et al., eds., *Papers of Madison*, 12:453. For the letter in question, see James Manning to James Madison, Aug. 20, 1789, ibid., pp. 365–66.

MICHAEL LIENESCH

Reinterpreting Rights
Antifederalists and the
Bill of Rights

IN THE EVENTS leading up to the creation of the Bill of Rights,
Antifederalists played an ambivalent and ultimately uncertain
role. From the time of the Philadelphia Convention, they were
ardent advocates for the protection of rights, and their efforts
throughout the period of ratification and into the First Congress were critical to the formation of the first ten amendments. At the same time, Antifederalists were first to admit
that the amendments that became known as the Bill of Rights,
a list of liberties proposed by the Federalist James Madison,
amended and passed by the Federalist First Congress, and
ratified with some deletions with strong Federalist support by
the state legislatures, were not entirely of their own choosing. In fact, most of the rights contained in the final form of
the first ten amendments were different from the ones they
had originally proposed. Moreover, the rights that eventually
emerged were based on a different conception of rights, and
a different way of thinking about rights, than the one they
had advocated at the start. And because they played a part in
the debates from which these rights emerged, Antifederalists
were themselves at least partly responsible. Thus their role
remains, as Herbert J. Storing says, "an ambiguous legacy."[1]

Antifederalists saw the debate over the Bill of Rights as both
political and philosophical, a contest not only to create rights
but also to define them. Insisting on a bill of rights, and sug-

[1] Herbert J. Storing, "What the Anti-Federalists Were *For*," Storing, ed.,
The Complete Anti-Federalist, 7 vols. (Chicago, 1981), 1:65 (hereafter cited
as *CAF*).

gesting long lists of liberties to be contained therein, they talked incessantly of rights, and the record that they left is rich with references to them. They spoke of all kinds of rights: the rights of states, of citizens, and of men; the rights of "peoples" and of "the people"; the rights of "humanity" and of "mankind."[2] They described these rights in an abundance of ways, as "essential" and "fundamental"; as "inalienable," "inherent," and "inviolable"; as "natural" and "perpetual"; as "sacred."[3] In defining rights, they distinguished many different kinds: "civil" and "constitutional," "public" and "political," "private" and "personal."[4] Claiming them all, they insisted on reserving rights of every conceivable kind, "the whole catalogue of rights."[5] And when the lists got long, they implied still more, "many other rights."[6] For Antifederalists, the debates about the Bill of Rights were debates about the meaning and purpose of rights themselves. In this regard, they can be seen as a capstone to the civic discourse of the Founding Era,

[2] "Letter from a Delegate Who Has Catched Cold," *CAF,* 5:273; "Essays of Brutus" (II), ibid., 2:372; "Speeches of Patrick Henry in the Virginia State Ratifying Convention," June 12, 1788, ibid., 5:239; "Essays by the Impartial Examiner" (I), ibid., 5:175.

[3] "Essays of Brutus" (II), ibid., 2:373; "South Carolina Proposed Amendments," 1788, Bernard Schwartz, comp., *The Roots of the Bill of Rights,* 5 vols. (New York, 1980), 4:757; "Essays of Philadelphiensis" (III), *CAF,* 3:110; "Speeches of Henry," June 16, 1788, *CAF,* 5:247, 246; "Essays of Brutus" (II), *CAF,* 2:373; "South Carolina Proposed Amendments," Schwartz, comp., *Roots of the Bill of Rights,* 4:757; "Essays of Philadelphiensis" (IX), *CAF,* 3:129.

[4] "Essays by the Impartial Examiner" (I), *CAF,* 5:185; "Letters from the Federal Farmer" (VI), ibid., 2:261; Melancton Smith, "Address to the People of New York on the Necessity of Amendments to the Constitution," 1788, Schwartz, comp., *Roots of the Bill of Rights,* 3:574; "Letters of Agrippa" (XV), *CAF,* 4:109; "The Address and Reasons of Dissent of the Minority of the Convention of the State of Pennsylvania to Their Constituents," 1787, Schwartz, ed., *Roots of the Bill of Rights,* 3:671; Samuel Chase, "Notes of Speeches Delivered to the Maryland Ratifying Convention," *CAF,* 5:82.

[5] "Essays by the Impartial Examiner" (I), *CAF,* 5:185.

[6] Aristocrotis [William Petrikin], "The Government of Nature Delineated," ibid., 3:205.

which Forrest McDonald has called "an ongoing public forum on the meaning of liberty."[7]

Over the course of the debates, Antifederalists changed their thinking about rights. Federalists did too, and the records reveal a remarkable scene of partisans on both sides listening to and learning from one another and revising their views accordingly. The transformations were by no means total, and from beginning to end conceptions of rights on both sides were complicated and often confused, combining communitarian and libertarian strains in sometimes self-contradictory ways. On balance, however, for reasons both political and philosophical, Antifederalists appear to have changed more. For in the debates, their thinking followed a pattern in which fundamental republican principles were reformulated into the more specific standards and more enforceable rules of liberal law. Collective and communitarian concepts of compact, in which rights were seen as the powers and obligations of citizens to act publicly, were transformed into individualistic ideas of contract, designed to protect persons and to defend their private possessions. Moral "oughts" became legal "shall nots." So it was, writes Storing, that "the Bill of Rights became what it is today: not the broad principles establishing the ends and limits of government, not 'maxims' to be learned and looked up to by generations of Americans, not statements of those first principles to which a healthy people should, according to the Virginia Declaration of Rights, frequently resort; but specific protections of traditional civil rights."[8]

This essay considers the Antifederalist reinterpretation of rights. Taking their thinking about rights seriously, it reviews a selection of their writings over the period from the close of the Philadelphia Convention to the adoption of the Bill of Rights. These writings include essays, pamphlets, and letters

[7] Forrest McDonald, *Novus Ordo Seclorum: The Intellectual Origins of the Constitution* (Lawrence, Kans., 1985), p. 10.

[8] Herbert J. Storing, "The Constitution and the Bill of Rights," in Robert A. Goldwin and William A. Schambra, eds., *How Does the Constitution Secure Rights?* (Washington, D.C., 1985), p. 32.

written for audiences "out-of-doors," as well as speeches in the state ratifying conventions and from the floor of the First Congress. They represent the work of influential writers such as "The Federal Farmer," "An Old Whig," Agrippa, "A Maryland Farmer," and "The Impartial Examiner," and of lesser lights as well. Taken from every region of the country, they are chosen to reveal a range of Antifederalist thinking. Considering these sources chronologically and in context, focusing on turning points in the debates, the essay charts changes in Antifederalist conceptions of rights, suggests some of the reasons for them, and considers their implications for the way Americans think about rights today.

THE FOUNDATIONS OF FREEDOM

For Antifederalists, the debate began in the dying days of the Philadelphia Convention, when the redoubtable George Mason, author of the Virginia Declaration of Rights, rose to demand that the proposed Constitution be prefaced with a bill of rights. Rejected roundly by the Federalist-controlled Convention, Mason's demand became the cornerstone of Antifederalist politics throughout the period of ratification.[9] Moreover, premised as it was on time-tested republican principles, it set the philosophical preconditions of Antifederalist thinking as well. For Antifederalists, freedom required that citizens declare their rights. History, by which they meant mostly Anglo-American history, was for them a story of liberty-loving republicans prying powers from the grasp of their rulers, forcing them to relinquish their prerogatives, in the form of rights, to the people. Over the course of this continuing conflict, citizens won some significant concessions, which they proceeded to declare in documents such as Magna Charta, the Declaration of Independence, and the declarations of rights that were contained in the constitutions of most of the original American states. While seeming to be lists of liberties, these declarations were more significantly statements of self-

---

[9] For background on the Philadelphia Convention, see Robert Allen Rutland, *The Birth of the Bill of Rights, 1776–1791* (Chapel Hill, 1955), pp. 106–25.

definition, in which citizens announced their intentions to govern themselves. In other words, declarations were compacts, binding citizens together into self-governing states.[10] Writing in early October 1787, in one of the first of his letters commenting on the Philadelphia Constitution, the able Antifederalist "Federal Farmer" described declarations in this way: "There are certain unalienable and fundamental rights," he wrote, "which in forming the social compact, ought to be explicitly ascertained and fixed."[11] In declaring these rights, citizens saw themselves as acting in a constitutive role, not as protecting themselves from the power of their rulers, but as defining those very powers. "Federal Farmer" explained that "a free and enlightened people, in forming this compact, will not resign all their rights to those who govern, and they will fix limits to their legislators and rulers, which will soon be plainly seen by those who are governed, as well as by those who govern."[12] In essence, declarations were founding documents, creating republics by stating the right of their people to rule themselves. "Rights," "Farmer" summed up, were "the basis of every constitution: and if a people be so situated, or have such different opinions that they cannot agree in ascertaining or fixing them, it is a very strong argument against their attempting to form one entire society, to live under one system of laws only."[13]

To Antifederalists, declarations of rights were declarations of fundamental principles. In most of the existing state constitutions they were listed first, above the articles establishing the forms of government, and they served a foundational purpose, setting forth the founding precepts or (as republicans liked to call them) the "first principles" on which these states rested. As Antifederalists saw them, these principles, which they also called "axioms," "maxims," or simply "truths," existed prior to the creation of their states, and for that mat-

[10] On compacts, see Donald S. Lutz, *The Origins of American Constitutionalism* (Baton Rouge, La., 1988), esp. pp. 31–34.

[11] "Letters from the Federal Farmer" (II), *CAF,* 2:231.

[12] Ibid.

[13] Ibid., p. 232.

ter, prior to the creation of free government itself. In an entry written in January 1788, "Federal Farmer" made this point: "We do not by declarations change the nature of things, or create new truths, but we give existence, or at least establish in the minds of the people truths and principles which they might never otherwise have thought of, or soon forgot."[14] Rights were self-evident truths, existing not on paper, in constitutions or documents, but in principles, in timeless and transcendent truths. In articulating these truths, once and for all, in their declarations of rights, citizens did not so much create rights as create a self-consciousness about them among themselves, inscribing them, as "Federal Farmer" put it, "in the front page of every family book."[15] Furthermore, because rights belonged not only to citizens of the present but also to posterity, declarations were transhistorical documents. In essence, Antifederalists saw declarations as texts, required readings in a process of civic education in which citizens of all times were repeatedly reminded of their rights and constantly encouraged to claim them. Through this pedagogical process, timeless truths could be brought to bear on the changing circumstances of contemporary politics. Thus, these declarations were meant to be both philosophical and practical in purpose. As "Federal Farmer" put it, "What is the usefulness of a truth in theory, unless it exists constantly in the minds of the people and has their assent?"[16]

In thinking of rights as truths, Antifederalists tended to see them as articles of faith, the basis of the covenant on which their republican civil religion rested. Frequently they referred to their rights as their American "palladium," for the statue of Pallas Athena, protector of the public order, which was seen as a kind of republican ark of the covenant, passed symbolically from Troy to Greece, Rome, England, and eventually to America. Even more often they described their rights as "sacred," meaning not only that they were handed down from on high but also, and probably more important, that they

[14] Ibid. (XVI), p. 324.

[15] Ibid.

[16] Ibid.

were paid for with the blood of patriots and tyrants. For them, to declare these rights was to recall the sacrifices of those who had won them, and it was also to commit themselves to protecting their legacy. Reminding his readers that Magna Charta itself was read twice a year in public places, "Federal Farmer" suggested a similar process, a kind of republican religious ritual, to enliven America's liberties. He wrote, "Men, in some countries do not remain free, merely because they are entitled to natural and unalienable rights; men in all countries are entitled to them, not because their ancestors once got together and enumerated them on paper, but because, by repeated negociations and declarations, all parties are brought to realize them, and of course to believe them to be sacred." [17] For Antifederalists, declarations were civic creeds. Ascribed to collectively by citizens, they were the basis of a common civic faith. Acting like commandments, or moral "oughts," they served as standards toward which citizens could strive. Above all, they suggested a set of obligations, for rights had to be protected, a process that required citizens to be constantly conscious of them. "Federal Farmer" concluded, "Were it necessary, I might shew the wisdom of our past conduct, as a people in not merely comforting ourselves that we were entitled to freedom, but in constantly keeping in view, in addresses, bills of rights, in news-papers, &c. the particular principles on which our freedom must always depend." [18]

As Antifederalists saw it, to found government was to lay the foundations of freedom. The one and only purpose in founding republics was to secure rights. Thus it was that citizens created compacts, declaring solemnly to one another their common commitment to defend any and all their liberties. Thinking rhetorically rather than analytically or deductively, Antifederalists defined rights broadly and expansively, in open-ended and universalistic ways. In their minds, rights were inalienable and indivisible, coming not singly but tied together, in what Forrest McDonald calls "congeries" or complex and contradictory combinations of rights, powers, and

[17] Ibid., p. 325.

[18] Ibid.

obligations.[19] Relying on rhetoric, which they used skillfully
in both political and philosophical ways, they called on citizens to claim all of these rights simultaneously. To do any less,
they argued, would be to break the compact and to destroy
the foundations of the republic. So it was that from the beginning Antifederalists assumed, as self-evident, that the Constitution must begin with a declaration of rights, insisting, in the
words of Richard Henry Lee, that "the new constitution . . .
be bottomed upon a declaration or bill of rights, clearly and
precisely stating the principles upon which this social compact
is founded."[20]

LISTING LIBERTIES

For Antifederalists, Pennsylvania provided a turning point in
the debate over the Bill of Rights. Calling themselves "Constitutionalists," or supporters of the state constitution of 1776,
Antifederalists considered ratification to be a referendum on
their state's constitutional rights. Overwhelmed by high-
handed Federalists in the ratifying convention, they took their
case to the streets, demanding that the Constitution begin
with a declaration of rights.[21] Here they were met by the Federalist James Wilson who, in his famous "state house yard
speech," delivered in early October 1787, countered the demands of the Pennsylvania minority by making a case against
bills of rights that threw the opposition into confusion and
drove the debate over ratification from that time on. Taking
the offensive, Wilson contrasted state constitutions, where all
rights not expressly reserved to citizens were considered to
be granted (as powers) to their representatives, to the federal

[19] See McDonald, *Novus Ordo Seclorum*, p. 13. He describes early Americans as thinking about liberty as "a complex and subtle combination of
many rights, powers, and duties, distributed among individuals, society,
and the state."

[20] Richard Henry Lee to Gov. Edmund Randolph, Oct. 16, 1787, *CAF*,
5:116. See also "Letters of Centinel" (I), ibid., 2:143.

[21] On Pennsylvania, see Robert Allen Rutland, *The Ordeal of the Constitution: The Antifederalists and the Ratification Struggle of 1787–1788* (Norman,
Okla., 1966), pp. 49–65.

Constitution, a document of expressed powers, in which all powers not expressly granted to representatives were presumed to be reserved (as rights) to the people. Thrown onto the defensive, Antifederalists responded by criticizing Wilson's blithe reliance on reserved rights. In countering his conclusions, however, many of them accepted his claim about the distinction between reserved and expressed rights and in fact took it even further, suggesting that rights not expressly reserved were not rights at all. Thus, writing in the fall of 1787 in the Philadelphia *Independent Gazetteer*, "An Old Whig" said that without a bill of rights, government is always in danger of degenerating into tyranny, "for it is certainly true, that [here quoting Wilson] 'in establishing the powers of government, the rulers are invested with every right and authority, which is not in explicit terms reserved.'"[22] While the quotations are out of context, as well as confused (Wilson referred to "representatives" rather than "rulers"), the conclusions are clear: unless expressly reserved, rights revert to rulers. "Hence it is," continued "Old Whig," "that we find the patriots, in all ages of the world, so very solicitous to obtain explicit engagements from their rulers, stipulating, expressly, for the preservation of particular rights and privileges."[23]

Rights expressly reserved were different from rights declared. Antifederalists assumed that rights arose out of a continuing series of struggles between the people and their rulers. For "Old Whig," however, these struggles seemed less important than their constitutional consequences, the "grants or reservations of privileges appealed to in the struggles between the rulers and the people."[24] Thus he could condense the course of English liberty into a list of documents, including Magna Charta, the Petition of Right, and the 1689 Bill of Rights, along with "other instances to shew the care and watchfulness of that nation . . . to obtain the most explicit declarations in favor of their liberties."[25] "Old Whig" connected

[22] "Essays of an Old Whig" (IV), *CAF,* 3:33.

[23] Ibid.

[24] Ibid.

[25] Ibid., p. 34.

these documents to the American context, describing how the people of this country "in forming the constitutions of the several states, took care to secure themselves by bills of rights, so as to prevent, as far as possible, the encroachment of their future rulers upon the rights of the people."[26] The descriptions echo with traditional republican terminology. Yet in describing rights, "Old Whig" defined them differently—at least slightly differently—from earlier republican writers: as "privileges" rather than powers; as protecting the people from the "encroachments" of their rulers rather than securing their right to govern themselves; as "bills" rather than compacts. Rejecting Wilson's contention that any expression of reserved rights was redundant, and therefore unnecessary, "Old Whig" went so far as to imply that rights must be expressed to be rights. He wrote: "Some of these rights are said to be *unalienable,* such as the rights of conscience: yet even these have been often invaded, where they have not been carefully secured by express and solemn bills and declarations in their favor."[27]

Expressed rights differ from declared rights in another way as well. The act of expressing rights requires a process of discrimination, of distinguishing different rights and evaluating their respective claims. In declarations, rights are self-evident and are conceived as both inalienable and indivisible. Usually they are summed up in sweeping rhetorical terms, as in the Declaration of Independence, where any and all rights are contained in the claims to life, liberty, and the pursuit of happiness. After Pennsylvania, however, for Antifederalists like "Old Whig," rights are described as separable, being manifested in what he calls "particular rights and privileges."[28] Being distinguishable, they are also different, so that some can be seen as more precious than others. At least a few of these, he suggested, the people "have not even the right to surrender."[29] Appearing to criticize Wilson's argument that to list rights would be not only unnecessary but also unwise, leaving

[26] Ibid.

[27] Ibid.

[28] Ibid., p. 33.

[29] Ibid., p. 34.

important liberties unlisted, "Old Whig" made clear that bills of rights are compilations not only of rights but of absolutely essential rights. He concluded in this vein, arguing that "we ought carefully to guard ourselves by a BILL OF RIGHTS, against the invasion of those liberties which it is essential for us to retain, which it is of no real use to government to strip us of; but which in the course of human events have been too often insulted with all the wantonness of an idle barbarity."[30]

Yet to the extent that expressing rights means distinguishing them, Antifederalists were forced to face a number of questions. What rights were most essential? How would these rights be determined? And what was to become of other rights, the "inessential" ones? Antifederalists were quick to point out that the Constitution begged such questions, since it protected certain rights such as habeus corpus, while leaving others unmentioned, consigning them to be protected by the respective states. Yet they themselves were forced to confront these problems, for as "Old Whig" admitted, "the same argument which proves the necessity of securing one of them shews also the necessity of securing others."[31] Thus began the process of constructing lists of liberties. For "Old Whig," the list included freedom of conscience, liberty of the press, the right to trial by jury, and protection against seizure and search without warrants.[32] For his colleague "A Democratic Federalist" it consisted of protections against a federal judiciary and a standing army.[33] For the pamphleteer "Federal Republican," it required a declaration that whatever rights were not deeded to Congress were reserved to the states.[34] Others added their own contributions, so that by late December, with the publication of the Address of the Minority of the Convention of Pennsylvania, the outlines of a bill of rights was already emerging in the form of a list of fifteen separate

[30] Ibid.

[31] Ibid. (V), p. 37.

[32] Ibid.

[33] See "Essay of a Democratic Federalist," ibid., 3:58–63.

[34] See "A Review of the Constitution Proposed by the Late Convention by a Federal Republican," ibid., p. 85.

amendments, establishing those rights, in the words of the Minority, "without the full, free, and secure enjoyment of which there can be no liberty, and over which it is not necessary for a good government to have the controul." [35]

"THE PEOPLE'S" PREROGATIVES

In Massachusetts, the first state convention to adopt the strategy of formally recommending amendments to the proposed Constitution, the debates focused once more on the role of rights. Among the American states, few if any could claim so long a legacy of republican self-rule. Beginning with the 1641 Body of Liberties, the earliest and most extensive of the colonial charters of liberties, and continuing through the 1780 state constitution, with its distinctive call for the reservation of state rights, Massachusetts had acted as a model in protecting the prerogatives of the people. [36] Antifederalists in particular, led by living legends like Samuel Adams and John Hancock, saw ratification as a struggle to secure Revolutionary rights, including especially the rights of states to govern themselves. In the postwar period, these concerns were economic as well as political, for commerce-conscious citizens of Massachusetts, in alliance with their New England neighbors, saw themselves as economic rivals of Philadelphia and the Mid-Atlantic states and of the South. Fearful that the new Constitution would threaten their tenuous place in the economy of the new nation, Antifederalists in Massachusetts began with a ringing defense of the Confederation and of the sovereign rights of states under it. In his letter of January 29, 1788, apparently written in response to broadsides from Connecticut conservatives like the "Landholder," Agrippa criticized the consolidating effects of the new Constitution, especially the powers of Congress to regulate commerce and to tax, and of the federal courts to preside over property cases, including those involving citizens of a single state. He wrote, "To any

[35] "The Address and Reasons of Dissent of the Minority of the Convention of Pennsylvania to Their Constituents," ibid., p. 157.

[36] See Bernard Schwartz, *The Great Rights of Mankind: A History of the American Bill of Rights* (New York, 1977), pp. 35–38, 82–85, 125–29.

body who will be at the trouble to read the new system, it is evidently in the same situation as the state constitutions now possess. It is a compact among the *people* for the purposes of government, and not a compact between states. It begins in the name of the people, and not of the states."[37]

In accepting the assumption that the Constitution was created through a compact of the people rather than of the states, Massachusetts Antifederalists were forced to face a hard choice. Politically, they could accept the new Constitution, adding amendments afterward, or they could reject it outright, holding fast to the existing confederation. Philosophically the choice was even harder, and most, like Agrippa, were ambivalent: fearful of the loss of state power beyond their boundaries, they saw advantages to consolidation at home. In truth, Massachusetts was more like two states than one, divided between city and country, east and west, creditor and debtor. So deep were the divisions, in fact, that they had recently rent the state apart in a virtual civil war, the tax protests that culminated in Shays's Rebellion.[38] Predisposed to side with the popular party against the more exclusive eastern elite but repelled by the excesses of the recent protests, Antifederalists like Agrippa found themselves caught in the middle. On the one hand, they feared strong government, having little sympathy for people in power. "Let us not flatter ourselves that we shall always have good men to govern us," Agrippa wrote. "If we endeavour to be like other nations we shall have more bad men than good ones to exercise extensive powers. That circumstance alone will corrupt them. While they fancy themselves the viceregents of God, they will resemble him only in power, but will always depart from his wisdom and goodness."[39] On the other hand, consolidation did offer some prospect of social order, along with expanded economic opportunities. In fact, assuming that rights could be protected, a self-confident and strong federal government might well do better than a divided and weak state in protecting the

[37] "Letters of Agrippa" (XV), *CAF,* 4:108.

[38] For background, see Rutland, *Ordeal of the Constitution,* pp. 66–68.

[39] "Letters of Agrippa" (XV), *CAF,* 4:109.

liberties of the people. Writing about the Massachusetts bill of rights, Agrippa made the case: "Though our bill of rights does not, perhaps, contain all the cases in which power might be safely reserved, yet it affords a protection to the persons and possessions of individuals not known in any foreign country. In some respects the power of government is a little too confined. In many other countries we find the people resisting their governours for exercising their power in an unaccustomed mode. But for want of a bill of rights the resistance is always by the principles of their government, a rebellion which nothing but success can justify."[40] Applied to the new Constitution, Agrippa's argument suggested that a federal bill of rights might be the key to a consolidated government that could provide both liberty and order. For frightened Antifederalists like Agrippa, who had personally volunteered to lead troops against Shays, the prospect was pleasing. "It is a stale contrivance to get the people into a passion, in order to make them sacrifice their liberty," he continued. "Repentance always comes, but it comes too late."[41]

In the arguments of Agrippa, ironies run rampant, as he criticized the Constitution for failing to protect the people, while accepting, seemingly without realizing it, constitutional conceptions of "the people." Arguing backwards, as it were, and steadily retreating from Revolutionary republican principles, he admitted that the people are not always committed to a common cause. Within the body politic, he continued, there are clear-cut differences between citizens. He wrote, "I know it is often asked against whom in a government by representation is a bill of rights to secure us? I answer, that such a government is indeed a government by ourselves; but as a just government protects all alike, it is necessary that the sober and industrious part of the community should be defended from the rapacity and violence of the vicious and idle."[42] Sounding less like an Antifederalist than a Federalist

[40] Ibid.

[41] Ibid.

[42] Ibid. (XVI), p. 111.

and anticipating *Federalist* No. 10, Agrippa distinguished minorities from majorities and made clear that minorities needed to be protected in their rights. "A bill of rights, therefore, ought to set forth the purposes for which the compact is made, and serves to secure the minority against the usurpation and tyranny of the majority."[43] Quoting John Adams, the godfather of Massachusetts Federalism, he argued that political passions are destructive of rights, be they the passions of the king, the nobility, or the mob. It followed that even in republics, the rights of minorities must be protected. Warning of majority tyranny, Agrippa carried the argument to its logical conclusion: "The experience of all mankind has proved the prevalence of a disposition to use power wantonly. It is therefore as necessary to defend an individual against the majority in a republick as against the king in a monarchy."[44]

Nor was Agrippa alone. For many Massachusetts Antifederalists, perceiving themselves as standing between reactionary rulers and an unmanageable mob, the new Constitution had undeniable advantages, especially when rights were properly protected. Hence the strategy of accepting the Constitution and recommending amendments to it, a strategy that was followed by most of the states from this point on.[45] Yet in taking this political position, Antifederalists were forced to take a revised philosophical position as well, redefining both their notion of the people and of their rights. "A Columbian Patriot," thought to be the Antifederalist author and intellectual Mercy Otis Warren, denounced the decision in her "Observations on the New Constitution," branding the document as a blend of aristocracy and monarchy, the worst of all worlds. Power, she wrote, must reside with the people: "It will be allowed by every one that the fundamental principle of a free government

[43] Ibid.

[44] Ibid.

[45] On the role of this "conciliatory proposition" in the ratification process, see Michael Allen Gillespie, "Massachusetts: Creating Consensus," in Michael Allen Gillespie and Michael Lienesch, eds., *Ratifying the Constitution* (Lawrence, Kans., 1989), pp. 138–67.

is the equal representation of a free people."[46] In defining "the people," however, the "Columbian Patriot" presupposed no compact, no collectivity, no citizenry pursuing its common good. Instead, quoting Blackstone, she assumed the contractual character of civil society: "That the principal aim of society is to protect individuals in the absolute rights which were vested in them by the immediate laws of nature, but which could not be preserved in peace, without the mutual intercourse which is gained by the institution of friendly and social communities."[47] In Massachusetts, Antifederalists continued to demand a bill of rights, but their demands were different from before. Although the amendments adopted by the convention concerned mostly matters of state prerogatives, those that were not adopted, a list offered by Samuel Adams, included a long list of liberties that were both public and personal, including guarantees of a free press. Changing terms, subtle but significant, suggest changing concepts: "the people," defined in the singular, are now the people, an aggregation and a plural term; "the citizenry" has become simply citizens; "freemen" are free men. As for rights, they are described more commonly as belonging to minorities, to groups, and ultimately to individual citizens. Said "Columbian Patriot," "The rights of individuals ought to be the primary object of all government, and cannot be too securely guarded by the most explicit declarations in their favor."[48]

THE PRIVILEGES OF PERSONS

Following Massachusetts, the attention of Antifederalists turned to Maryland, where antiaristocratic sentiments and a long tradition of toleration led to strong support for a bill of rights. In this colonial proprietary colony, closely controlled by the Calvert family until the eve of the Revolution, citizens had a history of relying upon the common law to protect

[46]"Observations on the New Constitution, and on the Federal and State Conventions. By a Columbian Patriot," *CAF,* 4:275.

[47]Ibid.

[48]Ibid., p. 279.

themselves against their aristocratic rulers. Most prominent of these protections was the 1649 Toleration Act, which provided freedom of worship to the Catholics and other Dissenters who found Maryland to be a relative haven of religious freedom. Although the act itself was repealed and subsequently revived, Marylanders would come to conceive of themselves as a part of a pluralistic political culture, a tolerant and welcoming society affording protection not only to citizens, of whom there were few, but also to all inhabitants (or at least all Christian inhabitants) of the colony.[49] Among Antifederalists, who included some of the state's leading lawyers— Samuel Chase, Luther Martin, and William Paca—the common law commitment to antiaristocratic resistance and toleration ran strong. But it was "A [Maryland] Farmer," thought to be John Francis Mercer, who best captured their thinking in a series of letters written in the early spring of 1788. In an answer to the Federalist pamphleteer Aristides, the pseudonym of Alexander Contee Hanson, "A Farmer" denounced him for his aristocratic arguments, and in particular for his claim that bills of rights consisted of concessions of the king. Pointing to the English Bill of Rights, "A Farmer" argued it was the product of citizens acting in convention, "the concession of no Prince," he wrote, "but the Prince of Heaven— whom alone they acknowledged as the author of their liberties."[50] Where others saw rights as the result of resistance, the outcome of a continuing struggle in which the people wrested rights from their rulers, "A Farmer" seemed to see them more as a consequence of the social compact, "an enumeration of those conditions on which the individuals of the empire agreed to confirm the social compact."[51] Most important, "A Farmer" defined the social compact as an agreement among citizens, acting as individuals, through which they limit not only their rulers but also themselves, and protect not just their own rights, but the rights of all persons. In essence, he saw the compact as contractual, a social contract. As he put

---

[49] See Schwartz, *Great Rights of Mankind*, pp. 33–34, 39–40.

[50] "Essays by a Farmer" (I), *CAF*, 5:11.

[51] Ibid.

it, "no power, which they thus conditionally delegated to the majority (in whatever form organized) should be so exercised as to infringe and impair these their natural rights—not vested in SOCIETY, but reserved to each member thereof."[52]

Seeing themselves as a small state surrounded by large neighbors, and as a state cut off from expansion westward, Marylanders were particularly concerned about protecting the rights of small states in the new union and, if possible, adding to them. Luther Martin had made this case at Philadelphia, and he continued to think of himself as champion of the smaller states in the lost cause of preventing ratification.[53] It was "A Farmer," however, who crafted a more moderate and more persuasive Antifederalist position, one that seemed to secure states' rights while at the same time expanding the protection of personal liberties. Thus when Aristides argued that a bill of rights would have usurped the sovereign rights of the states, "A Farmer" answered that adding rights to the new Constitution, far from usurping the rights of states, would be underlining them and adding extra protection. "The convention have actually engrafted some of these natural rights," he argued, referring apparently to protections against bills of attainder and ex post facto laws, "yet no one calls it an usurpation."[54] Indeed, the problem is not that the creators of the Constitution had added too many protections, but too few. "But says Aristides, it would have been a work of great difficulty, if not impossible to have ascertained them—Are the fundamental rights of mankind at this day unknown? Are they so soon forgot? If they are not imprinted on our hearts, they are in several of the constitutions—Although various in form, they are certainly not contradictory in substance."[55] Ironically, while fearing expansion, "A Farmer" set forth an expansive vision of rights. Accepting the Constitution to be

[52] Ibid.

[53] On Maryland's "small state" psychology and on the role of Luther Martin, see Peter S. Onuf, "Maryland: The Small Republic in the New Nation," in Gillespie and Lienesch, eds., *Ratifying the Constitution*, pp. 171–200.

[54] "Essays by a Farmer" (I), *CAF,* 5:13.

[55] Ibid.

a creation not of states but of the people, he argued that its bill of rights must protect not only citizens but persons. Extending beyond state boundaries, rights exist not in politics, because of state compacts, but in society, because of the social contract. These rights, residing not in politics but in society, should be the basis of a federal bill of rights. Said "A Farmer": "If a citizen of Maryland can have no benefit of his own bill of rights in the confederal courts, and there is no bill of rights of the United States—how could he take advantage of a natural right founded in reason, could he plead it and produce Locke, Sydney, or Montesquieu as authority?"[56]

Maryland Antifederalists were predisposed to see rights as personal protections. Prevented by proprietary rule from playing an extensive role in the state's politics, Marylanders found it difficult—outside their experience—to think of rights as popular prerogatives. Unlike their counterparts in states such as Massachusetts or New Hampshire, where traditions of local self-rule were stronger, and where rights tended to be seen as civic obligations, Marylanders had little conception of rights as responsibilities. Instead, drawing on their tradition of toleration, they tended to define rights more defensively, as protections.[57] "A Farmer" showed their thinking in arguing against the claim of Aristides that bills of rights, while useful in monarchies, were unnecessary in representative governments. Taking the opposite argument, "A Farmer" contended that in popular government the danger is even greater, given that the people are subject to "heated passions."[58] Applying the argument to the realm of religion, long a concern of Maryland Catholics, he argued that tyranny is equally detestable whether it be in "the garb of a despot" or the "plain coat of a quaker."[59] Presenting a kind of paradox, that rights are particularly precious in republics, since they protect people from "the people," he made a strong case for the rights of conscience. He closed: "The truth is, that the

---

[56] Ibid.

[57] See Rutland, *Birth of the Bill of Rights*, pp. 48–55.

[58] "Essays by a Farmer" (I), *CAF,* 5:15.

[59] Ibid.

rights of individuals are frequently opposed to the apparent interests of the majority—For this reason the greater the portion of political freedom in a form of government the greater the necessity of a bill of rights."[60]

In Maryland, Antifederalists came to speak of rights as personal possessions. In the debates, they championed all of the rights recommended by Massachusetts and added more, concentrating on those of conscience. Throughout, they tended to talk of liberty, as did Samuel Chase, as *personal* liberty."[61] Defeated decisively in the convention and prevented from recommending amendments, they presented their views in a pamphlet, including a list of some fifteen liberties. Important among these was a provision, the first in the ratification process, to prevent the establishment of a national religion and to allow the free exercise of religious liberty. Significantly, it protected all persons equally and cast religious freedom as an entitlement: "that all persons be equally entitled to protection in their religious liberty."[62] In Maryland, public rights gave way to private ones, prerogatives to protections, "oughts" to "shall nots." In the words of the Maryland minority, rights had become "precautions and securities."[63]

CONSTITUTIONAL CLAIMS

In Virginia, Antifederalists staged their final stand in defense of rights. Inspired by the ringing rhetoric of Patrick Henry and encouraged from afar by Thomas Jefferson, they saw themselves as the last remnant of Revolutionary resistance, protectors of a libertarian past. They also saw themselves as defenders not only of their own state but also of the South,

---

[60] Ibid.

[61] Samuel Chase, "Notes of Speeches," ibid., p. 82.

[62] "Address of a Minority of the Maryland Ratifying Convention," ibid., p. 97.

[63] Ibid., p. 100, and see pp. 96–97. On "positive" and "negative" freedom, see Isaiah Berlin, "Two Concepts of Liberty," in Berlin, *Four Essays on Liberty* (London, 1969), pp. 118–72.

and sometimes the two tended to blur together.[64] Ironically in a state dominated by some extraordinary elites, their thinking was captured best by an anonymous Antifederalist, "The Impartial Examiner," in a series of letters sent to the *Virginia Independent Chronicle* in early 1788. Appearing to respond to Madison's Publius, "Impartial Examiner" contended that republics exist for one reason only: to secure rights. Following Jefferson, he saw these rights as inherent, "pertaining to all mankind in a state of natural liberty."[65] To better secure them, civil compacts are created, agreements among individuals through which they pledge themselves to mutual protection of the rights of one another and by which they create civil society. "Men, therefore, agree to enter into society, that by the united force of *many* the rights of *each* individual may be protected and secured." In short, according to "Examiner," civil compacts are social contracts, public commitments to protect mutual private liberties. The compact, he summed up, is "a *covenant* between *each* with *all*."[66]

Antifederalists in Virginia believed that law existed to limit public power. As libertarian rebels, products of the colonial period, they saw rulers as corrupt and devious, always seeking to extend their power at the expense of the people. Being legalistic in their thinking, they considered legal limitations to provide the surest checks on these rapacious rulers. Moreover, perhaps because many of them were lawyers, they preferred that these legal limits be clearly and expressly codified. So it was that their state Declaration of Rights had gone out of its way to omit any reference whatsoever to the common law, preferring to rely for protection on express written provisions.[67] "Impartial Examiner" explained the theory. With the

[64] On Virginia, see Schwartz, *Great Rights of Mankind*, pp. 67–72; Rutland, *Birth of the Bill of Rights*, pp. 35–40; and Lance Banning, "Virginia: Sectionalism and the General Good," in Gillespie and Lienesch, eds., *Ratifying the Constitution*, pp. 261–99.

[65] "Essays by the Impartial Examiner" (I), *CAF,* 5:175.

[66] Ibid.

[67] See Schwartz, *Great Rights of Mankind*, pp. 67–72.

265

creation of the social contract, persons give up all of their powers over others. These powers are placed in the hands of the state, which serves as a watchman, overseeing the contract by protecting persons from one another. Said "Examiner," each member must "be presumed to give up all those powers into the hands of the state by submitting his whole conduct to the direction thereof."[68] Yet how are persons to be protected from the state itself? "Examiner" stated that they must make the clearest of constitutional claims, demanding their rights through bills and declarations of rights. "Properly defined," he wrote, a right is "a power of claim established by law, to act, or to possess, or to obtain something from others."[69] Without such claims, public power can never be restrained. "Hence results the necessity of an *express stipulation* for all such rights as are intended to be exempted from the civil authority."[70]

Applied to America, the argument is unequivocal. The Constitution creates arbitrary rule. Only with a bill of rights, legally limiting those in power, can it claim to establish free government. According to "Examiner," bills of rights create constitutional boundaries, past which those who hold power cannot pass. Without such boundaries, he wrote, "it cannot be alledged in any case whatsoever, that a breach has been committed—that a right has been violated; as there will be no standard to resort to—no criterion to ascertain the breach, or even to find whether there has been any violation at all. Hence it is evident that the most flagrant acts of oppression may be inflicted; yet, still there will be no apparent object injured: there will be no unconstitutional infringement."[71] Put simply, bills of rights are documents of fundamental law, setting legal standards against which subsequent legislation can be measured. In this regard, "Examiner" made it clear that they pose limitations on popular power. Sounding less like an Antifederalist than a Federalist, he asked how Con-

[68] "Essays by the Impartial Examiner" (I), *CAF,* 5:177.

[69] Ibid.

[70] Ibid.

[71] Ibid., p. 185.

gress can be checked "when no responsibility on the part of Congress has been required by the constitution?"[72] Moreover, although less explicitly than Hamilton or Iredell, "Examiner" seemed to be suggesting some process of constitutional review. At least, he advised, without a bill of rights, laws could be passed that were "totally derogatory to the whole catalogue of rights."[73]

In Virginia, Antifederalists drew the line, insisting on the inclusion of a bill of rights. Not content to continue the Massachusetts strategy of recommending amendments, Virginians made the case for prior amendments, refused to compromise, and were outvoted.[74] Speaking eloquently, at times seeming to speak endlessly, as in one seven-hour speech, Patrick Henry rallied the opposition. Without a bill of rights, he told the delegates, ratification would be an absurdity, an abandonment of the power of the people to their rulers. Worse, it would be an abdication "without check, limitation, or controul."[75] For Henry, bills of rights were barriers and barricades, existing less to set forth the people's prerogatives than to provide them with a set of protections, what he called "checks and guards."[76] Far from precepts or principles, rights were restrictions, legal limitations embedded in fundamental law. He asked: "What barriers have you to oppose to this most strong energetic Government? To that Government you have nothing to oppose. All your defence is given up. This is a real actual defect."[77] According to Henry, bills of rights protected persons and their property. Not lost on some southerners was the implication that among the possessions they protected were slaves. Concluding his final speech to the Virginia convention, Henry chastised those who believed that in "securing the slave trade," they would "sufficiently secure their liber-

[72] Ibid.

[73] Ibid.

[74] See Rutland, *Ordeal of the Constitution,* pp. 218–34.

[75] "Speeches of Henry," June 16, 1788, *CAF,* 5:247.

[76] Ibid.

[77] Ibid., p. 248.

ties."[78] He closed on an uncompromising note: "My mind will not be quieted till I see something substantial come forth in the shape of a Bill of Rights."[79]

Nor did Henry's demands die with the defeat in Virginia. Following in his footsteps, Antifederalists in North Carolina continued to argue that the addition of a bill of rights was not negotiable, and in North Carolina they won, as that state refused to ratify without specific protections for rights. In fact, North Carolinians led by Judge Samuel Spencer took the argument another step further, insisting not only on constitutional protections but also on the strictest constitutional construction of those protections.[80] As Spencer told the convention, there were "certain human rights that ought not to be given up, and which ought in some manner to be secured. With respect to these great essential rights, no latitude ought to be left."[81] With the future Supreme Court justice James Iredell dominating the debates, carving out an expanded role for the Court in carrying out the process of constitutional review, Antifederalists found themselves on the defensive, attempting to control constitutional powers though specific statements of rights. Continuing to press for a bill of rights, Spencer insisted that it be both extensive and explicit: "There is no express negative—no fence against their being trampled upon. They might exceed the proper boundary without being taken notice of. When there is no rule but a vague doctrine, they might make great strides, and get possession of so much power that a general insurrection of the people would be necessary to bring an alteration about. But if a boundary were set up, when the boundary is passed, the people would take notice of it immediately."[82] In the minds of North Carolina Antifeder-

[78] Ibid., June 17, 1788, p. 251.

[79] Ibid.

[80] On the North Carolina debates, see Michael Lienesch, "North Carolina: Preserving Rights," in Gillespie and Lienesch, eds., *Ratifying the Constitution*, pp. 343–67.

[81] "North Carolina Convention Debates," Schwartz, comp., *Roots of the Bill of Rights*, 4:946 (speech of Samuel Spencer, July 29, 1788).

[82] Ibid., p. 952.

alists, rights were neither broad philosophical principles nor high moral maxims. Their role was not to inspire and not to teach. They existed to protect, and the more precise they were, the better they protected. Observed Spencer's colleague, Gen. Joseph McDowall, "I wish to see everything fixed."[83]

LAW AND LEGITIMATION

By the time that Madison introduced his proposed amendments in the First Congress, Antifederalists had become reconciled to their role as an opposition party. While still committed to a bill of rights, they seemed resigned to ratification and to the role they played in ruling under the new Constitution. In fact, with the exception of Elbridge Gerry, who still showed some of the old fire, most appeared to have lost interest or at least to have lost the initiative in securing a bill of rights. Almost alone, Madison carried on the cause. Having become personally persuaded of the importance of a bill of rights and having promised his constituency in the last election that he would introduce one, on June 8, 1789, Madison called on Congress for immediate consideration of his proposed amendments.[84] Opposed by many in his own party, and opposed strongly by those such as Connecticut's Roger Sherman and Georgia's James Jackson, who preferred to attend to issues involving commercial duties and the collection of taxes, he got little help from the other side. Hesitant to be hurried and fearful that Madison could seize the initiative with his less ambitious set of amendments, Antifederalists urged delay. In doing so, they found themselves in the peculiar position of arguing that the most important business at hand was not rights but the collection of revenues. In essence, rights had become secondary to the establishment of an efficient govern-

---

[83] "North Carolina Convention Debates," Schwartz, comp., *Roots of the Bill of Rights*, 4:943 (speech of Joseph McDowall, July 28, 1788).

[84] On James Madison's role, see Schwartz, *Great Rights of Mankind*, pp. 162–71; Rutland, *Birth of the Bill of Rights*, pp. 190–218; and Stuart Leibarger, "James Madison and Amendments to the Constitution, 1787–1789," M.A. Thesis, University of North Carolina at Chapel Hill, 1989.

ment. Said Gerry, who also spoke on June 8: "Whatever might have been my sentiments of the ratification of the constitution without amendments, my sense now is, that the salvation of America depends upon the establishment of this Government, whether amended or not. If the constitution which is now ratified should not be supported, I despair of ever having a government of these United States."[85]

Antifederalists continued to call for the addition of amendments. In advocating delay, Gerry argued that by putting off the debate, supporters of a bill of rights would be in a stronger position. In particular, by delaying the debate they could keep it on the floor of Congress, preventing any bill from being bottled up in a Federalist-controlled committee. At the same time, debate could continue in the public forum, where popular opinion was strongly in favor of a bill of rights. In fact, Antifederalists pointed repeatedly to the role of the public, arguing that the new government would win popular support only by adding protections for rights. Gerry made the case to Congress: "But from the view which we have already had of the disposition of the Government, we seem really to be afraid to administer the powers with which we are invested, lest we give offence. We appear afraid to exercise the constitutional powers of the Government, which the welfare of the State requires, lest a jealousy of our powers be the consequence. What is the reason of this timidity? Why, because we see a great body of our constituents opposed to the constitution as it now stands, who are apprehensive of the enormous powers of Government."[86] Clearly, these Antifederalist arguments were political, intended as they were for the ears of their Federalist counterparts. But they were also philosophical; from this point on, Antifederalists would describe rights differently, not as ends, the purpose of republican self-rule, but as means, practical procedures to establish an efficient form of government. While perhaps important as principles, rights now served the practical purpose of creating legitimacy. Without them, the new government could not govern. As to the goal

[85] "House of Representatives Debates," Schwartz, comp., *Roots of the Bill of Rights*, 5:1037 (speech of Elbridge Gerry, June 8, 1789).

[86] Ibid.

of government, Gerry suggested, it was not freedom, but efficiency. "Thus, and thus only," he argued for amendments, "the Government will have all due energy, and accomplish the end for which it was instituted."[87]

Even as Antifederalists continued to call for rights, they continued to reinterpret them. Antifederalists applauded when, following a six-week delay and a diversion into committee, Madison reintroduced his amendments. Supporting Madison's proposals, they sought to add more of their own, including all of the amendments recommended by all of the state ratifying conventions. Arguing at length for additional amendments, Gerry gently chided Madison: "It is natural, sir, for us to be fond of our own work. We do not like to see it disfigured by other hands."[88] Yet even as they sought more rights, they tended to downplay their significance. Typical was the case of an amendment offered by Representative Thomas Tudor Tucker of South Carolina allowing citizens the right to instruct their representatives. Arguing against Madison, who claimed that instruction could not require a representative to cast a vote in violation of the Constitution, Gerry supported the right to instruct. In the process, however, he found himself admitting that the Constitution was prior to the power of the people: "I admit, sir, that instructions contrary to the constitution ought not to bind, though the sovereignty resides in the people."[89] Continuing the case for instruction, Gerry accepted Madison's argument that the people have no constitutional right to rebel. He went on: "The same gentleman asks if we are to give the power to the people in detached bodies to contravene the Government while it exists. Certainly not; nor does the proposed proposition extend to that point; it is only intended to open for them a convenient mode in which they may convey their sense to their agents."[90] For Gerry, making the assumption that government will be good, rights had become conveniences: "The gentleman therefore

[87] Ibid., p. 1038.

[88] Ibid., 5:1098 (speech of Elbridge Gerry, Aug. 15, 1789).

[89] Ibid., p. 1099.

[90] Ibid.

takes for granted what is inadmissable, that Congress will always be doing illegal things, and make it necessary for the sovereign to declare its pleasure."[91]

Antifederalists were not impressed with the twelve amendments that emerged from the congressional debate. Blocked from adding others, they resigned themselves to making piecemeal revisions and to accepting the rights that had been won. North Carolina's Representative Thomas Burke admitted that the amendments were "very far from giving satisfaction to our constituents; "they are not those solid and substantial amendments which the people expect; they are little better than whip syllabub, frothy and full of wind, formed only to please the palate; or they are like a tub thrown out to a whale, to secure the freight of the ship and its peaceable voyage."[92] For those like Burke, an unreconstructed advocate of rights, all the essential rights had been forgotten. "Upon the whole, I think it will be found that we have done nothing but lose our time, and that it will be better to drop the subject now."[93] In truth, however, there was no going back. Beaten and bitter, Burke confessed to Congress the weakness of the Antifederalist strategy. "He said the people knew, and were sensible, that in ratifying the present constitution, they parted with their liberties; but it was under a hope that they would get them back again. Whether this was to be the case or not, he left it to time to discover."[94]

CONCLUSION

Antifederalists had reason to celebrate when, after revisions in the Senate, Madison's amendments were submitted to the states, where ten of the original twelve were ratified, and the Bill of Rights became law. Throughout the process, from the earliest essay to the last of the votes in the state legislatures, they had been unrelenting in their insistence on a bill

[91] Ibid.

[92] Ibid., 5:1103 (speech of Thomas Burke, Aug. 15, 1789).

[93] Ibid.

[94] Ibid., p. 1106.

of rights. With final ratification, they succeeded, and because of them, our rights became clearer, stronger, and more easily enforceable.

Yet Antifederalists could not celebrate too much. The Bill of Rights that eventually emerged was not their bill of rights. Moreover, the conceptions of rights that it contained were not exactly theirs, although they had played a part in bringing them into being. After 1789 rights became constitutional claims, not fundamental principles, moral standards, or lessons to be learned in the course of civic education. They were seen as protecting persons, not empowering citizens or demanding civic duties from them. Ironically, they allowed for the growth of government by providing procedures to limit its intrusion into the private realm. So it was that Antifederalists were ambivalent. For them, the Bill of Rights was at best a mixed blessing and, at worst, the best of a bad bargain. Making the situation even worse, they knew that they were partly responsible.

Yet Antifederalists did leave a legacy. Since the Civil War, and especially in the course of this century, constitutional rights have been clarified, formalized, and strengthened. In the process, the protections afforded by the Bill of Rights have been extended, especially to African-Americans, to women, and to the poor. Today, the Bill of Rights is stronger than ever. Antifederalists would probably be pleased. Yet they might also suggest that in extending rights, we ought also to be extending the way we think about rights. Remembering these thinkers, we might do well to recall some of their lost lessons: that the purpose of government is to foster freedom, not efficiency; that power belongs to the people, and not to those who serve them; that citizenship is a duty rather than an entitlement; that rights empower as well as protect. With these lessons in mind, we may be inspired to claim more of our rights, which, as the Antifederalists knew, were ours all along.

AKHIL REED AMAR

The Bill of Rights
as a Constitution

To MANY AMERICANS, the Bill of Rights stands as the center-
piece of our constitutional order—and yet constitutional
scholars lack an adequate account of it. Instead of being studied holistically, the Bill has been chopped up into discrete
chunks of text, with each bit examined in isolation. In a typical law school curriculum, for example, the First, Ninth, and
Tenth Amendments are integrated into an introductory survey course on "Constitutional Law"; the Sixth, Eighth, and
much of the Fifth are taught in "Criminal Procedure"; the
Seventh is covered in "Civil Procedure"; the takings clause is
featured in "Property"; the Fourth becomes a course unto itself, or is perhaps folded into "Criminal Procedure" or "Evidence" (because of the judicially created exclusionary rule);
and the Second and Third are ignored.[1]

When we turn from law school classrooms to legal scholarship, a similar pattern emerges. Each clause is typically considered separately, and some amendments—again, the Second
and Third—are generally ignored by mainstream constitutional theorists.[2] To my knowledge no legal academic in the

[1] For a more detailed discussion of how law school teachers have carved
up the Bill of Rights, see Howard W. Gutman, "Academic Determinism: The
Division of the Bill of Rights," *Southern California Law Review* 54 (1981):295,
328–31. Gutman closes his essay with a suggestion that legal discourse
about rights be severed from analysis of constitutional structure (pp. 379–
81). Although this plea stands directly opposed to my own approach, Gutman's little-known essay is the font of many important insights. It deserves
a place on the "must read" list of all serious students of the Bill of Rights.

[2] Sanford Levinson has powerfully documented the general lack of interest in the Second Amendment among mainstream constitutional theorists
("The Embarrassing Second Amendment," *Yale Law Journal* 99 [1989]:637–

twentieth century has attempted to write in any comprehensive way about the Bill of Rights as a whole.[3] So too, today's scholars rarely consider the rich interplay between the original Constitution and the Bill of Rights. Leading constitutional casebooks treat "the structure of government" and "individual rights" as separate blocks[4] (facilitating curricular bifurcation of these subjects into different semesters), and the conventional wisdom seems to be that the original Constitution was concerned with the former; the Bill of Rights, the latter.

In this essay I seek to challenge the prevailing practice by offering an integrated overview of the Bill of Rights as originally conceived, an overview that illustrates how its myriad provisions related to each other and to those of the original Constitution. In the process I hope to refute the prevailing notion that the Bill of Rights and the original Constitution represented two very different types of regulatory strategies.

Conventional wisdom acknowledges that the original Constitution proposed by the Philadelphia Convention focused primarily on issues of organizational structure and democratic self-governance: federalism, separation of powers, bicameralism, representation, and constitutional amendment. By contrast, the Bill of Rights proposed by the First Congress is generally read to have little to say about such issues. Its dominant approach, according to conventional wisdom, was

---

42). Levinson criticizes this lack of interest, but even one so catholic as he is willing to allow the Third Amendment to languish in obscurity (see p. 641).

[3] Accord Gutman, "Academic Determinism," p. 328 and n. 146 ("No work since [the 1890s] has provided an integrated analysis of the Bill of Rights"). The best modern account of the Bill is a book by a practitioner: Edward Dumbauld, *The Bill of Rights and What It Means Today* (Norman, Okla., 1957). The book contains a wealth of historical material about the Bill and its antecedents, but offers little in the way of comprehensive constitutional theory.

[4] See, for example, Gerald Gunther, *Constitutional Law,* 11th ed. (Mineola, N.Y., 1985), pp. 70–402 ("Part II: The Structure of Government") and 403–1633 ("Part III: Individual Rights"). Professor Gunther's casebook is far from unique in this respect (see Gutman, "Academic Determinism," p. 372 and n. 424).

rather different: to vest individuals and minorities with substantive rights against popular majorities. I disagree.

Of course, individual and minority rights did constitute a motif of the Bill of Rights—but not the sole, or even the dominant, motif. A close look at the Bill reveals structural ideas tightly interconnected with language of rights: states' rights and majority rights alongside individual and minority rights, and protection of various intermediate associations—church, militia, and jury—designed to create an educated and virtuous electorate. The main thrust of the Bill was not to downplay organizational structure, but to deploy it; not to impede popular majorities, but to empower them.

Consider, in this regard, Madison's famous assertion in *Federalist* No. 51 that "it is of great importance in a republic not only to guard the society against the oppression of its rulers, but to guard one part of the society against the injustice of the other part."[5] The conventional understanding of the Bill seems to focus almost exclusively on the second issue (protection of minority against majority) while ignoring the first (protection of the people against self-interested government). Yet as I shall show, this first issue was indeed first in the minds of those who framed the Bill of Rights. To borrow from the language of economics, the Bill of Rights was centrally concerned with controlling the "agency costs" created by the specialization of labor inherent in a republican government. In such a government the people (the "principals") delegate power to run day-to-day affairs to a small set of specialized government officials (the "agents"), who may try to rule in their own self-interest, contrary to the interests and expressed wishes of the people. To minimize such self-dealing ("agency costs"), the Bill of Rights protected the ability of local governments to monitor and deter federal abuse, ensured that ordinary citizens would participate in the federal administration of justice through various jury-trial provisions, and preserved the transcendent sovereign right of a majority of the people themselves to alter or abolish government and thereby pronounce the last word on constitutional questions. The essence

[5] *Federalist* No. 51 (Madison), Clinton Rossiter, ed., *The Federalist Papers* (New York, 1961), p. 323.

of the Bill of Rights was more structural than not, and more majoritarian than counter.

MODERN BLINDERS

Before we fix our gaze on the eighteenth-century Bill of Rights, let us briefly consider how nineteenth- and twentieth-century events and ideas have organized our legal thinking, predisposing us to see certain features of the constitutional decalogue and to overlook others.

The Ideology of Nationalism

We inhabit a world whose constitutional terrain is dominated by landmark Supreme Court cases invalidating state laws and administrative practices in the name of individual constitutional rights. Living in the shadow of *Brown* v. *Board of Education* and the second Reconstruction of the 1960s,[6] many lawyers embrace a tradition that views state governments as the quintessential threat to individual and minority rights, and federal officials—especially federal courts—as the special guardians of those rights.[7]

This nationalist tradition has deep roots. Over the course of two centuries, the Supreme Court has struck down state action with far more regularity than it has invalidated acts of coordinate national branches.[8] Early in this century, Justice Oliver Wendell Holmes declared, "I do not think the United States would come to an end if we lost our power to declare an Act of Congress void. I do think the Union would be im-

[6] 347 U.S. 483 (1954).

[7] See, for example, Jesse H. Choper, *Judicial Review and the National Political Process: A Functional Reconsideration of the Role of the Supreme Court* (Chicago, 1980), pp. 252–54. I too am guilty. See, for example, Akhil Reed Amar, "A Neo-Federalist View of Article III: Separating the Two Tiers of Federal Jurisdiction," *Boston University Law Review* 65 (1985):205.

[8] For an elegant discussion of the differences between judicial invalidations of congressional statutes and other forms of judicial review, see Charles L. Black, Jr., *Structure and Relationship in Constitutional Law* (Baton Rouge, La., 1969), pp. 67–93.

periled if we could not make that declaration as to the laws of the several States."[9] James B. Thayer's famous 1893 essay on judicial review also embraced an expansive role for federal courts in reviewing state legislation, even as Thayer preached judicial deference to congressional acts of doubtful constitutionality.[10] Holmes and Thayer had reached maturity during the Civil War era, and they understood from firsthand experience that the constitutional amendments adopted following the war—particularly the Fourteenth Amendment—evinced a similar suspicion of state governments.

In fact, the nationalist tradition is far older than Reconstruction; its deepest roots lie in Philadelphia, not Appomattox. One of the Federalists' most important goals was to forge a strong set of federally enforceable rights against abusive state governments, a goal dramatized by the catalog of rights in Article I, Section 10—the Federalist forebear of the Fourteenth Amendment.[11] Indeed, the very effort to create a strong central government drew much of its life from the Federalists' dissatisfaction with small-scale politics and their belief that an "enlargement" of the government's geographic "sphere" would improve the caliber of public decision-making.[12] The classic statement of this view, of course, is James Madison's *Federalist* No. 10.

Alongside this nationalist tradition, however, lay a states' rights tradition—also championed by Madison—extolling the ability of local governments to protect citizens against abuses by central authorities. Classic statements of this view include Madison's *Federalist* No. 46, his *Virginia Resolutions of 1798,* and his *Report of 1800.* Heavy traces of these ideas ap-

[9] Oliver Wendell Holmes, *Collected Legal Papers* (New York, 1920), pp. 295–96.

[10] James B. Thayer, "The Origin and Scope of the American Doctrine of Constitutional Law," *Harvard Law Review* 7 (1893):129.

[11] See, for example, Akhil Reed Amar, "Of Sovereignty and Federalism," *Yale Law Journal* 96 (1987):1425, 1440–41, and sources cited therein.

[12] See generally Gordon S. Wood, *The Creation of the American Republic, 1776–1787* (Chapel Hill, 1969), pp. 463–67 ("The Abandonment of the States").

pear even in the work of the strong centralizer Alexander Hamilton.[13]

The foundations of this states' rights tradition are even older than those of the nationalist tradition—indeed, older than the Union itself. During the fateful years between the end of the French and Indian War and the beginning of the Revolutionary one, it was colonial governments that took the lead in protecting Americans from perceived parliamentary abuses. Colonial legislatures kept a close eye on the central government; sounded public alarms whenever they saw oppression in the works; and organized political, economic, and (ultimately) military opposition to perceived British abuses.[14] The rallying cry of the Revolution nicely illustrates how states' rights and citizens' rights were seen as complementary, rather than conflicting: "No taxation without representation" sounds in terms of both federalism and the rights of Englishmen.[15]

The complementary character of states' rights and personal rights was dramatized yet again by the Virginia and Kentucky Resolutions of 1798–1800. Self-consciously echoing their colonial forebears, legislators in these two states sounded the alarm when they saw the central government taking actions that they deemed dangerous and unconstitutional.[16] Like its

[13] See generally Amar, "Sovereignty," pp. 1492–1520.

[14] Ibid., pp. 1500–1503.

[15] See also Andrew C. McLaughlin, "The Background of American Federalism," *American Political Science Review* 12 (1918):215, 222, noting overlap between "states' rights" and "individual rights" rhetoric in colonial arguments against Parliament; Alexander H. Pekelis, *Law and Social Action: Selected Essays of Alexander H. Pekelis* (New York, 1950), pp. 94–95.

[16] Eight years earlier, the Virginia legislature had adopted resolutions denouncing as unconstitutional the federal government's assumption of state war debts. See "Virginia Resolutions on the Assumption of State Debts," Henry Steele Commager, ed., *Documents of American History*, 9th ed., 2 vols. (New York, 1973), 1:155–56, describing state legislators as "guardians . . . of the rights and interests of their constituents" and "sentinels placed by them over the ministers of the federal government, to shield it from their encroachments, or at least to sound an alarm when it is threatened with invasion." This 1790 declaration is an important link in the historical chain

predecessor, the "Revolution of 1800" fused rhetoric of federalism and freedom: the Alien and Sedition Acts were seen as violating both the First and the Tenth Amendments.[17] Although many other state legislatures rejected Kentucky's open-ended claims that a state could nullify a federal law, state legislatures as a whole played a central role in the denouement of the new nation's first constitutional crisis. Through their power to select senators and presidential electors, state lawmakers helped sweep the high-Federalist friends of the Alien and Sedition Acts out of national office in the election of 1800, replacing them with Jeffersonians who allowed the repressive acts to expire.

Madison was quite careful to identify the limits, as well as the affirmative scope, of states' rights. State governments could monitor the federal one and mobilize political opposition to federal laws seen as oppressive, but no state entity could unilaterally nullify those laws or secede from the Union.[18] Moreover, Madison's scheme gave the federal government a crucial role in protecting citizens from abusive state governments. Later spokesmen for the states' rights position, such as John C. Calhoun, Jefferson Davis, and Alexander Stephens, disregarded these vital limits to states' rights. Not only did their arguments on behalf of nullification and secession misread the Constitution's federal structure,[19] but these arguments were deployed on behalf of slavery, the ultimate violation of human dignity. Once again, a war was fought on American soil over intertwined issues of states' rights and human rights, but with a critical difference. In sharp contrast to the Revolutionaries' rhetoric of the 1770s, the South's rhetoric of federalism in the 1860s came to

---

connecting the antiparliamentary activity of colonial legislatures before 1776 with the resolutions of 1798. Note especially the use of the revealing word *ministers* to describe federal officers.

[17] See, for example, Philip B. Kurland and Ralph Lerner, eds., *The Founders' Constitution*, 5 vols. (Chicago, 1987), 5:132 (Kentucky Resolution No. 3, intertwining First and Tenth Amendment arguments).

[18] See Amar, "Sovereignty," pp. 1451–66, 1492–1520.

[19] See ibid., pp. 1451–66.

be seen as conflicting with, rather than supportive of, true freedom.

Twentieth-century Americans are still living with the legacy of the Civil War, with modern rhetorical battle lines tracking those laid down a century ago. Thus, in the tradition of Thaddeus Stevens, twentieth-century nationalists recognize the need for a strong national government to protect individuals against abusive state governments but often miss the threat posed by a monstrous central regime unchecked by competing power centers. Conversely, in the tradition of Jefferson Davis, twentieth-century states' rightists wax eloquent about the dangers of a national government run rampant but regularly deploy the rhetoric of states' rights to defend states' wrongs. Sadly, "states' rights" and "federalism" have often served as code words for racial injustice and disregard for the rights of local minorities[20]—code words for a world view far closer to Jefferson Davis's than James Madison's.

What has been lost in this twentieth-century debate is the crucial Madisonian insight that localism and liberty can sometimes work together, rather than at cross-purposes. This is one of the themes that I hope will emerge from a fresh look at Madison's Bill of Rights.

The Logistics of Incorporation

Through the Fourteenth Amendment, almost all the provisions of the Bill of Rights have come to be "incorporated" against the states.[21] Although generally sound,[22] the process of incorporation has had the unfortunate effect of blinding us to the ways in which the Bill has thereby been transformed. Originally a set of largely structural guarantees applying only against the federal government, the Bill has become a body of rights against all government conduct. Originally centered on protecting a majority of the people from a possibly un-

[20] See, for example, ibid., pp. 1425–29, 1488 n. 252; Pekelis, *Law and Social Action*, p. 127.

[21] See Gunther, *Constitutional Law*, pp. 422–40.

[22] But see text accompanying notes 127–40, below (questioning incorporation of establishment clause).

representative government, the Bill has been pressed into the service of protecting vulnerable minorities from dominant social majorities. Given the core concerns of the Fourteenth Amendment, all this is fitting, but because of the peculiar logistics of incorporation, the Fourteenth Amendment itself often seems to drop out of the analysis. We *appear* to be applying the Bill of Rights directly; the Civil War amendment is mentioned only in passing or not at all.[23] Like people with spectacles who often forget they are wearing them, most lawyers read the Bill of Rights through the lens of the Fourteenth Amendment without realizing how powerfully that lens has refracted what they see.

It is time, then, to take off these spectacles and try to see how the Bill of Rights looked *before* Reconstruction. Only then can we fully appreciate some of its most important features, as originally conceived. And only after we understand this original vision can we begin to assess, in a self-conscious and systematic way, how much—if any—of this vision has survived subsequent constitutional developments.[24]

THE ORIGINAL BILL OF RIGHTS

Let us begin by considering two provisions that are not part of our Bill of Rights, but were part of Madison's.

Lost Causes and Forgotten Clauses

Size and representation: first things first. The First Congress proposed a Bill of Rights containing twelve amendments, but only the last ten were ratified by the requisite three-fourths of state legislatures, thereby becoming "valid to all Intents and Purposes, as Part of [the] Constitution."[25] Thus, the words that we refer to as the "First" Amendment really weren't

[23] See, for example, note 94, below.

[24] As shall become clear, this essay only sets the stage for, but does not undertake, this systematic assessment. See text accompanying notes 310–15, below.

[25] U.S. Constitution, Art. V.

"First" in the minds of the First Congress. Hear, then, the words that began *their* Bill of Rights:

> Article the first. . . . After the first enumeration required by the first Article of the Constitution, there shall be one Representative for every thirty thousand, until the number shall amount to one hundred, after which, the proportion shall be so regulated by Congress, that there shall be not less than one hundred Representatives, nor less than one Representative for every forty thousand persons, until the number of Representatives shall amount to two hundred, after which the proportion shall be so regulated by Congress, that there shall not be less than two hundred Representatives, nor more than one Representative for every fifty thousand persons.[26]

This would-be First Amendment obviously is primarily structural; it is an explicit modification of the structural rule set out in Article I, Section 2, mandating that the "number of Representatives shall not exceed one for every thirty Thousand" constituents.[27] Had this original First Amendment been adopted instead of narrowly defeated during the ratification period—it fell one state short of the requisite three-fourths—it would no doubt be much harder for twentieth-century citizens and scholars to ignore the Bill of Rights' emphasis on structure, for the Bill would begin and end with obviously structural provisions. As it stands instead, the fact that the most evident structural provision (our Tenth, their Twelfth, Amendment) sits at the end of the decalogue may mislead us into viewing it as an afterthought, discontinuous with the perceived individual rights theme of the earlier provisions. The original First Amendment suggests otherwise. It is not surprising that *this* amendment was first, for it responded to perhaps the single most important concern of the Antifederalists. Part of this concern focused on demography and geography—on the numerical size of the polity and the spatial

[26] *Documentary History of the Constitution of the United States of America, 1787–1870*, 5 vols. (Washington, D.C., 1894–1905), 2:321–22 (ellipsis in original).

[27] Under this formula, each slave was counted as three-fifths of a free person (U.S. Constitution, Art. I, Sec. 2, Cl. 3).

size of the nation. Classical political theory had suggested that republics could thrive only in geographically and demographically small societies, where citizens would be shaped by a common climate and culture, would have homogeneous worldviews, would know each other, and could meet face-to-face to deliberate on public issues. Models of such republics included the Greek city-states and pre-imperial Rome.[28]

The Federalists' contribution. The Federalists stood this orthodoxy on its head by claiming that a large and modestly heterogeneous society could actually produce a more stable republic than could a small city or state. Madison's *Federalist* No. 10 is today recognized as the most elegant and incisive presentation of this revolutionary idea, but in fact the entire introductory section of *The Federalist Papers* is devoted to confronting the Antifederalist concern about size. In *Federalist* No. 2, John Jay notes the many ways in which (white) Americans shared a basic homogeneity that constituted them as one people, ethnically, culturally, linguistically, historically, commercially, and geographically. Over the next seven papers, Jay and Hamilton sketch the inability of small republics to defend themselves against external threats while maintaining internal democracy. This is primarily a geopolitical and military argument for an extended nation. Finally, Madison takes the stage in *Federalist* Nos. 10 and 14, stressing the purely domestic reasons for preferring a large state.[29]

Madison's first two *Federalist* essays demonstrate the rich interplay among the issues of national size, legislative size, and representation. (The last issue, of course, had played a central role in the debates leading up to and growing out of the American Revolution; anyone claiming that the new Constitu-

---

[28] The best-known exponent of this view, of course, was Montesquieu. This view resounds throughout Antifederalist speeches and writings. For a smattering, see Cecelia M. Kenyon, ed., *The Antifederalists* (Indianapolis, 1966), pp. 24, 39, 101–2, 132–33, 208, 302, 324, reprinting work of Centinel, "The Pennsylvania Minority," John DeWitt, Agrippa, "The Federal Farmer," Cato, and Brutus.

[29] For more discussion, see Akhil Reed Amar, "Marbury, Section 13, and the Original Jurisdiction of the Supreme Court," *University of Chicago Law Review* 56 (1989):443, 469–78.

tion vindicated rather than betrayed that Revolution had to address the subject of representation head on.) Direct democracy, Madison argued, was impossible in any society more expansive than a small city-state.[30] Even in tiny Rhode Island, the mass of citizens could not assemble regularly to decide matters of state; instead, citizens had to rely on a smaller body of government agents to represent them.[31] Rather than cause for alarm, representation was a great blessing in Madison's eyes. A small, select group of representatives could "refine"[32] public opinion and produce more virtuous, wise, and stable decisions. The image here is akin to skimming a small amount of cream (the representatives) off the top of a bucket of milk (the polity).[33] Just as representative systems were better (creamier) than direct democracies, so a large society was preferable to a small one. In order to get the same absolute amount of cream, we need skim an even thinner (and thus richer) layer off the top of a bigger bucket. This last argument, of course, presupposes an absolute numerical limit on the size of the legislature: no matter how large the polity, the legislature could not expand beyond a certain number (just as direct democracy could not expand beyond a certain size), after which deliberation and discussion would be impossible.[34]

Yet even Madison noted that the skimming principle should not be carried to extremes: "By enlarging too much the number of electors [per representative], you render the

[30] *Federalist* No. 14 (Madison), Rossiter, ed., *Federalist Papers*, p. 100.

[31] Compare *Federalist* No. 63 (Madison), ibid., p. 387 ("true distinction . . . [of] the American governments lies *in the total exclusion of the people in their collective capacity,* from any share" in day-to-day governance).

[32] *Federalist* No. 10 (Madison), ibid., p. 82.

[33] For a more elaborate discussion of Madison's precise imagery of "refinement," see Garry Wills, *Explaining America: The Federalist* (Garden City, N.Y., 1981), pp. 223–47.

[34] See, for example, *Federalist* No. 10, Rossiter, ed., *Federalist Papers*, p. 82; *Federalist* No. 55 (Madison), ibid., p. 342; *Federalist* No. 58 (Madison), ibid., p. 360; *Federalist* No. 62 (Madison), ibid., p. 379. See also text accompanying notes 58–61, below.

representative too little acquainted with all their local circumstances and lesser interests."[35]

The Antifederalist's critique. Probably the deepest Antifederalist objection to the Constitution was that the document took the skimming principle too far: Congress was too small, too "refined." Indeed, this *structural* concern underlay most of the Antifederalists' other arguments. Because the legislature was so small, the Antifederalists feared that only "great" men with reputations over wide geographic areas could secure election.[36] Thus, for Antifederalists, the Constitution was at heart an "aristocratic" document, notwithstanding its ringing populist proclamations ("We the People . . .") and the process of ratification itself, which was far more democratic than the process by which the Articles of Confederation and most state constitutions had been adopted.[37] Antifederalists feared that the aristocrats who would control Congress would have an insufficient sense of sympathy with, and connectedness to, ordinary people. Unlike state legislators, "lordly" men in Congress would disdain their lowly constituents, who would in turn lose confidence in the national government. In the end, the new government would be obliged to rule through corruption, force, and fear—with monopolies and standing armies—rather than through mutual confidence.[38] Thus,

[35] *Federalist* No. 10, ibid., p. 83.

[36] This was, of course, part of the Federalists' design. See Wood, *Creation of the American Republic*, pp. 471–518 ("The Worthy against the Licentious"); Wills, *Explaining America*, pp. 216–47.

[37] See, generally, Amar, "Sovereignty"; idem, "Philadelphia Revisited: Amending the Constitution outside Article V," *University of Chicago Law Review* 55 (1988):1043.

[38] See Carol M. Rose, "The Ancient Constitution vs. the Federalist Empire: Anti-Federalism from the Attack on 'Monarchism' to Modern Localism," *Northwestern University Law Review* 84 (1989):74, 90–91, and sources cited therein; Kenyon, ed., *Antifederalists*, p. xl; "Essays of Brutus" (IV), Herbert J. Storing, ed., *The Complete Anti-Federalist*, 7 vols. (Chicago, 1981), 2:382–84 (hereafter cited as *CAF*); "Letters from the Federal Farmer" (II), *CAF*, 2:233–34; Bernard Schwartz, comp., *The Bill of Rights: A Documentary History*, 2 vols. (New York, 1971), p. 1187 (letter from Richard Henry Lee and William Grayson to Speaker of the Virginia House of Representatives, Sept. 28, 1789).

Antifederalists rejected the novel logic of *Federalist* No. 10 in favor of more orthodox political science: because of the attenuated chain of representation, Congress would be far *less* trustworthy than state legislatures.

The Antifederalists' lack of confidence in the federal legislature's ability to truly represent the people made them all the more insistent on popular representation in the judicial branch. Precisely because ordinary citizens could not aspire to serve as national legislators, there was a vital need to guarantee their role as jurors. This was especially true because national laws, adopted by persons unfamiliar with local circumstances, would need to be modified in their application by representatives better acquainted with local needs and customs.[39]

The Antifederalists were not simply concerned that Congress was too small *relatively*—too small to be truly representative of the great diversity of the nation. Congress was also too small *absolutely*—too small to be immune from cabal and intrigue. As Gilbert Livingston pointed out during the New York ratifying convention, the extraordinary powers of the Senate were vested in twenty-six men, fourteen of whom would constitute a quorum, of which eight would make up a majority.[40] Although the House of Representatives looked much better, with its initial allocation of sixty-five members, it could conceivably end up even worse, as Patrick Henry noted in the Virginia ratifying convention: "In the clause under consideration, there is the strangest language that I can conceive. . . . 'The number shall not exceed one for every thirty thousand.' This may be satisfied by one representative from each state. Let our numbers be ever so great, this immense continent may, by this artful expression, be reduced to have but thirteen representatives."[41] And of course, by logic similar to Livingston's, seven representatives could con-

[39] Rose, "Ancient Constitution," p. 91; "Essays by a Farmer" (IV), *CAF,* 5:38.

[40] Jonathan Elliot, ed., *The Debates in the Several State Conventions, on the Adoption of the Federal Constitution,* 2d ed., 5 vols. (New York, 1888), 2:287.

[41] Ibid., 3:46.

ceivably form a quorum, four of whom would constitute a majority!

Friends of the Constitution were not oblivious to these concerns, as Madison's own language in *The Federalist Papers* shows.[42] Indeed, the "thirty thousand" clause set the scene for a dramatic finale to the Philadelphia Convention in which George Washington, for the first and last time, took center stage to address his fellow delegates on a substantive issue.

The date was September 17, 1787—the final day of the Convention. Two days earlier the Convention had unanimously agreed to a final text and had authorized the engrossment of the parchment for signing.[43] This final version provided that the number of representatives not exceed "one for every *forty* thousand." Moments before the copy was finally voted upon and signed, Nathaniel Gorham of Massachusetts "said if it was not too late he could wish, for the purpose of lessening objections to the Constitution, that the clause . . . might be yet reconsidered, in order to strike out 40,000 & insert 'thirty thousand.'"[44] The irregularity of this eleventh hour motion only underscored the importance of the issue. Equally irregular was the response of presiding officer Washington, who had until then officially maintained a scrupulous silence on all substantive issues:

> When the President rose, for the purpose of putting the question, he said that although his situation had hitherto restrained him from offering his sentiments on questions depending in the House, and it might be thought, ought now to impose silence on him, yet he could not forbear expressing his wish that the alteration proposed might take place. It was much to be desired that the objections to the plan recommended might be made as few as possible—The smallness of the proportion of Representatives had been considered by many members of the Convention, an insufficient security for the rights & interests of the people. He

[42] See text accompanying note 35, above.

[43] On the details of engrossing and signing, see Akhil Reed Amar, "Our Forgotten Constitution: A Bicentennial Comment," *Yale Law Journal* 97 (1987):281–83.

[44] Max Farrand, ed., *The Records of the Federal Convention of 1787*, rev. ed., 4 vols. (New Haven, 1937), 2:643–44.

acknowledged that it had always appeared to himself among the exceptionable parts of the plan; and late as the present moment was for admitting amendments, he thought this of so much consequence that it would give much satisfaction to see it adopted.[45]

With the weight of its president behind the measure, the Convention unanimously adopted the amendment. An erasure was made in the parchment, the word "thirty" was inserted where "forty" had been, and the document was then finally approved and signed. Thus, even before the ratification struggle, Federalist supporters of the Constitution were sensitive to the structural issue of congressional size.

During the ratification debates Antifederalists seized upon the issue, taking up Publius's challenge to frame their opposition in *structural* terms: "And the adversaries of the plan promulgated by the convention would have given a better impression of their candor if they had confined themselves to showing that the internal structure of the proposed government was such as to render it unworthy of the confidence of the people."[46] And, again, "All observations founded upon the danger of usurpation ought to be referred to the composition and structure of the government, not to the nature or extent of its powers."[47]

Nowhere was the concern with size more evident than in the ratification conventions themselves. Of the six states where conventions endorsed various amendments prior to the meeting of the First Congress—Massachusetts, New Hampshire, New York, North Carolina, South Carolina, and Virginia—all but one (South Carolina) proposed a secure minimum size for the House of Representatives.[48] This proposal was never placed lower than second on a typically long list of desired amendments. Only one principle ever ranked higher—the idea of limited federal power that eventually

---

[45] Ibid., p. 644.

[46] *Federalist* No. 23 (Hamilton), Rossiter, ed., *Federalist Papers*, p. 156.

[47] *Federalist* No. 32 (Hamilton), ibid., p. 196.

[48] Dumbauld, *Bill of Rights*, pp. 161, 175–76, 181, 185–86, 193, 202.

made its way into our Tenth (their Twelfth) Amendment.[49] In the words of leading Antifederalist Melancton Smith at the New York ratifying convention, "We certainly ought to fix, in the Constitution, those things which are essential to liberty. *If any thing falls under this description, it is the number of the legislature.*"[50]

The First Amendment compromise. Given all this, it is not surprising that the First Congress's *First* Amendment attempted further fine tuning of the structure of representation in the lower house. Nor is it surprising that Virginia, the home state of both Madison and Henry, ratified this amendment separately, weeks before approving the rest of the Bill of Rights.[51] What remains to be explained is why the amendment failed, even by a single vote.[52] Although the legislative history on this

[49] Ibid., pp. 163, 175, 180, 181, 185, 189, 201–2.

[50] Elliot, ed., *Debates*, 2:249 (emphasis added). For a sample of similar concerns about congressional size voiced by other Antifederalists, see Kenyon, ed., *Antifederalists*, pp. lii (introductory essay), 12 (Centinel), 37, 49 ("Pennsylvania Minority"), 79–80, 86 (Philadelphiensis), 107–9 (John De-Witt), 192 (George Mason), 209, 213, 216, 222–30 ("The Federal Farmer"), 242, 263 (Patrick Henry), 307, 310–11 (Cato), 361 ("Albany Manifesto"), 375–89 (Melancton Smith), and 396 (Thomas Tredwell). On the size of state legislatures during the Revolution era, see Wood, *Creation of the American Republic*, p. 167.

[51] See *Documentary History of the Constitution*, 2:385–90.

[52] See ibid., pp. 321–90. The ratification tally in this official document corresponds with that in Herman V. Ames, *The Proposed Amendments to the Constitution of the United States during the First Century of Its History* (Washington, D.C., 1897), p. 320, and suggests that the tallies in Schwartz, comp., *Bill of Rights*, 2:1203, and Elliot, ed., *Debates*, 1:339–40, reprinted in Kurland and Lerner, eds., *Founders' Constitution*, 5:41, are in error. Elliot omits both Vermont's ratification of all twelve amendments and Pennsylvania's eventual decision to ratify the (original) First Amendment on Sept. 21, 1791. Elliot also erroneously states that Rhode Island ratified Congress's Second Amendment. Schwartz ignores Pennsylvania's ratification of the First Amendment and mistakenly implies that both Rhode Island and Pennsylvania ratified the original Second Amendment (apparently they did not). Compare Schwartz 2:1203 with 2:1197, 1200–1201. The Holmes Devise account of ratification is also faulty. See Julius Goebel, *History of the Supreme Court of the United States: Antecedents and Beginnings to 1801* (New York, 1971), p. 456.

point is sparse, a close analysis of the text itself yields a couple of possible explanations.

First, the amendment's intricate mathematical formula made little sense. If the population rose from eight to nine million in a decade, the requirement that there be at least two hundred representatives would be inconsistent with the requirement that there be not more than one representative for every fifty thousand people. In effect, the amendment required the population to jump from eight to at least ten million in a single decade! The mathematical oddness of the text is confirmed by the lean legislative history that does exist. When initially passed by the House of Representatives, the amendment was worded identically to its final version with one exception: its last clause provided for "not . . . *less* than one Representative for every fifty thousand persons."[53] So worded, the proposal was sent to the Senate, along with all the other amendments proposed by the House. When the Senate adopted a Bill of Rights whose wording and substance diverged from the House version, the two chambers convened a joint committee to harmonize the proposed bills.[54] At this conference, the word *more* was inexplicably substituted for *less,* and the conference paste-job was hurriedly adopted by both houses under the shadow of imminent adjournment, apparently without deep deliberation about the substitution's (poor) fit with the rest of the clause.[55] Thus it is quite possible that the technical glitches in the First Amendment's formula became evident only during the later process of ratifying Congress's proposed amendments.

Second, and related, what the First Amendment promised in the short term—increased congressional size—it took back in the long run. Its final clauses established a maximum, not a minimum, on congressional size. Even worse, this maximum was more stringent than that in the existing Constitution. In effect, the amendment dangled the bait of more "democracy"

[53] Dumbauld, *Bill of Rights,* p. 213 (emphasis added); *Annals of Congress,* 1st Cong., 1st sess., 1:802 (Aug. 21, 1789).

[54] *Annals of Congress,* 1st Cong., 1st sess., 1:939 (Sept. 21, 1789).

[55] Ibid., p. 948 (Sept. 24, 1789).

now in exchange for more "aristocracy" in the future. Some committed democrats may have been wary of snatching that bait. Tellingly, not a single state ratifying convention had proposed a stricter constitutional maximum on the size of the House.[56]

Why, then, did the joint House-Senate committee insert a maximum? The lack of extant records of the committee's deliberations requires us to speculate, but the most plausible culprit is James Madison, one of three representatives (the other two being John Vining and Roger Sherman) appointed by the House. As we have seen,[57] Madison's *Federalist Papers* presupposed an absolute maximum on the size of the legislature: "Sixty or seventy men may be more properly trusted with a given degree of power than six or seven. But it does not follow that six or seven hundred would be proportionably a better depositary. And if we carry on the supposition to six or seven thousand, the whole reasoning ought to be reversed. . . . In all very numerous assemblies, of whatever characters composed, passion never fails to wrest the scepter from reason. Had every Athenian citizen been a Socrates, every Athenian assembly would still have been a mob."[58]

Unsurprisingly, when Madison initially offered up to the First Congress his proposed amendments to the Constitution, he integrated both minimum and maximum: "the number shall never be less than ____, nor more than ____."[59] Although the full House eventually rejected the idea of a maximum,[60] Madison may well have seen his appointment to the joint committee as a chance to slip his pet provision back in—especially given the previously expressed views of fellow committee member Sherman in support of his earlier provision.[61]

---

[56] Dumbauld, *Bill of Rights*, pp. 175–76, 181, 185–86, 193, 202.

[57] See text accompanying note 34, above.

[58] *Federalist* No. 55, Rossiter, ed., *Federalist Papers*, p. 342.

[59] *Annals of Congress*, 1st Cong., 1st sess., 1:451 (June 8, 1789).

[60] Ibid., p. 802 (Aug. 22, 1789).

[61] Ibid., p. 753 (Aug. 14, 1789).

A final, more obvious explanation for the failure of the First Amendment focuses on Delaware, the only state that ratified the last ten amendments while rejecting the first.[62] Since each state was guaranteed at least one seat in the House of Representatives, Delaware, with its small population and limited room for growth, had selfish reasons to favor as small a House as possible—indeed to endorse the hypothetical congressional bill that Patrick Henry had conjured up in the Virginia ratifying debates *decreasing* the size of the House from sixty-five members to thirteen.[63] Under Henry's nightmare bill, Delaware could achieve equality of representation in both branches, as its delegates had strenuously urged in the Philadelphia Convention during the summer of 1787.[64] Prior to the Convention, the Delaware legislature had gone so far as to issue binding instructions to its delegates to oppose all attempts to modify the one state, one vote rule of the Articles of Confederation.[65] This political explanation for Delaware's vote against the original First Amendment gains added support from the conduct of Delaware Representative Vining. When an early version of Madison's First Amendment initially came up for debate on the floor of the House of Representatives, Vining unsuccessfully sought to amend it in a way that would assure small states more than proportional representation in an expanded House.[66]

Whatever Delaware's reasons for ultimately rejecting Madison's First Amendment, we do well to remember that only a single state—and a tiny one at that—stood between the ten "success stories" of Amendments III-XII, and the "failure" of Amendment I.

Economic self-dealing. The Second Amendment proposed by the First Congress also went down to defeat in the ratification

[62] See note 52, above.

[63] See text accompanying note 41, above.

[64] See, for example, Farrand, ed., *Records of the Convention,* 1:37, 490–92, 500–502.

[65] Ibid., pp. 4, 37; 3:574–75 and n. 6.

[66] *Annals of Congress,* 1st Cong., 1st sess., 1:747 (Aug. 14, 1789).

period, but by a wider margin—only six state legislatures[67] ratified its words: "Article the second. . . . No law, varying the compensation for the services of the Senators and Representatives, shall take effect, until an election of Representatives shall have intervened."[68]

As with the First Amendment, the Second obviously dealt centrally with an issue of governmental structure rather than substantive individual right. The original First Amendment tried to reduce the general danger that federal lawmakers would lack knowledge of and sympathy with their constituents, whereas the concern of the Second was more specific: economic self-interest among senators and representatives, a concern also evident in the emolument clause of the original Constitution's Article I, Section 6. Despite this difference, both amendments shared a fundamentally similar outlook. At base, both addressed the "agency cost" problem of government—possible self-dealing among government "servants" who may be tempted to plunder their "masters," the people—rather than the analytically distinct problem of protecting minorities of ordinary citizens from tyrannical majorities. If anything, both amendments were attempts to strengthen majoritarianism rather than check it since both tried to tighten the link between representatives and their constituents.

Interestingly, of the three states whose ratifying conventions had suggested a congressional salary amendment in 1787–88—Virginia, New York, and North Carolina[69]—only the two southern states voted to ratify the idea when it formally came before their legislatures. Perhaps this was an issue about which New York state legislators felt more natural sympathy with future congressmen than had the specially called, ad hoc convention of the people of New York in 1788. Because the First Congress's First Amendment had focused on a key difference between an "aristocratic" Congress and more "demo-

---

[67] Maryland, North Carolina, South Carolina, Delaware, Vermont, and Virginia. *Documentary History of the Constitution*, 2:321–90; Ames, *Proposed Amendments*, p. 317; see also note 52, above.

[68] *Documentary History of the Constitution*, 2:322 (ellipsis in original).

[69] Dumbauld, *Bill of Rights*, pp. 161, 188, 195, 204–5.

cratic" state legislatures, the latter bodies could cheerfully support that amendment without calling into question their own legitimacy. But the issue of legislative salaries hit closer to home—close to *their own* pocketbooks. How could state legislators vote for Congress's Second Amendment without also triggering public demand for similar amendments to their respective state constitutions regulating their own salaries? Thus, the lukewarm reaction of state legislatures to the original Second Amendment is itself mildly suggestive of a possible "agency cost" gap between the interests of constituents and legislators.

The events of 1816 are also suggestive. When Congress enacted the first increase in congressional pay since 1789, and refused to defer the increase until after the next election, an enraged electorate responded by voting congressional incumbents out of office in record numbers. Opposition to the act found voice not simply in newspapers, but in grand jury presentments, petitions, and local resolutions—all adopted by ordinary citizens.[70]

Our First Amendment

Political rights. The first Congress's first two proposed amendments offer an illuminating perspective on their Third (our First) Amendment. From this perspective, we can see features of that amendment that tend to be obscured by conventional wisdom. Let us begin by considering the second half of the amendment: "Congress shall make no law . . . abridging the freedom of speech, or of the press; or of the right of the people peaceably to assemble, and to petition the Government for a redress of grievances."

Speech and press. Like its two predecessors, this declaration obviously deals with structure and focuses (at least in part) on the representational linkage between Congress and its constituents. Notwithstanding conventional wisdom, several leading scholars have noted the structural role of free speech and

[70] See John Bach McMaster, *A History of the People of the United States from the Revolution to the Civil War*, 8 vols. (New York, 1927), 4:357–62. At least one state legislature also denounced the congressional act (ibid., p. 361).

a free press in a working democracy.[71] Yet many others tend to view these rights as fundamentally minority rights—rights of paradigmatically unpopular individuals or groups to speak out against a hostile and repressive majority.[72] To be sure, even here there is often a weak brand of majoritarianism at work. Political action by today's minority may eventually persuade some members of today's majority or members of the next generation, thus enabling a new majority to emerge in the future. Fittingly, the classic First Amendment dissents of Holmes and Louis Brandeis[73] were themselves exercises of free speech by a minority inspired by the hope of persuading a future majority (of the Court, of course).

However, the perspective furnished by the first two proposed amendments suggests that an even stronger kind of majoritarianism underlies our First Amendment. The body that is restrained is not a hostile majority of the people, but Congress; and the earlier two amendments remind us that congressional majorities may in fact have "aristocratical" and self-interested views in *opposition* to views held by a majority of the people. Thus, while the amendment's text is broad enough to protect the rights of unpopular minorities (such

[71] See, for example, Alexander Meiklejohn, *Political Freedom: The Constitutional Powers of the People* (New York, 1960); Black, *Structure and Relationship,* pp. 33–50.

[72] See, for example, Ronald K. L. Collins and David M. Skover, "The Future of Liberal Legal Scholarship," *Michigan Law Review* 87 (1988):189, 214. The authors' identification of the First Amendment with minority rights is especially revealing in light of their view, to which I subscribe, that the Bill of Rights is less centrally focused on minority rights than on protecting "the entire citizenry from governmental abuses of power." See also William T. Mayton, "Seditious Libel and the Lost Guarantee of a Freedom of Expression," *Columbia Law Review* 84 (1984):91, 127 n. 189 (presenting First Amendment as in large part a federalism provision; but nevertheless implying that its core concern was to prevent majority tyranny). But see text accompanying notes 75–76, below.

[73] *Abrams* v. *United States,* 250 U.S. 616, 624–31 (1919) (Holmes dissenting); *Gitlow* v. *New York,* 268 U.S. 652, 672–73 (1925) (Holmes and Brandeis dissenting); see also *Whitney* v. *California,* 274 U.S. 357, 372–80 (1927) (Brandeis and Holmes concurring).

as Jehovah's Witnesses and Communists),[74] the amendment's historical and structural core was to safeguard the rights of popular majorities (such as the Republicans of the late 1790s) against a possibly unrepresentative and self-interested Congress.

Consider once again Madison's distinction in *Federalist* No. 51 between the two main problems of republican government—first, protecting citizens generally from government officials pursuing their own self-interested agendas at the expense of their constituents, and second, protecting individuals and minorities from tyrannical majority factions of fellow citizens.[75] As did the First Congress's first two amendments, their Third (our First) Amendment betrayed more concern about the first issue than the second. To begin to see this, we need only reflect on the amendment's first word. *Congress* was restrained but not state legislatures. Yet, as Madison's *Federalist* No. 10 reminds us, the danger of majority oppression of minorities (the second issue) was far greater at the state than at the national level. Of course, this was largely because state legislative representation was so much less attenuated than congressional representation, making state legislative majorities far more likely to reflect the unrefined sentiments of popular majorities. Thus, the fact that our First Amendment restrained only Congress suggests that its primary target was attenuated representation, not overweening majoritarianism.[76] Congress was singled out precisely because it was *less* likely to reflect majority will.

Madison himself had a rather different goal. As part of his initial proposed Bill of Rights, he included an amendment

[74] See, for example, *Kingsley Pictures Corp.* v. *Regents,* 360 U.S. 684, 688–89 (1959) (amendment's "guarantee is not confined to the expression of ideas that are conventional or shared by a majority").

[75] See text accompanying note 5, above.

[76] Compare Michael W. McConnell, "Contract Rights and Property Rights: A Case Study in the Relationship between Individual Liberties and Constitutional Structure," *California Law Review* 76 (1988):267, 288–93 (similar structural analysis of contracts and takings clauses based on framework of *Federalist* Nos. 10 and 51 (Madison), Rossiter, ed., *Federalist Papers*).

proscribing states from violating "freedom of the press"[77] and went on to declare, "But I confess that I do conceive, that in a Government modified like this of the Untied States, the great danger lies rather in the abuse of the community than in the legislative body. The prescriptions in favor of liberty ought to be levelled against the quarter where the greatest danger lies, namely, that which possesses the highest prerogative of power. But this is not found in either the executive or the legislative departments of Government, but in the body of the people, operating by the majority against the minority."[78] Madison's proposed amendment also obliged state governments to protect "equal rights of conscience" and "trial by jury in criminal cases" and was soon reworded to protect "speech" as well as "press" from state interference.[79] When the package came up for discussion on the floor of the House, Madison described it as "the most valuable amendment in the whole list. If there was any reason to restrain the Government of the United States from infringing upon these essential rights, it was equally necessary that they should be secured against the State Governments."[80]

[77] *Annals of Congress,* 1st Cong., 1st sess., 1:452 (June 8, 1789); Dumbauld, *Bill of Rights,* p. 208.

[78] *Annals of Congress,* 1st Cong., 1st sess., 1:454–55 (June 8, 1789). Madison had previously expressed the same view in a letter to Thomas Jefferson on the subject of a possible bill of rights: "In our Governments the real power lies in the majority of the Community, and the invasion of private rights is *cheifly* [sic] to be apprehended, not from acts of Government contrary to the sense of its constituents, but from acts in which the Government is the mere instrument of the major number of the constituents" (see Madison to Jefferson, Oct. 17, 1788, William T. Hutchinson et al., eds., *The Papers of James Madison,* 22 vols. to date [Chicago and Charlottesville, Va., 1962-], 11:298). Yet Madison's views were atypical, as his next sentence reveals: "This is a truth of great importance, but not yet sufficiently attended to." Madison went on to say that a bill of rights would probably be most effective where unpopular and unrepresentative government action was at issue. "There may be occasions on which the evil may spring from [government self-interest]; and on such, a bill of rights will be a good ground for an appeal to the sense of the community" (p. 299).

[79] Dumbauld, *Bill of Rights,* pp. 208, 211.

[80] *Annals of Congress,* 1st Cong., 1st sess., 1:784 (Aug. 17, 1789).

Madison's proposal passed the House of Representatives (as the original Fourteenth Amendment!)[81] but died in the Senate.[82] Of course, to the extent that principles of free speech and a free press were implicit in the republican structure of the original Constitution,[83] state legislatures were already bound to observe those principles—especially where citizens sought to speak out about issues of national concern. (Any state effort to stifle this debate would seem vulnerable on supremacy clause grounds.)[84] However, full vindication of the Madisonian vision did not occur until the adoption of *our* Fourteenth Amendment after the Civil War. The equal protection clause of that amendment, directed at state governments, obviously focuses more on overweening majoritarianism that attenuated representation. And strong arguments support a reading of the privileges or immunities clause as incorporating most of the provisions of the Bill of Rights, including the speech and press clauses, against the states.[85]

[81] Dumbauld, *Bill of Rights*, p. 215.

[82] Ibid., pp. 217–19.

[83] See, for example, U.S. Constitution, Art. IV, Sec. 4 (guaranteeing republican government at state level).

[84] See generally Black, *Structure and Relationship*, pp. 33–50. Interestingly, when abolitionist congressmen sought to codify this rule in the 36th Congress, they were voted down 36–20 by a straight party line vote. Their bill was worded as follows: "But the free discussion of the morality and expediency of slavery shall never be interfered with by the laws *of any State* or of the United States; and the freedom of speech and of the press, on this and every other subject of domestic *and national* policy, should be maintained inviolate in all the States" (Alan P. Grimes, *Democracy and the Amendments to the Constitution* [Lexington, Mass., 1978], p. 40, emphasis added).

[85] See generally Michael Kent Curtis, *No State Shall Abridge: The Fourteenth Amendment and the Bill of Rights* (Durham, N.C., 1986); *Adamson* v. *California*, 332 U.S. 46, 92–123 (1947) (Black dissenting). Indeed, incorporation of free speech and free press principles makes especially strong sense in light of the free speech crusade that the (often unpopular) abolitionists had waged from the 1830s on, fighting discriminatory gag rules on abolitionist petitions in Congress, and censorship of abolitionist literature by both southern state governments and a Democrat-controlled federal postal service. See Stephen Higginson, "A Short History of the Right to Petition Gov-

Although many modern speech theorists echo Madison's 1789 fear of popular majorities, we must remember that the First Amendment tradition of "uninhibited, robust, and wide-open" criticism of government celebrated by *New York Times* v. *Sullivan*[86] was born when Madison and Thomas Jefferson successfully appealed to a popular majority during 1798–1800. No court invalidated the Alien and Sedition Acts (unless one cheats by counting the *Sullivan* court itself, 150 odd years later, or the "court of history"[87] it invoked). Rather, a popular majority adjudicated the First Amendment question in the election of 1800 by throwing out the haughty and aristocratic rascals who had tried to shield themselves from popular criticism. (The Sedition Act itself was a textbook example of attempted self-dealing among the people's agents; it criminalized libel of incumbents, but not challengers. Yet another dead giveaway: the act conveniently provided for its own expiration after the next election.)[88] If we see the First Amendment as primarily about minority rights, Jefferson's strategy of appealing to a popular majority seems odd indeed. But once we see the amendment's populist roots, its vindication

---

ernment for the Redress of Grievances," *Yale Law Journal* 96 (1986):142, 158–66; Clement Eaton, *The Freedom-of-Thought Struggle in the Old South* (New York, 1964); Russel Blaine Nye, *Fettered Freedom: Civil Liberties and the Slavery Controversy, 1830–1860* (East Lansing, Mich., 1963); W. Sherman Savage, *The Controversy over the Distribution of Abolition Literature, 1830–1860* (Washington, D.C., 1938). To recast the historical argument into a textual one: at the heart of the Fourteenth Amendment is the idea that no state shall "abridge" the freedoms of free(d)men; it would be odd indeed to refuse to apply the one pair of clauses of the Bill of Rights whose explicit battle cry is "freedom" and whose language prohibiting "abridging" explicitly tracks the "abridg[ment]" language of the privileges or immunities clause (accord Meiklejohn, *Political Freedom*, p. 530).

[86] 376 U.S. 254, 270 (1964).

[87] 376 U.S. at 276.

[88] Contemporary critics of the act highlighted its self-dealing features. See, for example, James Madison, "Report on the Virginia Resolutions," January 1800, Kurland and Lerner, eds., *Founders' Constitution*, 5:141, 144–45; see also *Annals of Congress*, 5th Cong., 2d sess., 8:2153 (July 1798) (remarks of Edward Livingston stressing "majorit[arian]" thrust of speech and press clauses).

by the election of 1800 borders on the poetic. The election of 1816 was less dramatic, but it too highlighted the core role of the press in alerting popular majorities to the dangers of congressional self-dealing.[89]

It becomes even more clear that popular speech was the paradigm of our First Amendment when we recall its historic connection to jury trial; popular bodies outside regular government would protect popular speech criticizing government. The historic common law rule against "prior restraint"[90]—courts could not enjoin a publisher from printing offensive material, but could entertain civil and criminal prosecutions for libel and sedition afterwards—had bite largely because of the structural differences between the two proceedings. The former could occur in equity courts, presided at by permanent government officials on the government payroll (chancellors),[91] but the latter would require the intervention of ordinary citizens (jurors) who could vote for the publisher without reprisal. In the colonies, the celebrated 1730s trial of the New York publisher John Peter Zenger had placed the issue of the jury's role at center stage in libel cases—and it continued to remain there even after the Revolution and Constitution.[92] As we shall see in more detail below,[93] publishers prosecuted under the Alien and Sedition Acts in the late 1790s tried to plead their First Amendment

[89] See text accompanying note 70, above.

[90] See Sir William Blackstone, *Commentaries on the Laws of England*, 4:150–53; Elliot, ed., *Debates*, 2:449–50 (remarks of James Wilson at Pennsylvania ratifying convention); Joseph Story, *Commentaries on the Constitution of the United States*, 3 vols. (Boston, 1833), vol. 3, sec. 1879.

[91] Before *Bloom* v. *Illinois*, 391 U.S. 194 (1968), it appears that American judges, following English authorities, claimed a right to enforce injunctions through contempt proceedings from which juries were excluded, even in cases resulting in serious punishment of the contemner. See Vincent Blasi, "Toward a Theory of Prior Restraint: The Central Linkage," *Minnesota Law Review* 66 (1981):11, 23, 44–45.

[92] See, for example, "Letters of Centinel" (I), *CAF*, 2:136 ("If I use my pen with the boldness of a freeman, it is because I know that *the liberty of the press yet remains unviolated, and juries yet are judges*." Emphasis in original).

[93] See text accompanying notes 265–84, below.

defense to jurors. The judges, after all, had been appointed by the very same (increasingly unpopular) Adams administration that the defendants had attacked in the press.

This episode contrasts sharply with today's practice, where friends of the First Amendment often seek to limit the power of juries on speech questions, such as obscenity vel non, by appealing to Article III judges. Since the First Amendment's center of gravity has (appropriately in light of the later Fourteenth Amendment) shifted to protection of unpopular, minority speech, its natural institutional guardian has become an insulated judiciary rather than the popular jury.[94]

Similarly, today's First Amendment champions tend to see state and local "community standards" of discourse as the paradigmatic threat to free speech, but the amendment's defenders in the 1790s turned to local juries and state legislatures for refuge. After congressional enactment of the Sedition Act, where could opponents vigorously voice their criticism of the act without fear of prosecution under the act itself? In state legislatures, of course. Even if, as the high Federalists claimed, freedom for partisan publishers was not absolute but limited to freedom from prior restraint, who would dare claim that absolute "freedom of speech" did not obtain within constitutionally recognized legislative bodies?[95] Indeed, the very notion of free speech for citizens had grown out of an older tradition establishing *legislative* "speech and debate" immunity from prosecution.[96] The Articles of Confederation had explicitly used the phrase "freedom of speech"

[94] Professors Monaghan and Schauer have both noted this shift, but neither points to the Fourteenth Amendment to justify or explain it—yet another illustration, perhaps, of the invisibility of the incorporation doctrine. See Henry P. Monaghan, "First Amendment 'Due Process,'" *Harvard Law Review* 83 (1970):518, 526–32; Frederick Schauer, "The Role of the People in First Amendment Theory," *California Law Review* 74 (1986):761, 765.

[95] Compare Meiklejohn, *Political Freedom,* pp. 34–35 (discussing absolute right of free political speech and debate in Congress).

[96] See, for example, the Maryland constitution of 1776 (Declaration of Rights), Art. VIII; Massachusetts constitution of 1780, Pt. I, Art. XXI; New Hampshire constitution of 1784, Pt. I, Art. I, Sec. XXX; see also an act for declaring the rights and liberties of the subject and settling the succession

to immunize members of the federal Congress from state libel law,[97] and the Virginia and Kentucky legislatures in 1798 were simply returning the compliment. Thus, even as the Virginia and Kentucky legislators themselves invoked both First and Tenth Amendment protections in arguing that the Alien and Sedition Acts were unconstitutional,[98] their own speech was specially protected by a states' rights gloss on the free speech clause.

In the end, the individual rights vision of the speech and press clauses powerfully illuminates a vital part of our constitutional tradition, but only by obscuring other parts. The special structural role of freedom of speech in a representative democracy; the localist and majoritarian accent of the First Amendment circa 1800; the massive transformation brought about by the Fourteenth Amendment; the competing claims of judge, jury, and electorate to define the boundaries of "free speech"; the obvious "agency" problem of incumbent self-dealing at the heart of the Sedition Act; the special role of free speech in state legislatures—all this and much more are simply bleached out of the standard sketch drawn from the individual rights perspective.

Assembly and petition. When we turn our attention to the assembly and petition clauses, a similar pattern emerges. Both clauses obviously protect individuals and minority groups, but the clauses contain a majoritarian core that contemporary scholarship has virtually ignored. The right *of the people* to assemble does not simply protect the ability of self-selected clusters of individuals to meet together; it is also an express reservation of the *collective* right of We the People to assemble

---

of the crown (Bill of Rights), 1689, 1 W. and M. chap. 2, sec. 9; Leonard W. Levy, *Emergence of a Free Press* (New York, 1985), pp. 102–3. Indeed, of the original thirteen colonies, only Pennsylvania's 1776 constitution extended "freedom of speech" beyond the legislature (Levy, *Emergence of a Free Press*, p. 5). And as Gordon S. Wood has shown, the unusual unicameral legislative system in Pennsylvania can be understood as constituting the citizens themselves as the implicit lower house. See Wood, *Creation of the American Republic*, pp. 231–32, 249–51.

[97] Articles of Confederation (1781), Art. V, Cl. 5.

[98] See text accompanying notes 16–17, above.

in a future convention and exercise our sovereign right to alter or abolish our government by a simple majority vote. In the words of Rousseau's 1762 treatise on the social contract, "The sovereign can act only when *the people are assembled*." [99]

Listen carefully to the remarks of President Edmund Pendleton of the Virginia ratifying convention of 1788:

> *We, the people,* possessing all power, form a government, such as we think will secure happiness: and suppose, in adopting this plan, we should be mistaken in the end; where is the cause of alarm on that quarter? In the same plan we point out an easy and quiet method of reforming what may be found amiss. No, but, say gentlemen, we have put the introduction of that method in the hands of our servants, who will interrupt it from motives of self-interest. What then? . . . Who shall dare to resist *the people?* No, *we* will *assemble in Convention*; wholly recall our delegated powers, or reform them so as to prevent such abuse. [100]

This rich paragraph has it all: primary attention to the "agency" problem of government self-dealing, dogged unwillingness to equate Congress with a majority of the people, and keen appreciation of the collective rights of the people to bring wayward government to heel by *assembling* in convention. Pendleton saw that the "agency" problem of government meant that future amendments might be necessary to bring government under control. Obviously, ordinary government officials—Congress, state legislatures, and so on—could not be given a monopoly over the amendment process, for that would enable them to thwart desperately needed change by self-interested inaction. Hence the need to keep open the special channel of the popular convention acting outside of all ordinary government, convenable, if necessary, by popular petition. [101] (Indeed, it was the very threat of a second constitutional convention that induced many Federalists in the

---

[99] Jean-Jacques Rousseau, *Du Contrat Social* (1762), chap. 12 (emphasis added in my translation; in original, "le Souverain ne sauroit agir que quand le peuple est assemblé").

[100] Elliot, ed., *Debates,* 3:37 (emphasis added).

[101] See text accompanying notes 116–19, below.

First Congress to support a Bill of Rights limiting their own powers, lest a new convention propose even more stringent amendments.)[102]

Pendleton's language reveals the obvious bridge between the Preamble's invocation of "the People" and the reemergence of that phrase in our First Amendment. The Preamble's dramatic opening words, quoted by Pendleton, trumpeted the Constitution's underlying theory of popular sovereignty.[103] Those words and that theory implied a right of "the People" (acting by majority vote in special conventions) to alter or abolish their government whenever they deemed proper: what "the People" had "ordain[ed] and establish[ed]" (by majority vote in special conventions), they or their "posterity" could disestablish at will (by a similar mode).[104] To good lawyers of the late 1780s, Pendleton was merely restating first principles, Madison's very first proposed amendment was a prefix to the Preamble that similarly declared: "*The people* have an indubitable, unalienable, and indefeasible right to reform or change their Government."[105] Not a single representative quarreled with Madison on the substance of this claim, although some considered any prefix superfluous.[106] When Congress eventually decided to add amendments to the end of the document rather than interweave them into the original text, the prefix was abandoned; but the underlying idea survived, repackaged as a guarantee of the right of "*the people* to assemble." Members of the First Congress shared Pendleton's understanding that constitutional conventions

[102] See, for example, *Annals of Congress,* 1st Cong., 1st sess., 1:446 (remarks of John Page, June 8, 1789); Goebel, *History of the Supreme Court,* pp. 413–30.

[103] See Amar, "Sovereignty," p. 1439.

[104] I have elsewhere attempted to develop this argument in much greater detail; my seemingly counterintuitive but increasingly confident view is that Article V does not specify the exclusive mode of lawful constitutional alteration. See Amar, "Philadelphia Revisited."

[105] *Annals of Congress,* 1st Cong., 1st sess., 1:451 (June 8, 1789; emphasis added).

[106] See, for example, ibid., pp. 741, 746 (remarks of James Jackson, Page, and Madison, Aug. 13–14, 1789).

were paradigmatic exercises of this right.[107] As Gordon S. Wood has observed, "Conventions . . . of the people . . . were closely allied in English thought with the people's right to assemble."[108] Thus, our First Amendment's language of "the right of the people to assemble" simply made explicit at the end of the Constitution what Pendleton and others already saw as implicit in its opening. (Many other provisions of the Bill of Rights were also understood as declaratory, inserted simply out of an abundance of caution to clarify preexisting constitutional understandings.)[109]

Pendleton's language about the people's right to assemble was echoed by the Declaration of Rights adopted by the Virginia convention, which included the following language: "That the people have a right peaceably to assemble together to consult for the common good, or to instruct their representatives."[110] This was neither the first nor the last time that the people's asserted rights of assembly and instruction were yoked together. The same pairing had appeared in the Pennsylvania and North Carolina state constitutions of 1776, the Vermont constitutions of 1777 and 1786, the Massachusetts constitution of 1780, and the New Hampshire constitution of 1784, and would later appear in the declarations of rights of the New York, North Carolina, and Rhode Island ratifying

---

[107] See, for example, ibid., p. 446 (reference to "assembling of a convention," remarks of Page, June 8, 1789); see also Amar, "Philadelphia Revisited," p. 1058, and sources cited therein (linking ideas of convention and assembly); James Gray Pope, "Republican Moments: The Role of Direct Popular Power in the American Constitutional Order," *University of Pennsylvania Law Review* 139 (1990):287 (connecting people's right to assemble to conventions and other forms of popular sovereignty and mass mobilization).

[108] Wood, *Creation of the American Republic*, p. 312.

[109] Indeed, the congressional resolution accompanying the Bill explicitly described it as containing "declaratory" as well as "restrictive" provisions (*Documentary History of the Constitution*, 2:321). Our Tenth Amendment is of course an obvious example and was so understood from the outset. See *Annals of Congress*, 1st Cong., 1st sess., 1:458–59 (remarks of Madison admitting that his proto-Tenth Amendment "may be considered as superfluous," June 8, 1789).

[110] Elliot, ed., *Debates*, 3:658–59.

conventions.[111] When Madison proposed the assembly clause
to the First Congress, Thomas Tudor Tucker of South Carolina quickly moved to add to it an express right of the people
"to instruct their Representatives."[112]

The juxtaposition of assembly and instruction is illuminating. Both clauses have strong majoritarian components and
reflect the Antifederalist concern with attenuated representation in Congress. Yet there is a vital difference between the
two rights—a difference that led Madison and his fellow Federalists to embrace the former while successfully opposing the
latter. Instruction would have completely undermined the
Madisonian system of deliberation among refined representatives. All the advantages of "skimming" would be lost if each
representative could be bound by his relatively uninformed
and parochial constituents rather than his conscience, enlightened by full discussions with his fellow representatives
bringing information and ideas from other parts of the country.[113] As Garry Wills has pointed out, all of Madison's central
arguments in *Federalist* No. 10 are premised on a repudiation
of the idea of instruction.[114]

By contrast, Madison and his fellow Federalists could embrace the idea of a popular right to assemble in convention.

[111] Pennsylvania constitution of 1776 (Declaration of Rights), Art. XVI;
North Carolina constitution of 1776 (Declaration of Rights), Art. XVIII;
Vermont constitution of 1777, Chap. 1, Sec. XVIII; Massachusetts constitu-
tion of 1780, Pt. I, Art. XIX; New Hampshire constitution of 1784, Pt. I,
Art. I, Sec. XXXII; Vermont constitution of 1786, Chap. 1, Sec. XXII; El-
liot, ed., *Debates*, 1:328 (New York), 335 (Rhode Island), and 4:244 (North
Carolina).

[112] *Annals of Congress*, 1st Cong., 1st sess., 1:761 (Aug. 15, 1789).

[113] See, for example, ibid., p. 767 (remarks of Michael Jenifer Stone that
instruction "would change the Government entirely" from one "founded
upon representation" into a "democracy of singular properties," Aug. 15,
1789). Stone's formulation precisely tracks Madison's *Federalist* No. 10 distinction between representative republics and direct democracies.

[114] Wills, *Explaining America*, pp. 216–30; see also *Federalist* No. 63, Rossiter, ed., *Federalist Papers*, p. 387. Only after the instruction debate in the
First Congress did state constitutions begin to sever the rights of instruction
and assembly. See, for example, Kentucky constitution of 1792, Art. XII,
Sec. 22.

Unlike instruction, such a right would not continually under-mine ordinary congressional deliberation on day-to-day af-fairs, but would simply reserve to the people the right to meet in future conventions to consider amending the Constitu-tion—just as the people had assembled in convention in the previous months to ratify the Constitution proposed by Madi-son and his fellow Federalists. Under the Federalists' "two track" scheme, ordinary legislation during moments of "nor-mal politics" should be reserved to the legislature, but We the People could take center stage during "constitutional mo-ments."[115] Thus, like the rights *of the people* explicitly reserved in the Ninth and Tenth Amendments, discussed below, the assembly clause has important implications for the structural process of constitutional amendment.

So too with the petition clause. I have argued elsewhere that whenever a majority of voters so petitioned, Congress would be obliged to convene a constitutional convention, just as it would be when presented with "Application of the Leg-islatures of two thirds of the several States" under Article V.[116] The key textual point here is that the Amendment explicitly guarantees "the right of *the people*" to petition—a formulation that decisively signals its connection to popular sovereignty theory and underscores Gordon Wood's observation that the ideas of petition, assembly, and convention were tightly inter-twined in eighteenth-century America.[117] The precursors of the petition clause suggested by state ratifying conventions

[115] I borrow here the phrasing of my colleague Bruce Ackerman (see Ack-erman, "The Storrs Lectures: Discovering the Constitution," *Yale Law Jour-nal* 93 [1984]:1013). Elsewhere I have explained more precisely the extent of my agreements and disagreements with his theory of constitutional amendment (Amar, "Philadelphia Revisited").

[116] Amar, "Philadelphia Revisited," pp. 1065–66.

[117] Wood, *Creation of the American Republic,* p. 312. See also Edward Dumb-auld, *The Declaration of Independence and What It Means Today* (Norman, Okla., 1950), pp. 103–5 (linking assembly, petition, conventions, and rights "of the people"); Norman B. Smith, "'Shall Make No Law Abridging . . .': An Anal-ysis of the Neglected, but Nearly Absolute, Right of Petition," *University of Cincinnati Law Review* 54 (1986):1153, 1179 (petition right "inextricably linked to the emergence of popular sovereignty").

had obscured these connections. Each of the four conventions spoke of the "people's" right to "assemble" or to alter or abolish government (and as we have seen, these two rights were closely linked); yet each convention described the right of petition in purely individualistic language—a right of "every freeman," "every person," or "every man." [118] Under these formulations, petition appeared less a political than a civil right, akin to the right to sue in court and receive due process. [119] The language and structure of our First Amendment suggest otherwise. As with assembly, the core petition right is collective and popular.

To be sure, like its companion assembly clause, the petition clause also protects individuals and minority groups. Stephen Higginson has persuasively shown that the clause was originally understood as giving extraordinary power to even a single individual, for the right to petition implied a corresponding congressional duty to respond, at least with some kind of hearing. [120]

But to focus only on minority invocations of the right to petition is to miss at least half of the clause's meaning, even if we put to one side its momentous implications for constitutional amendment. Like the other provisions of the First Amendment, the clause is not primarily concerned with the problem of overweening majoritarianism; it is at least equally concerned with the danger of attenuated representation. Higginson shows that part of the purpose and effect of the petitions was to help inform representatives about local con-

[118] Elliot, ed., *Debates*, 1:328 (New York), 2:553 (proposals of Maryland convention committee minority), 3:658–59 (Virginia), 4:244 (North Carolina).

[119] On the political rights–civil rights distinction, see text accompanying note 152, below.

[120] Higginson, "Short History," pp. 155–58. So too a single individual can, merely by drafting and filing a complaint, compel both a defendant to answer upon pain of default, and a judge to provide a judicial opinion applying the law to a set of facts. Less dramatically, a mere fifth of a single house may compel the recording of any vote in the house journal (U.S. Constitution, Art. I, Sec. 5, Cl. 3).

ditions.[121] In eighteenth-century Virginia, for example, more than half of the statutes ultimately enacted by the legislature originated in the form of popular petitions.[122] And as we have seen, Congress's small size gave rise to special concern about whether representatives would have adequate knowledge of their constituents' wants and needs. If we seek historical examples illustrating this point, we need look no further than the 1816 election, when citizens used petitions to Congress as one of several devices to educate their "agents" and each other.[123]

Indeed, the populist possibilities implicit in the petition clause should be evident from a simple side-by-side comparison of the First Amendment's language with English precedent. According to Blackstone's *Commentaries*, in England "*no petition to the king, or either house of parliament, for any alterations in church or state, shall be signed by above twenty persons,* unless the matter thereof be approved by three justices of the peace or the major part of the grand jury, in the country; and in London by the lord mayor, alderman, and common council; *nor shall any petition be presented by more than ten persons at a time.*"[124] In his American edition of Blackstone, St. George Tucker took obvious satisfaction in reminding his readers that, "in America, there is no such restraint."[125]

Like their speech and press clause counterparts, the rights of petition and assembly became applicable against state gov-

[121] Higginson, "Short History," pp. 153–55; accord Smith, "'Shall Make No Law Abridging,'" pp. 1178–79.

[122] Raymond C. Bailey, *Popular Influence upon Public Policy: Petitioning in Eighteenth-Century Virginia* (Westport, Conn., 1979), p. 64.

[123] See text accompanying note 70, above.

[124] Blackstone, *Commentaries*, 1:139 (emphasis added). One scholar has questioned whether these restrictions were rigorously enforced after the Glorious Revolution (Smith, "'Shall Make No Law Abridging,'" p. 1162. But see p. 1166, noting 1781 ruling by Lord Mansfield that restrictions were still in effect).

[125] St. George Tucker, *Blackstone's Commentaries: With Notes of Reference to the Constitution and Laws of the Federal Government of the United States and of the Commonwealth of Virginia*, 4 vols. (Philadelphia, 1803), 1:299–300 app.

ernments only after the adoption of the Fourteenth Amendment. As suggested above, incorporation of these guarantees against state governments makes a good deal of sense in light of the text of the amendment's privileges or immunities clause, its historical purpose of safeguarding vulnerable minorities against majority oppression, and the overall structure of federalism implied by that amendment—namely, that those citizen rights formerly protected against the national government should also be protected against state governments. Nor should we forget the central role the right of petition played in abolitionist thought and practice in the antebellum era.[126] What makes less sense, however, is the Supreme Court's attempt to fully "incorporate" the First Amendment's establishment clause against states. To that clause, and its free exercise counterpart, we now turn.

Religion Clauses

Religion and federalism. The establishment clause did more than prohibit Congress from establishing a national church. Its mandate that Congress shall make no law "*respecting* an establishment of religion" also prohibited the national legislature from interfering with, or trying to *dis*establish, churches established by state and local governments.[127] The key point is not simply that, as with the rest of the First Amendment, the establishment clause limited only Congress and not the states. As we have seen, that point is obvious on the face of the amendment and is confirmed by its legislative history. (It

---

[126] See sources cited note 85, above.

[127] For much more support and elaboration than is possible here, see Dumbauld, *Bill of Rights*, p. 104 and n. 5; Joseph M. Snee, "Religious Disestablishment and the Fourteenth Amendment," *Washington University Law Quarterly* (1954):371; Clifton B. Kruse, Jr., "The Historical Meaning and Judicial Construction of the Establishment of Religion Clause of the First Amendment," *Washburn Law Journal* 2 (1962):65, 84–85, 127–30; Michael A. Paulsen, "Religion, Equality, and the Constitution: An Equal Protection Approach to Establishment Clause Adjudication," *Notre Dame Law Review* 61 (1986):311, 321–23; William K. Lietzau, "Rediscovering the Establishment Clause: Federalism and the Rollback of Incorporation," *De Paul Law Review* 39 (1990):1191.

also, of course, has the imprimatur of Chief Justice John Marshall's opinion in *Barron* v. *Baltimore*.)[128] Nor is the main point exhausted once we recognize that state governments are in part the special beneficiaries of, and rights-holders under, the clause. As we have also seen, the same thing could be said, to some degree, about the free speech clause.[129] The special prick of the point is this: the nature of the states' establishment clause right against federal disestablishment makes it quite awkward to "incorporate" the clause against the states via the Fourteenth Amendment. Incorporation of the free speech clause against states does not negate state legislators' own First Amendment rights to freedom of speech in the legislative assembly. But incorporation of the establishment clause has precisely this kind of effect; to apply the clause against a state government is precisely to eliminate its right to choose whether to establish a religion—a right explicitly confirmed by the establishment clause itself!

To put the point a slightly different way, the structural reasons that counsel caution in attempting to incorporate the Tenth Amendment against the states seem equally valid here. What's more, one of the strongest historical arguments for incorporation is that (contrary to *Barron*) various key drafters of the Fourteenth Amendment thought the Bill of Rights, properly interpreted, generally applied to state governments as well.[130] Yet this argument is equally unavailing for the establishment clause and the Tenth Amendment. There is little evidence that any of the architects of Reconstruction thought that either provision was originally designed to limit state governments.[131] Indeed, the incorporationists' historical exhibit

---

[128] 32 U.S. (7 Pet.) 243 (1833).

[129] See text accompanying notes 95–98, above.

[130] See Curtis, *No State Shall Abridge*.

[131] On the other hand, because states had dissolved their formal establishments well before the Civil War, and at least one state had adopted a state establishment clause with "respecting" language tracking that of the federal First Amendment, the original federalism dimension of the federal clause was probably less obvious in the 1860s than in the early 1800s (see Iowa constitution of 1857, Art. I, Sec. 3).

A—Senator Jacob M. Howard's famous catalog of "personal rights" that should always have applied, and henceforth would apply, against the states—meticulously mentioned each of the four "political" rights under the First Amendment (speech, press, assembly, and petition) but omitted nonestablishment.[132] It of course also omitted the Tenth Amendment.

To my knowledge no scholar or judge has argued for incorporating the Tenth Amendment, but few seem critical of, or even concerned about, the blithe manner in which the establishment clause has come to apply against the states. The apparent reason for this lack of concern, and for the Supreme Court's initial decision to incorporate the clause, is our old friend, conventional wisdom. If we assume that virtually all the provisions of the Bill of Rights, except the Tenth Amendment, were essentially designed to protect individual rights, total incorporation of the first nine[133] amendments seems eminently sensible and wonderfully clean to boot. Unfortunately, that assumption is false.

There is, however, another clean solution to the problem that may well do more justice to history and structure. The Fourteenth Amendment might best be read as incorporating free exercise, but not establishment, principles against state governments. Like the "political rights" clauses we have already considered, the free exercise clause was paradigmatically about citizen rights, not state rights; it thus invites

---

[132] *Congressional Globe,* 39th Cong., 1st sess., 2765–66 (1866). Senator Howard omitted mention of the free exercise clause as well, but as we shall see below, there are stronger structural reasons for incorporating that clause (see text accompanying notes 134–35, below). What's more, other architects of Reconstruction *did* mention "free exercise" or "conscience" while omitting all mention of establishment. See, for example, *Congressional Globe,* 42d Cong., 1st sess., 475–76 (remarks of Henry Dawes, 1871) and 84–85 app. (remarks of John Bingham, 1871). Early judicial opinions also mentioned free exercise while ignoring nonestablishment. See, for example, *The Slaughter-House Cases,* 83 U.S. (16 Wall.) 36, 118–19 (1872) (Bradley dissenting); *United States* v. *Hall,* 26 F. Cas. 79, 81 (C.C.S.D. Ala. 1871; No. 15, 282) (Woods).

[133] On the issue of incorporating the Ninth Amendment, see note 139, below.

incorporation. Indeed, this clause was specially concerned with the plight of minority religions and thus meshes especially well with the minority-rights thrust of the Fourteenth Amendment. Yet unlike incorporation of the establishment clause, application of free exercise principles does not wholly negate states' rights under the original establishment clause. A state would be free to establish one or several churches but would be obliged to respect the free exercise rights of dissenters to opt out. Official establishment is of course not necessarily incompatible with freedom of worship and religious toleration, as England today attests. The American experience confirms this. Although Massachusetts had state-supported churches until 1833, her constitution of 1780 explicitly guaranteed freedom of conscience for religious dissenters—in a provision that immediately preceded language authorizing government-supported churches.[134]

Fittingly, the substitute synthesis of First and Fourteenth Amendment principles I am suggesting here closely tracks James Madison's initial proposals in 1789. As we have already seen, Madison was ahead of his time in his concern for minority rights and his desire for federally enforceable constitutional rights against state governments. Thus he sponsored a quite modern-looking (but unsuccessful) amendment that would have limited state governments' ability to abridge their citizens' freedom of speech, press, and conscience, but that would have allowed state establishment of religion—precisely the same result as my suggested synthesis.[135]

Jefferson, too, understood the states' rights aspects of the original establishment clause. While he argued for an absolutist interpretation of the First Amendment—the federal government should have *nothing* to do with religion, control of which was beyond its limited delegated powers—he was more willing to flirt with governmental endorsements of religion at the state level, especially where no state coercion would impinge on the freedom of conscience of dissenters. The two ideas were logically connected; it was especially easy to be an

---

[134] Massachusetts constitution of 1780, Pt. I, Arts. II-III.

[135] See text accompanying notes 77–80, above.

absolutist about the federal government's involvement in religion if one understood that the respective states had broad authority over their citizens' education and morals. Thus, while *President* Jefferson in 1802 refused to proclaim a day of religious thanksgiving, he had done just that as *Governor* Jefferson some twenty years before.[136] Interestingly, a virtually identical view was voiced in the First Congress on September 25, 1789—the very day the Bill of Rights cleared both houses. When New Jersey Representative Elias Boudinot introduced a bill recommending "a day of public thanksgiving and prayer," South Carolina's Thomas Tudor Tucker rose up in opposition: "It is a religious matter, and as such, is proscribed to us. If a day of thanksgiving must take place, let it be done by the authority of the several States."[137]

Everson v. *Board of Education,* the first Supreme Court case to apply the establishment clause against the states, invoked the views of Madison and Jefferson on religious freedom without so much as noting their views on the interconnected issue of federalism.[138] It is hardly surprising that the author of the Court opinion, Justice Hugo Black, sought to gloss over the special difficulties in applying the establishment clause against the states, given his longstanding commitment to "total incorporation" of the Bill of Rights.[139] More surprising,

[136] Compare Proclamation Appointing a Day of Thanksgiving and Prayer (Nov. 11, 1779), Julian P. Boyd et al., eds., *The Papers of Thomas Jefferson,* 28 vols. to date (Princeton, 1950-), 3:177, with Thomas Jefferson to Attorney General Levi Lincoln, Jan. 1, 1802, Paul Leicester Ford, ed., *The Writings of Thomas Jefferson,* 10 vols. (New York, 1892–99), 8:129; see also Jefferson's Second Inaugural Address, Mar. 4, 1805, Ford, ed., *Writings of Jefferson,* 8:341, 344 (suggesting that states have power over religion where the federal government has none).

[137] *Annals of Congress,* 1st Cong., 1st sess., 1:949–50.

[138] 330 U.S. 1, 11–16 (1947). *Everson's* incorporation drew support from dicta in earlier cases in which the Court held that free exercise principles applied against states (330 U.S. at 15 and n. 22).

[139] See *Adamson* v. *California,* 332 U.S. 46, 68–123 (1947) (Black dissenting). Black appeared to define the Bill of Rights as encompassing only the first eight amendments, 332 U.S. at 72 n. 5, 98, 110. The federalism-based awkwardness of incorporating the Tenth Amendment has already been noted, and Black's disinclination to incorporate the Ninth is sup-

however, is the failure of any other member of the Court, then or since, to raise a serious challenge.[140]

Religion and education. It is apt that the incorporation of the establishment clause first arose in a school case and has had its most visible—if problematic—impact in public schools.

---

ported by some of the historical evidence he cites but is inconsistent with other portions of that evidence (compare 332 U.S. at 105–6, 113–15, quoting speeches referring to "first eight" amendments, with 121–22, quoting material referring to "ten amendments . . . so far as they recognize rights of persons"). Justice Black, of course, read the Ninth Amendment quite narrowly. See *Griswold* v. *Connecticut,* 381 U.S. 479, 518–20 (1965) (Black dissenting). His strongest structural argument against incorporating that amendment—that it's tough to transmogrify a provision "enacted to protect state powers against federal invasion" into "a weapon of federal [judicial] power to prevent state legislatures from passing laws they consider appropriate to govern local affairs" (381 U.S. at 520) relies on a plausible yet debatable reading of the Ninth Amendment. See note 307, below, and sources cited therein. It's a structural argument, however, that applies in spades against Black's own commitment to incorporating the establishment clause.

[140]Abandoning *Everson* would not necessarily destabilize existing understandings. Although a detailed discussion of the possible applications of my substitute synthesis of First and Fourteenth Amendment principles is beyond the scope of my remarks here, consider the example of voluntary school prayer. In the absence of establishment clause constraints, state-supported prayer might not be deemed per se unconstitutional. Yet under the well-established principles of *Board of Education* v. *Barnette,* 319 U.S. 624 (1943) (school pledge case), and *Wooley* v. *Maynard,* 430 U.S. 705 (1977) ("live free or die" case)—free speech cases with heavy free exercise overtones—the First and Fourteenth Amendments would nevertheless require the state to allow any student who objected to opt out without penalty. In some situations—for example, involving children of tender age, or specially strong social pressure from the dominant religious community—even the existence of a formal "no hassle pass" might not be deemed sufficient to render the state-led prayer "voluntary" and thus permissible. Yet if a court were to make this claim about prayer, why treat the Pledge of Allegiance any differently? Once we disregard the ill-fitting establishment clause, the issues implicated by pledges and prayers in public schools tend to converge. If we insist on keeping the ban on school-sponsored prayer in all its strictness by emphasizing the inherently coercive atmosphere of elementary school classrooms, *Barnette* must be expanded to prohibit the Pledge altogether, rather than simply requiring an opt-out. This seems even clearer in light of the post-*Barnette* insertion of the words "under God" into the Pledge.

From one perspective, the twentieth-century state school is designed to serve a function very similar to that of the eighteenth-century state church: imparting community values and promoting moral conduct among ordinary citizens, upon whose virtue republican government ultimately rests.[141] For example, the Pennsylvania constitution of 1776 dealt with public schools and religious organizations in back-to-back sections and treated "religious societies" as entities designed for the "encouragement of virtue" and "for the advancement of religion *or learning*."[142] The Massachusetts constitution of 1780 likewise spoke of "public instructions" and "public teachers" in its provisions for establishing churches and declared that "the happiness of a people, and the good order" of society "depend upon piety, religion, and morality."[143] Consider also its language concerning Harvard College: "Our wise and pious ancestors . . . laid the foundation of Harvard College. . . .

So too, at some point, equal protection principles—which undeniably apply to state governments—might limit the ability of a state to privilege one religion over another. Even without the establishment clause, a court could plausibly hold that a statute declaring that "this is a Christian state" denies equal concern and respect to discrete social minority groups—but only if the court were willing to think in a similar way about a statute declaring English to be the state's "official" language.

Thus, the main reason for abandoning *Everson* is not that it necessarily leads to the wrong results but simply that it rests on faulty history and shaky structural analysis. Emphasizing free exercise, free speech, and equal protection instead of nonestablishment, my substitute synthesis focuses on the key issues of *equality* and *freedom* from coercion. These are obviously the issues at the heart of Reconstruction and should be central to any application of the Fourteenth Amendment, yet, as noted earlier, the Fourteenth Amendment itself too often drops out of the analysis altogether. Ironically, its core themes of equality and freedom are often obscured and even violated by the byzantine edifice of establishment clause doctrine in which the modern Court has imprisoned itself.

The ideas in this note have been importantly influenced by Michael Paulsen. See generally Paulsen, "Religion, Equality, and the Constitution."

[141] See Wood, *Creation of the American Republic*, p. 427 ("Religion was the strongest promoter of virtue, the most important ally of a well-constituted republic").

[142] Pennsylvania constitution of 1776, Secs. 44–45 (emphasis added).

[143] Massachusetts constitution of 1780, Pt. I, Art. III.

Encouragement of arts and sciences, and all good literature, tends to the honor of God, the advantage of the Christian religion, and the great benefit of this and the other United States of America."[144] Harvard, of course, was hardly unique; most of the leading centers of learning in eighteenth-century America had religious roots.[145] Perhaps it is not coincidental that Massachusetts phased out its formal church establishments in the 1830s—precisely the same time that state lawmakers such as Horace Mann began to reinvigorate the complementary institution of public schools.

But to see the analogy between today's public schools and yesterday's state churches is to see once again the federalism dimension of the original establishment clause. The possibility of national control over a powerful intermediate association self-consciously trying to influence citizens' worldviews, shape their behavior, and cultivate their habits obviously struck fear in the hearts of Antifederalists. Yet local control over such intermediate organizations seemed far less threatening, less distant, less aristocratic, less monopolistic—just as local banks were far less threatening than a national one and local militias less dangerous than a national standing army. On a more positive note, allowing state and local establishments to exist would encourage participation and community spirit among ordinary citizens at the grass roots—a vision not too different from that underlying parent-teacher associations or local school boards of our own era. (The Massachusetts constitution of 1780, it should be noted, devolved the designation of established churches upon "the several towns, parishes, precincts, and other bodies politic" within the state.)[146]

The educational importance of religious intermediate asso-

---

[144] Ibid., Pt. II, Chap. V, Art. I.

[145] The linkage between education and religion was so obvious that when Madison proposed giving Congress explicit textual authority to establish a national university, he felt compelled to explicitly deny power to make that university sectarian. The proposal failed (Farrand, ed., *Records of the Convention,* 2:616).

[146] Massachusetts constitution of 1780, Pt. I, Art. III.

ciations resurfaces in the free exercise clause. For if state-established churches in the eighteenth century were in some ways like today's public schools, other churches also played the role of educators, as Alexis de Tocqueville stressed: "Almost all education is entrusted to the clergy."[147] Thus, the free exercise clause protected not simply the "private" worship of an individual but also the nongovernmental yet "public" (Tocqueville's word)[148] education of citizens—the very foundation of democracy.

The Military Amendments

The militia amendment. The Second Amendment reads as follows: "A well regulated Militia, being necessary to the security of a free State, the right of the people to keep and bear Arms, shall not be infringed." As with our First Amendment, the text of the Second is broad enough to protect rights of discrete individuals or minorities, but the amendment's core concerns are populism and federalism.

Populism. We have already noted the populist and collective connotations of the rights of the people to petition and assemble in conventions, rights intimately bound up with the people's transcendent right to alter or abolish their government. Whenever self-interested government actors abused their powers or shirked their duties, "the people" could "assemble" in convention and reassert their sovereignty. "Who shall dare to resist the people?" asked Pendleton with obvious flourish.[149]

To many Antifederalists, the answer seemed both obvious and ominous. An aristocratic central government, lacking sympathy with and the confidence of ordinary constituents, might dare to resist—especially if that government were propped up by a standing army of lackeys and hirelings (mer-

---

[147] Alexis de Tocqueville, *Democracy in America,* 2 vols., ed. Phillips Bradley (New York, 1945), 1:320 n. 4.

[148] Ibid., p. 320.

[149] See text accompanying note 100, above.

cenaries, vagrants, convicts, aliens, and the like). Only an armed populace could deter such an awful spectacle. Hence the need to bar Congress from disarming freemen.

Thus, the Second Amendment was closely linked to the First Amendment's guarantees of petition and assembly. One textual tip-off is the use of the loaded Preamble phrase "the people" in both contexts, thereby conjuring up the Constitution's bedrock principle of popular sovereignty and its concomitant popular right to alter or abolish the national government. More obvious, of course, is the preamble to the amendment itself, and its structural concern with democratic self-government in a "free State." Compare this language with a proposed amendment favored by some Pennsylvania Antifederalists: "The people have a right to bear arms for the defence of themselves and their own State, or the United States, *or for the purpose of killing game.*" [150] Unlike our Second Amendment, this text puts individual and collective rights on equal footing.

History also connected the right to keep and bear arms with the idea of popular sovereignty. In John Locke's influential *Second Treatise of Government,* the people's right to alter or abolish tyrannous government invariably required a popular appeal to arms.[151] To Americans in 1789 this was not merely speculative theory. It was the lived experience of their age. In

---

[150] Dumbauld, *Bill of Rights,* p. 174 (emphasis added).

[151] Apparently, the violent nature of revolution induced John Locke strictly to limit the legitimate occasions for the exercise of the people's right to revolt. The people, said Locke, could reclaim their sovereignty only when government action approached true and systematic tyranny (*The Second Treatise of Government,* ed. Thomas P. Peardon [New York, 1952], secs. 221–43). Between 1776 and 1789, Americans domesticated and defused the idea of violent revolution by channeling it into the newly renovated legal instrument of the peaceful convention. Through the idea of conventions, Americans *legalized* revolution, substituting ballots for bullets. As a result, by 1789 Americans could expand the Lockean right to "revolt"— to alter or abolish government—into a right the people could invoke (by convention) at any time and for any reason. See, for example, Wood, *Creation of the American Republic,* pp. 342–43; Robert Green McCloskey, ed., *Works of James Wilson,* 2 vols. (Cambridge, Mass., 1967), 1:77–79; Elliot, ed., *Debates,* 2:432–33 (remarks of Wilson at Pennsylvania ratifying convention). Yet as the Second Amendment reminds us, even the new legal institutions

their lifetimes they had seen the Lockean words of the Declaration made flesh (and blood) in a Revolution wrought by arms.

To see the connection between arms and populism from another angle, consider the key nineteenth-century distinction between political rights and civil rights. The former were rights of members of the polity—call them Citizens—whereas the latter belonged to all (free) members of the larger society. Alien men and single white women circa 1800 typically could enter into contracts, hold property in their own name, sue and be sued, and exercise sundry other civil rights, but typically could not vote, hold public office, or serve on juries. These last three were political rights, reserved for Citizens. So too, the right to bear arms had long been viewed as a political right, a right of Citizens.[152] Thus, the "people" at the core

---

ultimately rested on force—force that ideally would never need to be invoked yet whose latent existence would nevertheless deter.

[152] There is some fuzziness at the edges, but arms-bearing and suffrage were intimately linked two hundred years ago and have remained so for two centuries. Thus, Abraham Lincoln's initial decision to propose the Thirteenth Amendment, and the Republicans' eventual decision to endorse the black franchise in the Fifteenth Amendment, were importantly influenced by the fact that black soldiers had served the Union during the Civil War (Derrick A. Bell, Jr., "Racial Remediation: An Historical Perspective on Current Conditions," *Notre Dame Law Review* 52 [1976]:5, 9–11). Indeed, Section 2 of the Fourteenth Amendment defined a state's presumptive electorate as all males over twenty-one. This was virtually identical to the definition of the general militia, which encompassed all adult males capable of bearing arms. In our own century, Woodrow Wilson and other national politicians explicitly endorsed women's suffrage in recognition of women's roles as "partners" in the war effort against Germany (Wilson, *War and Peace: Presidential Messages, Addresses, and Public Papers [1917–1924]*, ed. Ray Stannard Baker and William E. Dodd, 2 vols. [New York, 1927], 1:263, 265; Aileen S. Kraditor, *The Ideas of the Woman Suffrage Movement, 1890–1920* [Garden City, N.Y., 1971], p. 166; Grimes, *Democracy and the Amendments*, p. 92). Even more recently, the Twenty-sixth Amendment extending the franchise to eighteen-year-olds grew out of the perceived unfairness of any gap between the Vietnam draft age and the voting age (pp. 141–47). For an extraordinarily rich discussion of the *political* connotations of arms-bearing, see Elaine Scarry, "War and the Social Contract: Nuclear Policy, Distribution, and the Right to Bear Arms," *University of Pennsylvania Law Review* 139 (1991).

of the Second Amendment were Citizens—the same "We the People" who in conventions had "ordain[ed] and estab-lish[ed]" the Constitution and whose right to reassemble in convention was at the core of the First Amendment. Apart from the Preamble, the words "the People" appeared only once in the original Constitution, just a single sentence removed from the Preamble and in a context where "the People" unambiguously connoted *voters*: "The House of Representatives shall be . . . chosen every second Year by the People of the several States."

In emphasizing the structural and populist core of the Sec-ond Amendment, I do not deny that the phrase "the people" can be read broadly, beyond what I have called "the core." As with the language of petition and assembly, other concerns can be comfortably placed under the language's spacious can-opy.[153] But to see the amendment as primarily concerned with an individual right to hunt or protect one's home is like view-ing the heart of the speech and assembly clauses as the right of persons to meet to play bridge or to have sex.[154]

Federalism. Even if armed, unorganized citizens would face an uphill struggle when confronting a disciplined and profes-sional standing army. In *Federalist* No. 28 Alexander Hamilton described a typical nonfederal regime: "If the persons in-trusted with supreme power become usurpers, the differ-ent parcels, subdivisions, or districts of which [the nation]

---

[153] For arguments supporting a broad reading of the amendment as pro-tecting arms-bearing outside of military service, see Stephen P. Halbrook, "What the Framers Intended: A Linguistic Analysis of the Right to 'Bear Arms,'" *Law and Contemporary Problems* 49 (1986):151. But see, for example, *Aymette v. The State*, 21 Tenn. (2 Hum.) 154, 161 (1840) ("The phrase *'bear arms,'* . . . has a military sense, and no other. . . . A man in the pursuit of deer, elk and buffaloes, might carry his rifle every day, for forty years, and, yet, it would never be said of him, that he had *borne arms*"); accord Don B. Kates, Jr., "Handgun Prohibition and the Original Meaning of the Second Amendment," *Michigan Law Review* 82 (1983):204, 219–20, 267. Kates has subsequently modified his position in response to Halbrook's evidence. See idem, "The Second Amendment: A Dialogue," *Law and Contemporary Prob-lems* 49 (1986):143, 149.

[154] See Scarry, "War and the Social Contract."

consists, having no distinct government in each, can take no regular measures for defense. The citizens must rush tumultuously to arms, without concert, without system, without resource."[155] In the federal system of America, however, Article I, Section 8, clause 16 of the Constitution explicitly devolved upon state governments the power of "Appointment of the Officers, and the Authority of training the Militia according to the discipline prescribed by Congress." In the event of central tyranny, state governments could do what colonial governments had done in 1776: organize and mobilize their Citizens into an effective fighting force capable of beating even a large standing army. Wrote Madison in *Federalist* No. 46, "The State governments with the people on their side would be able to repel the danger. . . . [A standing army] would be opposed [by] a militia amounting to near half a million of citizens with arms in their hands, officered by men chosen from among themselves, fighting for their common liberties and united and conducted by governments possessing their affections and confidence."[156]

Yet the "military check of federalism"[157] built into the original Constitution did not quiet Antifederalist fears. Many pointed a suspicious finger at earlier language in clause 16 empowering Congress "to provide for organizing, arming, and disciplining, the Militia." Might Congress try to use the power granted by these words, they asked darkly, to *dis*arm the militia?[158] The Second Amendment was designed to make clear that any such congressional action was off limits.

The obvious importance of federalism to the Constitution's original allocation of military power prompts key questions about federalism's role in the Second Amendment's clarifying gloss. A good many modern scholars have read the Amendment as protecting only arms-bearing in organized "state mili-

---

[155] *Federalist* No. 28 (Hamilton), Rossiter, ed., *Federalist Papers*, p. 180.

[156] *Federalist* No. 46 (Madison), ibid., p. 299.

[157] See generally Amar, "Sovereignty," pp. 1494–1500.

[158] See, for example, Elliot, ed., *Debates*, 3:48, 52 (remarks of Henry at Virginia ratifying convention).

tias," such as SWAT teams and National Guard units.[159] If this reading were accepted, the Second Amendment would be at base a right of state governments rather than Citizens. If so, the amendment would be analogous to the establishment clause and similarly resistant to incorporation against state governments via the Fourteenth Amendment.[160]

Though in some ways congenial to my overall thesis about the Bill of Rights, this reading doesn't quite work. The states' rights reading puts great weight on the word *militia,* but this word appears only in the amendment's subordinate clause. The ultimate right to keep and bear arms belongs to "the people," not the "states." As the language of the Tenth Amendment shows, these two are of course not identical and when the Constitution means "states," it says so.[161] Thus, as noted above, "the people" at the core of the Second Amendment are the same "people" at the heart of the Preamble and the First Amendment, namely Citizens. What's more, the "militia" as used in the amendment and in clause 16 had a very different meaning two hundred years ago than in ordinary conversation today. Nowadays, it is quite common to speak loosely of the National Guard as "the state militia," but two hundred years ago any band of paid, semiprofessional, part-time volunteers, like today's Guard, would have been called "a *select* corps" or "*select* militia"—and viewed in many quarters as little better than a standing army.[162] In 1789, when used without any qualifying adjective, "the militia" referred

[159] See, for example, John Hart Ely, *Democracy and Distrust: A Theory of Judicial Review* (Cambridge, Mass., 1980), pp. 94–95, 227 n. 76; Laurence H. Tribe, *American Constitutional Law,* 2d ed. (Mineola, N.Y., 1988), p. 299 n. 6. For a more detailed catalog of Second Amendment scholarship, see Kates, "Original Meaning," pp. 206–7.

[160] Tribe, *American Constitutional Law,* p. 299 n. 6.

[161] See U.S. Constitution, Amend. X (distinguishing between "States respectively" and "the people").

[162] See, for example, Kates, "Original Meaning," pp. 214–18; David T. Hardy, "Armed Citizens, Citizen Armies: Toward a Jurisprudence of the Second Amendment," *Harvard Journal of Law and Public Policy* 9 (1986):559, 623–28; "Letters from the Federal Farmer" (III, XVIII), *CAF,* 2:242, 341–42.

to all Citizens capable of bearing arms.[163] The seeming tension between the dependent and the main clauses of the Second Amendment thus evaporates on closer inspection—the "militia" is identical to "the people" in the core sense described above. Indeed, the version of the amendment that initially passed in the House, only to be stylistically shortened in the Senate, explicitly defined the "militia" as "composed of the body of the People."[164] This is clearly the sense in which *"the* militia" is used in clause 16 and throughout *The Federalist Papers,*[165] in keeping with standard usage[166] confirmed by contemporaneous dictionaries, legal and otherwise.

A more plausible bit of text to stress on behalf of a states' rights reading is "well regulated."[167] It might be asked, who, of not state governments, would regulate the militia and organize them into an effective fighting force capable of deterring would-be tyrants in Washington? And does not the right to "regulate" subsume the right to prohibit, as the Supreme Court has explicitly recognized in commerce clause cases such as *Champion* v. *Ames*?[168] And, if so, how can a provision designed to give state governments broad regulatory power over their Citizens' arms-bearing be incorporated against states to limit that very power?

---

[163] In addition to sources cited in note 162, see Stephen P. Halbrook, *That Every Man Be Armed: The Evolution of a Constitutional Right* (Albuquerque, N.Mex., 1984); William E. Nelson, "The Eighteenth-Century Background of John Marshall's Constitutional Jurisprudence," *Michigan Law Review* 76 (1978):893, 920.

[164] Dumbauld, *Bill of Rights,* p. 214.

[165] See, for example, *Federalist* No. 25 (Hamilton), Rossiter, ed., *Federalist Papers,* p. 166; *Federalist* No. 29 (Hamilton), ibid., p. 184; *Federalist* No. 46, ibid., p. 299.

[166] See, for example, Elliot, ed., *Debates,* 3:425 (remarks of Mason at Virginia ratifying convention: "Who are the Militia? They consist now of the whole people"); "Letters from the Federal Farmer" (XVIII), *CAF,* 2:341 ("A militia, when properly formed, are in fact the people themselves . . . and include . . . all men capable of bearing arms").

[167] See, for example, Ely, *Democracy and Distrust,* p. 227 n. 76; Tribe, *American Constitutional Law,* p. 299 n. 6.

[168] 188 U.S. 321 (1903).

Though much stronger than the standard states' rights reading, this chain of argument has some weak links of its own. First, it appears that the adjective "well regulated" did not imply broad state authority to disarm the general militia; indeed, its use in various state constitutional antecedents of the Second Amendment suggests just as the opposite.[169] Second, and connected, the notion that congressional power in clause 16 to "organiz[e]" and "disciplin[e]" the general militia logically implied congressional power to *disarm* the militia entirely is the very heresy the Second Amendment was designed to deny. How, then, can we use the amendment's language to embrace the same heresy vis-à-vis state regulation?[170] What's more, in dramatic contrast to the establishment clause and the Tenth Amendment, the right to keep and bear arms was viewed by key framers of the Fourteenth Amendment as a "privilege of national citizenship" that henceforth would apply, and perhaps should always have applied, against states.[171] Senator Howard, for example, explicitly invoked "the right to keep and bear arms" in his important speech cataloging the "personal rights" to be protected by the Fourteenth Amendment.[172] Howard and others may have been influenced by the antebellum constitutional commentator William Rawle, who had argued in his 1825 treatise that the Second Amendment as written limited both state and federal government—a view embraced by at least one (post-*Barron*) state supreme court in the 1840s.[173]

---

[169] See, for example, Virginia Declaration of Rights (1776), Sec. 13; Delaware Declaration of Rights (1776), Sec. 18; Maryland constitution of 1776 (Declaration of Rights), Art. XXV; New Hampshire constitution of 1784, Pt. I, Art. I, Sec. XXIV; see also Hardy, "Armed Citizens, Citizen Armies," p. 626 n. 328.

[170] Compare *State* v. *Reid*, 1 Ala. 612, 616–17 (1840) (distinguishing between arms regulation and arms prohibition).

[171] See, generally, Halbrook, *That Every Man Be Armed*, pp. 107–53; Stephen P. Halbrook, "The Jurisprudence of the Second and Fourteenth Amendments," *George Mason University Law Review* 4 (1981):1.

[172] *Congressional Globe*, 39th Cong., 1st sess., 2765–66 (1866).

[173] William Rawle, *A View of the Constitution of the United States of America* (Philadelphia, 1829), pp. 120–30; accord *Nunn* v. *State*, 1 Ga. 243 (1846);

There is, however, another area in which the Second Amendment can be seen as analogous to the establishment clause, imposing limits on the federal government but not the states: the draft. Under this reading, the federal government cannot directly draft ordinary Americans into its army but state governments can conscript, organize, and train their respective Citizens—the militia—who can in times of emergency be called into national service. Consider first the key texts in Article I, Section 8: "The Congress shall have Power ... To raise and support Armies ... To provide for calling forth the Militia to execute the Laws of the Union, suppress Insurrections and repel Invasions; To Provide for organizing, arming, and disciplining, the Militia, ... reserving to the States respectively, the Appointment of the Officers, and the Authority of training the Militia according to the discipline prescribed by Congress."

By itself, the authority to "raise" armies no more naturally subsumed a power to conscript soldiers than the authority to "lay and collect Taxes [and] Duties" and to "constitute Tribunals inferior to the supreme Court" naturally subsumed power to draft tax collectors, customs officers, judges, and bailiffs.[174] (Similarly, more than mere implication from the naked text authorizing a navy would seem necessary to allow the Congress to engage in the historically odious practice of impressment.)[175] In 1789 the word *army*—in contradistinction

---

see also *State* v. *Chandler,* 5 La. Ann. 489 (1850) (state regulation of arms case with dictum, "This is the right guaranteed by the Constitution of the United States").

[174] U.S. Constitution, Art. I, Sec. 8, Cls. 1, 9. See Elliot, ed., *Debates,* 4:210 (remarks of Richard Spaight in North Carolina ratifying convention: "Men are to be *raised* by bounty"; emphasis added).

[175] British impressment in the 1770s was one of the major grievances triggering the American Revolution and was explicitly denounced by the Declaration of Independence. In the later impressment debate leading to the War of 1812, Secretary of State James Monroe declared that impressment "is not an American practice, but is utterly repugnant to our Constitution" (*Annals of Congress,* 13th Cong., 3d sess., 28:81 [1814] [remarks of Senator Jeremiah Mason]). Yet even if naval impressment were deemed permissible, army conscription power would not necessarily follow. Historically the two were distinct issues—the British government before the Revolution "did

to *militia*—connoted a *mercenary* force, as even a casual glance at contemporaneous dictionaries reveals.[176] Of course, this was largely why an "army" was feared. It was *not* composed of a randomly conscripted cross-section of the general militia (all Citizens capable of bearing arms), but was instead filled with *hired* guns. These men, full-time soldiers who had sold themselves into virtual bondage to the government, were typically considered the dregs of society—men without land, homes, families, or principles. Full-time service in the army further weakened their ties to civil(ized)/(ian) society, and harsh army "discipline" increased their servility to the government.

Small wonder, then, that many traditional republicans opposed standing armies, at least in peacetime. (Perhaps in war, with the very survival of the nation at stake, an army was the lesser of two evils—"America's" army might be marginally less threatening to domestic liberty than the enemy's army.) Thus, mainstream republican thought in the late eighteenth century saw a "well regulated *Militia*" as the best "security of a free State." Article I clearly gave Congress authority in actual emergencies to federalize the militia instead of raising an

---

attempt to exercise in this country the supposed right of impressment for the Navy, which it never did for the Army." As explained below, the word *army*, in contradistinction to *militia*, connoted a volunteer force. The word *navy* was more ambiguous, as illustrated by the British-American tussles over impressment. These textual and historical points can be recast into a structural argument: impressing "private" sailors who had already voluntarily agreed to abandon ordinary civilian life and submit to the harsh discipline and command on a merchant ship involved a smaller marginal deprivation of liberty than wrenching Citizen farmers from their families and lands through an army draft.

[176] See, for example, *Federalist* No. 24 (Hamilton), Rossiter, ed., *Federalist Papers*, p. 161 (defining "army" as "permanent corps in the pay of government"); *Webster's American Dictionary* (1828). In addition to the sources cited in notes 162–63, above, see John Remington Graham, *A Constitutional History of the Military Draft* (Minneapolis, 1971); Harrop A. Freeman, "The Constitutionality of Direct Federal Military Conscription," *Indiana Law Journal* 46 (1971):333, 337 n. 14; Leon Friedman, "Conscription and the Constitution: The Original Understanding," *Michigan Law Review* 67 (1969):1493; Alan Hirsch, "The Militia Clauses of the Constitution and the National Guard," *University of Cincinnati Law Review* 56 (1988):919, 958–59; Story, *Commentaries*, 3:1179.

army—but only under a system of cooperative federalism designed to maintain the integrity of the militia. Clause 16 painstakingly prescribed the precise role that state governments had to play in training and organizing the militia and in appointing its officers. These carefully wrought limitations in clause 16 were widely seen in 1789 as indispensable bulwarks against any congressional attempt to misuse its power over Citizen militiamen. Yet these bulwarks would become trivial—a constitutional Maginot Line—if Congress could outflank them by relabeling militiamen as army "soldiers" conscriptable at will, in times of war and peace, under the plenary power of the army clause.[177] Seen from another angle, the Constitution's explicit invocation of "the Militia" in clause 16, in contradistinction to its use of "Armies" in clause 12, makes clear that each word is used in its ordinary language sense: "Arm[y]" means *enlisted* soldiers, and "Militia" means Citizen conscripts.[178]

[177] But see Michael J. Malbin, "Conscription, the Constitution, and the Framers: An Historical Analysis," *Fordham Law Review* 40 (1972):805, 824. Malbin claims that although Congress can conscript under the army clause, the militia clause is not thereby rendered trivial. According to him, had Congress not been able to rely on the militia as a backup military force, Congress would have been tempted to keep a large (and thus dangerous) *standing* army at all times. The militia clause removes this temptation and thus adds something valuable, he claims. Malbin's argument fails miserably. If Congress did have army conscription power, as he claims, surely it would have the lesser power under the *army* clause to draft backup army "reserves" obviating the need for large standing armies—but once again, this contingent draft violates the cooperative federalism safeguards imposed by the militia clause.

[178] The idea of a national army based on a national draft is a distinctly modern one, born in Napoleonic France in 1798—a decade after ratification of our Constitution (Harrop A. Freeman, "The Constitutionality of Peacetime Conscription," *Virginia Law Review* 31 [1944]:40, 68; Friedman, "Conscription and the Constitution," pp. 1498–99 and n. 20; Malbin, "Conscription, the Constitution, and the Framers," p. 811). Tellingly, although many leading Antifederalists voiced loud fears about the federal government's power to mistreat conscripted militiamen, virtually nothing was said about possible mistreatment of conscripted army soldiers—the very idea bordered on oxymoron. Put another way, even the most suspicious Antifederalists generally seemed to assume that the federal government could not use the army clause to justify conscription, and no Federalists, of course,

Structure confirms this technical parsing of text. Wretches miserable enough to volunteer as hired guns might deserve whatever treatment that they got at the hands of army officers, but Citizens wrenched by conscription from their land, their homes, and their families deserved better. They were entitled to be placed in units with fellow Citizens from their own locality, and officered by local leaders—men chosen by state governments closest to them and most representative of them, men who were likely to be persons of standing in their communities (indeed, likely to be elected civilian officials), men whom they were likely to know directly or indirectly from civilian society and who were likely to know them.[179] The ordinary harshness of military discipline would be tempered by the many social, economic, and political linkages that preexisted military service, and that would be reestablished thereafter. Officers would know that, in a variety of ways, they could be called to account back home after the fighting was over.

Nor should we forget the relationship among militiamen at the bottom ranks. Men serving alongside their families, friends, neighbors, classmates, and fellow parishioners—in short, their community—would be constantly reminded of civil(ian)/(ized) norms of conduct.[180] They were less likely to

---

ever supported such a reading (Friedman, "Conscription and the Constitution," pp. 1525–33; see also "Essay by Deliberator," *CAF,* 3:178–79. But see "Essays of Brutus" [VIII], *CAF,* 2:406, questioning whether Congress might have impressment power under the army clause but referring to this as a draft "from the militia"). Elsewhere, Brutus took the extreme position that the Article I enumeration of powers imposed no meaningful or sincere limits on congressional authority.

[179] Friedman, "Conscription and the Constitution," p. 1508. States' rights advocates viewed the state appointment of officers as vital. When Madison proposed to limit states to appointments "under the rank of General," the Philadelphia convention voted overwhelmingly against him. Roger Sherman called the modification "absolutely inadmissible," and Elbridge Gerry sarcastically suggested that the convention might as well abolish state governments altogether, create a king, and be done with it (Farrand, ed., *Records of the Convention,* 2:388).

[180] The social aspects of militias are nicely captured in the following account of a typical militia muster in late seventeenth-century Massachusetts:

become uncivilized marauders or servile brutes. Thus, the transcendent constitutional principle of civilian control over the military[181] would be beautifully internalized in the everyday mindset of each militiaman.

In the end, the militia system was carefully designed to protect liberty through localism. Here, as with the Virginia and Kentucky Resolutions, freedom and federalism pulled together. Just as the establishment clause saw a national establishment as far more likely to oppress than state and local establishments—and in the worst-case scenario, it was always easier to flee an oppressive locality or state than the nation as a whole—so here, national conscription was far more dangerous than the state and local militia system. Like the jury of the vicinage, which we shall examine shortly, the militia was a local institution, bringing together representative Citizens to preserve popular values of their society.

Thus far my federalism argument has stressed the language and structure of Article I. Why have I advertised this as a

---

"On the training days, a town's militia company generally assembled on public grounds, held roll call and prayer, practiced the manual of arms and close order drill, and passed under review and inspection by the militia officers and other public officials. There might also be target practice and sham battles followed in the afternoon—when times were not too perilous—by refreshments, games, and socializing" (Russell F. Weigley, *History of the United States Army* [New York, 1967], p. 6). Note how the reference to prayer fits well with the role of local religious establishments in Massachusetts (see text accompanying notes 143–46, above).

[181] At least seven Revolution-era constitutions or bills of rights echoed— almost in haec verba—the language of the Virginia Declaration of Rights (1776), Sec. 13: "In all cases the military should be under strict subordination to, and governed by, the civil power." These provisions were invariably placed alongside paeans to "the militia" and guarantees of the right of "the people" to keep and bear arms. See Pennsylvania constitution of 1776 (Declaration of Rights), Art. XIII; Delaware Declaration of Rights (1776), Sec. 20; Maryland constitution of 1776 (Declaration of Rights), Art. XXVII; North Carolina constitution of 1776 (Declaration of Rights), Art. XVII; Vermont constitution of 1777, Chap. 1, Sec. XV; Massachusetts constitution of 1780, Pt. I, Art. XVII; New Hampshire constitution of 1784, Pt. I, Art. I, Sec. XXVI. See generally Tocqueville, *Democracy in America*, 2:279–302. Although not explicitly analyzing the allocation of military power under the U.S. Constitution, Tocqueville's account of civilian versus professional armies strongly supports my analysis.

Second Amendment argument? Because for me, it is the Second Amendment's gloss on Article I—a synthesis of original Constitution and Bill of Rights, if you will—that is decisive. For the stylized portrait of "army" and "militia" I have just presented was not universally subscribed to in 1789. Hamilton, for example, painted a less affectionate picture of the militia[182] and might well have pointed to the expansive language of the necessary and proper clause to support a national army draft. In contrast, I have up to now omitted all reference to that clause and have read federal power strictly, emphasizing structural arguments that resonate best with Antifederalist and republican ideology. My warrant for this interpretive posture is the Second Amendment. I have read clause 16 jealously and have been especially vigilant about congressional circumvention of its terms because, as we saw above, jealousy and vigilance are at the heart of the amendment's gloss on clause 16.[183] I have emphasized republican ideology about militias and armies because that ideology was expressly written into the amendment's preamble.[184] Truly, no other clause in the Constitution is so obviously, so self-consciously, didactic and ideological, save perhaps the (other) Preamble. If the amendment is not about the critical difference between the vaunted "well regulated Militia" of "the people" and the despised standing army, it is about nothing. And to ask what *makes* this militia "well regulated"—a protector of, rather than a threat to, civilian society—is to confront the social and structural vision outlined above. To put the point yet another way, the Second Amendment takes the expansive word *necessary*—

[182] See, for example, *Federalist* Nos. 25, 29 (Hamilton), Rossiter, ed., *Federalist Papers*.

[183] See text accompanying notes 157–58, above; see also note 179, above.

[184] See *Annals of Congress*, 1st Cong., 1st sess., 1:777 (remarks of Gerry: "What, sir, is the use of the militia? It is to prevent the establishment of a standing army, the bane of liberty"); compare Malbin, "Conscription, the Constitution, and the Framers," p. 824 n. 69 (criticizing overreliance on republican ideology in interpreting militia and army clauses of Article I). Interestingly, at the Philadelphia convention Mason proposed an anti-standing-army preamble to the Article I militia clause but the proposal failed (Farrand, ed., *Records of the Convention*, 2:617).

originally a word on the congressional power side of the ledger, as Chief Justice Marshall stressed in *McCulloch* v. *Maryland*[185]—and puts that word to work as a restriction on Congress. It is a well-regulated militia, and not an army of conscripts, that is *"necessary* to the security of a free State"; the Second Amendment estops Congress from claiming otherwise.

Postconstitutional history supports the foregoing analysis. During the War of 1812 various sorts of federal draft bills were introduced, setting the scene for an important congressional debate over the army and militia clauses of Article I and the gloss of the Second Amendment. Opposition to these bills in the House of Representatives was led by none other than Daniel Webster, who argued that any federal draft under the army clause impermissibly evaded the constitutional limitations on federal use of the militia. The plan was an illegitimate attempt to raise "a standing army out of the militia by draft." [186] Webster's vivid image of the evils of such an evasion of clause 16 should by now be familiar:

> Where it is written in the Constitution, . . . that you may take children from their parents, and parents from their children. . . .
>
> . . . . .
>
> But this father or this son . . . goes to the camp. With whom do you associate him? With those only who are sober and virtuous and respectable like himself? No, sir. But you propose to find him companions in the worst men of the worst sort. Another bill lies on your table offering a bounty to deserters from your enemy. Whatever is most infamous in his ranks you propose to make your own. . . . In the line of your army, with the true levelling of [Napoleonic] despotism, you propose a promiscuous mixture of the worthy and the worthless, the virtuous and the profligate; the husbandman, the merchant, the mechanic of your own country, with [the dregs of Europe] who possess neither interest, feeling, nor character in common with your own people, and who have no other recommendation . . . than their propensity to crimes.[187]

[185] 17 U.S. (4 Wheat.) 316, 419–21 (1819).

[186] Charles M. Wiltse, ed., *Papers of Daniel Webster: Speeches and Formal Writings,* 2 vols. to date (Hanover, N.H., 1986-), 1:21.

[187] Ibid., pp. 25–29.

Webster closed with an invocation of the libertarian localism of the Virginia and Kentucky Resolutions and a quotation of the Right of Revolution clause of the New Hampshire constitution:

> It will be the solemn duty of the State Governments to protect their own authority over their own militia, and to interpose between their citizens and arbitrary power. These are among the objects for which the State Governments exist; and their highest obligations bind them to the preservation of their own rights and the liberties of their people. . . . [My constituents and I] live under a constitution which teaches us that "the doctrine of nonresistance against arbitrary power and oppression is absurd, slavish, and destructive of the good and happiness of mankind." [188]

In the tradition of the Virginia and Kentucky Resolves, representatives of various New England states met in the Hartford Convention of 1814–15 to denounce as unconstitutional any national "drafts, conscriptions, or impressments." [189] The eventual republican triumph on this issue—none of the proposed draft bills passed [190]—should be as central a precedent for our Second Amendment as the 1800 triumph over the Sedition Act is for our First.

Only in the twentieth century did the Supreme Court uphold a federal draft, in the *Selective Draft Law Cases* [191] decided

[188] Ibid., pp. 30.

[189] "Report and Resolutions of the Hartford Convention," reprinted in Richard Hofstadter, ed., *Great Issues in American History: A Documentary Record*, 2 vols. (New York, 1958), 1:237, 240.

[190] The precise degree to which constitutional scruples contributed to the bills' defeat is the subject of some dispute. Compare Malbin, "Conscription, the Constitution, and the Framers," pp. 820–21 and n. 56, with Friedman, "Conscription and the Constitution," pp. 1541–44, and Freeman, "Constitutionality of Conscription," pp. 341–42. See, generally, Jack Franklin Leach, *Conscription in the United States: Historical Background* (Rutland, Vt., 1952), pp. 30–126.

[191] 245 U.S. 366 (1918). During the Civil War, the federal government adopted a draft bill of sorts, although many of its supporters conceded that the army clause might not allow direct conscription. These supporters tried to characterize the bill as akin to a tax and denied that it established illegiti-

during World War I. The arguments of the Court can be charitably described as unpersuasive. Less charitably, the Court's opinion is no more worthy of deference today than the Court's contemporaneous First Amendment jurisprudence, epitomized by now-malodorous cases such as *Debs*[192] and *Abrams*.[193] The "Revolution of 1800" had been all but forgotten until *New York Times* v. *Sullivan*[194] made it a pole star of the First Amendment; so today, the central lessons of 1812–14 lie dormant, waiting to be rediscovered and resurrected.

The quartering amendment. Consider next the Third Amendment: "No Soldier shall, in time of peace be quartered in any house, without the consent of the Owner, nor in time of war, but in a manner to be prescribed by law."

Like the Second, the Third is centrally focused on the structural issue of protecting civilian values against the threat of an overbearing military. No standing army in peacetime can be allowed to dominate civilian society, either openly or by subtle insinuation. The Second Amendment's militia could thwart any open military usurpation—say, a siege—but what about more insidious forms of military occupation, featuring federal soldiers cowing civilians by psychological guerrilla warfare, day by day and house by house? Bostonians who had lived under the hated British Quartering Act of 1774 knew that this was no wild hypothetical. Hence the Third Amend-

---

mate conscription, pointing to its provisions allowing money payment in lieu of personal military service (Fred A. Shannon, *The Organization and Administration of the Union Army, 1861–1865*, 2 vols. [Cleveland, 1928], 1:308). In the end, less than one-fifth of the men "drafted" personally served (Freeman, "Constitutionality of Peacetime Conscription," p. 72 n. 102). In an unpublished sketch in preparation for a proper judicial case that never materialized, Chief Justice Roger B. Taney nevertheless declared the act unconstitutional as an impermissible circumvention of the militia clause (Taney, "Thoughts on the Conscription Law of the United States," Martin Anderson, ed., *The Military Draft: Selected Readings on Conscription* [Stanford, Calif., 1982], pp. 207–18).

[192] *Debs* v. *United States*, 249 U.S. 211 (1919).

[193] *Abrams* v. *United States*, 250 U.S. 616 (1919).

[194] 376 U.S. 254, 273–76 (1964).

ment was needed to deal with military threats too subtle and stealthy for the Second's "well regulated Militia."

Note also how the Third reinforces the federalism argument against the draft inspired by the Second. Since the Third flatly forbids Congress to conscript civilians as involuntary innkeepers and roommates of soldiers in peacetime, what sense does it make to read the army clause as giving Congress peacetime power to exercise even more drastic coercion by conscripting civilians into the army itself? It would be odd indeed to say that Congress has absolutely no peacetime power to force soldiers upon civilians, but virtually total peacetime power to force civilians into soldiers. I stress peacetime, because the army clause makes no distinction between war and peace. If its text allows a wartime draft, peacetime conscription must likewise be deemed necessary and proper. The militia clause, by contrast, limits Congress's conscription power to specified national emergencies[195]—just as the Third Amendment limits Congress's quartering power to wartime.

The strict limits in both places derive from the awesome nature of the conscription power. Like a criminal sanction, conscription can take over much of a person's life. This leads to my final structural point about the Third Amendment. Just as criminal law requires special legislative and judicial safeguards (as we shall see below) to protect against possible executive overreaching, so too the Third Amendment requires a special legislative finding before a civilian's house can be conscripted. Military use must be explicitly prescribed by national law, and as the *Youngstown* Court pointedly observed in an analogous context, only Congress can pass such a law.[196] Surprisingly, only one of the seven opinions in *Youngstown* even mentioned that Third Amendment;[197] as with federalism, the separation of powers implications of the Bill of Rights

[195] The national government may call out the militia only to "execute the Laws of the Union, suppress Insurrections and repel Invasions" (U.S. Constitution, Art. I, Sec. 8, Cl. 15).

[196] *Youngstown Sheet and Tube Co.* v. *Sawyer,* 343 U.S. 579, 587–88 (1952).

[197] 343 U.S. at 644 (Jackson concurring).

often go unnoticed because of our modern day fixation on individual rights.

To the extent modern lawyers think about the Third Amendment at all, they are likely to see it as an affirmation of the general right of individual privacy thought to pervade the penumbras and inhabit the interstices of the Bill of Rights. The most notable Supreme Court mention of the amendment in the modern era, Justice Douglas's opinion of the Court in *Griswold* v. *Connecticut*,[198] epitomizes this perspective. But as we have seen, this is not the whole story—indeed perhaps not even the headline. To be sure, there is an important connection between the Third and Fourth Amendments. Both explicitly protect "houses" from needless and dangerous intrusions by governmental officials. But the obvious connections between the Third Amendment and the one which immediately follows it—to which we now turn—must not be allowed to obscure the equally significant but typically unmentioned linkages between the Third Amendment and the words that immediately *precede* it in the Second Amendment.[199]

The Fourth Amendment

"The right of the people to be secure in their persons, houses, papers, and effects, against unreasonable searches and seizures, shall not be violated, and no Warrants shall issue, but upon probable cause, supported by Oath or affirmation, and particularly describing the place to be searched, and the persons or things to be seized." So reads our Fourth Amendment.

---

[198] 381 U.S. 479, 484 (1965).

[199] A LEXIS search of Supreme Court citations to the Third Amendment since *Youngstown* reveals seven attempts to associate the amendment with privacy and only one (dissenting) invocation of the amendment in a context involving alleged military overreaching. See *Laird* v. *Tatum*, 408 U.S. 1, 22 (1972) (army surveillance case; Douglas dissenting). By contrast, the precursors of the Third Amendment proposed by state ratifying conventions invariably linked the quartering amendment with its militia counterpart (Dumbauld, *Bill of Rights*, pp. 182, 185, 201).

We have already noted that the First and Second Amendments' references to "the people" implied a core *collective* right, echoing the Preamble's commitment to the ultimate sovereignty of "We the People of the United States." So too, as we shall see, with the Ninth and Tenth Amendments' use of that phrase. Indeed, the historian Lawrence Cress has argued that in constitutions in "state after state, [the phrases] 'the people' or 'the militia' [were used to connote] the sovereign citizenry, described collectively." In contrast, "the expression, 'man' or 'person' [was typically] used to describe individual rights such as freedom of conscience."[200] The Virginia ratifying convention's declaration of rights followed a similar pattern, invoking "the people's" rights to assembly, instruction, speech, press, and arms-bearing—political rights all—but using "every freeman" and "man" language in connection with a variety of civil rights involving due process and criminal procedure safeguards.[201] The Virginia prototype of the Fourth Amendment fell in the latter category—"every *freeman* has a right to be secure from all unreasonable searches and siezures [*sic*] of his *person*."[202] This formulation followed the general outlines of the search and seizure clause of the highly influential Massachusetts constitution of 1780 and its New Hampshire look-alike, and was in turn echoed by ratifying conventions in New York and North Carolina.[203] Madison was surely aware of these formulations, given his leading role in the Virginia convention, but his initial proposal instead invoked "the people"[204]—language that survived all subsequent congressional modifications. In the search and seizure context, this formulation had appeared in only a single state

---

[200] Lawrence Cress, "An Armed Community: The Origins and Meaning of the Right to Bear Arms," *Journal of American History* 71 (1984):22, 31.

[201] Dumbauld, *Bill of Rights*, pp. 182–85.

[202] Ibid., p. 184 (emphasis added).

[203] Massachusetts constitution of 1780, Pt. I, Art. XIV; New Hampshire constitution of 1784, Pt. I, Art. I, Sec. XIX; Dumbauld, *Bill of Rights*, p. 191 (New York), p. 200 (North Carolina).

[204] Dumbauld, *Bill of Rights*, p. 207.

constitution—the rather atypical Pennsylvania constitution of 1776, penned before the American reconceptualization of English popular sovereignty theory reached full flower.[205]

There is, even here, a way that we can—if we try hard enough—read "the people" as a collective noun. For the Fourth Amendment creates an explicit textual shield against any improper governmental interference with the proceedings of a constitutional convention—quite literally, a *house* of *the people*. Seen from this angle, the amendment resembles Article I's speech and debate and arrest clauses,[206] which immunize representatives in Congress from improper interference by executive or judicial agents. More broadly, the amendment's language reminds us that we must be specially watchful of government efforts to use search and seizure powers to interfere with the people's political activities—circulating petitions (literally *the people's papers*), attending political meetings (with their literal *persons*), and so on.

Madison's choice of language here may well have been influenced by the celebrated 1763 English case of *Wilkes* v. *Wood*,[207] one of the two or three most important search and seizure cases on the books in 1789.[208] *Wood* involved a famous

[205] Pennsylvania constitution of 1776 (Declaration of Rights), Art. X. Vermonters copied Pennsylvania's language; see the Vermont constitution of 1777, Chap. 1, Sec. IX, and the Vermont constitution of 1786, Chap. 1, Sec. XII. The legal status of Vermont's statehood had not been definitively resolved in 1789.

[206] U.S. Constitution, Art. I, Sec. 6, Cl. 1.

[207] 98 Eng. Rep. 489 (C.P. 1763), Kurland and Lerner, eds., *Founders' Constitution*, 5:230.

[208] The other leading case here was *Entick* v. *Carrington*, 95 Eng. Rep. 807 (K.B. 1765), ibid., p. 233. The Boston writs of assistance case appears to have played very little role in the discussion leading up to the Fourth Amendment. The leading historical account of that amendment uncovered only one reference to the writs of assistance (Nelson B. Lasson, *The History and Development of the Fourth Amendment to the United States Constitution* [Baltimore, 1937], p. 89 n. 40). Lasson attributed the pseudononymous pamphlet containing this reference to Gerry. In fact, Charles Warren has shown that this pamphlet was written by Mercy Otis Warren, the sister of the colonial lawyer James Otis who argued the writs of assistance case (Warren,

cast of characters. Both the target of the government search, John Wilkes, and the author of the opinion, Lord Chief Justice Pratt (soon to become Lord Camden), were folk heroes in the colonies. (Pennsylvania residents named the town of Wilkes-Barre after the plaintiff; New Jersey and South Carolina each dedicated a city in Camden's honor.)[209] No less famous were the facts of the case. Wilkes, a champion of the people and a member of Commons (the people's house), had used the press to communicate with his constituents and criticize George III's ministry and majesty. When the government reacted by trying to use general warrants to suppress his political activity, Wilkes brought suit in *Wood* and successfully challenged the legality of those warrants. Wilkes also brought suit to challenge the "seizure" of his "person." (The government had imprisoned him in the Tower of London.) In a companion case to *Wood*, the Lord Chief Justice ordered Wilkes released on habeas corpus on the ground of his parliamentary privilege from arrest.[210]

In the Fourth Amendment, as elsewhere, we need not view the phrase "the people" as sounding solely in collective, political terms; once again, the language is broad enough to radiate beyond its core. Indeed, it is less than clear that populism *is* the core here. To begin with, the collective reading of "people" and "houses," though textually defensible and historically buttressed by the facts of *Wood*, seems strained—a bit too cute, perhaps. Even more important, in the Fourth

---

"Elbridge Gerry, James Otis, and Mercy Warren, and the Ratification of the Constitution," *Massachusetts Historical Society Proceedings* 64 [1930–32]: 143–64).

[209] On John Wilkes, see Raymond W. Postgate, *That Devil Wilkes* (New York, 1929); George F. E. Rudé, *Wilkes and Liberty: A Social Study of 1763 to 1774* (Oxford, 1962); Pauline Maier, *From Resistance to Revolution: Colonial Radicals and the Development of American Opposition to Britain, 1765–1776* (New York, 1972), pp. 162–69; *Powell* v. *McCormack*, 395 U.S. 486, 527–31 (1969). On *Camden* see Telford Taylor, *Two Studies in Constitutional Interpretation* (Columbus, Ohio, 1969), p. 184 n. 35. On *Wood* and its companion cases, see Taylor, *Two Studies*, pp. 29–35 and accompanying endnotes; Lasson, *History and Development*, pp. 43–49.

[210] *Rex* v. *Wilkes*, 95 Eng. Rep. 737 (C.P. 1763), Kurland and Lerner, eds., *Founders' Constitution*, 5:231.

Amendment, as nowhere else in the Constitution, the collective-sounding phrase "the people" is immediately qualified by the use and subsequent repetition of the more individualistic language of "persons." The amendment's text seems to move quickly from the public to the private, from the political to the personal, from "the people" out-of-doors to "persons" very much in-doors, in their private homes.

Yet even here, in talking the familiar talk of individual rights, we must be wary of anachronism and must not automatically assume that the right was essentially countermajoritarian. As with virtually every Bill of Rights provision thus far examined, the Fourth Amendment evinces more concern with the "agency" problem of protecting the people generally from self-interested government policy than with protecting minorities against majorities of fellow Citizens.

Reflect, for a moment, on the fact that the amendment actually contains two different commands. First, all government *searches* and *seizures* must be *reasonable*. Second, no *warrants* shall issue without *probable cause*. The modern Supreme Court has intentionally collapsed the two requirements, treating all unwarranted searches and seizures—with a few categorical exceptions, such as exigent circumstances—as per se unreasonable.[211] Otherwise, the Court has reasoned, the requirement that a neutral magistrate verify probable cause ex ante would be obviously frustrated—the special safeguards of the warrant requirement would be all but meaningless.

If we assume that the amendment is primarily about protecting minority rights, and further assume that judges and magistrates are best institutional guardians of those rights, this reading seems to make sense. Why should government officials be allowed greater latitude (general reasonableness rather than the stricter probable cause) when they intentionally avoid the courtroom and intrude on individuals in a judicially unwarranted manner? Hence the need, under these assumptions, to engraft a constructive second sentence onto the amendment: "Absent special circumstances, no search or seizure shall occur without a warrant."

But the fact that the amendment does *not* contain such a

---

[211] See, for example, *Johnson* v. *United States*, 333 U.S. 10 (1943).

sentence should invite us to rethink our assumptions. (So too, should the combination of the silliness of the engrafted sentence without the "special circumstances" escape hatch, and the extraordinary difficulty of specifying the appropriate size and shape of the hatch.) To do this, consider the paradigmatic way in which Fourth Amendment rights would be enforced. Virtually any search or seizure by a federal officer would involve a physical trespass under common law principles. An aggrieved target could use the common law of trespass to bring suit for damages against the official—just as Wilkes brought a trespass action in *Wood.* If the search or seizure were deemed lawful in court, defendant would prevail; but if, as in *Wood,* the search were found unlawful, defendant government officials would be held strictly liable. There was no such thing as "good faith" immunity.[212]

Given this, many officials would obviously prefer to litigate the lawfulness of a contemplated search or seizure before it occurred—to seek a judicial warrant authorizing the intrusion. Such a warrant, if strictly complied with, would act as a sort of declaratory judgment whose preclusive effect could be subsequently pled in any later damage action. A lawful warrant, in effect, would compel a sort of directed verdict for the defendant government official in any subsequent lawsuit for damages.[213]

But note what has happened. A warrant issued by a *judge* or *magistrate*—a permanent government official, on the gov-

[212]See, generally, Amar, "Sovereignty," pp. 1486–87, 1506–7, and sources cited therein; William E. Nelson, *Americanization of the Common Law: The Impact of Legal Change upon Massachusetts Society, 1760–1830* (Cambridge, 1975), p. 17; see also *Entick v. Carrington,* 95 Eng. Rep. 807 (K.B. 1765).

[213]See, for example, Nelson, *Americanization of the Common Law,* pp. 190 n. 57 (citing Massachusetts case with jury verdict that officer not guilty "If this Warrant be Lawfull in This Case," but guilty otherwise) and 92 ("due issuance of a [judicial] warrant was an absolute defense to an officer who was sued for an unlawful search or arrest"). In *Wood* and *Entick,* had the warrants been lawful, each surely would have been a good defense (Blackstone, *Commentaries,* 4:286–90 [general warrant "is therefore in fact no warrant at all: for it will not justify the officer who acts under it; whereas a lawful warrant will at all events indemnify the officer, who executes the same ministerially"]).

ernment payroll—has had the effect of taking a later trespass action away from a *jury* of ordinary Citizens. Because juries could be trusted far more than judges to protect against government overreaching (the "agency" problem), warrants were generally *dis*favored. Judges and warrants are the heavies, not the heroes, of our story.

We can now see the Fourth Amendment with fresh eyes. Searches without warrants are not presumptively illegitimate. Rather, whenever such a search or seizure occurred, a jury could subsequently assess its reasonableness. If the jury deemed the search "unreasonable," the plain words of the Fourth Amendment would render the search unlawful. Defendant official could thus be held strictly liable in damages (though he might well in turn be indemnified by the government). Reasonableness vel non was a classic question of fact for the jury;[214] and the Seventh Amendment, in combination with the Fourth, would require the federal government to furnish a jury to any plaintiff-victim who demanded one and protect that jury's finding of fact from being overturned by any judge or other government official.[215] Judicial warrants, however, were another matter. Precisely because they were granted by government officials and had the effect of taking the reasonableness issue away from the jury, they had to be strictly limited.[216] Such a warrant must meet stricter requirements (probable cause, etc.) than mere reasonableness. Thus, contrary to the modern Court's approach, the words of the Fourth Amendment mean what they say: the probable cause requirement applies only if and when a warrant issues.[217] Put

[214] Compare Antonin Scalia, "The Rule of Law as a Law of Rules," *University of Chicago Law Review* 56 (1989):1175, 1180–86.

[215] Compare Elliot, ed., *Debates*, 2:550 (amendment proposed by committee at Maryland ratifying convention requiring jury trial in "all cases of trespasses" and prohibiting appellate relitigation of jury's factual findings).

[216] See ibid., pp. 551–52 (general warrants should be "forbidden to those *magistrates* who are to administer the general government"; emphasis added).

[217] Accord Taylor, *Two Studies*, pp. 21–50. Professor Taylor offers a wealth of historical evidence against collapsing the Fourth Amendment's distinct requirements but nowhere suggests the possible relevance of jury trial is-

another way, the Court has simply reversed the original linkage between the Fourth Amendment's two different commands. It is not that a search or seizure *without* a warrant was presumptively *un*reasonable, as the Court has assumed; rather, a search or seizure *with* a warrant was presumed reasonable as a matter of law—and thus immune from jury oversight.[218]

There is an obvious connection here to the common law rule against prior restraint, which we noted in the First Amendment context.[219] Just as judges were barred ex ante from restraining the press, but juries ex post could impose damages on publishers, so here judges and magistrates acting before a search were much more strictly limited than juries acting afterwards. This connection would hardly have been lost on the Fourth Amendment framers. In sixteenth- and seventeenth-century England, general warrants were the very devices by which various schemes of prior restraint and printer licensing were enforced.[220] Indeed, in *Wood* itself the secretary of state, Lord Halifax, had issued a general warrant against Wilkes in an attempt to enforce the seditious libel laws, an area of law where the proper role of the jury was a hot topic.

As with the First Amendment, the central role of the jury

---

sues. Although Professor Nelson suggests that arrests and searches always required warrants in colonial Massachusetts (Nelson, *Americanization of the Common Law,* pp. 17–18, he elsewhere cites two early nineteenth-century cases holding that no arrest warrant was needed "in cases of treason and felony, and . . . to preserve the peace and to prevent outrage" (p. 226 n. 126). The later cases accord with Professor Taylor's extensive evidence and with Blackstone (Blackstone, *Commentaries,* 4:286–90).

[218] I owe this alternative formulation to a conversation with Michael A. Paulsen.

[219] See text accompanying notes 90–93, above.

[220] Stephen A. Saltzburg, *Cases and Commentary on American Criminal Procedure,* 2d ed. (St. Paul, 1984), p. 47; Lasson, *History and Development,* pp. 24–50; Story, *Commentaries,* vol. 3, sec. 1895; see also Elliot, ed., *Debates,* 2:551 (Maryland convention recognition that general warrants were "the great engine by which power may destroy those individuals who resist usurpation").

in the Fourth Amendment should remind us that the core rights of "the people" were popular and populist rights—rights which the popular body of the jury as well suited to vindicate.[221] To see the amendment as centrally concerned with countermajoritarian rights is to miss the later transformation brought about by the Fourteenth Amendment, with its core concerns about minority rights and its heavy reliance on federal judges.

Nor should we ignore the Fourth Amendment's image of federalism. The reasonableness requirement limited all federal officers, and the warrant requirement imposed special restrictions on federal judges and magistrates, but vindication of these restrictions would largely come from state bodies. State statutes and state common law, after all, would typically define and protect ordinary individuals' property rights to their "persons, houses, papers, and effects." Thus, *state* law would initially create the cause of action that would enable ordinary men and women to challenge unconstitutional actions by *federal* officials.[222] And even if these actions were tried in federal court (because they raised federal questions arising under the Fourth Amendment),[223] a Seventh Amendment jury composed of local Citizens, rather than a judge appointed in Washington, D.C., would decide the general ques-

---

[221] The linkage between juries and Fourth Amendment interests was most vividly articulated in the following passage from an Antifederalist essayist: "[If a federal constable searching] for stolen goods, pulled down the clothes of a bed in which there was a woman and searched under her shift . . . a trial by jury would be our safest resource, heavy damages would at once punish the offender and deter others from committing the same; but what satisfaction can we expect from a lordly [judge] always ready to protect the officers of government against the weak and helpless citizens." See John Bach McMaster and Frederick D. Stone, eds., *Pennsylvania and the Federal Constitution, 1787–1788* (Philadelphia, 1888), p. 154; see also pp. 781–82 (remarks of Robert Whitehill at Pennsylvania ratifying convention). Immediately after criticizing the Constitution's inadequate provisions for jury trial, Whitehill invoked "The Case of Mr. Wilkes"—a trespass action that had been tried to a jury—and argued that "the Doctrine of general Warrants show[s] that *Judges* may be corrupted" (emphasis added).

[222] See Amar, "Sovereignty," pp. 1504–10.

[223] See ibid., pp. 1510–12.

tion of reasonableness. Here too, localism would protect liberty.

The Judicial Process Amendments

Let us now turn to the Fifth through Eighth Amendments, which we shall consider as a block. Each of the provisions in this block can be understood as regulating the structure and procedure of federal courts—each, that is, except for the takings clause of the Fifth Amendment.

Takings clause. "Nor shall private property be taken for public use, without just compensation."

This prohibition seems primarily to protect individuals and minority groups. After all, any government action imposing a financial burden on a majority of the populace would look more like a legitimate "tax" than an unconstitutional "taking." In this respect, the provision runs counter to the dominant majoritarian thrust of other Bill of Rights provisions we have seen thus far. The clause also seems distinctly modern in proclaiming that limits should be imposed on government action, even when government agents are acting on behalf of their constituents, rather than pursuing their own self-interest. Thus, the clause requires private compensation even if property is taken for "public" use.[224]

The concerns underlying the takings clause were deeply felt by James Madison, who, we should recall, was ahead of his time in arguing that the dominant danger in America came from a possibly overweening majority rather than from self-interested government agents. But as we saw in considering Madison's original Fourteenth Amendment—a prescient precursor of our own—he was unsuccessful in bringing the

---

[224] But see McConnell, "Contract Rights," pp. 288–93 (using *Federalist* No. 51 framework and federalism analysis to argue that takings clause was primarily motivated by agency cost concerns about remote and self-interested federal officials, especially military officers). Professor McConnell's analysis helps to explain why the takings clause applied only against the federal government. To the extent his explanation works, the takings clause is that much smaller an exception to my overall thesis about the Bill of Rights.

needed majorities in Congress around to his way of thinking.[225] How, then, did he manage to slip the takings clause through?

In part by clever bundling, tying the clause to a variety of other provisions that commanded more enthusiasm (in large part because they rested on a somewhat different worldview, as we shall see). One key bit of evidence in support of the clever-bundling hypothesis has already been noted: the subject of the clause seems to have very little in common with the other clauses of the Fifth Amendment, each of which deals centrally with criminal procedure. Even more dramatic is the fact that unlike every other clause in the First Congress's proposed Bill, the just compensation restriction was not put forth in any form by any of the state ratifying conventions.[226] So too with Madison's original but unsuccessful Fourteenth Amendment,[227] which was more vulnerable to attack precisely because it was not as cleverly bundled as the takings clause. On these two provisions, then, Madison was putting forth his own somewhat prophetic ideas, rather than distilling the zeitgeist.

Jury clauses. Unlike the takings clause, most other provisions of Amendments Five through Eight were centrally concerned with the "agency" problem of government officials' attempting to rule in their own self-interest at the expense of their constituents' sentiments and liberty. There was, for example, a special historical connection between the First and Eighth Amendments. The most gruesome punishments in England had typically been imposed on those who spoke out against the government. Justice Hugo Black noted one example in his James Madison Lecture on the Bill of Rights. For the crime of "writing books and pamphlets," the English lawyer William Prynne's "ears were first cut off by court order and . . . subsequently, by another court order, . . . his remaining ear stumps [were] gouged out while he was on a pil-

---

[225] See text accompanying notes 77–82, above.

[226] See Dumbauld, *Bill of Rights,* pp. 53, 162 (item 14).

[227] Ibid., p. 162 (item 23).

lory."[228] Even more gruesome was the typical sentence in treason:

> That you, and each of you, (here his Lordship named the prisoners severally,) be taken to the place from whence you came, and from thence you are to be drawn on hurdles to the place of execution, where you are to be hanged by the neck, but not until you are dead; for while you are still living, your bodies are to be taken down, your bowels torn out, and burnt before your faces; your heads are to be then cut off, and your bodies divided each into four quarters, and your heads and quarters to be then at the King's disposal; and may the Almighty God have mercy on your souls.[229]

Just as the awesome power of conscription, if not strictly regulated, could give runaway government officials near-despotic control over the general citizenry,[230] so criminal law inspired dread and jealousy. Thus, the deep concerns underlying the Second and Third Amendments are at work here too—as should be evident from the specific aside on military justice in the opening clause of the Fifth Amendment: "No person shall be held to answer for a capital, or otherwise infamous crime, unless on a presentment or indictment of a Grand Jury, except in cases arising in the land or naval forces, or in the Militia, when in actual service in time of War or public danger." The dominant strategy to keep agents of the central government under control was to use the populist and local institution of the jury.

Jurors as populist protectors. Guaranteed in no less than three amendments, juries were at the heart of the Bill of Rights. The Fifth safeguarded the role of the grand jury; the Sixth, the criminal petit jury; and the Seventh, the civil jury. In addi-

---

[228] Hugo L. Black, "The Bill of Rights," *New York University Law Review* 35 (1960):865, 870; see also *Adamson* v. *California,* 332 U.S. 46, 70–71 (1947) (Black dissenting, noting connection between First Amendment and limitations on "arbitrary court action" imposed by Fifth, Sixth, and Eighth Amendments).

[229] Trials for High Treason of Lieut. Col. Edward Marcus Despard et al. 46 (Birmingham 1803), quoted in Taylor, *Two Studies,* p. 180 n. 41.

[230] See text accompanying notes 196–97, above.

tion, Madison's unsuccessful Fourteenth Amendment would have explicitly guaranteed jury trial against state governments.[231] What's more, trial by jury in all criminal cases had earlier been mandated by the clear words of Article III: "The Trial of all Crimes, except in Cases of Impeachment, shall be by Jury." Indeed, the entire debate at the Philadelphia Convention over whether to add a Bill of Rights was triggered when George Mason picked up on a casual comment from another delegate that "no provision was yet made for juries in civil cases."[232] Between the close of the Philadelphia Convention and the opening of the First Congress, five of the six state ratifying conventions that proposed amendments put forth two or more jury-related proposals.[233] State constitutions further confirm the centrality of the jury. According to Leonard W. Levy's tally, the only right secured in all state constitutions penned between 1776 and 1787 was the right of jury trial in criminal cases.[234]

Spanning both civil and criminal proceedings, the key role of the jury was to protect ordinary individuals against governmental overreaching. Jurors would be drawn from the community; like the militia they were ordinary Citizens, not permanent government officials on the government payroll. Just as the militia could check a paid professional standing army, so too the jury could thwart overreaching by powerful and ambitious government officials.

The grand jury, for example, could thwart any prosecution it deemed unfounded or malicious—especially if it suspected that the executive was trying to use the powers of incumbency illegitimately to entrench itself in power by prosecuting its political critics. Note how the Fifth Amendment differs from the Fourth. In contrast to the Fourth's warrant clause, the decision whether sufficient cause exists to prosecute a felony can never under the Fifth be made solely by permanent government officials. Perhaps because of this, the Fifth nowhere ex-

[231] See text accompanying note 79, above.

[232] See Farrand, ed., *Records of the Convention*, 2:587–88.

[233] See Dumbauld, *Bill of Rights*, pp. 176, 181–84, 188, 190–91, 200, 204.

[234] Levy, *Emergence of a Free Press*, p. 227.

plicitly requires that the indictment be supported by a given level of "probable cause" or that the indictment or present-ment "particularly describ[e]" the factual offenses charged. Because the decision was to be made by a popular body, perhaps more flexibility was allowed, as within the Fourth Amendment itself.

More broadly, the grand jury had sweeping proactive and inquisitorial powers to investigate suspected wrongdoing or coverups by government officials and make its findings known through the legal device of "presentment"—a public document stating its accusations. Presentments were not lim-ited to indictable criminal offenses. The grand jury had a rov-ing commission to ferret out official malfeasance of self-dealing of any sort and bring it to the attention of the public at large. In the words of James Wilson, "The grand jury are a great channel of communication, between those who make and administer the laws, and those for whom the laws are made and administered. All the operations of government, and of its ministers and officers, are within the compass of their view and research. They may suggest publick improve-ments and the modes of removing publick inconveniences: they may expose to publick inspection, or to publick punish-ment, publick bad men, and publick bad measures."[235] This vision of the grand jury was nicely illustrated by the events of 1816; the congressional pay increase noted earlier was the target of several grand jury proceedings that helped inform and mobilize the electorate about "publick bad men, and pub-lick bad measures."[236]

In cases where an indictable criminal offense had occurred, the grand jury was unable to compel prosecution on its own initiative without the concurrence of the executive, but could nonetheless use presentments to publicize to the people at large any suspicious executive decisions to decline prosecu-tion.[237] The image here is akin to that of modern-day blue

[235] McCloskey, ed., *Works of Wilson*, 2:537.

[236] See text accompanying note 70, above.

[237] See *United States* v. *Cox*, 342 F. 2d 167, 185–96 (1965) (Wisdom con-curring).

ribbon commissions and special prosecutors called to investigate in areas where regular government officials may have conflicts of interest. By focusing public attention on otherwise low-visibility executive decisions, the grand jury could deter executive self-dealing and enhance executive accountability.

Though not as proactive as its "grand" counterpart, the criminal petit jury could interpose itself on behalf of "the people's" rights by refusing to convict when the executive sought to trump up charges against its political critics. Once again, more than a permanent government official—even an independent Article III judge—was required to safeguard liberty. In England, judges had too often acquiesced in government tyranny, as the cases of Prynne and Wilkes (tried to absentia for seditious libel) graphically illustrated.[238] Even in America, federal judges would be appointed by the central government and might prove reluctant to rein in their former benefactors and current paymasters—as illustrated by the brazenly partisan conduct of some Federalist judges during the Sedition Act controversy.[239] Thus, in those aspects of a criminal case that might involve a judge acting without a jury—issuing arrest warrants, setting bail, and sentencing—additional *restrictions* came into play via the Fourth Amendment warrant clause and the Eighth Amendment.

The petit jury's power would be especially great if it could lawfully refuse to convict a defendant charged under any federal law *it* deemed unconstitutional. As we shall see below, this

[238] See *Adamson* v. *California*, 332 U.S. 46, 70–71 (1947) (Black dissenting); *Green* v. *United States*, 356 U.S. 165, 209 (1957) (Black, dissenting); compare "Essays by a Farmer" (IV), *CAF,* 5:39 ("Whenever therefore the trial by juries has been abolished, . . . the judiciary power is immediately absorbed, or placed under the direction of the executive"). On Wilkes, see Irving Brant, *The Bill of Rights: Its Origin and Meaning* (Indianapolis, 1965), pp. 189–91.

[239] See George Lee Haskins and Herbert A. Johnson, *Foundations of Power: John Marshall, 1801–15,* History of the Supreme Court of the United States, vol. 2 (New York, 1981), pp. 140, 159; James Morton Smith, *Freedom's Fetters: The Alien and Sedition Laws and American Civil Liberties* (Ithaca, N.Y., 1956), pp. 139–417.

right of "jury review" was advocated by many constitutional theorists in the late eighteenth and early nineteenth centuries and was invoked by publishers accused of violating the Sedition Act.[240]

A Sixth Amendment right of "jury review" gains added plausibility when we remember the central role of the Seventh Amendment civil jury in adjudicating the Fourth Amendment issue of "reasonableness." Here, the order of the parties was typically reversed—the target of government harassment would be the plaintiff, and a government official the defendant—but the basic idea was the same. Ordinary Citizens would check executive overreaching and monitor the professional judiciary.

As Tocqueville observed, the overall jury system was fundamentally populist and majoritarian: "The institution of the jury . . . places the real direction of society in the hands of the governed, . . . and not in that of the government. . . . [It] invests the people, or that class of citizens, with the direction of society. . . . The jury system as it is understood in America appears to me to be as direct and as extreme a consequence of the sovereignty of the people as universal suffrage. They are two instruments of equal power, which contribute to the supremacy of the majority."[241]

Jurors as provincials. The jury was not simply a popular body, but a local one as well. Indeed, the Sixth Amendment explicitly guaranteed a jury "of the State and district wherein the crime shall have been committed," going a step beyond the language of Article III, which required only that jury trials be held somewhere within *the state* where the crime occurred. Early in the Philadelphia Convention, Madison captured an important truth in a telling analogy, arguing for the need to "preserve the State rights, as carefully as the trials by jury."[242] Just as state legislators could protect their constituents against central oppression, so too jurors could obviously "interpose" themselves against central tyranny through the devices of pre-

---

[240] See text accompanying notes 265–84, below.

[241] Tocqueville, *Democracy in America*, 1:293–94.

[242] Farrand, ed., *Records of the Convention*, 1:490.

sentments, nonindictments, and general verdicts. As with the militia, the jury would be composed of Citizens from the same community, and its actions were expected to be informed by community values.

Jurors as pupils. The jury was also to be informed by judges—most obviously in the judges' charges. As Ralph Lerner has shown in his essay "The Supreme Court as Republican Schoolmaster," judges often seized the occasion to educate the jurors about legal and political values, ranging well beyond the narrow issues before them.[243] Like the church and the militia, the jury was in part an intermediate association designed to educate and socialize its members into virtuous thinking and conduct. Churches stressed religious and moral virtues, militias struck a proper balance between civilian and martial virtues, and juries instilled republican legal and political virtues.

No one understood all this better than Tocqueville, a keen student of American constitutional law and the leading theorist on the importance of intermediate associations:

> The jury, and more especially the civil jury, serves to communicate the spirit of the judges to the minds of all the citizens; and this spirit, with the habits whch attend it, is the soundest preparation for free institutions. It imbues all classes with a respect for the thing judged and with the notion of right. . . . It teaches men to practice equity; every man learns to judge his neighbor as he would himself be judged. . . .
>
> . . . *It may be regarded as a gratuitous public school,* ever open, in which every juror learns his rights, enters into daily communication with the most learned and enlightened members of the upper classes, and becomes practically acquainted with the laws, which are brought within the reach of his capacity by the efforts of the bar, the advice of the judge, and even the passions of the parties. . . .
>
> . . . I look upon [the jury] as one of the most efficacious means for the education of the people which society can employ.[244]

[243] See Ralph Lerner, "The Supreme Court as Republican Schoolmaster," *Supreme Court Review* (1967):127.

[244] Tocqueville, *Democracy in America,* 1:295–96 (emphasis added). Francis Lieber, one of the leading constitutional commentators of the mid-

Through the jury, Citizens would learn self-government by doing self-government. In Tocqueville's memorable phrase, "The jury, which is the most energetic means of making the people rule, is also the most efficacious means of teaching it how to rule well."[245] In 1789 the Antifederalist "Maryland Farmer" noted that although ordinary folk were "much degraded in the powers of the mind," jury service would uplift them. *"Give them power and they will find understanding to use it."*[246]

Jurors as political participants. Unable to harbor any realistic expectations about serving in the small House of Representatives or the even more aristocratic Senate, ordinary Citizens could nevertheless participate in the application of national law through their service on juries.[247] In the words of the "Federal Farmer," the leading Antifederalist essayist of the ratification period, through juries "frequently drawn from the body of the people . . . we secure to the people at large, their just and rightful controul in the judicial department."[248] Juries, wrote another republican in 1791, give the people "a share of Judicature which they have reserved for themselves."[249] As the most prominent historian of Antifederalist thought, Herbert J. Storing, has written, "The question was not fundamentally whether the lack of adequate provision for jury trial would weaken a traditional bulwark of individual rights (although that was also involved) but whether it would

---

nineteenth century, shared Tocqueville's assessment. See Lieber, *On Civil Liberty and Self-Government* (London, 1853), p. 250.

[245] Tocqueville, *Democracy in America,* 1:297.

[246] "Essays by a Farmer" (IV), *CAF,* 5:39.

[247] "Letters from the Federal Farmer" (IV), ibid., 2:249; compare "Letters of Cato" (V), ibid., p. 119 ("the opportunity you will have to participate in government [is] one of the principal securities of a free people").

[248] "Letters from the Federal Farmer" (XV), ibid., p. 320.

[249] Quoted in Wythe Holt, "'The Federal Courts Have Enemies in All Who Fear Their Influence on State Objects': The Failure to Abolish Supreme Court Circuit-Riding in the Judiciary Acts of 1792 and 1793," *Buffalo Law Review* 36 (1987):301, 325.

fatally weaken the role of the people in the *administration* of government."[250]

Analogies between legislatures and juries abounded.[251] Wrote the "Federal Farmer":

> It is essential in every free country, that common people should have a part and share of influence, in the judicial as well as in the legislative department.
>
> . . . . .
>
> The trial by jury in the judicial department, and the collection of the people by their representatives in the legislature . . . have procured for them, in this country, their true proportion of influence, and the wisest and most fit means of protecting themselves in the community. Their situation, as jurors and representatives, enables them to acquire information and knowledge in the affairs and government of the society; and to come forward, in turn, as the centinels and guardians of each other.[252]

So too, Jefferson declared in 1789 that "it is necessary to introduce the people into every department of government. . . . Were I called upon to decide whether the people had best be omitted in the Legislative or Judicial department, I would say it is better to leave them out of the Legislative."[253]

---

[250] Herbert J. Storing, "What the Anti-Federalists Were *For*," *CAF*, 1:19 (footnote omitted). Storing's language here closely tracks that of the Antifederalist essayist Centinel. See "Letters of Centinel" (II), ibid., 2:149 (jury trial "preserves in the hands of the people, that share which they ought to have in the administration of justice"); accord Schwartz, comp., *Bill of Rights*, 2:1174 (quoting speech of Gov. John Hancock to Massachusetts legislature: jury trial provisions "appear to me to be of great consequence. In all free governments, a share in the administration of the laws ought to be vested in, or reserved to the people"). The centrality of the jury is nowhere more evident than in Hancock's speech on Congress's proposed Bill of Rights. No clauses are mentioned other than the three dealing with juries.

[251] Storing, "What the Anti-Federalists Were *For*," p. 19.

[252] "Letters from the Federal Farmer" (IV), *CAF*, 2:249–50.

[253] Jefferson to L'Abbé Arnoux, July 19, 1789, Boyd et al., eds., *Papers of Jefferson*, 15:282–83; see also Charles Francis Adams, ed., *The Works of John Adams, Second President of the United States: With a Life of the Author*, 10 vols. (Boston, 1850–56), 2:253 (diary entry, Feb. 12, 1771, "the common people should have as complete a control" over judiciary as over legislature).

Tocqueville later made much the same point: "The jury is, above all, a political [and not a mere judicial] institution. . . . The jury is that portion of the nation to which the execution of the laws is entrusted, as the legislature is that part of the nation which makes the laws; and in order that society may be governed in a fixed and uniform manner, the list of citizens qualified to serve on juries must increase and diminish with the list of electors."[254]

Even more elaborate was the vision of the jury conjured up by John Taylor of Caroline, one of the early republic's leading constitutional theorists. The jury, wrote Taylor, was the "lower judicial bench" in a bicameral judiciary.[255] The judicial structure mirrored that of the legislature, with an upper house of greater stability and experience and a lower house to represent popular sentiment more directly. In a similar vein, the "Maryland Farmer" defined the jury as *the democratic branch of the judiciary power*—more necessary than representatives in the legislature."[256]

Tocqueville explicitly defined the jury as "a certain number of citizens chosen by lot and invested with a temporary" commission[257]—the analogy to militias suggests itself once again—and the "Federal Farmer" also seemed to stress the *rotating* quality of jury service, as evidenced by his final reference, quoted above, to Citizens coming forward "in turn." The idea of mandatory rotation once again illustrates the connec-

[254] Tocqueville, *Democracy in America*, 1:293–94. Professor Nelson writes that jurors were typically selected "by lot from a list of freeholders, elected by the voters of a jurisdiction, or summoned by the sheriff from among the bystanders at court" (Nelson, "John Marshall's Constitutional Jurisprudence," p. 918 n. 140). Jefferson was harshly critical of this last method, which he believed vested too much discretion in permanent executive officials. See Petition on Election of Jurors, October 1798, Ford, ed., *Writings of Jefferson*, 7:284–85; First Annual Message, Dec. 8, 1801, ibid., 8:108, 123–24; Jefferson to Samuel Kercheval, July 12, 1816, ibid., 10:37, 39.

[255] John Taylor of Caroline, *An Inquiry into the Principles and Policy of the Government of the United States*, new ed. (New Haven, 1950), p. 209.

[256] "Essays by a Farmer" (IV), *CAF,* 5:38.

[257] Tocqueville, *Democracy in America*, 1:293.

tions between juries and legislators, for many Antifederalists wanted compulsory rotation in the legislature as well.[258] Indeed, Thomas Jefferson's two biggest objections to the original Constitution were its lack of a bill of rights and its abandonment of the republican principle of mandatory rotation.[259] At the New York ratifying convention Gilbert Livingston criticized the lack of mandatory rotation in the legislature, but his comments fit the jury context as well: "[Rotation] will afford opportunity to bring forward the genius and information of the states, and will be a stimulus to acquire political abilities. It will be the means of diffusing a more general knowledge of the measures and spirit of the administration. These things will confirm the people's confidence in government."[260] Like so many other ideas we have seen, the mandatory rotation principle drew its strength from structural concerns about attenuated representation rather than elaborate ideas about minority rights.

The centrality of the jury. If we seek a paradigmatic image underlying the Bill of Rights, we cannot go far wrong in picking the jury. Not only was it featured in three separate amendments (the Fifth, Sixth, and Seventh), but its *absence* strongly influenced the judge-restricting doctrines underlying three other amendments (the First, Fourth, and Eighth). So too, the double jeopardy clause, which makes no explicit mention of juries, should be understood to safeguard not simply the individual defendant's interest in avoiding vexation but also the integrity of the initial petit jury's judgment (much like the

[258] See, for example, Wood, *Creation of the American Republic*, pp. 521–22; "Essays of Brutus" (XVI), *CAF,* 2:444–45; Elliot, ed., *Debates,* 2:309–11 (remarks of Melancton Smith at New York ratifying convention). On the possible use of lotteries to achieve *legislative* rotation, see Akhil Reed Amar, "Choosing Representatives by Lottery Voting," *Yale Law Journal* 93 (1984):1283.

[259] Jefferson to George Washington, May 2, 1788, Boyd et al., eds., *Papers of Jefferson,* 13:124, 128; Jefferson to Madison, July 31, 1788, ibid., pp. 440, 442–43; Jefferson to Madison, Dec. 20, 1787, ibid., 12:438, 440–41; Jefferson to Francis Hopkinson, Mar. 13, 1789, ibid., 14:649–50.

[260] Elliot, ed., *Debates,* 2:288.

Seventh Amendment's rule against "re-examin[ation]" of the civil jury's verdict.[261] The due process clause also implicated the jury, for its core meaning was to require lawful indictment or presentment (thus triggering the Fifth Amendment grand jury clause).[262] Even those amendments that at first seem rather far afield appear on closer inspection to resonate with the values underlying the jury. We have seen important parallels between the jury and the Second Amendment's vaunted "well regulated Militia." The vision underlying the jury also harmonizes well with Congress's first two (unsuccessful) amendments, which reflected suspicion of government agents

[261] The only state constitutional precursor of the double jeopardy clause conjoined this provision to its criminal jury trial guarantee (New Hampshire constitution of 1784, Pt. I, Art. I, Sec. XVI). The Maryland state ratifying convention—one of only two that raised the double jeopardy issue—made this linkage even more explicit: "That there shall be a trial by jury in all criminal cases . . . and that there be no appeal from matter of fact, or second trial after acquittal." This clause was immediately followed by a proto–Seventh Amendment bar on appellate relitigation of facts found by a *civil* jury (Elliot, ed., *Debates*, 2:550; see also Story, *Commentaries*, vol. 3, sec. 1781 [double jeopardy clause prohibits second trial after defendant "has once been convicted, or acquitted of the offence charged, by the verdict of a jury. . . . But it does not mean, that he shall not be tried for the offence a second time, if the jury have been discharged without giving any verdict; or, if, having given a verdict, judgment has been arrested upon it, or a new trial has been granted in his favor"]). Story's position is in some tension with current double jeopardy doctrine in America but appears well supported by British practice, both then and now. See Jay A. Sigler, *Double Jeopardy: The Development of a Legal and Social Policy* (Ithaca, N.Y., 1969), pp. 15–16, 32 n. 138, 126–28. It also may well make more sense than current doctrine (ibid., pp. 42, 127, 223).

[262] See, for example, Harold A. Syrett and Jacob E. Cooke, eds., *The Papers of Alexander Hamilton*, 27 vols. (New York, 1961–87), 3:485 (1784 "Letter of Phocion" defining "due process of law" as *"indictment or presentment of good and lawful men* and trial and conviction in consequence," quoting Sir Edward Coke in italicized language); James Kent, *Commentaries on American Law*, 2d ed., 4 vols. (New York, 1832), 2:13 (parroting Coke's definition of due process of law, quoted above); Story, *Commentaries*, vol. 3, sec. 1783 (similar). Here, as elsewhere, I do not argue that the clause cannot be applied beyond what I have called its "core" meaning. Indeed, refusal to do so here would render the provision wholly redundant, as the Supreme Court has noted (*Murray's Lessee* v. *Hoboken Land and Improvement Co.*, 59 U.S. [18 How.] 272, 276 [1856]).

on the permanent payroll and too far removed from the people. The jury summed up—indeed embodied—the ideals of populism, federalism, and civic virtue that were the essence of the original Bill of Rights.

If the foregoing picture of the jury seems somewhat unconventional, perhaps the reason is that the present day jury is only a shadow of its former self. First Amendment doctrine has evolved beyond the prohibition against prior restraint, while the judge-created and judge-enforced exclusionary rule has displaced the jury trial for damages as the central enforcement mechanism of the Fourth Amendment—in part because of judge-created doctrines of government officials' immunity from damages.[263] As we shall now see, even the core role of the jury in criminal trials has been seriously eroded over the last two centuries.

Jury review. Consider first the issue of jury review. Let us begin by defining the question with precision. First, the issue is not the general one of jury nullification (can a jury disregard a law it thinks unjust?) but the narrower question of whether a jury can refuse to follow a law if and only if it deems that law *unconstitutional.*[264] The concept is exactly analogous to the idea of judicial review, as traditionally understood. Judges may not ignore a law simply because they think it wrong, or unjust, or silly; but they may—indeed must—do so if they deem it unconstitutional. Second, the question is not whether a jury has the raw *power* of review by entering a general verdict and "getting away with it"—that is, escaping sanctions that would affect the Holmesian "bad man." Rather, the question is whether a jury has the legal right—perhaps even the duty—to refuse to follow a law it deems unconstitutional. As a practical matter, the issue often boils down to whether

[263] Most current immunity doctrines are of a distinctly modern vintage. See Amar, "Sovereignty," p. 1487 and sources cited therein.

[264] These issues are unhelpfully conflated in Alan W. Scheflin, "Jury Nullification: The Right to Say No," *Southern California Law Review* 45 (1972): 168. See, for example, ibid., p. 169 n. 2 (equating jury decision that statute is "unconstitutional" with judgment that statute is "wrong"). But see McCloskey, ed., *Works of Wilson,* 2:542 (jury, in deciding legal questions, is bound by rules of legal reasoning).

an attorney should be allowed to argue unconstitutionality, typically as a defense, to a jury.

This is exactly how the issue arose in perhaps the most famous of all Sedition Act prosecutions, *United States* v. *Callender*,[265] tried in 1800 in a federal circuit court. When publisher James Callender's attorney, William Wirt, tried to argue the statute's unconstitutionality to the jury, he was cut off by presiding Circuit Justice Samuel Chase. Chase was later impeached for his overall handling of *Callender*, and for refusing to allow defense counsel in another criminal case to argue law to the jury. About half of the Senate voted to convict, several votes short of the two-thirds required by the Constitution.[266] Wirt, by contrast, went on to become "one of the greatest Supreme Court advocates of all time and the man who holds the record for years of service as Attorney General."[267] Here is an edited transcript of the Chase-Wirt exchange:

> Here CHASE, Circuit Justice—Take your seat, sir, if you please. If I understand you rightly, you offer an argument to the petit jury, to convince them that the . . . Sedition Law is contrary to the constitution of the Untied States and, therefore, void. Now I tell you that this is irregular and inadmissible; it is not competent to the jury to decide on this point. . . .
>
> . . . . .
>
> . . . We all know that juries have the right to decide the law, as well as the fact—and the constitution is the supreme law of the land, which controls all laws which are repugnant to it.
>
> Mr. Wirt.—Since, then, the jury have a right to consider the law, and since the constitution is law, the conclusion is certainly syllogistic, that the jury have a right to consider the constitution.
>
> CHASE, Circuit Justice.—A non sequitur, sir.
>
> Here Mr. Wirt sat down.[268]

---

[265] 25 F. Cas. 239 (C.C.D. Va. 1800) (No. 14,709).

[266] See materials in Stephen B. Presser and Jamil S. Zainaldin, *Law and Jurisprudence in American History*, 2d ed. (St. Paul, 1989), pp. 228–47.

[267] "Commemoration of the 200th Anniversary of the Supreme Court's First Sitting," *Supreme Court Review* (1990):738, 741.

[268] 25 F. Cas. at 253.

Chase went on to try to explain his ruling, but if anything, it is his arguments that border on non sequitur. At times he seemed to say that if the jury could consider constitutionality, it would necessarily follow that judges could not. But nothing in the idea of judicial review, or in the subsequent *Marbury* case, requires that *only* judges consider constitutionality.[269] Surely, for example, President Jefferson was within his constitutional rights—perhaps duties—when he pardoned those convicted under the Sedition Act because he deemed the act unconstitutional, notwithstanding that Article III circuit courts had held to the contrary in cases involving the very convicts in question. Judges took oaths to uphold the Constitution, as *Marbury* emphasized, but so did presidents and jurors. In his celebrated 1791 lectures on law, James Wilson, who had been second (if that) only to Madison in his contributions to the Constitution, declared: "Whoever would be obliged to obey a constitutional law, is justified in refusing to obey an unconstitutional act of the legislature. . . . When a question, even of this delicate nature, occurs, every one who is called to act, has a right to judge."[270] Though Wilson did not single out juries by name, surely they were "called to act" when requested to send Callender to jail. Theophilus Parsons, who would one day sit as chief justice of his state supreme court, was even more explicit in the Massachusetts ratifying convention: "But, sir, the people themselves have it in their power effectually to resist usurpation, without being driven to an appeal to arms. An act of usurpation is not obligatory; it is not law; and any man may be justified in his resistance. Let him be considered as a criminal by the general government, yet only his own fellow-citizens can convict him; they are his jury, and if they pronounce him innocent, not all the powers of Congress can hurt him; and innocent they certainly will pronounce him, if the supposed law he resisted was an act of usurpation."[271]

---

[269] See *Marbury* v. *Madison*, 5 U.S. (1 Cranch) 137 (1803). See, generally, Amar, "Original Jurisdiction," pp. 445–46 and sources cited therein.

[270] McCloskey, ed., *Works of Wilson*, 1:186.

[271] Elliot, ed., *Debates*, 2:94.

Likewise, *Marbury*'s sonorous claim that "it is emphatically the province and duty of the judicial department to say what the law is"[272] does not necessarily support Chase. As Taylor's bicameral image illustrates, juries can be seen as part of the judicial department—the lower (and if anything, presumptively more legitimate, because more popular) house.[273] Just as both House and Senate had to agree the Sedition Bill was constitutional before it became law, why shouldn't both judge and jury be required to agree on its constitutionality before Callender was sent to jail? Nor was today's strict law-fact distinction between the roles of upper and lower judicial houses so clear in 1800. On the contrary, it was widely believed in late eighteenth-century America that the jury, when rendering a general verdict, could take upon itself the right to decide both law and fact.[274] So said a unanimous Supreme Court in one of its earliest cases (decided before *Callender*),[275] in language that resonates with the writings of some of the most eminent American lawyers of the age—Jefferson, John Adams, and Wilson, to mention just three.[276] Indeed, Chase himself went

[272] 5 U.S. (1 Cranch) at 177.

[273] Taylor, *Inquiry*, pp. 200–201.

[274] Mark DeWolfe Howe, "Juries as Judges of Criminal Law," *Harvard Law Review* 52 (1939):582. Nelson, "John Marshall's Constitutional Jurisprudence," pp. 904–17; "The Changing Role of the Jury in the Nineteenth Century," *Yale Law Journal* 74 (1964):170.

[275] *Georgia* v. *Brailsford*, 3 U.S. (3 Dall.) 1, 4 (1794).

[276] See, for example, Jefferson to L'Abbé Arnoux, July 19, 1789, Boyd et al., eds., *Papers of Jefferson*, 15:282–83; Petition on Election of Jurors, October 1798, Ford, ed., *Writings of Jefferson*, 7:284, Jefferson to Kercheval, July 12, 1816, 10:37, 39; Adams, ed., *Works of Adams*, 2:254–55 (diary entry, Feb. 12, 1771); McCloskey, ed., *Works of Wilson*, 2:540. This view of the power of American juries was articulated as early as 1692 (Levy, *Emergence of a Free Press*, pp. 24–25). Even Alexander Hamilton seems to have believed that juries in criminal cases could decide both law and fact and disregard the bench's instructions on law—or so he argued as defense counsel in 1803. See *Sparf and Hansen* v. *United States*, 156 U.S. 51, 147–48 (1895) (Gray and Shiras dissenting). But compare Edith Guild Henderson, "The Background of the Seventh Amendment," *Harvard Law Review* 80 (1966):289

out of his way to concede that juries were judges of law as well as of fact.[277] Perhaps, however, this concession had to do with the peculiarities of sedition law and its somewhat unusual procedures—driven, it will be recalled, by the struggle between judge and jury. In any event, the line between constitutional law and constitutional fact is often hazy, as illustrated by the "reasonableness" issue in Fourth Amendment jurisprudence.[278]

Chase also suggested that decentralized jury review would undermine the idea of uniform national law—one jury might acquit on constitutional grounds, another might not—but the same thing can be said of Article III judicial review.[279] Through its power to make exceptions to the Supreme Court's appellate jurisdiction, Congress can vest the last word in constitutional cases in lower federal courts who, like juries, might disagree among themselves.[280] The *Callender* case was itself a remarkable example of this truth, for under the Judiciary Act of 1789 the Supreme Court lacked jurisdiction to hear this or any other criminal appeal from circuit courts.[281] (Thus, the most important constitutional issue of the Federalist era never reached the Supreme Court.) Truly, the situation under the Judiciary Act of 1789 was even more decentralized than this. Trials in circuit court, such as Callender's, were presided over by two or even three judges. In the event these judges disagreed among themselves, whose instructions must

---

(distinguishing between civil and criminal juries and dismissing *Georgia* v. *Brailsford* as anomalous).

[277] See text accompanying note 268, above.

[278] See Scalia, "Rule of Law," p. 214.

[279] Professor Scheflin apparently fails to understand this. See Scheflin, "Jury Nullification: Right to Say No," p. 169 n. 2; Alan W. Scheflin and John Van Dyke, "Jury Nullification: The Contours of a Controversy," *Law and Contemporary Problems* 43 (1980): 51, 56.

[280] See, generally, Amar, "A Neo-Federalist View."

[281] See Akhil Reed Amar, "The Two-Tiered Structure of the Judiciary Act of 1789," *University of Pennsylvania Law Review* 138 (1990):1499.

the jury follow? If anything, the very structure of the judges' hierarchy implied a radical decentralization and nonuniformity wholly consistent with jury review.[282]

But would not such a decentralized system lead to confusion and anarchy? Not in any single case, given the Constitution's rather clear procedural structure for aggregating substantive disagreement. In general, these rules work in a systematically antigovernmental, propopulist way. In the event any major institutional actor at the federal level deems a federal law unconstitutional, that institution is typically able to make its constitutional objection stick—at least in criminal law, where persons' lives, liberties, and property are most vulnerable. If either House or Senate deems a criminal bill unconstitutional, it cannot become law; and no person can be convicted in the absence of such a law, because there is no such thing as a "federal common law" of crimes.[283] If the president deems the bill unconstitutional, he may veto or pardon (even before indictment). So too, if judges deem the law unconstitutional, they may order the defendant released and make their decision stick through the Great Writ of habeas corpus. By symmetric logic, juries too should be allowed to

---

[282] See Nelson, *Americanization of the Common Law,* pp. 19, 26, 28, 166; "Changing Role of the Jury," p. 174 n. 27.

[283] See *United States* v. *Hudson and Goodwin,* 11 U.S. (7 Cranch) 32 (1812). The *Hudson* case raises many complications, but I would distill its central insight as follows: In the absence of express congressional authorization, federal courts may not fashion general criminal rules—especially where *Congress's* constitutional authority to enact identical rules is in question. I would defend this insight by invoking the structure of the original Constitution (that is, separation of powers, federalism, and their intersection through "the political safe-guards of federalism"), the Constitution's own heightened procedural rules governing criminal sanctions, and general rules requiring strict construction where penal policy is involved. Thus, various earlier federal judicial decisions in tension with *Hudson* were dubious precedents indeed, defensible only if Congress in the First Judiciary Act meant to delegate its own (limited) criminal authority to federal courts, and such a sweeping statutory grant somehow did not violate constitutional norms of nondelegation. See Judiciary Act of 1789, chap. 20, sec. 11 (giving circuit courts "exclusive cognizance of all crimes and offences cognizable under the authority of the United States" subject to certain exceptions).

use their power to issue a general verdict for defendant to achieve the same result.

Chase's final argument simply asserted the jury's lack of "competence" to decide the Sedition Act's (un)constitutionality. Judges were learned in law, and juries were not. Though this may seem quite obvious today, perhaps the reason is that we have lost the powerful and prevailing sense of two hundred years ago that the Constitution was *the people's* law. Even if juries generally lacked competence to adjudicate intricate and technical "lawyer's law," the Constitution was not supposed to be a prolix code. It had been made, and could be unmade at will, by We the People of the United States—Citizens acting in special single-issue assembles (ratifying conventions), asked to listen, deliberate, and then vote up or down. How, it might be asked, were juries different from conventions in this regard? If ordinary Citizens were competent to make constitutional judgments when signing petitions or assembling in conventions, why not in juries too? Is there not an important truth in Jefferson's exuberant 1789 definition of jury trials as "trials by the people themselves"?[284]

In setting forth the strong arguments for jury review, I do not mean to suggest that I am wholly persuaded. But the mere fact of their strong plausibility shows how strikingly powerful the jury might have become, had post-1800 history unfolded differently. As previously noted, the Supreme Court never heard *Callender* or any other Sedition Act case and, indeed, did not definitively address the issue of jury review until the 1895 case of *Sparf and Hansen* v. *United States*.[285] In upholding Chase's approach, the *Sparf* Court added no real arguments beyond those canvassed above. The strongest defense of its holding comes from provisions never cited by the Court, namely, the Civil War amendments. These amendments did not repeal the fundamentally populist philosophy of the original Constitution and Bill of Rights, but they did radically transform the nature of American federalism. As Jefferson

---

[284] Jefferson to David Humphreys, Mar. 18, 1789, Boyd et al., eds., *Papers of Jefferson*, 14:676–79.

[285] 156 U.S. 51 (1895).

and Taylor understood all too well, acceptance of Wirt's argument for jury review would have created in fundamentally local bodies a power that approached de facto nullification in a wide range of situations. Existence of such a power in local bodies to nullify Congress's Reconstruction statutes might have rendered the Civil War amendments a virtual dead letter. Thus it is plausible to think that these amendments implicitly qualified the (equally implicit) power of local juries to thwart national laws. This, however, was hardly an argument that lay in the mouth of the *Sparf* Court. In the previous two decades, the Supreme Court had *itself* systematically destroyed congressional Reconstruction with the scalpel of stingy statutory construction and the sledgehammer of judicial review.[286]

Waivability of jury trial. For whose benefit did the right to jury trial exist? For Tocqueville, the answer was easy—the core interest was that of the Citizens rather than the parties: "I do not know whether the jury is useful to those who have lawsuits, but I am certain it is highly beneficial to those who judge them."[287] Similarly, Justice Harry Blackmun has written that the public has interests, independent of a criminal defendant, in monitoring judges, police, and prosecutors—and in being "educat[ed about] the manner in which criminal justice is administered."[288] Though speaking of the gallery's right to a "public" trial within the meaning of the Sixth Amendment, Justice Blackmun's insight would seem to apply a fortiori to the jury's right, for every trial in which a jury sits is to that extent a *public* trial, of and by the people, and not just for them.

Nevertheless, in 1930 the Supreme Court held that the jury trial right was defendant's alone, to waive if he pleased. The Court explicitly framed the question as whether jury trial was "only [a] guaranty to the accused" instead of a component of

---

[286] See, for example, *United States* v. *Cruikshank,* 92 U.S. 542 (1876); *The Civil Rights Cases,* 109 U.S. 3 (1883).

[287] Tocqueville, *Democracy in America,* 1:296.

[288] *Gannett Co.* v. *De Pasquale,* 443 U.S. 368, 428–29 (1979) (Blackmun dissenting in part).

the structure of "a tribunal as a part of the frame of government."[289] If the latter, the Court seemed to concede, a judge acting without a jury was simply not a court capable of trying a defendant, just as the Senate acting without the House is not a legislature capable of passing laws.

But as we have seen, the bicameral analogy is historically apt; it is anachronistic to see jury trial as an issue of individual right rather than (also, and, more fundamentally) a question of government structure. None of the arguments in *Patton* v. *United States* survives close scrutiny. Predictably, the Court stressed the words of the Sixth Amendment guaranteeing to "*the accused*" the right of jury trial. But this ignores the clear words of Article III mandating that "the trial of *all* Crimes . . . *shall* be by Jury"—a command no less mandatory and structural than its companion commands that the judicial power of the United States "*shall* be vested in" federal courts, whose judges "*shall*" have life tenure and undiminished salaries, and whose jurisdiction "*shall* extend to *all*" cases in certain categories.[290] The words in the Article III jury clause were plainly understood during the ratification period as words of obligation.[291] Nothing in the Sixth Amendment repeals those words—as would have been the case, for example, had the amendment explicitly conferred upon "the accused" a (waivable?) right to a *non*-jury trial. Before *Patton*, the Supreme Court was on record in *Callan* v. *Wilson* as affirming that the amendment was not "intended to supplant" Article III's jury

[289] *Patton* v. *United States,* 281 U.S. 276, 293 (1930).

[290] On the mandatory character of these other words of Article III, see Amar, "Neo-Federalist View"; idem, "Judiciary Act." Joseph Story, whose opinion of the Court in *Martin* v. *Hunter's Lessee,* 14 U.S. (1 Wheat.) 304 (1816), emphasized the plain meaning of "shall" and "all" in Article III's jurisdictional and tenure provisions, also deemed these words mandatory in the criminal jury context. *United States* v. *Gibert,* 25 F. Cas. 1287, 1305 (C.C.D. Mass. 1834) (No. 15,204).

[291] See, for example, *Federalist* No. 83 (Hamilton), Rossiter, ed., *Federalist Papers,* p. 496; Elliot, ed., *Debates,* 3:520–21 (remarks of Edmund Pendleton at Virginia ratifying convention); 4:145, 171 (remarks of James Iredell in North Carolina ratifying convention), and 290 (remarks of Rawlins Lowndes at South Carolina ratifying convention); Kenyon, ed., *Antifederalists,* p. 51 (report of Pennsylvania convention minority).

clause.[292] In *Callan,* decided in 1888, the Court held that the undiminished words of Article III required jury trials in the District of Columbia, even though the Sixth Amendment speaks only of "State[s]." Nor have any other parts of Article III's jury clause—such as its impeachment exception—been deemed repealed by implication. *Patton's* reading is thus at odds with precedent as well as with the plain words of the Ninth Amendment that the expression of some rights (such as "the accused's" right to jury trial) must never "be construed" by sheer implication to "deny or disparage" other rights guaranteed by the preexisting Constitution (such as the *people's* right to jury trial).[293]

By why, then, was the jury trial language of the amendment necessary? If Article III is as clear as I have suggested, and was so understood in 1789, why did the First Congress add the jury clause of the Sixth Amendment? The historical answer is unequivocal: to guarantee a right to a trial *within the district* of the crime. Article III had not specified jury trial of "the vicinage," as per the prevailing common law, and many Antifederalists wanted an explicit guarantee that juries would be organized around local rather than statewide communities.[294] (Once again, we see the local communitarian spirit of the Bill of Rights.) Thus, perhaps the special Sixth Amendment right to a jury from the "district" is solely the accused's, waivable at will—but the underlying mandate of jury trial itself cannot be waived.

[292] 127 U.S. 540, 549 (1888) (Harlan).

[293] One of the core purposes of the Ninth Amendment was to prevent this sort of misconstruction. See McAffee, "Original Meaning of the Ninth Amendment," p. 1215. For other applications, see text accompanying notes 304–7, below.

[294] See, for example, "Letters from the Federal Farmer" (II-IV), *CAF,* 2:230–31, 244–45, 249; Kenyon, *Antifederalists,* pp. 36, 51 (report of Pennsylvania convention minority); Elliot, ed., *Debates,* 3:578–79 (remarks of Henry in Virginia ratification debates); 4:154 (remarks of Samuel Spencer in North Carolina ratifying convention); 2:400 (remarks of Tredwell in New York ratifying convention); Dumbauld, *Bill of Rights,* pp. 183, 190, 200 (declarations of rights of Virginia, New York, and North Carolina ratifying conventions).

The Sixth Amendment's legislative history overwhelmingly confirms this. Until the mysterious House-Senate conference we earlier noted in conjunction with the First Congress's original First Amendment, the jury clause used language identical to that of Article III ("the trial of all crimes shall be . . .").[295] When House and Senate failed to agree about whether explicitly to introduce the "vicinage" formulation, the compromise language of "district" was chosen,[296] and the clause was dropped into a catchall criminal procedure amendment that used language of the right of "the accused" to various nonstructural benefits including speedy trial, assistance of counsel, confrontation, and compulsory process. To put the historical point in its strongest light, it would be perverse in the extreme to take a clause in the Bill of Rights designed to strengthen jury trial as evincing a desire to weaken it. Had this been the intended or even a plausible reading of the clause of 1789, there would have been howls of protest from Antifederalists like the "Federal Farmer." Instead, there is not a scrap of evidence that anyone thought that the Article III mandate could be slyly undone by the Sixth Amendment.

Ignorance is indeed a great law reformer, but surely there are limits. *Patton* claimed that no one at the Founding viewed jury trial as going beyond the protection of the accused—a statement that ignores the writings of the "Federal Farmer," the "Maryland Farmer," Jefferson, and many others.[297] Thus, *Patton*'s claim that no third-party rights were at stake simply begs the question of jurors' rights. Also question-begging is

---

[295] Dumbauld, *Bill of Rights*, pp. 208, 212, 215.

[296] Ibid., pp. 49 and n. 22, 54; Goebel, *History of the Supreme Court*, pp. 449, 454–55.

[297] Compare Patton, 281 U.S. at 296–97, with material quoted in text accompanying notes 247–60, above. Patton suggested that the colonies allowed bench trials in criminal cases (281 U.S. at 306), but more recent historical studies have called into question the evidence underlying Patton's claims. See Susan C. Towne, "The Historical Origins of Bench Trial for Serious Crime," *American Journal of Legal History* 26 (1982):123. In any event, this history is of only tangential relevance to the meaning of Article III and the Sixth Amendment, whose wording differed considerably from various colonial and state constitutional antecedents.

reliance on the fact that other Sixth Amendment rights are waivable, since these concededly do not go to the structure and status of the court as a properly constituted tribunal and do not implicate any Article III mandate. Nor can reliance be placed on the "greater" power of defendant to waive trial altogether by pleading guilty; for surely that would not allow the alleged "lesser" power of permitting a criminal defendant who pled not guilty to be tried by a federal "judge" who lacked Article III status—say, the Speaker of the House, in clear violation of the bill of attainder clause. Equally unavailing is the argument that civil jury trial is waivable. Indeed, the clear language of the Supreme Court's earliest treatment of the waiver issue cuts exactly the opposite way. In 1819 the Court wrote, "Had the terms been, that 'the *trial* by jury shall be preserved,' it might have been contended, that they were imperative, and could not be dispensed with. But the words [of the Seventh Amendment] are, that the *right* of trial by jury shall be preserved, which places it on the foot of [waivable rights]."[298] As noted before, the language of Article III is imperative in just the way the Court appeared willing to acknowledge. Indeed, as late as 1898, the Supreme Court, per Justice John Marshall Harlan, was squarely on record as declaring that a criminal defendant could not waive jury trial.[299] *Patton* breezily dismissed the 1898 discussion as "dictum" (it wasn't) and failed even to mention an 1874 Supreme Court case whose unambiguous language squarely addressed the precise issue in *Patton:* "In a criminal case, [defendant] cannot

---

[298] *Bank of Columbia* v. *Okely,* 17 U.S. (4 Wheat.) 235, 244 (1819). In dramatic contrast to the universal view during the ratification debates that Article III did mandate jury trial in all criminal cases—and properly so— various proposals for civil jury were expressly limited to situations where "the parties, or either of them request it" (Dumbauld, *Bill of Rights,* pp. 176, 182 [proposed amendments of Massachusetts and New Hampshire ratifying conventions]).

[299] *Thompson* v. *Utah,* 170 U.S. 343, 353–54 (1898). Unanimity on this point is evident as late as 1904, even as the Court split on the analytically distinct issue of the degree to which petty crimes fell within the scope of the Article III mandate. *Schick* v. *United States,* 195 U.S. 65 (1904).

. . . be tried in any other manner than by a jury of twelve men, although he consent in open court to be tried by a jury of eleven men."[300]

Nevertheless, it would be a mistake to put all the blame for the vanishing significance of the jury on the shoulders of the *Patton* Court. The issue in *Patton* was a rather narrow one: could a defendant who pled not guilty be tried without a (twelve-person) jury? Even had *Patton* said no, back door evasion of jury trial was possible through the device of the guilty plea. Historically, the petit jury had a role only at trial; a guilty plea occurred prior to, and precluded, any trial (although even a guilty plea could occur only after a different jury— the grand jury—had authorized the charge).[301] As a practical matter, the back door opened by guilty pleas was of little significance two hundred years ago, for as Albert W. Alschuler has shown, such pleas were then highly atypical, and plea bargaining was generally viewed with suspicion, if not hostility.[302] Today, by contrast, roughly 90 percent of criminal defendants convicted in American courts plead guilty, and plea bargaining has the explicit sanction of the Supreme Court.[303]

The Popular Sovereignty Amendments

In light of the strongly populist cast of all the preceding amendments, it is wholly fitting that the Bill of Rights ends with back-to-back invocations of "the people": "The enumeration in the Constitution, of certain rights, shall not be con-

[300] *Insurance Co.* v. *Morse*, 87 U.S. (20 Wall.) 445, 451 (1874) (dictum).

[301] See, for example, *United States* v. *Gibert*, 25 F. Cas. 1287, 1304 (C.C.D. Mass. 1834) (No. 15,204) (Story); Schick, 195 U.S. at 81–82 (Harlan dissenting); Francis Howard Heller, *The Sixth Amendment to the Constitution of the United States* (Lawrence, Kans., 1951), p. 71.

[302] Albert W. Alschuler, "Plea Bargaining and Its History," *Columbia Law Review* 79 (1979):1–24; see also Nelson, *Americanization of the Common Law*, p. 100 (noting judicial discouragement of guilty pleas in capital cases).

[303] Alschuler, "Plea Bargaining," pp. 1, 40 (citing statistics and Supreme Court cases).

strued to deny or disparage others retained by the people," and "The powers not delegated to the United States by the Constitution, nor prohibited by it to the States, are reserved to the States respectively, or to the people."

The popular sovereignty motif of the Tenth Amendment could not be more obvious. We the People, acting collectively, have delegated some powers to the federal government, have allowed others to be exercised by state governments, and have withheld some things from all governments. The Preamble and the Tenth Amendment are perfect bookends, fittingly the alpha and omega of the Founding and its gloss.

The obviously collective meaning of "the people" in the Tenth Amendment (and everywhere else) should alert us that its core meaning in the Ninth is similarly collective. As I have explained in detail elsewhere,[304] the most obvious and inalienable right underlying the Ninth Amendment is the collective right of We the People to alter or abolish government, through the distinctly American device of the constitutional convention. We have already seen that this clarifying gloss—with antecedents in virtually every state constitution—was initially proposed as a prefix to the Preamble, only to be dropped for stylistic reasons and resurrected in the First Amendment's explicit right of "the people" to assemble in convention.[305] So too, with both the Ninth and Tenth Amendments' use of that phrase. Indeed, Hamilton in *Federalist* No. 84 explicated the Preamble in language that perfectly foreshadowed the later amendments' wording: "[Our Constitution is] professedly founded on the power of *the people*. Here, in strictness, *the people* surrender nothing; and as they *retain* everything they have no need of particular *reservations*, 'WE, THE PEOPLE of the United States, to secure the blessings of liberty to ourselves and our posterity, do ordain and establish this Constitution for the United States of America.' Here is a [clear] recognition of *popular rights*."[306] To see the Ninth as

---

[304] Amar, "Philadelphia Revisited," pp. 1044–60.

[305] See text accompanying notes 103–9, above.

[306] *Federalist* No. 84 (Hamilton), Rossiter, ed., *Federalist Papers*, p. 513 (emphasis altered).

centrally about countermajoritarian individual rights—such as privacy—is to engage in anachronism.[307]

Finally, let us consider how the Tenth Amendment elegantly integrates popular sovereignty with federalism.[308] All government power derives from the people, but these grants are limited. The federal government has only powers "delegated" to it, expressly or by implication, and certain "prohibit[ions]" are imposed on state governments. How are these government agents to be kept within these limits? In part by mutual jealousy and monitoring, as we have seen throughout. State legislatures could alert the people to any perceived usurpations by central agents (consider the "sirens" sounded by the Virginia and Kentucky legislatures in 1798, or the Hartford Convention in 1814–15), state militias could thwart and thus deter a tyrannical standing army, state common law of trespass could help vindicate persons' Fourth Amendment rights, and so on. Once again, populism and federalism—liberty and localism—work together.

THE BILL OF RIGHTS AS A CONSTITUTION

It is now time to step back and see what larger lessons may be pieced together from the story thus far.

The Bill of Rights . . .

Reading old rights holistically. In this essay I have tried to suggest how much is lost by the clause-bound approach that now dominates constitutional discourse. The clause-bound approach misses the ways in which structure and rights mutually reinforce. It misses interesting questions *within* amendments,

---

[307] Accord McAffee, "Original Meaning of the Ninth Amendment." Although a source of many insights, Professor McAffee's essay seems to move a bit too quickly past the phrase "retained by the people" and the popular sovereignty theory underlying that phrase. For an equally insightful corrective, see "Was the Flag Burning Amendment Unconstitutional?" *Yale Law Journal* 100 (1991):1073. See generally Amar, *Philadelphia Revisited,* pp. 1043–76.

[308] For further elaboration, see Amar, "Sovereignty," pp. 1492–1519.

like "why is the takings clause lumped together with the rest of the Fifth Amendment?" It misses the thematic continuities *across* different amendments—such as the popular sovereignty motif sounded by repeated invocations of "the people," and the ways in which jury trial issues influenced the thinking behind the First, Fourth, and Eighth Amendments. It misses the many linkages between the original Constitution and the Bill—the importance of earlier invocations of "the people" in the Preamble and Article I, the connection between the free speech clause and the speech and debate clause, the relevance of the enumerated power philosophy of Article I for First Amendment absolutism, the subtle interplay between the militia and army clauses of Article I and the Second and Third Amendments, the implications of the Article III jury trial command for the Sixth Amendment, the nonexclusivity of Article V signaled by the First, Ninth, and Tenth Amendments, and so on.

How could we forget that our Constitution is a *single* document and not a jumble of disconnected clauses—that it is *a* Constitution we are expounding?

Taking new rights seriously. The Bill of Rights as I have sketched it here differs dramatically from its conventional image in the minds of both lawyers and lay folk. If my account is persuasive, must we abandon current folk wisdom and case law?

Not necessarily. As I have tried to emphasize at a number of strategic points, adoption of the Fourteenth Amendment appears to have transformed the nature of the Bill. The original Bill's strong emphasis on popular sovereignty theory makes it especially important to attend to the effect of subsequent constitutional amendments. For that theory requires interpreters to take "more modern [amendments] at least as seriously as more ancient ones."[309] In Bruce Ackerman's terminology, interpreters must try to "synthesize" the meanings of chronologically separated "constitutional moments."[310]

[309] See Amar, "Our Forgotten Constitution," p. 293.

[310] Bruce Ackerman, "Constitutional Politics/Constitutional Law," *Yale Law Journal* 99 (1989):453, 515–47; see also note 115, above.

This sort of synthesis—holism across time—is hardly mechanical. Indeed, to be done well, synthesis requires extraordinary legal and historical sensitivity.[311] But the first step is to recognize the problem: the worldview underlying the Bill of Rights was not dominated by the idea of individualistic, countermajoritarian rights. In this essay I have not gone much beyond this first step nor attempted to consider in any comprehensive way how much of the Bill, as originally understood, survives the subsequent adoption of Amendments Eleven through Twenty-six. For the problem of synthesis, of course, is by no means limited to the Fourteenth Amendment.

To take one obvious example, consider the fact that, as originally conceived, militias and juries were all male. Of course, the exclusion of women reflects the strong connections between these two institutions and suffrage—also all male two hundred years ago. But once We the People adopted the Nineteenth Amendment, guaranteeing women the vote, how could judges continue to permit sex discrimination in juries and militias? To be sure, the words *jury* and *militia* appear nowhere in the Nineteenth Amendment—but by the same token, the word *male* appears nowhere in the earlier references to these institutions. What remains constant across time is the underlying understanding that jury and militia service are *political* rights and duties, closely linked to suffrage.[312] Once suffrage rights are extended, corresponding and coextensive changes must occur in juries and militias. To put the point another way, could any law making women ineligible to hold

[311] For example, although the Fourteenth Amendment is aimed only at state governments, its attempt to bring citizen rights against both state and federal governments into sync may have interesting feedback effects on the character of rights against *federal* officials. Given that the original texts of many provisions are broad enough to encompass minority rights against the federal government, the gloss placed on these provisions by the Fourteenth Amendment may have inverted the "core" and the "peripheral" applications—even against the federal government.

[312] Indeed, President Wilson and many other lawmakers ultimately endorsed the proposed Nineteenth Amendment as a war measure, in recognition of the role of women as economic soldiers in the war effort. See note 152, above.

office be reconciled with the Nineteenth Amendment? I think the answer is no, even though the amendment does not explicitly speak of holding office.[313] The same should hold true for other political rights.[314]

Yet things have not seemed so clear to the Supreme Court. Not until 1975, more than a half century after the Nineteenth Amendment became the supreme law of the land, did the Court strike down sex discrimination on juries, in an opinion that nowhere mentioned the suffrage amendment.[315] In 1981 the Court upheld sex discrimination in draft registration. Once again, the Nineteenth Amendment went unmentioned.[316]

Part of the problem, I suggest, is that judges tend to view the original Bill of Rights as more modern than it really was. Once judges see how deeply the Bill was rooted in certain

[313] During debates preceding the Fifteenth Amendment, various leading congressmen took the sensible position that the right to hold office need not be explicitly mentioned, since, absent a clear statement to the contrary, the right to be voted for was implicit in the right to vote. See Grimes, *Democracy and the Amendments*, p. 57.

[314] See, for example, text accompanying note 254, above (Tocqueville's linkage of electorate and jury pool); Amar, "Choosing Representatives," p. 1290 n. 38 (discussing various modern statutes that "use voter registration rolls as a first approximation of" the pool of eligible jurors); see also *Palmer* v. *State*, 150 N.E. 917–18 (Ind. 1926) (post–Nineteenth Amendment case requiring that women be eligible to sit on state juries: "Where, by statute, jurors are to be selected from qualified electors, the adoption of a constitutional amendment making women electors qualifies them for jury duty" [citing cases]). Feminists in the early twentieth century appear to have clearly understood that women's capacity to serve on juries was intimately linked to the larger issue of women's suffrage. See, for example, Susan Glaspell's "A Jury of Her Peers," in E. J. H. O'Brien, ed., *The Best Short Stories of 1917* (London, 1918), pp. 256–82.

[315] *Taylor* v. *Louisiana*, 419 U.S. 522 (1975). Interestingly, the Nineteenth Amendment did get fleeting mention in one of the first postsuffrage Supreme Court cases involving sex discrimination on juries. See *Fay* v. *New York*, 332 U.S. 261, 290 (1947).

[316] *Rostker* v. *Goldberg*, 453 U.S. 57 (1981). Compare the views of the National Organization for Women: "Omission from the registration and draft ultimately robs women of the right to first-class citizenship," quoted in Scarry, "War and the Social Contract."

eighteenth-century assumptions, courts are likely to spend more time carefully reflecting on the words and spirit of later amendments that *are* more modern in their underlying vision.

. . . as a Constitution

Today, the very phrase "Bill of Rights" is virtually synonymous with a compilation of countermajoritarian personal rights. Cause and effect are hard to disentangle; does the definition drive, or is it driven by, the standard reading of *our* Bill of Rights? Either way, we should recognize how different standard usage was two hundred years ago. The virulent Antifederalist Luther Martin, for example, argued during 1788 for "a bill of rights" that would encompass "a stipulation in favour of the rights both of states and of men."[317] George Mason, the leading proponent of a Bill of Rights at the Philadelphia Convention, also linked the project to an express reservation of states' rights.[318] Another leading Antifederalist urged a "declaration in favour of the rights of states and of citizens."[319] In the New York ratifying convention, Thomas Tredwell lamented: "Here we find no security for the rights of individuals, no security for the existence of our state governments; here is no bill of rights."[320] In proposing provisions to be included in such a Bill, Tredwell emphasized populist provisions: "freedom of election, a sufficient and responsible representation, the freedom of the press, and the trial by jury both in civil and criminal cases."[321] In a similar populist spirit,

---

[317] Farrand, ed., *Records of the Convention,* 3:290 (Luther Martin's Reply to the Landholder).

[318] Ibid., 2:640 (George Mason's objections to Constitution); Elliot, ed., *Debates,* 3:444 (remarks of Mason in Virginia ratifying convention).

[319] "Letters of Agrippa" (XVI), *CAF,* 4:111.

[320] Elliot, ed., *Debates,* 2:401; see also 3:445–46 (similar remarks of Henry at Virginia ratifying convention); McAffee, "Original Meaning of the Ninth Amendment," pp. 1241–44 (discussing and quoting other Antifederalists linking Bill of Rights with states' rights).

[321] Elliot, ed., *Debates,* 2:399.

Thomas Jefferson wrote that "a bill of rights is what *the people* are entitled to against every *government* on earth."[322]

Gordon Wood sums up this Antifederalist spirit well:

> The Antifederalists' lack of faith was not in the people themselves, but only in the [regular government] organizations and institutions that presumed to speak for the people. . . . Enhancing the people out-of-doors as it correspondingly disparaged their elected officials, [Antifederalist thought] can never be considered undemocratic. [Antifederalists] were "localists," fearful of distant governmental, even representational, authority for very significant political and social reasons that in the final analysis must be called democratic.[323]

The Federalists also understood that calls for a Bill of Rights were driven by populist and localist concerns. In 1788 Madison wrote Jefferson that proponents of a Bill of Rights sought "further guards to *public liberty* & individual rights."[324] In *Federalist* No. 38 he noted that some critics "concur[red] in the absolute necessity of a bill of rights, but contend[ed] that it ought to be declaratory, not of the personal rights of individuals, but of the rights reserved to the States in their political capacity."[325] And in *Federalist* No. 84 Hamilton stressed that "one object of a bill of rights [is] to declare and specify the *political* privileges of the citizens in the *structure* and *administration* of the government."[326]

Hamilton's answer to the drumbeat for a Bill of Rights was to stress the ways in which the original Constitution fit the bill,

---

[322] Jefferson to Madison, Dec. 20, 1787, Boyd et al., eds., *Papers of Jefferson*, 12:438, 440 (emphasis added).

[323] Wood, *Creation of the American Republic*, p. 520; see also p. 516 (describing Antifederalists as populists emphasizing widespread participation in government). But see "Letters of Agrippa" (XVI), *CAF*, 4:111 (explicit argument for protections of "the minority against the usurpation and tyranny of the majority").

[324] Hutchinson et al., eds., *Papers of Madison*, 11:297 (letter of Oct. 17, 1788; emphasis added).

[325] *Federalist* No. 38 (Madison), Rossiter, ed., *Federalist Papers*, p. 235.

[326] *Federalist* No. 84, ibid., p. 515 (emphasis added).

so to speak. For Hamilton and many others, the Philadelphia Constitution was "itself, in every rational sense, and to every useful purpose, A BILL OF RIGHTS."[327] But this point can be flipped around. As I have tried to show throughout, the Bill of Rights can itself be seen as a *Constitution* of sorts—that is, as a document attentive to structure, focused on the "agency" problem of government, and rooted in the sovereignty of We the People of the United States.

Seeing the importance of structure. Like the original Constitution, the original Bill of Rights was webbed with structural ideas. Federalism, separation of powers, bicameralism, representation, amendment—these issues were understood as central to the preservation of liberty. My point is not that substantive "rights" are unimportant, but that these rights were intimately intertwined with structural considerations.

Consider, in this regard, Jesse H. Choper's thesis that courts should treat "structural" issues such as federalism and separation of powers as nonjusticiable and save their prestige for the protection of "individual rights."[328] For Choper, the only items that fall within the second category are those things that no government—state or federal—may do. Issues of federalism, Choper assures us, lie beyond the judicial ken because true liberty is not involved—the issue is simply *which* government can intrude.[329]

But two hundred years ago, the issue of which government often made all the difference in the world. The original Constitution specified only three things that neither federal or state government could do: pass bills of attainder, enforce ex post facto laws, and grant titles of nobility. To make matters even worse for Choper, the first two of these prohibitions obviously have structural overtones in the area of separation of

---

[327] Ibid.; see also McMaster and Stone, eds., *Pennsylvania and the Federal Constitution*, p. 252 (remarks of Thomas McKean in Pennsylvania ratifying convention: "The whole plan of government is nothing more than a bill of rights—a declaration of the people in what manner they choose to be governed").

[328] Choper, *Judicial Review.*

[329] Ibid., pp. 174–75.

powers.[330] When we look at the original Bill of Rights, an even starker pattern emerges: none of its provisions bound state governments. This regime, epitomized by *Barron* v. *Baltimore*,[331] a case Choper never even mentions in over four hundred pages of text—was the de jure constitutional framework for almost a century. De facto, *Barron* survived well into this century and was not decisively dethroned until the Warren Court. Only after the near-total incorporation of the Bill of Rights against states and the "reverse-incorporation" of equal protection principles against the federal government—both of which occurred after World War II—did it become natural to define "individual rights" as Choper does. Yet Choper nowhere signals his awareness of just how odd his ideas would have sounded to earlier generations. When Choper does purport to do history, his claims become even more outlandish: "The assertion that federalism was meant to protect . . . individual constitutional freedoms . . . has no solid historical or logical basis."[332]

Getting beyond the countermajoritarian difficulty. I have singled out Dean Choper for special criticism because his work is particularly clear in its effort to distill and defend widely held, but distinctly modern, ideas about the Constitution. The work of Alexander M. Bickel also epitomizes much modern thinking about the Constitution. "The root difficulty," Bickel wrote in one of his most quoted sentences, "is that judicial review is a counter-majoritarian force in our system."[333] By focusing so singlemindedly on one of the two main issues flagged by Madison in *Federalist* No. 51—the problem of minority rights—Bickel's work has unfortunately diverted our attention from

[330] See Ely, *Democracy and Distrust,* p. 90 (both "clauses prove on analysis to be separation of powers provisions, enjoining the legislature to act prospectively and by general rule [just as the judiciary is implicitly enjoined by Article III to act retrospectively and by specific decree]").

[331] 32 U.S. (7 Pet.) 243 (1833).

[332] Choper, *Judicial Review,* p. 244.

[333] Alexander M. Bickel, *The Least Dangerous Branch: The Supreme Court at the Bar of Politics* (Indianapolis, 1962), p. 16.

Madison's other chief concern, namely, the "agency" problem of government. As we have seen, only by taking seriously the "agency" issue can we fully understand the original Bill of Rights. Elsewhere I have tried to show how inattention to "agency" problems has led to profound misunderstandings about federalism, sovereign immunity, and the amendment process.[334] And this is only the beginning. Renewed scholarly attention to "agency" issues could shed new light on a vast number of other constitutional questions, just as renewed emphasis on "agency costs" has importantly energized the recent law and economics literature.

Putting the people back into the Constitution. Attention to the "agency" problem should remind us that all permanent government officials—even Article III judges—may at times pursue self-interested policies that fail to reflect the views and protect the liberties of ordinary Americans. As the Fourth Amendment warrant clause and the Eighth Amendment make clear, professional judges acting without Citizen juries can sometimes be part of the problem, rather than the solution.

Today it is commonplace to stress judicial review as the most natural enforcement mechanism of the Bill of Rights. But consider again the two historical quotations typically invoked for this idea. First, there is Madison's speech before the First Congress: "If [rights] are incorporated into the constitution, independent tribunals of justice will consider themselves in a peculiar manner the guardians of those rights; they will be an impenetrable bulwark against every assumption of power in the legislative or executive [branch]."[335]

Madison surely had Article III judicial review in mind here, but he may also have been thinking of juries. He speaks not of "judges" but "tribunals," which from one perspective can be seen as encompassing both the "upper" house of the judge and the "lower" house of the jury. If "independen[ce]" be the key to Madison's remarks, we must remember that juries were

---

[334] See Amar, "Sovereignty"; idem, "Philadelphia Revisited."

[335] *Annals of Congress,* 1st Cong., 1st sess., 1:457 (June 8, 1789).

arguably even less dependent on executive and legislature, since jurors had never been appointed by these branches, and did not draw any permanent salary from them. Emphasis on the populist and localist jury would fit perfectly with other things Madison said in the above-quoted speech. For example, in the sentence immediately after his mention of "independent tribunals" he stressed federalism as an enforcement device: "Besides this security, there is a great probability that such a declaration in the federal system would be enforced; because the State Legislatures will jealously and closely watch the operations of this Government, and be able to resist with more effect every assumption of power, than any other power on earth can do; and the greatest opponents to a Federal Government admit the State Legislatures to be sure guardians of the people's liberties."[336] Moments earlier, Madison had pointed to the importance of "public opinion" in making the Bill of Rights more than a mere "paper barrier."[337]

Now turn to Jefferson's comment that a bill of rights would put a "legal check . . . into the hands of the judiciary. This is a body, which if rendered independent, and kept strictly to their own department merits great confidence for their learning and integrity."[338] Here too, Jefferson plainly has in mind judicial review by judges. But elsewhere, he made clear that he viewed juries as part of the "judiciary." Indeed, only three months after his approving comments about judges and judicial review, and a full decade before *Callender,* Jefferson argued that where they suspected self-dealing or other "agency" bias on the bench, ordinary Citizen jurors could constitute themselves as judges of both fact and law: "But we all know that permanent judges acquire an Esprit de corps, that being known they are liable to be tempted by bribery, that they are misled by favor, by relationship, by a spirit of party, by a devotion to the Executive or Legislative. . . . It is left therefore to

---

[336] Ibid.

[337] Ibid., p. 455.

[338] Jefferson to Madison, Mar. 15, 1789, Boyd et al., eds., *Papers of Jefferson,* 14:659.

the juries, if they think the permanent judges are under any biass whatever in any cause, to take upon themselves to judge the law as well as the fact. They never exercise this power but when they suspect partiality in the judges."[339]

Beyond juries, both Madison and Jefferson emphasized public education as the remedy for, and deterrent to, unconstitutional conduct. Wrote Jefferson, "Written constitutions may be violated in moments of passion or delusion, yet they furnish a text to which those who are watchful may again rally and recall *the people;* the fix too for *the people* the principles of their political creed."[340] The words of the Bill of Rights would themselves educate Americans; hence the appropriateness of didactic, nonlegalistic phrases such as "a well regulated Militia [is] necessary to the security of a free State."[341] Such maxims were the heart and soul of early state constitutions.[342]

---

[339] Jefferson to L'Abbé Arnoux, July 19, 1789, ibid., 15:282 (citing book "Jurors judges both of law and fact by Jones"); for further evidence of Jefferson's views, see sources cited in note 276, above.

[340] Jefferson to Joseph Priestley, June 19, 1802, Ford, ed., *Writings of Jefferson*, 8:158–60.

[341] See, for example, Story, *Commentaries*, vol. 3, sec. 1859 (Bill of Rights "serves to guide, and enlighten public opinion"); "Letters from the Federal Farmer" (XVI), *CAF,* 2:324–25 ("If a nation means its systems, religious or political, shall have duration, it ought to recognize the leading principles of them in the front page of every family book. What is the usefulness of a truth in theory, unless it exists constantly in the minds of the people and has their assent. . . . education [consists of] a series of notions impressed upon the minds of the people by examples, precepts and declarations"); Tucker, *Blackstone's Commentaries*, 1:308 app. ("A bill of rights may be considered, not only as intended to give law, and to assign limits to a government, . . . but as giving *information to the people* [so that] every man of the meanest capacity and understanding may *learn* his own rights"; emphasis added).

[342] See Robert C. Palmer, "Liberties as Constitutional Provisions, 1776–1791," in William E. Nelson and Robert C. Palmer, *Liberty and Community: Constitution and Rights in the Early American Republic* (New York, 1987), p. 55; Brant, *Bill of Rights*, pp. 37–42. Recall Daniel Webster's language, noted earlier: "[My constituents and I] live under a [state] constitution which *teaches us*" certain maxims of democratic self-governance. See text accompanying note 188, above (emphasis added). Also recall the obviously didactic

Virginia's famous 1776 Declaration of Rights even featured a maxim about the need for maxims! "No free government, or the blessings of liberty, can be preserved to any people, but by . . . virtue, and by frequent recurrence to fundamental principles."[343] A Bill of Rights would crystallize these principles so that they could be memorized and internalized—much like scripture—by ordinary Citizens.[344] In the words of one 1788 commentator, a bill of rights "will be the first lesson of the young citizens."[345] Patrick Henry and John Marshall agreed on very little in the Virginia ratifying convention, but when Henry declared that "there are certain maxims by which every wise and enlightened people will regulate their conduct," Marshall went out of his way to agree that such maxims "are necessary in any government, but more essential to a democracy than to any other."[346]

Madison, too, stressed popular education and popular enforcement: "What use then it may be asked can a bill of rights serve in popular Governments? . . . 1. The political truths declared in that solemn manner acquire by degrees the character of fundamental maxims of free Government, and as they become incorporated with the national sentiment, counteract the impulses of interest and passion. 2. [Whenever] usurped

---

language of the Massachusetts constitutional provisions concerning Harvard and of virtually all state constitutions regarding civilian supremacy over the military, notes 144, 181, above.

[343] Virginia Declaration of Rights (1776), Sec. 15.

[344] Madison well understood the mnemonic benefits of maxims for ordinary Citizens. See *Federalist* No. 53 (Madison), Rossiter, ed., *Federalist Papers*, pp. 330–32. Hamilton, less of a true populist, was more critical. See *Federalist* No. 84, p. 513 (didactic "aphorisms which make the principal figure in several of our State bills of rights . . . would sound much better in a treatise of ethics than in a constitution of government"). Hamilton was of course also less enthusiastic about militias and juries. See *Federalist* Nos. 26 (Hamilton), 29, 83.

[345] Quotation in Herbert J. Storing, "The Constitution and the Bill of Rights," in Robert A. Goldwin and William A. Schambra, eds., *How Does the Constitution Secure Rights?* (Washington, D.C., 1985), p. 31.

[346] Elliot, ed., *Debates*, 3:137, 223.

acts of the Government [occur], a bill of rights will be a good ground for an appeal to the sense of the community."[347] In 1792 Madison—the great champion of internal checks and balances—noted that such checks "are neither the sole or the chief palladium of constitutional liberty. *The people* who are the authors of this blessing, must also be its guardians."[348]

The emphasis on popular enforcement would of course prove prescient. Less than a decade after the Bill of Rights became law, federal judges cheerfully sent men to jail for criticizing the government, but opponents of the Sedition Act—led by Jefferson and Madison—ultimately prevailed by "*appeal[ing]* to the sense of the community."[349] First, they attempted to "appeal" from judges to juries, who embodied this community sense. When blocked by judges, they used the media of state legislatures to transform the election of 1800 into a national public seminar on constitutional principles. Thus educated, ordinary Citizens on election day registered the "community sense" that the Act was usurpation.

Though their personal labors in founding the University of Virginia signaled the special depth of their commitment, Madison and Jefferson were hardly unique in seeing the centrality of public education. In 1775, for example, Moses Mather declared that "the strength and spring of every free government is the virtue of the people; virtue grows on knowledge, and knowledge on education."[350] After quoting Mather, Gordon Wood sums up the ethos of the era in his own words: "And education, it was believed, was the responsibility and agency of a republican government. So the circle

[347] Madison to Jefferson, Oct. 17, 1788, Hutchinson et al., eds., *Papers of Madison*, 11:298–99. Madison here closely tracked the remarks of Edmund Randolph concerning the Virginia Bill of Rights, quoted in Schwartz, comp., *Bill of Rights*, 1:249.

[348] *National Gazette* essay on U.S. government, Feb. 4, 1792, Hutchinson et al., eds., *Papers of Madison*, 14:218; accord Wood, *Creation of the American Republic*, pp. 33–35 (Constitution "ultimately sustained" by "the very spirit of the people"); p. 377 ("genius" and "habits" of people prevail over "paper . . . form[s]" in constitutions and bills of rights, quoting Noah Webster).

[349] See text accompanying note 347, above.

[350] Quoted in Wood, *Creation of the American Republic*, p. 120.

went."[351] "The most obvious republican instrument for . . . inculcating virtue in a people was education."[352] We should not be surprised, then, that each of the first six presidents of the United States urged the formation of a national university. In the didactic language of the Massachusetts constitution of 1780: "Wisdom and knowledge, as well as virtue, diffused generally among the body of the people, being necessary for the preservation of their rights and liberties; and as these depend on spreading the opportunities and advantages of education . . . it shall be the duty of legislatures and magistrates . . . to encourage [these ends]."[353]

The idea of popular education resurfaces over and over in the Bill of Rights. As we have seen, each of the three intermediate associations it safeguards—church, militia, and jury—was understood as a device for educating ordinary Citizens about their rights and duties. The erosion of these institutions over the last two hundred years has created a vacuum at the center of our Constitution. Thus, one of the main tasks for today's constitutional theorists should be to explore ways this vacuum might be filled. Revisiting the *Rodriguez* case[354] and establishing a constitutional right to public education might be one place to start.[355] An uneducated populace cannot be a truly sovereign populace.

Yet it is exactly such a truly sovereign people who constitute the rock on which our Constitution is built. The opening words of the Preamble, of course, dramatize this truth; but so do the words of the Bill of Rights. For I hope it has not escaped our notice that no phrase appears in more of the first ten amendments than "the people."

[351] Ibid.

[352] Ibid., p. 426.

[353] Massachusetts constitution of 1780, Pt. II, Chap. V, Sec. II.

[354] *San Antonio Independent School Dist.* v. *Rodriguez*, 411 U.S. 1 (1973).

[355] For some tentative thoughts, see Akhil Reed Amar, "Forty Acres and a Mule: A Republican Theory of Minimal Entitlements," *Harvard Journal of Law and Public Policy* 13 (1990):37.

FORREST McDONALD

The Bill of Rights
Unnecessary and Pernicious

AMIDST THE MANY paeans of praise for the Framers of the Constitution that were uttered during the bicentennial season, one scarcely heard a word to the effect that the Framers flatly rejected proposals to include a Bill of Rights as part of our organic law. Most Americans today, were they so informed, would be either disbelieving or totally confused, for most think in a vague sort of way that the Bill of Rights *is* the Constitution, even as they think that the First Amendment guarantees are the Bill of Rights and that among those rights are life, liberty, and the pursuit of happiness. Historians of the subject know better, but even they—or at least the vast majority of them—seem to believe that the Framers were wrong, and that the adoption of the Bill of Rights has secured American liberties far more firmly than our constitutional order could otherwise have done.

Yet the fact remains that the thirty-nine men who signed the Constitution thought that popular rights were adequately protected by the original document. Most of them believed, as well, that adding a bill of rights could produce little or nothing in the way of further protection and might well be pernicious in its consequences. Inasmuch as their ranks included such towering figures as George Washington, James Madison, Alexander Hamilton, Roger Sherman, John Dickinson, James Wilson, Gouverneur Morris, and John Rutledge—wise men all, most of whom had risked their lives, their fortunes, and their sacred honor in the cause of American liberty—it behooves us to examine their position more closely and to survey the course of American history to determine whether their judgment proved to be sound or unsound.

THE BILL OF RIGHTS

The heretical position that I shall take in the pages that follow is that they were far more nearly right than wrong.

Bills of rights were a hallowed part of the legacy Americans inherited from their English forebears. The first "bill of rights" was Magna Charta (1215); during the following four centuries, according to Sir Edward Coke, it was reenacted thirty-two times. Its principles were reiterated in the 1628 Petition of Right, acceded to at least nominally by Charles I, and again in the 1689 Bill of Rights.[1] All these, however, were irrelevant to American circumstances after Independence, for they had been guarantees of the rights of the people extracted from the sovereign, which is to say the Crown. In America, the people as citizens of the several states was the sovereign, and it were a solecism to speak of guaranteeing the rights of the people against the people.

Notwithstanding the incongruity, six of the eleven states that adopted new constitutions during the American Revolution included in those constitutions declarations of rights of one sort or another, and several others incorporated provisions for certain rights, such as freedom of religion for Christians, in the body of the document. Moreover, there was a logic to these inclusions, for the new state governments, unlike governments of delegated and enumerated powers, had (as representatives of the sovereign people) all powers not constitutionally forbidden them.

But these declarations and provisions were, by and large, mere statements of principles—the bill of rights to the Virginia constitution, for example, was a preamble—without substantive force in law. The only exception of consequence was involved in the Quock Walker Case (1783), in which the Massachusetts Supreme Court ordered the freedom of a slave on the ground that the state constitution of 1780 declared that "all men are born free and equal."[2]

---

[1] Irving Brant, *The Bill of Rights: Its Origin and Meaning* (Indianapolis, 1965), p. 7; Sir Edward Coke, *The Second Part of the Institutes of the Laws of England*, 4 vols. (1629; reprint ed., Buffalo, 1986).

[2] Francis Newton Thorpe, comp., *The Federal and State Constitutions, Colonial Charters, and Other Organic Laws . . .* , 7 vols. (1909; reprint ed., Washing-

Against that background, the action, or rather inaction, of the Federal Convention of 1787 in regard to a bill of rights is scarcely surprising. The subject first arose, after a fashion, on August 20, when Charles Pinckney of South Carolina introduced thirteen propositions on a variety of subjects including popular rights. The resolutions were turned over to a committee without debate, and though they never emerged from committee, some of them found their way into the text of the Constitution by other means. The matter arose again on September 12, when Elbridge Gerry of Massachusetts proposed and George Mason of Virginia seconded a motion to appoint a committee to draft a bill of rights. The motion elicited little comment and was rejected by a unanimous vote of the delegations present.[3]

Federalists in the state conventions that ratified the Constitution repeatedly spelled out the reasons why adding a bill of rights made no sense. In New York, John Jay pointed out the inappropriateness of the English experience to American circumstances. "In days and countries where monarchs and their subjects were frequently disputing about prerogative and privileges," he said, the subjects "found it necessary, as it were, to run out the line between them" and oblige the monarchs "to admit, by solemn acts, called bills of rights, that cer-

---

ton, D.C., 1977), 3:1889. The case was *Quock Walker* v. *Nathaniel Jennison* (1783). Henry Steele Commager, ed., *Documents of American History*, 7th ed., 2 vols. (New York, 1963), 1:110. Compare the Virginia constitution of 1776 (Thorpe, 7:3813), whose bill of rights, Section 1, read "that all men are by nature equally free and independent," but which did not result in freeing the slaves.

[3] Max Farrand, ed., *The Records of the Federal Convention of 1787*, rev. ed., 4 vols. (1937; New Haven, 1966), 2:334–35, 340–42, 587–88. The Elbridge Gerry–George Mason proposal for a bill of rights to preface the Constitution arose in the context of Hugh Williamson's objection that "no provision was yet made for juries in Civil cases." Nathaniel Gorham answered, "It is not possible to discriminate equity cases from those in which juries are proper. The Representatives of the people may be safely trusted in this matter." The comment after the motion was made came from Roger Sherman who said, "The State Declarations of Rights are not repealed by this Constitution; and being in force are sufficient—There are many cases where juries are proper which cannot be discriminated. The Legislature may be safely trusted" (2:587–88).

tain enumerated rights belonged to the people" and could not be encroached upon by the Crown. "But, thank God, we have no such disputes; we have no monarchs to contend with, or demand admissions from."[4]

In North Carolina, James Iredell repeated that argument and gave it another dimension. The English had no written constitution, "fixed and certain," that showed "plainly the extent of that authority which they were disputing about." Had they had such a constitution, "a bill of rights would have been useless." The American Constitution was different from the English, deriving its authority not from "remote antiquity" but from "a declaration of particular powers by the people to their representatives, for particular purposes." The people, through the Constitution, "expressly declare how much power they do give, and consequently retain all they do not." Iredell likened the Constitution to "a great power of attorney, under which no power can be exercised but what is expressly given."[5]

Many Federalists pointed out the difference between the state constitutions and the United States Constitution. Col. Joseph B. Varnum declared that in Massachusetts "the legislative have a right to make all laws not repugnant to the Constitution," and if that were true of the United States Constitution, "there would be a necessity for a bill of rights." But that was not the case; under Article I, Section 8, all powers were "express, and required no bill of rights." Edmund Randolph made the same argument, in different words, in the Virginia ratifying convention, as did James Wilson in Pennsylvania and others elsewhere.[6]

[4]Jonathan Elliot, ed., *The Debates in the Several State Conventions, on the Adoption of the Federal Constitution,* 5 vols. (Philadelphia, 1836–59), 1:498.

[5]Ibid., 4:148.

[6]Ibid., 2:78, 3:467, 2:436. Rufus King and Gorham responded to Gerry's objections in a similar fashion on Nov. 3, 1787. They wrote: "When the constitution vests in the Legislature 'full power & authority,' . . . a Declaration or Bill of Rights seems proper, But when the powers vested are explicitly defined both as to quantity & the manner of their Exercise," a bill of rights "is certainly unnecessary & improper" (James H. Hutson, ed., *Supplement to Max Farrand's The Records of the Federal Convention of 1787* [New Ha-

Wilson made additional points as well. He indicated that South Carolina, Delaware, New Jersey, New York, Connecticut, and Rhode Island had no bills of rights, despite the power of their legislatures to make all laws not prohibited, and yet those states were no less free than Pennsylvania, which did have a declaration of rights. He also made the comparison between England and America and rang a change upon that argument and upon the one about the difference between state and national constitutions. "A bill of rights to a constitution," he said, "is *an enumeration of the powers* reserved" by the people. "If we attempt an enumeration, every thing that is not enumerated is presumed to be given." Thus "an imperfect enumeration would throw all implied power into the scale of the government, and the rights of the people would be rendered incomplete." Almost no one, he declared, knew enough to formulate an all-inclusive list of people's rights. The great writers on natural law and natural rights, "from *Grotius* and *Puffendorf* down to *Vattel,* have treated on this subject; but in no one of those books, nor in the aggregate of them all, can you find a complete enumeration of rights appertaining to the people as men and as citizens."[7]

In Virginia several Federalists scoffed at the supposed efficacy of "parchment" guarantees of rights. Referring especially to a wartime incident in which a Virginia renegade had been convicted and executed by bill of attainder, Edmund Pendleton said, "I believe every gentleman will see that it is unconstitutional to condemn any man without a fair trial," for to do so violated principles of justice, the common law, and the Virginia Declaration of Rights, which declared "that no man shall be condemned without being confronted with his accusers and witnesses; that every man has a right to call for evidence in his favor, and, above all, to a speedy trial by an

---

ven, 1987], p. 284). As Alexander Hamilton wrote in *Federalist* No. 84, "The truth is . . . that the Constitution is itself, in every rational sense, and to every useful purpose, A BILL OF RIGHTS."

[7] Elliot, ed., *Debates,* 2:436–37, 453–54. The authorities cited are Hugo Grotius (1583–1645), author of *De Jure Belli ac Pacis,* Samuel von Pufendorf (1632–1694), author of *De Jure Naturae et Gentium,* and Emmerich de Vattel (1714–1767), author of *Le Droit des Gens.*

impartial jury of the vicinage, without whose unanimous consent he cannot be found guilty. These principles have not been attended to." Wilson Cary Nicholas declared that "that man who was killed, not *secundum artem,* was deprived of his life without the benefit of law, and in express violation of [the Virginia] declaration of rights. . . . This bill of rights was no security. It is but a paper check. It has been violated in many other instances. . . . If we had no security against torture but our declaration of rights, we might be tortured to-morrow."[8]

James Madison, in the same convention, discussed the matter of religious freedom, of which he was well known as a champion. Disdaining Antifederalist claims that a bill of rights was necessary for the protection of religious liberty, he employed reasoning similar to that which he used in regard to factions in his celebrated essay, *Federalist* No. 10. The country's religious freedom, he said, "arises from that multiplicity of sects which pervades America, and which is the best and only security for religious liberty in any society; for where there is such a variety of sects, there cannot be a majority of any one sect to oppress and persecute the rest." Besides, he added, no constitutional restraint was necessary because "there is not a shadow of right in the general government to intermeddle with religion. Its least interference with it would be a most flagrant usurpation."[9]

[8] Elliot, ed., *Debates,* 3:298–99, 450–51. Edmund Pendleton was referring to Section 8 of the Virginia bill of rights, which specified the rights of the accused in capital or criminal prosecutions (Thorpe, *Federal and State Constitutions,* 7:3813).

[9] Elliot, ed., *Debates,* 3:330. Edmund Randolph made a similar argument: "I am a friend to a variety of sects, because they keep one another in order. How many different sects are we composed of throughout the United States! How many different sects will be in Congress! . . . There are now so many . . . that they will prevent the establishment of any one sect, in prejudice to the rest, and will forever oppose all attempts to infringe religious liberty." Randolph extended the argument by pointing out that the constitutional prohibition of religious tests as requirements for office holding (Article VI) guarantees religious diversity in Congress and puts "all sects on the same footing" (2:204). Notice that in Jonas Phillips's letter to the Constitutional Convention (Sept. 7, 1787), as a Philadelphia Jew seeking the inclusion of what became Article VI, he expressed confidence that the pro-

The classical formulation of the Framers' argument against a bill of rights was that penned by Alexander Hamilton in *Federalist* No. 84. The whole Constitution, Hamilton wrote, was properly to be regarded as a bill of rights because of its checks and balances, the federal principle, and above all the strictly limited powers it vested in the central government, leaving all others to the states. Thus "a minute detail of particular rights is certainly far less applicable to a Constitution . . . which is merely intended to regulate the general political interests of the nation," than to the constitutions of the states, which had "the regulation of every species of personal and private concerns." But he went further and contended that an itemization of rights was "not only unnecessary in the proposed Constitution, but would even be dangerous." Such an itemization would contain "exceptions to powers not granted; and, on this very account, would afford a colorable pretext to claim more than were granted. For why declare that things shall not be done which there is no power to do?" For example, to say that liberty of the press shall not be violated "would furnish, to men disposed to usurp, a plausible pretence" for claiming a national power to regulate the press in other ways.[10]

---

hibition of religious tests would be a sufficient constitutional protection for Jews "to live under a goverment where all Relegious societys are on an Eaquel footing" (Farrand, ed., *Records of the Convention*, 3:79). James Madison, in a letter to Thomas Jefferson, Oct. 17, 1788, in addition to calling bills of rights "parchment barriers," noted that "experience proves the inefficacy of a bill of rights on those occasions when its control is most needed" (Gaillard Hunt, ed., *The Writings of James Madison*, 9 vols. [New York, 1900–1910], 5:271–75).

[10] Charles Cotesworth Pinckney made a similar argument before the South Carolina House of Representatives on Jan. 18, 1788. He said, "With regard to the liberty of the press, . . . It was fully debated, and the impropriety of saying any thing about it in the Constitution clearly evinced. The general government has no powers but what are expressly granted to it; it therefore has no power to take away the liberty of the press . . . and to have mentioned it in our general Constitution would perhaps furnish an argument, hereafter, that the general government had a right to exercise powers not expressly delegated to it. For the same reason, we had no bill of rights inserted in our Constitution; for, as we might perhaps have omitted

This argument was criticized at the time and has been criticized by some modern scholars on the ground that it is falsified by the Constitution itself. That is, Article I, Section 9, contains a list of things Congress or the national government in general may not do. The most thorough rebuttal to this charge was made by Edmund Randolph. Every exception contained in Section 9, Randolph said, was from powers granted to Congress in Article I, Section 8, and he went through them one by one. The first prohibited Congress from interfering with the slave trade for twenty years; otherwise Congress could have done so under "the power given them to regulate commerce." The second forbade suspending the writ of habeas corpus except during emergencies; otherwise the writ could have been suspended "by virtue of the power given to Congress to regulate courts." The third prohibited bills of attainder and ex post facto laws; these, Randolph pointed out, had "always been the engines of criminal jurisprudence." The prohibition was thus "an exception to the criminal jurisdiction" vested in Congress. The fourth prohibited the levying of capitation or other direct taxes, an exception from the enumerated power to tax, as was the fifth, banning taxes on exports; the sixth, prohibiting preference of ports in one state over another's and banning the taxation of interstate commerce; and the seventh, forbidding expenditures without appropriations. The eighth restriction prohibited granting titles of nobility. "If we cast our eyes to the manner in which titles of nobility first originated," Randolph said, "we shall find . . . these sprang from military and civil offices. Both are put in the hands of the United States," and therefore the restriction was "an exception to that power." Finally, Section 9 prohibited officers of the United States from receiving emoluments from foreign kings, princes, or states without the consent of Congress. "All men," Randolph indicated, "have a natural inherent right of receiving emoluments from any one, unless they be restrained by the regulations of

---

the enumeration of some of our rights, it might hereafter be said we had delegated to the general government a power to take away such of our rights as we had not enumerated" (Farrand, ed., *Records of the Convention*, 3:256).

the community." The restraint in the Constitution was necessary as a safeguard against corruption.[11]

In sum, the restrictions in Section 9 were qualitatively different from proposals to provide for freedom of religion or of the press, for the restrictions were against things that the national government otherwise would have been empowered to do.

Clearly, the Federalists had the better of the debate, both logically and historically. Be it remembered that they had the better of it politically, too, for the Constitution was ratified by eleven states before the Bill of Rights was even proposed and by all thirteen before it was adopted.

The proposal and adoption of the Bill of Rights came about not because of popular demand or the logic or persuasive powers of its advocates but as a tactical political response to the machinations of Antifederalist enemies of the Constitution, who were motivated by less exalted concerns than the liberties of the people. Antifederalists were unorganized during the early months of the campaign for ratification and lacked a positive program, with the result that Federalists carried the conventions of eight of the required nine states by the spring of 1788. But then the Antis agreed upon a strategy of stepping up propagandistic agitation for a bill of rights— only two states had actually called for amendments—and for a second constitutional convention, ostensibly to amend but in fact to undo the work of the first. They failed to achieve their initial aim, to make ratification by the remaining states conditional upon the calling of a second convention, but the movement had gained a large number of highly vocal adherents by the time the first presidential and congressional elections were held late in 1788. In the circumstances, most Federalists decided that they must head off the danger by reversing themselves and sponsoring a "safe" bill of rights.[12]

---

[11] Elliot, ed., *Debates*, 3:464–65.

[12] Forrest McDonald, *E Pluribus Unum: The Formation of the American Republic, 1776–1790* (1965; reprint ed., Indianapolis, 1979), pp. 334, 341, 345, 351–52, 359, 366–67. For a detailed study of Antifederalist tactics and

Among the leaders in adopting the new posture was James Madison, who had political axes to grind. Patrick Henry, the leading Antifederalist in Virginia and devout personal enemy of Madison, used his great influence in the state legislature to elect two Antifederalists to the United States Senate, thus closing that avenue to Madison's ambition. Then Henry induced the legislature to place Madison's home county, Orange, in a congressional district with six Antifederalist counties. Madison campaigned for the House seat anyway and won it by depicting himself as the arch-champion of a bill of rights, which the state's ratifying convention had recommended.[13]

True to his campaign promise, Madison served notice in the House on May 4, 1789, that he would in three weeks introduce a set of constitutional amendments (thus obviating the need for a convention to draw them), and on the twenty-fifth he did so. In the ensuing debates he was opposed by a handful of Federalists from New England, but the vast majority of Federalists supported him. To the surprise of no one, the opposition was led by Antifederalists who, until a few weeks earlier, had been crying loudly for a bill of rights. Madison prevailed, and the movement for a second constitutional convention collapsed.[14]

---

aims in one state, see Philip A. Crowl, "Anti-Federalism in Maryland, 1787–1788," *William and Mary Quarterly*, 3d ser. 4 (1947):446–69. See also Steven R. Boyd, *The Politics of Opposition: Antifederalists and the Acceptance of the Constitution* (Millwood, N.Y., 1979), pp. 20–22, 82; Brant, *Bill of Rights*, p. 39; and Herbert J. Storing, ed., *The Complete Anti-Federalist*, 7 vols. (Chicago, 1981), 1:67, 69. The best survey of the historical literature is James H. Hutson, "The Drafting of the Bill of Rights: Madison's 'Nauseous Project' Reexamined," *Benchmark* 3 (1987):309–20. For the shift by Federalists, see Ralph A. Rossum, "'To Render These Rights Secure': James Madison's Understanding of the Relationship of the Constitution to the Bill of Rights," *Benchmark* 3 (1987):11–13.

[13] McDonald, *E Pluribus Unum*, p. 366.

[14] Especially instructive as to Madison's reasoning and his line of argument is the speech he made in the House of Representatives, June 8, 1789. See *The Debates and Proceedings in the Congress of the United States*, 2 vols. (Washington, D.C., 1834–56), 1:449, 453, 459. See also Robert Allen Rutland, *The Birth of the Bill of Rights, 1776–1791* (Chapel Hill, 1955), pp. 190–216.

Madison had studied the subject with characteristic thoroughness. Proposals for amendments had come in from three additional ratifying conventions and from dissenters in four more; the total number of proposals was upwards of two hundred. Eliminating duplicates, Madison found eighty substantive proposals. Dismissing the most impractical and least popular, he condensed the remainder into nineteen. When these were passed by the House on August 24, they had been consolidated into seventeen. As they emerged from the House, the amendments would have applied to state governments as well as to the national government.[15]

The Senate took up the proposed amendments nine days later, almost its first action being to remove their applicability to the states. Otherwise it generally concurred, though it and a joint committee that met on September 25 consolidated the amendments into twelve. The first two, concerning the number and salaries of congressmen, were not ratified at that time by the requisite number of states. The other ten, known collectively as the Bill of Rights, became part of the Constitution on December 15, 1791.[16]

A special word concerning the Ninth and Tenth Amendments is in order. The Ninth provides that "the enumeration in the Constitution, of certain rights, shall not be construed to deny or disparage others retained by the people." Indisputably, that was designed to obviate the difficulty, pointed out by Wilson and others, of making an all-inclusive enumeration of rights, and the dangers inherent in that difficulty. The Tenth provides that "the powers not delegated to the United States by the Constitution, nor prohibited by it to the States, are reserved to the States respectively, or to the people." Clearly that was designed to ensure that the interpretation of the Constitution espoused by the Federalists during the contests over ratification—that it established a government of limited, delegated powers—would prevail. To Americans it would have appeared as a renunciation for all time of the infa-

[15] Edward Dumbauld, *The Bill of Rights and What It Means Today* (Norman, Okla., 1957), pp. 33–44.

[16] Ibid., pp. 46–48.

mous Declaratory Act of 1766, in which Parliament claimed a power to legislate for the colonies "in all cases whatsoever." Congress was to have no such power.

Another way of putting it is that the Ninth Amendment sought to guarantee that the first eight would not be dangerous, and the Tenth declared them to be unnecessary.

Before taking up the larger question, how much or how little protection the Bill of Rights has historically afforded, let us consider Hamilton's concern lest the prohibition of certain things serve as a handle for exerting powers that otherwise the national government would not have. In retrospect his caution may seem to have been misplaced, but during the early decades after the adoption of the amendments at least two were employed just as Hamilton had predicted.

The first concerned freedom of the press. As Hamilton said, the original Constitution gave Congress no power, express or implied, to legislate in regard to the press. The First Amendment declared that "Congress shall make no law . . . abridging the freedom of speech, or of the press." The operative word is *abridging:* to abridge is to reduce, to diminish. After the adoption of the amendment, then, Congress could by inference be empowered to legislate concerning freedom of the press so long as it did not diminish it.

The subject came up less than seven years after the ratification of the amendment. In the summer of 1798, amidst the frenzy for war against France that was set off by the publication of the XYZ correspondence, President John Adams and the Federalists in Congress were avid to muzzle their Republican critics—who, in Federalist eyes, were behaving in a downright subversive fashion. They might have done so by bringing indictments under the common law of seditious libel, which according to Blackstone prohibited "malicious defamations of any person, and especially a magistrate, made public . . . in order to provoke him to wrath, or expose him to public hatred, contempt, and ridicule." Both the Washington and the Adams administrations had brought common law indictments for assorted crimes in their efforts to keep the United States neutral in the French Revolutionary wars, and they had met with considerable success. But in April 1798, just days after the publication of the XYZ papers, Supreme Court Justice Samuel Chase, riding on circuit, ruled in the case of *United States* v. *Worrall* that there were no federal common law crimes, and he would hear no common law indictments. But for the First Amendment, the matter would have ended there.[17]

Instead, on July 14 Congress passed and Adams signed the Sedition Act, making it a federal crime to publish "any false, scandalous and malicious writing" against the president, Congress, or the United States government. The constitutional justification for the act is to be found in the use of the word *false*. Under the common law as received in every American state, truth was not a defense in cases of seditious libel, for as Chancellor James Kent would later write, "whether true or false, it was equally dangerous to the public peace." But under the Sedition Act truth was made a defense; therefore the act augmented rather than abridged freedom of the press.[18] The first of many instances in which the federal government suppressed freedom of the press was thus justified by the First Amendment.

The other early abuse of popular rights through the Bill of Rights grew out of the Seventh Amendment, which provides for jury trials in civil suits. It also provides that "no fact tried by a jury, shall be otherwise reexamined in any Court of the United States, than according to the rules of the common law."

Those provisions are not so simple and straightforward as they seem from a twentieth-century perspective. To understand them, one must review briefly the history of common

[17] Sir William Blackstone, *Commentaries on the Laws of England*, 4 vols. (London, 1795), 4:150. *United States* v. *Worrall*, 2 Dall. 384 (1798); Charles Warren, *The Supreme Court in United States History*, 2 vols. (Boston, 1922), 1:159n, 433–34. The question of a federal common law of crimes was a vexed one. For an excellent analysis of it, see Kathryn Preyer, "Jurisdiction to Punish: Federal Authority, Federalism and the Common Law of Crimes in the Early Republic," *Law and History Review* 4 (1986):223–323.

[18] Commager, ed., *Documents of American History*, 1:177. Forrest McDonald, *Novus Ordo Seclorum: The Intellectual Origins of the Constitution* (Lawrence, Kans., 1985), pp. 48–49. James Kent, *Commentaries on American Law*, 4 vols. (New York, 1844), 2:18.

law juries in England and America. For centuries juries were subordinate to judges, who could imprison and otherwise punish jurors for rendering verdicts contrary to law or to the judge's reading of the evidence. That power was terminated by the Bushell case in 1670, and for almost a century English juries ruled freely in matters of law as well as fact. Then, after Lord Mansfield became chief justice in 1756, English courts began to employ an assortment of technical pleas and procedures to curtail the powers of juries.[19]

But in America such procedures were largely unused or ineffective, and on a case-to-case basis juries continued to exercise virtually absolute power. In practice they were the government, declaring what the law was, finding its source in nature and in principles of natural equity. When they saw fit, they disregarded the instructions of the judge as to what the law was, and even the plain language of an act of Parliament or of a colonial or state legislative enactment.[20]

Enter the Seventh Amendment, with its provision that no *fact* tried by a jury could be reexamined in a higher court. By implication, limiting the exemption to reexamination of facts effectively confirmed the power of appellate courts to overturn jury findings in matters of law. Within a generation after the adoption of the amendment, the process of "Mansfieldizing" American juries would be well under way, and within another generation the power to decide questions of law had been almost totally taken away from juries.[21]

The next matter to consider is how efficacious the Bill of Rights has proved to be in practice. Obviously the various provisions are meaningful only if, in the case of substantive rights, they are protected, and in the case of procedural

---

[19] McDonald, *Novus Ordo Seclorum*, p. 40.

[20] Ibid., pp. 40–41 and n. 40.

[21] Morton J. Horwitz, *The Transformation of American Law, 1780–1860* (Cambridge, 1977), pp. 28–29, 84–85, 141–43, 155–59, 228. William E. Nelson, *Americanization of the Common Law: The Impact of Legal Change upon Massachusetts Society, 1760–1830* (Cambridge, 1975), pp. 165–71. Edith Guild Henderson, "The Background of the Seventh Amendment," *Harvard Law Review* 80 (1966):289–337.

rights, they are adhered to in courts of law, and ultimately in the Supreme Court. Measured by those criteria, three of the ten amendments can be dismissed at the outset. For a number of historical reasons the Third Amendment, concerning the quartering of troops in private homes, never arose, though Edward Dumbauld's observation is worth recalling. The armed services, he wrote, "have not put soldiers into the houses of citizens; they have simply removed the citizens from their houses and put them in the army, navy, and air force." The Ninth Amendment, the reserved rights one, was not invoked until quite recently, and never, so far, as the sole justification of a Supreme Court decision. There is, it should be added, a large and growing body of literature by legal scholars, arguing for or against activation of the Ninth. As for the Tenth Amendment, the reserved powers one, no less an authority than Edward S. Corwin believed that it proved effective for a time, though the cases he cited turned upon a narrow reading of the commerce clause rather than upon the amendment. In any event, those cases have long since been overturned, and despite Justice Sandra Day O'Connor's dalliance with the Tenth in *Gregory* v. *Ashcroft,* I know no one who would contend that the Tenth Amendment offers any real protection today.[22]

[22] Dumbauld, *Bill of Rights,* quotation p. 62; see also pp. 65–66; Thomas B. McAffee, "The Original Meaning of the Ninth Amendment," *Columbia Law Review* 90 (1990):1215–1320; Marshall L. DeRosa, *The Ninth Amendment and the Politics of Creative Jurisprudence* (New Brunswick, N.J., 1996); Louis Fisher, *American Constitutional Law* (New York, 1990), pp. 374, 433–37; Charles A. Lofgren, "The Origins of the Tenth Amendment: History, Sovereignty, and the Problem of Constitutional Intention," in Ronald K. L. Collins, ed., *Constitutional Government in America* (Durham, N.C., 1980); Raoul Berger, *Federalism: The Founders' Design* (Norman, Okla., 1987); Eugene W. Hickok, Jr., "On Federalism," *Benchmark* 3 (1987):229–38; Paul J. Mishkin, "The Current Understanding of the Tenth Amendment," in Eugene W. Hickok, Jr., ed., *The Bill of Rights: Original Meaning and Current Understanding* (Charlottesville, Va., 1991), pp. 465–73. In *Report to the Attorney General: The Constitution in the Year 2000: Choices Ahead in Constitutional Interpretation,* Oct. 11, 1988, the Office of Legal Policy notes that in *Garcia* v. *San Antonio Metropolitan Transit Authority,* 469 U.S. 528 (1985) "the Court held that state sovereignty was adequately and more properly protected by the national political process and that issues of federalism were most appropriately debated and

THE BILL OF RIGHTS

The Supreme Court has sometimes used portions of the other seven amendments to protect people against excesses committed by the national government, but as a rule it has done so only in circumstances in which there is no serious threat of such excesses. To put it the other way around, the Court has not been willing to enforce or honor the Bill of Rights whenever one or more of seven sometimes overlapping conditions are present: (1) the justices feel that the integrity and independence of the judiciary are in danger of compromise or destruction by the political branches; (2) the president and Congress are united in support of particular policy objectives; (3) the Court sympathizes with or is indifferent to specific violations of the Bill of Rights; (4) the nation is gripped by a widespread sense of emergency, local or national; (5) the country is at war; (6) groups or individuals targeted by repressive policies are extremely unpopular; and (7) the revenues of the national government are at stake. To repeat, whenever any of these conditions is present—which is to say, precisely the circumstances in which individual rights are most imperiled—the Supreme Court tends to look the other way, at least until the conditions disappear. Let us take up each set of conditions, one at a time.

Grave threats to the Court by the political branches have arisen three times in American history, and on each occasion the Court pulled in its horns and allowed the government to do whatever it pleased. The first came early in the nineteenth century: Jeffersonian Republicans, outraged by the Judiciary Act of 1801, by John Adams's "midnight appointments," and by the Court's daring to declare a part of an act of Congress unconstitutional in *Marbury* v. *Madison,* virtually declared war on the federal judiciary. The most serious attempt was a scheme to purge the bench through the impeachment process. As a trial run, a Pennsylvania judge was removed by impeachment and conviction; next Congress impeached and removed a federal district judge in New Hampshire; and

---

resolved within such a legislative context" (p. 132). The report concludes that the Court "could decide to reverse its current course," but that "for those who view federalism as a serious concern ... the Supreme Court's law in this area is troubling" (p. 139).

402

then, in 1804, the House impeached Justice Samuel Chase. Pending the trial in the Senate, Republicans made it plain that they intended to clear the Court completely and replace the judges with Jeffersonian appointees.[23]

Chase was not convicted, the movement collapsed, and the independence of the judiciary remained intact. It is significant, however, that more than half a century elapsed before the Supreme Court declared another act of Congress unconstitutional. During that period the national government repeatedly violated the Bill of Rights, but the Court declined to intervene. Interestingly, one Bill of Rights case did reach the Court during John Marshall's long tenure as chief justice. The city of Baltimore seized for public use certain property of a man named Barron, who challenged the action on the ground that it deprived him of property without due process of law and just compensation, in violation of the explicit guarantees in the Fifth Amendment. The Marshall Court ruled against him, holding that the Bill of Rights did not limit the powers of local or state governments; it applied only to the federal government.[24]

When the Supreme Court again grew so bold as to declare another act of Congress unconstitutional—in the Dred Scott case (1857)—it soon learned anew that it was (as Hamilton had said in *Federalist* No. 78) "beyond comparison the weakest of the three departments of power." The decision elicited new demands for impeachment, but the greater threats to the Court came during the Civil War and shortly afterward. As will be seen, both the Bill of Rights and the Constitution were trampled into dust during the war; when Chief Justice Roger Brooke Taney sought to protect the rights of individuals, President Lincoln simply ignored him. After the war, when radical Republicans in Congress enacted a host of measures of questionable constitutionality, the Supreme Court held its peace; when it suggested that it might rule in a politically incorrect way in a particular case, Congress summarily removed

[23] *Marbury v. Madison*, 5 U.S. 137 (1803); Forrest McDonald, *The Presidency of Thomas Jefferson* (Lawrence, Kans., 1976), pp. 35–36, 49–51, 81–82, 89–93.

[24] *Barron v. Baltimore*, 32 U.S. (7 Pet.) 243 (1833).

its jurisdiction. Only after all danger to the Court had passed did it resume its full powers and duties.[25]

The other major threat to the integrity of the Court came in the 1930s. In 1937 Franklin Roosevelt, irate because the Court had declared unconstitutional several of his New Deal measures, proposed his "court-packing plan." The plan was not passed into law: it suddenly became unnecessary, for two conservative justices prudently switched sides, converting a 5–4 majority into a 3–6 minority, and other justices resigned or died. During the next generation, however, despite countless overt violations of the Bill of Rights, the Court held only one act of Congress and one action of a president unconstitutional.

A second circumstance under which the courts and the Bill of Rights are unlikely to provide protection is when Congress unites behind a strong president who is determined to pursue a policy at all costs. A stunning case is afforded by the efforts of the Jefferson administration to enforce the embargo enacted in December 1807 and strengthened by additional statutes in the first few months of 1808. Defiance of the embargo began as soon as northern ports started to thaw in February and March, whereupon Jefferson asked for and obtained from Congress legislation empowering collectors of the revenues to seize ships and cargoes, without a warrant or the prospect of a trial, upon the mere formation of a suspicion that a shipper or merchant *contemplated* a violation of the embargo. This was in direct violation of the Fourth and Fifth Amendments. He also asked for and obtained congressional authorization to use the army and navy to enforce the law. Contemporaneously, Jefferson declared the region around Lake Champlain—where some entrepreneurs from Vermont and upstate New York were transporting goods to Canada on rafts—to be in a state of insurrection. He ordered state and federal officials, "and all other persons, civil and military, who shall be found within the vicinage," to suppress the supposed rebellion "by all means in their power, by force of arms or

---

[25] *Dred Scott* v. *Sandford,* 60 U.S. (19 How.) 393 (1857); *Ex parte McCardle,* 74 U.S. (7 Wall.) 506 (1869).

otherwise." Local residents protested in vain at being sub-jected wholesale to the stigma of insurrection for the viola-tions of a few.[26]

The enforcement policy was challenged in the courts, and to Jefferson's mortification it was overruled by one of his Re-publican appointees. The collector at Charleston had im-pounded a ship and its cargo not because he suspected any intention to violate the law but because he was bound by exec-utive order. The owners brought suit to clear the vessel, and Supreme Court Justice William Johnson, sitting on circuit court, issued the appropriate writ late in May. Jefferson's at-torney general, Caesar Rodney, promptly issued and released to the press a contrary opinion, including a scathing rebuke of Johnson; the administration thenceforth followed Rodney's opinion in disregarding adverse rulings by lower courts.[27]

As the summer wore on, defiance of the embargo spread, and Jefferson and Secretary of the Treasury Albert Gallatin became convinced that judges and juries were totally unrelia-ble. Instead of going to the courts, they increasingly resorted to martial law and the armed forces. Gallatin advised the pres-ident that "arbitrary powers," which were "equally dangerous and odious," would be necessary to enforce the embargo. Jef-ferson agreed, insisting that "Congress must legalize all *means* which may be necessary to obtain its *end*"—and then pro-ceeded as if all possible means had already been legalized. Throughout the summer and fall the army and navy were deployed against American citizens, pitched battles erupted frequently, and scores of civilians were wounded and some killed. Whole towns were declared under the taint of treason. By November, when Congress was scheduled to reconvene,

[26] McDonald, *Presidency of Jefferson*, p. 149; Leonard W. Levy, *Jefferson and Civil Liberties: The Darker Side* (New York, 1973), pp. 107, 130–31; Dumas Malone, *Jefferson the President: Second Term, 1805–1809* (Boston, 1974), p. 585. For the embargo in general, see Walter W. Jennings, *The American Em-bargo, 1807–1809* (Iowa City, 1921), and Louis M. Sears, *Jefferson and the Embargo* (Durham, N.C., 1927).

[27] McDonald, *Presidency of Jefferson*, pp. 150–51; Levy, *Jefferson and Civil Liberties*, pp. 126–30; Donald G. Morgan, *Justice William Johnson: The First Dissenter* (Columbia, S.C., 1954).

Jefferson was preparing a final solution to the problem of un-cooperative courts: persons accused of violating or intending to violate the embargo would in effect be deprived of the right to offer any defense. The president suggested to one congressman that historically, in times of emergency, "the universal resource is a dictator."[28]

Still another circumstance under which the Court is passive in the face of violations of the Bill of Rights arises when it regards particular infringements with indifference or approval. That the Court does so might surprise novices in the field, but specialists are aware that what the Court cares about varies from time to time; it is prone to be preoccupied with one kind of rights for a generation or two and then lose interest in the subject. For example, it was intensely concerned with protecting property rights between the 1890s and the 1930s, at which time interest in such rights went out of fashion. In 1944 it overturned a large body of public utility regulatory law it had fashioned over the decades, now ruling that the Federal Power Commission could set rates so low as to be confiscatory, despite the taking clause of the Fifth Amendment.[29] A little earlier, the Court had upheld the presidential seizure of the property of certain Russian-Americans on the strength of an executive agreement, the so-called Litvinov Assignment of 1933—again despite the Fifth Amendment. On the basis of that and two related decisions, the president might theoretically bargain away the rights of all citizens merely by agreeing to do so with a foreign head of state.[30]

[28] McDonald, *Presidency of Jefferson*, pp. 151–52; Levy, *Jefferson and Civil Liberties*, pp. 115–19; Jefferson to James Brown, Oct. 27, 1808, Andrew A. Lipscomb and Albert Ellery Bergh, eds., *The Writings of Thomas Jefferson*, 20 vols. (Washington, D.C., 1904–5), 12:183.

[29] Forrest McDonald, *A Constitutional History of the United States* (Malabar, Fla., 1986), p. 203; *Federal Power Commission* v. *Hope Natural Gas Co.*, 320 U.S. 584 (1944).

[30] *United States* v. *Curtiss-Wright Export Corp.*, 299 U.S. 304 (1936); *United States* v. *Belmont*, 301 U.S. 324 (1937); *United States* v. *Pink*, 315 U.S. 203 (1942). For the Court's more recent failure to protect private property rights, see *Hawaii Housing Authority* v. *Midkiff*, 467 U.S. 229 (1984); Fisher, *American Constitutional Law*, p. 471.

Similarly, the Court was for several decades not so concerned with First Amendment rights as it has been in recent years. In 1842 Congress passed an act prohibiting the importation of "indecent and obscene prints, paintings, lithographs, engravings, and transparencies," and in 1865 it prohibited the mailing of any "obscene book, pamphlet, picture, print, or other publication of a vulgar and indecent character." In 1872 Congress added to the banned material "disloyal devices printed or engraved." None of these enactments was successfully challenged in the Court; indeed, the Court explicitly declared that Congress could refuse the use of the mails "for the distribution of matter deemed injurious to the public morals." In 1912 Congress saw fit to protect the public's morals by making it illegal to import or ship in interstate commerce or send through the mails films of prize fights intended for purposes of exhibition. Such statutes and the Court decisions that upheld them laid the foundation for the development of an enormous federal police power, not contemplated by the original Constitution, that enables the federal bureaucracy to flout the Bill of Rights wantonly.[31]

A fourth set of circumstances under which the Bill of Rights is apt to be trampled upon arises whenever there is a general sense of emergency, justified or unjustified, local or national. On the local level, the city of New Orleans offers instructive examples. In the winter of 1806–7 Gen. James Wilkinson, commander of the small American army in the Louisiana Territory, asked Territorial Governor William Claiborne to declare martial law, on the ground (which Wilkinson knew to be false) that Aaron Burr was about to invade New Orleans with his rebel band. Claiborne refused, whereupon Wilkinson imposed martial law anyway; and in the name and authority of the United States, he proceeded to crush the Constitution and

[31] O. John Rogge, *The First and Fifth: With Some Excursions into Others* (New York, 1971), pp. 76–77. The development of a federal police power arose slowly. As late as 1891 in *In re Rahrer*, 140 U.S. 545, 554 (1891), the Court held that the police power "is a power originally and always belonging to the States, not surrendered by them to the general government nor directly restrained by the Constitution of the United States, and essentially exclusive" (Fisher, *American Constitutional Law*, p. 472).

the Bill of Rights beneath his boot. He arrested without warrants and held incommunicado three of Burr's associates, and when writs of habeas corpus were obtained in their behalf he had them chained and sent by sea to Washington. In addition, he jailed their attorney, the judge, the judge's closest friend, a newspaper editor, former Senator John Adair, and about sixty other citizens. None was charged with a specific crime, none was allowed his constitutional rights, and a number were transported from the vicinage, where they had a constitutional right to a speedy and public trial, and were shipped in secret to Washington. The president of the United States approved of these doings, his only reservation being that Wilkinson must stay within the limits, not of the Constitution, but of what public opinion would bear.[32]

Eight years later in the same city, *after* he had won the Battle of New Orleans, General Andrew Jackson also imposed martial law. A newspaper dared publish an article criticizing him, and Jackson had the editor arrested. A lawyer procured a writ of habeas corpus from the federal district judge, and Jackson had both of them arrested. A certain Mr. Holander ventured to criticize some of these doings, and he promptly found himself in a military prison with the others.[33]

On the national level, flagrant violations of the Bill of Rights during times of perceived peril accompanied the great red scares after the First and Second World Wars. After the first, revolutions, terrorism, and violent strikes swept the entire globe, and socialists, anarchists, and communists sought to transform the disruptions into a world revolution. Beginning in April 1919, terrorists in a number of American cities planted and exploded bombs. The American people, their hostilities already enflamed by wartime government propaganda, overreacted. President Woodrow Wilson added to the near-hysteria by denouncing enemies of his proposed peace settlement as dupes of the Bolsheviks, and he asked Congress

[32] McDonald, *Presidency of Jefferson*, p. 127; Levy, *Jefferson and Civil Liberties*, pp. 81–89.

[33] Michael Linfield, *Freedom under Fire: U.S. Civil Liberties in Times of War* (Boston, 1990), p. 27.

to enact a peacetime sedition act. His attorney-general, Thomas W. Gregory, arrested and deported 249 radicals, and when Gregory was replaced by A. Mitchell Palmer, persecutions of radicals and suspected radicals began in earnest. Throughout 1920 Palmer's agents conducted raids in thirty-three cities from coast to coast. Several thousand people were jailed briefly without formal arrest or trial and then released. Formally, Palmer and his agents arrested more than 5,000, released about a third of them to the states for prosecution, and deported 556.[34]

It is to be observed that whenever government or a demagogic politician engages in such crusades, far more people suffer at the hands of unofficial vigilante-style groups than from official activity. As it happened, when Palmer was making his raids a goodly number of the socialists in the United States were Jews from eastern Europe and a goodly number of the anarchists were of Italian origin. These people were highly visible, and in the unofficial persecution they had to endure, the Bill of Rights was utterly meaningless. The same is true of people who were victimized by the new version of the Ku Klux Klan that the wave of nativism washed up.

Private persecutions similarly accompanied the anti-communist crusade conducted during the early phases of the Cold War, but official activity was quite bad enough. Even before Sen. Joseph McCarthy began to grab headlines with his sensational charges that communists had infiltrated the State Department and the army, President Harry Truman had instituted a comprehensive loyalty review program that resulted in the resignations of 7,000 government employees and the discharge of 560 more. Others were fired during the early 1950s, and many reputations were destroyed by reckless and unsubstantiated charges levied by demagogues who jumped on McCarthy's bandwagon.[35]

[34] McDonald, *Constitutional History*, p. 191; Robert K. Murray, *Red Scare: A Study in National Hysteria, 1919–1920* (Minneapolis, 1955); Linfield, *Freedom under Fire*, pp. 56–58.

[35] McDonald, *Constitutional History*, p. 214; Alfred H. Kelly and Winfred A. Harbison, *The American Constitution: Its Origins and Development* (New York, 1970), pp. 886–88, 893–95; Linfield, *Freedom under Fire*, p. 108.

But the gravest damage came in the form of direct attacks upon the First Amendment, made by Congress and upheld by the Supreme Court. One of the earliest such attacks came with the passage of the Taft-Hartley Act of 1947, which contained a provision requiring labor union officials to take an oath that they were not communists. The communications union, well known to be dominated by communists, challenged the provision on the grounds that it violated the First Amendment guarantees of freedom of speech and assembly and also that it amounted to a bill of attainder. The Supreme Court, in *American Communications Association* v. *Douds,* ruled to the contrary. The Wagner Act, said the Court, had been aimed at removing impediments to the flow of interstate commerce in the form of labor strife; Taft-Hartley had the same end, eliminating communist leadership to stop the threat of "political strikes." The right to be a communist was not at stake, the Court declared; what was at issue was only whether the government, from whose support the power of unions derived, could deny its support to communists.[36]

The right to be a communist soon became the issue, however. In 1948 the Justice Department obtained indictments against eleven top communist officials under the 1940 Smith Act, which had made it illegal to "advocate, abet, advise, or teach" the violent overthrow of any government of the United States and had prohibited publishing materials, organizing groups, or engaging in a conspiracy to commit such acts. The communists were found guilty in federal district court in New York and appealed to circuit court, where Judge Learned Hand abandoned the "clear and present danger" doctrine formulated by Oliver Wendell Holmes in 1919. There was no serious likelihood, Hand declared, that the communists would succeed in overthrowing the government, but the consequences if they did would be so horrendous that the First Amendment must not be allowed to prevent the government from protecting itself. This "sliding scale" rule for deciding

[36] Kelly and Harbison, *American Constitution,* pp. 888–89; *American Communications Assn.* v. *Douds,* 339 U.S. 382 (1950); Fisher, *American Constitutional Law,* p. 536.

sedition cases was approved by the Supreme Court on appeal in 1951.[37]

In the meantime, in 1950 Congress had passed the McCarran Internal Security Act, declaring that the "world Communist conspiracy" sought to establish a dictatorship in America and thus that American communists did constitute a "clear and present danger." Communists and communist-front organizations were required to register with a Subversive Activities Control Board; the president was authorized to declare at any time an "internal security emergency" during which anyone who "probably will conspire with others to engage in acts of espionage and sabotage" could be held indefinitely in one of the detention camps created by the act. The Communist Party refused to register, and a long court battle followed. It was not until eight years after Senator McCarthy died in 1957 and the atmosphere had become discharged that the Supreme Court screwed up the courage to declare the McCarran Act unconstitutional.[38]

The greatest threat to Bill of Rights guarantees comes, of course, during times of war. Except for occasional confiscations of private property by military commanders there were few if any violations of private rights during the War of 1812 and the Mexican War, but the Lincoln administration violated them on a grand scale during the Civil War. The national government took over telegraph service and censored telegrams throughout the conflict. When newspapers published articles or editorials critical of the government or its policies, troops were repeatedly dispatched to close the papers, arrest the editors, or seize the presses.[39]

[37] Kelly and Harbison, *American Constitution*, pp. 889–93; *Dennis* v. *United States*, 341 U.S. 494 (1951); *Schenck* v. *United States*, 249 U.S. 47 (1919); Fisher, *American Constitutional Law*, pp. 536, 554–56, 568–73.

[38] Kelly and Harbison, *American Constitution*, pp. 981–85; *Albertson* v. *Subversive Activities Control Board*, 382 U.S. 70 (1965); Fisher, *American Constitutional Law*, p. 537.

[39] Linfield, *Freedom under Fire*, pp. 24–25.

Far more serious was Lincoln's policy of subjecting suspect persons to military arrests. There were, it is true, many disloyal people in the four border slave states and in the southern parts of Ohio, Indiana, and Illinois, and these often propagandized against the war, discouraged enlistments in the army, spied for the Confederacy, and even engaged in paramilitary harrassment of Union troops. To keep them in check, Lincoln declared vast areas to be under martial law and ordered provost marshals and other military officers to arrest and detain the suspicious without charges or trials. When civilian judges ordered the release of prisoners, they were ignored.[40]

In September 1862 Lincoln issued a proclamation that governed such matters during the remainder of the war. It declared that all persons resisting the newly authorized draft, discouraging enlistments, or engaging in any other "disloyal practice affording aid and comfort to rebels . . . shall be subject to martial law, and liable to trial and punishment by courts-martial or military commissions." The substantive rights nominally guaranteed by the First Amendment and the procedural rights nominally guaranteed by the Fourth, Fifth, Sixth, Seventh, and Eighth Amendments were effectively suspended by this proclamation, as was the writ of habeas

[40] Kelly and Harbison, *American Constitution,* pp. 437–38; Linfield, *Freedom under Fire,* pp. 23–32. Linfield notes the irony that the Confederacy, despite containing pockets of Union supporters, never suspended the writ of habeas corpus. The case of *Ex parte Merryman,* 17 F. Cas. 144 (1861), is particularly instructive. Merryman, a Maryland citizen, was arrested and detained by the military at Fort McHenry. When Chief Justice Roger B. Taney issued a writ of habeas corpus, the commanding general of the fort refused to obey it and said he was acting under the authority of the president. Taney then cited the general for contempt, but the general refused to receive the citation. Taney filed an opinion on this affair, the last paragraph of which read: "I have exercised all the power which the Constitution and laws confer on me, but that power has been resisted by a force too strong for me to overcome. . . . I shall therefore order all the proceedings in this case, with my opinion, to be filed and recorded . . . and direct the clerk to transmit a copy . . . to the President. . . . It will then remain for that high officer, in fulfillment of his constitutional obligation to 'take care that the laws be faithfully executed' to determine what measure he will take to cause the civil process of the United States to be respected and enforced" (Commager, ed., *Documents of American History,* 1:401).

corpus. Under its provisions perhaps 20,000 people were summarily arrested and imprisoned throughout the Union. In combat zones such arbitrary action may have been justified, at least most of the time; but military courts also overran civil courts in areas far removed from the fighting, especially in the middle west.[41]

Two well-known Supreme Court cases illustrate the inefficacy of the Court and the Bill of Rights during wartime. In 1863 Gen. Ambrose Burnside, commander of the military department of Ohio, ordered the arrest of former congressman Clement Vallandigham for denouncing Lincoln's conduct of the war; Vallandigham was tried by a military commission and sentenced to close confinement for the duration of the war. He appealed to the Supreme Court for a writ of certiorari to review the sentence, but the Court dodged the issue on the ground that it had no jurisdiction in appeals from military tribunals. Then in 1866, the war safely over, the Court reversed its position, reviewing and overturning a sentence of L. P. Milligan for subversive activity in Indiana in 1864.[42]

Constitutional liberty fared even less well during the First World War. The legal foundation for what happened was two acts, the 1917 Espionage Act, providing severe penalties for statements or actions promoting insubordination, disloyalty, disunity, or interference with the draft; and the 1918 Sedition Act, providing the same penalties for writing, printing, or uttering profane or abusive language about the flag, the Constitution, the government, or the armed services or tending to reduce production. Under these acts more than a thousand persons, most of them innocent pacifists, were imprisoned, and a number of newspapers were suppressed. Additionally, under a presidential proclamation several thousand enemy aliens were temporarily detained, and 6,000 more were arrested and many were detained for the duration.[43]

---

[41] Kelly and Harbison, *American Constitution,* pp. 439, 443–44.

[42] *Ex parte Vallandigham,* 1 Wall. 243 (1864); *Ex parte Milligan,* 71 U.S. (4 Wall.) 2 (1866).

[43] Linfield, *Freedom under Fire,* pp. 33–67. The May 16, 1918, act not only made it a criminal offense to "utter, print, write, or publish" any "disloyal,

These were small affairs compared to what was done by two congressionally created propaganda and vigilante agencies, the Committee on Public Information and the State Councils of Defense. The first exercised censorship and distributed propaganda that went so far as to expunge from high school history books favorable references to Germany or the German people. The State Councils of Defense organized networks of vigilance committees to investigate, spy upon, and harrass the inhabitants of every neighborhood in the country. Much of what they did was petty, such as breaking the windows of German-American shopkeepers and banning the playing of Bach and Beethoven at concerts, but much of it was far from petty. In July 1918, for example, vigilance committees in Chicago alone seized and searched 150,000 men, detained 20,000 in jails and warehouses, and triumphantly announced that 14 of the men were draft dodgers. Indeed, for nineteen months the nation was policed by controlled hysteria, by government-sponsored mob action, and by totalitarian democracy. The Supreme Court lifted not a finger in protest, and shortly after the war it confirmed the constitutionality of most of what had happened.[44]

During the Second World War there was less hysteria, but the Bill of Rights was effectively suspended whenever its guarantees were deemed by government to conflict with the conduct of the war. The grossest violation was the incarceration in "Relocation Centers" of 115,000 persons of Japanese descent, of whom about 70,000 were American citizens. It is be-

---

profane, scurrilous, or abusive language" against the government, the Constitution, the military, the uniforms of the military, and the flag, it extended criminality to "whoever shall wilfully advocate, teach, defend, or suggest the doing of any of the acts"; to make "defending" an act of criminal espionage is to deny accused persons of right to counsel and to create a rather chilling lawyer-client atmosphere (Commager, ed., *Documents of American History*, 2:146).

[44] Kelly and Harbison, *American Constitution*, pp. 674–80; Forrest McDonald, *Insull* (Chicago, 1962), pp. 168–72. As to the cases, see *Schenck* v. *United States*, 249 U.S. 47 (1919); *Frohwerk* v. *United States*, 249 U.S. 204 (1919); *Debs* v. *United States*, 249 U.S. 211 (1919); *Abrams* v. *United States*, 250 U.S. 616 (1919); *Schaefer* v. *United States*, 251 U.S. 466 (1920); *Pierce* v. *United States*, 252 U.S. 239 (1920); *Gilbert* v. *Minnesota*, 254 U.S. 325 (1920).

side the point that many of the noncitizens professed loyalty
to the Japanese emperor and willingness to engage in covert
action in the Japanese cause; that it was difficult if not impossible to distinguish loyal Japanese-Americans from the others;
that detention doubtless saved some victims from mob action;
and that no one was maltreated at the detention centers. The
episode was scarcely the Bill of Rights' finest hour. Three
cases reached the Supreme Court regarding the internments:
in the first the Court hedged its decision but refused to act,
in the second it upheld the internments, and in the third it
ordered the release of one female.[45]

Lest anyone suppose that these horror stories are ancient history, and that the "rights revolution" perpetrated by the libertarian Warren and Burger courts has finally enshrined the
Bill of Rights as the law of the land, let us consider in present
terms the remaining circumstances under which the amendments are suspended. One of these is when the targets of government persecution are all but universally reckoned to be
"bad guys."

Consider RICO, the Racketeer Influenced and Corrupt
Organizations Act. This statute, aimed at suppressing organized crime, turns the criminal justice system upside down. It
provides that if a person is guilty of a "pattern of crime," con-
sisting of two or more "predicate acts," or if one is engaged
in a "criminal enterprise," these activities constitute another
crime, and the guilty party must forfeit all assets used or
gained in the pattern or enterprise. Predicate acts are defined
as certain specific criminal acts for which one has been convicted during the previous ten years. The real catch comes
with the definition of a criminal enterprise: any coordinated
activity of two or more persons in which any of the participants has been convicted of a crime during the preceding ten
years. Suppose, for example, fifty investors pool their re-
sources to build a shopping mall. If it turns out that one of
them, unknown to the others, had earlier been convicted of

[45] The cases were *Hirabayashi* v. *United States,* 320 U.S. 81 (1943); *Kore-matsu* v. *United States,* 323 U.S. 214 (1944); *Ex parte Endo,* 323 U.S. 283 (1944).

one of the specified crimes, then all are guilty of the crime of violating the RICO statute, and their property is forfeit. A more flagrant violation of due process, of the presumption of innocence, of excessive fines, and of the right to counsel can scarcely be imagined. Yet the Supreme Court held in two decisions rendered in 1989 that the constitutional right to the assistance of counsel is not violated when government seizes "ill-gotten gains."[46]

As indicated, RICO was originally aimed at the Mafia, and though that organization is now virtually defunct, the statute is still used in the so-called war on drugs. But it has also been employed against another group widely perceived as bad guys, namely, the very rich. The prejudice that anyone who makes obscenely large sums of money must necessarily be a crook is deeply rooted in American tradition, and government prosecutors seem to share it. Moreover, the mere threat of a RICO prosecution is sufficient to force targeted firms or individuals to settle out of court for exorbitant fines, lest they lose everything. Such was the case when Shearson-Lehman, which was guilty of no crime, took over E. F. Hutton, one of whose branch managers was.[47]

Another way in which the wealthy are treated as bad guys, not protected by the Constitution, arises from the revolution in tort law—personal damage suits and product liability cases. Perhaps the wildest example is the California case in which the telephone company was required to pay damages when a drunk driver crashed into a telephone booth and injured a man who was inside it. State courts have repeatedly, over the past two decades, employed the "deepest pocket" rule, meaning that when a product liability award is given by a jury, the

---

[46] The cases were *United States* v. *Monsanto*, 109 S.Ct. 2657 (1989) and *Caplin and Drysdale* v. *United States*, 109 S.Ct. 2647 (1989); Fisher, *American Constitutional Law*, p. 799; Kathleen F. Brickley, "The Current Understanding of the Sixth Amendment Right to Counsel," in Hickok, ed., *Bill of Rights*, pp. 382–90.

[47] In 1988 E. F. Hutton paid a $1.01 million fine for an "alleged" money laundering scheme involving a Rhode Island branch office. For prosecution of corporations as "bad guys," see Milton Eisenberg, *Corporate Criminal Liability: Is It Time for a New Look?* (Washington, D.C., 1991).

richest defendant, no matter how remotely involved, must pay the damages. The Supreme Court has not seen fit to judge such awards as "excessive fines," prohibited by the Eighth Amendment, even though they have amounted to death sentences for many corporations.[48]

Most Americans, of course, are neither filthy rich nor corporations; but they should remember that the definition of the designated bad guy can change and has changed from time to time. Any of us might be next.

Finally, there is the suspension of the Bill of Rights in regard to a matter that affects all Americans, namely the collection of federal income taxes. The First Amendment is suspended by the provision against filing "frivolous returns." What that means is that, though you have a right to burn the flag as political speech, you do not have the right to write "I protest" above your name on your tax return. You do not have the right to remain silent, as a common mugger has, for you must give all the information the Internal Revenue Service requires of you. You do not have immunity against self-incrimination, as a drug dealer has, for you must report all income obtained illegally. And when the IRS accuses you of fraud, the burden of proof is upon you.

One more point needs to be made. Enough has been said above to demonstrate that the Bill of Rights has never been an especially effective guarantor of the rights of people vis-à-vis the national government, and indeed that it has tended to be least effective in those circumstances wherein its protection was most needed. But the question remains, what about protection against abuses by state and local governments?

That question arises because of the development of the doctrine of incorporation—the proposition, first posited in a Supreme Court decision in the 1920s but seriously implemented only since the 1960s, that the due process and equal protec-

[48] The California case was *Bigbee* v. *Pacific Tel. and Tel. Co.*, 665 P.2d 947 (Cal. 1983). See also, for example, National Legal Center for the Public Interest, *Pernicious Ideas and Costly Consequences: The Intellectual Roots of the Tort Crisis* (Washington, D.C., 1990); and L. Gordon Crovitz, "Torturing Torts: Common Law Activism in the States," *Benchmark* 4 (1988):35–43.

tion clauses of the Fourteenth Amendment extended to the states such of the first nine amendments as were "fundamental to ordered liberty." Unfortunately the selective application of that doctrine has resulted, in fact, in an undermining of the very ordered liberty it professes to protect.[49]

Because an adequate summary treatment of this subject would more than double the size of this essay, I shall confine myself to a few general comments. First, the application of the doctrine of incorporation has effectively completed the destruction of the federal system. This means that the power to make decisions in matters of local concern has been taken from local governmental and nongovernmental institutions—where it can be most intelligently, efficiently, and humanely exercised—and has been placed instead in the hands of remote, faceless, unelected bureaucrats and judges who are rarely sensitive to local needs and preferences.

Secondly, the Court has, through the incorporation doctrine, used the Fourth, Fifth, and Sixth Amendments—which were designed to protect the people in their rights to life, liberty, and property—to protect instead the activities of vicious criminals and to render life, liberty, and property unsafe against such sociopaths. In other words, the rights of society have been sacrificed to the rights of certain individuals.

Thirdly, the Court has been utterly capricious in its application of the Bill of Rights to the states and has simultaneously exempted the federal government from its rulings. The result has been to undermine the very idea of the rule of law as

[49] Fisher, *American Constitutional Law*, pp. 393–94, has a table of the incorporation of the Bill of Rights. Notice, however, that in *Gitlow* v. *New York*, 268 U.S. 652 (1925), although the Court maintained that part of the First Amendment was incorporated through the due process clause of the Fourteenth Amendment, the Court upheld the conviction of Gitlow for violating the New York laws of criminal anarchy. In *Palko* v. *Connecticut*, 302 U.S. 319 (1937), the Court admitted that the line of incorporation "may seem to be wavering and broken if there is a hasty catalogue of the cases on the one side and the other." But the Court went on to say that there is a "rationalizing principle," in that those rights that are incorporated are "of the very essence of a scheme of ordered liberty." The Court then ruled against Palko, answering the question if the prohibition against double jeopardy was one of the "fundamental principles of liberty and justice" with a resounding "no."

the antithesis of arbitrary government. Consider the matter of religion alone. The First Amendment provides that "Congress shall pass no law respecting an establishment of religion, or prohibiting the free exercise thereof." By a process of reasoning that would have thrilled medieval theologians concerned with angels and pin heads, the Supreme Court has construed that language to prohibit the display of the Ten Commandments on a Kentucky elementary school wall,[50] the opening of a high school football game in Georgia with a prayer for the safety of the players, and the presence of a nativity scene on the lawn of a county courthouse. A nativity scene accompanied by plastic effigies of Frosty the Snow Man and Rudolph the Red-Nosed Reindeer, on the other hand, is acceptable. We do not have freedom of religion, only freedom from religion, on the local level. All the while, the confusion is compounded because on the national level Congress can open its sessions with prayers, the United States mint can print "In God We Trust" on the currency, the words "under God" remain in the pledge of allegiance, and the White House can display a Christmas tree without the protective coloration of Frosty or Rudolph.

Fourthly, the Court's posture as the champion of individual liberties through the Bill of Rights has given birth to the widespread impression, mentioned at the outset, that the Constitution for practical purposes *is* the Bill of Rights.[51] That, in turn,

---

[50] Local defiance and the innate common sense of most Americans result in some interesting compliance with what the Supreme Court says is the supreme law of the land: "In Liberty, Kentucky, for instance, a school forbidden to post the Ten Commandments in classrooms posted instead a page from the *Congressional Record*—on which were found the Ten Commandments" (John Shelton Reed, *Whistling Dixie: Dispatches from the South* [Columbia, Mo., 1990], p. 133).

[51] Rossum opens his article "To Render These Rights Secure," with a quotation from a dedicatory speech for the Bill of Rights Room, Subtreasury Building, 1964, by John Marshall Harlan: "We are accustomed to speak of the Bill of Rights . . . as the principal guarantee of personal liberty. Yet it would surely be shallow not to recognize that the structure of our political system accounts no less for the free society we have. The Framers staked their faith that liberty would prosper in the new nation not primarily upon declarations of individual rights but upon the kind of government the Union was to have."

has obscured the erosion of the substance of the Constitution. One by one, the provisions that made the Constitution a body of rules governing the exercise of power—a law governing government itself, prescribing what government can do and how—have been eaten away, and nobody seems to have noticed or cared. The illusion is liberty. The reality is Leviathan.

BERNARD SCHWARTZ

Experience versus Reason

"Beautiful Books and Great Revolutions"

THERE IS A passage by Alexis de Tocqueville that strikingly illustrates the difference between the American and French Revolutions: "When we study the history of our Revolution, we see that it was led in precisely the same spirit that produced so many abstract books on government. The same attraction for general theories; complete systems of legislation and exact symmetry in laws; the same disdain for existing facts; the same confidence in theory; . . . the same desire to remake the constitution at one stroke according to the rules of logic and following one single plan, instead of seeking to amend its parts. Frightening spectacle! For what is a quality in the writer is usually a vice in the statesman, and the same things that often make for beautiful books can lead to great revolutions."[1] Those who made the French Revolution, Tocqueville goes on, desired "to rebuild the society . . . according to an entirely new plan, which each of them derived from the exclusive light of his own reason."[2]

The American theme was a different one. It was neatly stated by John Dickinson during the Philadelphia Convention: "Experience must be our only guide. Reason may

[1] Alexis de Tocqueville, *L'Ancien Régime et la Revolution* (Paris, 1967), author's translation.

[2] Ibid., p. 232.

mislead us."[3] Here was a succinct summary of the American
constitution maker's creed. It was at the opposite extreme
from Voltaire's famous exclamation demanding the total destruction of all existing law: "Do you want good laws? Burn
yours and make new ones!"[4]

In his statement, of course, Dickinson was not denigrating
reason as the basis of government and law. He only insisted
that it had to be tempered by experience. And it was *American*
experience that was to govern—not that of ancient Greece or
Rome or even Britain. Even the common law was to be modified to meet conditions on this side of the Atlantic. As Dickinson put it in his *Farmer Letters,* "Some of the *English* rules are
adopted, others rejected."[5] To men like Dickinson, the law
was reason, as codified by the American experience with it—
an essentially conservative approach that emphasized the
rights protected by the law. When it came time to safeguard
those rights by organic guarantees, the rights listed were
those that experience had shown were suitable for constitutional protection, and they were secured by inclusion in a
legally enforceable bill of rights.

FRENCH DECLARATIONS OF
RIGHTS COMPARED

The attitude described by Tocqueville can be illustrated by
the declarations of rights that were important by-products of
the French Revolution. Two of these will be discussed—one
enacted by the legislature, the other a proposed declaration
by one of the revolutionary leaders.

---

[3] Max Farrand, *The Framing of the Constitution of the United States* (New Haven, 1913), p. 204.

[4] Quoted in C. J. Friedrich, "The Ideological and Philosophical Background," in Bernard Schwartz, ed., *The Code Napoleon and the Common-Law
World: The Sesquicentennial Lectures Delivered at the Law Center of New York University, December 13–15, 1954* (New York, 1956), p. 1.

[5] Paul Leicester Ford, ed., *The Writings of John Dickinson*, vol. 1, *Political
Writings, 1764–1774* (Philadelphia, 1895), p. 370.

In August 1789, a month before the federal Bill of Rights was passed by Congress, the Declaration of the Rights of Man was voted by the French National Assembly. Rightly considered one of the principal accomplishments of the French Revolution, the 1789 Declaration is a very different document from that drawn up by James Madison and his colleagues. The French Declaration is less a legally enforceable protection of specific guaranteed rights than an abstract statement of natural rights, which provides a standard that "may serve as a constant reminder of . . . rights and duties; to the end that the acts of the legislative power and those of the executive power [may be] compared with the end of every political institution."[6]

The rights guaranteed by the French Declaration are stated in most general terms. For example, Article 2 reads, "The end of every political association is the preservation of the natural and imprescriptible rights of man. These rights are liberty, property, security and resistance to oppression."

The rights listed are not specified in legally enforceable form. Thus, according to Article 4, "Liberty consists in being able to do anything which does not injure another: therefore, the exercise of the natural rights of each man has no limits other than those which assure to the other members of society the enjoyment of these same rights. These limits may be determined only by the law."

This is, of course, so general that it can scarcely form the basis of any action to challenge governmental restrictions upon liberty. Indeed, Article 4 appears to be but an early version of Herbert Spencer's "law of equal freedom"[7]—that

[6] Declaration of the Rights of Man and of the Citizen of August 26, 1789, Preamble. The quotations in the text are from the translation in Henry P. de Vries, Nina M. Galston, and George A. Berman, *French Law: Constitution and Selective Legislation* (Ardsley on Hudson, N.Y., 1989), p. 1. For the original text, see *Petits Codes Dalloz: Code Administratif,* 20th ed. (Paris, 1989), p. 16.

[7] See Sidney Fine, *Laissez-Faire and the General-Welfare State: A Study of Conflict in American Thought, 1865–1901* (Ann Arbor, Mich., 1964), p. 33.

"every man has freedom to do all that he wills, provided he infringes not the equal freedom of any other man."[8] Such a principle may serve as the foundation for a system of political philosophy, but it can scarcely be the basis by itself for legal protection of specific personal rights and liberties.

To an American constitutional lawyer, personal liberty is safeguarded by the constitutional protections against arrest and imprisonment except after a criminal trial and conviction governed by the procedural and other guarantees contained in the Bill of Rights. Those guarantees are stated in concrete legally enforceable terms: the right to be accused by a grand jury, to be immune from double jeopardy, not to be deprived of life or liberty without due process of law, to a speedy and public trial by jury, to be informed of the accusation, to be confronted with the witnesses against him, to call his own witnesses, and to have the assistance of counsel.[9]

The comparable guarantees in the French Declaration are contained in two articles. Article 7 reads: "No man may be accused, arrested or detained except as determined by the law, and according to the forms which it has prescribed." And, Article 9, "Every man being presumed innocent until he has been declared guilty, if it becomes unavoidable to arrest him any severity which is not necessary to secure his person must be strictly repressed by law."

These are broad declarations of principle. They do not descend to the level of practical enforcement; their provisions are too general to be made the basis of judicial decision in specific cases.

The same is true of the French Declaration's provisions on freedom of religion and speech and press. According to Article 10, "No one may be harassed because of his opinions, even his religious opinions, provided their expression does not disturb the public order established by law." Article 11 provides: "The free communication of thoughts and opinions

[8] Herbert Spencer, *Social Statics, or, The Conditions Essential to Human Happiness Specified, and the First of Them Developed* (London, 1851), p. 103, italics omitted.

[9] Compare Zechariah Chafee, Jr., *How Human Rights Got into the Constitution* (Boston, 1952), p. 53.

is one of the most precious rights of man; every citizen may therefore speak, write and publish freely, provided he shall be liable for the abuse of this freedom in such cases as are determined by law."

Both articles, to be sure, declare noble principles, but they scarcely do so in legally enforceable form. In addition, they contain provisions that appear all but to nullify the rights so resoundingly proclaimed. The rights given may be exercised only so far as they are not "abused" or do not "disturb the public order."

Nor is the protection of property rights in the French Declaration more effective. According to Article 17, "Property being an inviolable and sacred right, no one may be deprived thereof except where a public need, lawfully established, clearly requires, and on condition of a just and prior indemnity." This appears to provide only a French equivalent of the Fifth Amendment's takings clause.[10] Aside from a requirement of just compensation for deprivations by eminent domain, property rights are not safeguarded in the Declaration. True, it expresses the lofty sentiment that property is "an inviolable and sacred right." But there is no legally enforceable protection for that right and the abstract declaration of inviolability had no effect, deterrent or otherwise, upon the widespread confiscations that characterized the French Revolutionary period.

Even further removed from the American conception of a bill of rights was the Proposed Declaration of the Rights of Man and Citizen presented to the French Convention in 1793.[11] It contained thirty-seven articles, not one of which guaranteed specific rights in legally enforceable terms. The articles, in the main, state abstract principles that, however high-sounding, add nothing to the practical rights possessed by Frenchmen. Thus, Article 7 declares: "The law may forbid only whatever is injurious to society; it may order only what-

[10] For a recent discussion of the takings clause, see Bernard Schwartz, *The New Right and the Constitution: Turning Back the Legal Clock* (Boston, 1990), chap. 4.

[11] For its text, see George F. E. Rudé, ed., *Robespierre* (Englewood Cliffs, N.J., 1967), p. 54.

ever is useful thereto." And Article 8 states: "Every law which violates the inalienable rights of man is essentially unjust and tyrannical; it is not a law at all." Even more abstract is Article 34: "The men of all countries are brothers, and the different peoples must help one another, according to their power, as citizens of the same State."

In addition, the proposed Declaration illustrates the tendency that was warned against by one of the greatest American jurists, Thomas M. Cooley: "Don't in your constitution making legislate too much."[12] The proposed French Declaration includes provisions not suitable for organic instruments. Thus, Article 13 provides: "Society is obliged to provide for the subsistence of all its members either by procuring work for them or by assuring the means of existence to those who are unable to work." Aside from the fact that, once again, the provision is stated in general nonenforceable terms, one may doubt that the right to work and that to welfare assistance are rights that should be included in a constitution or bill of rights. By American conceptions at least, these are matters for the legislature, not the constitution maker.

The French declarations illustrate the crucial difference between American and French constitutional thinking at the end of the eighteenth century. The French declarations lay down not practical rules but only general principles deemed fundamental to man and hence universally applicable. Their provisions are not set forth as legal rules, enforceable as such by the courts. The rights safeguarded by the first ten amendments, on the other hand, include the basic rights appropriate for protection by constitutional guaranty, at least as they were understood at the end of the eighteenth century. There is nothing like that in the French declarations, drafted only in the hortatory terms of the general rights mankind ought to have. The French documents do not contain mandatory inhibitions that must be respected by the agents of government, nor do they descend to the level of practical enforcement

[12] Alan Jones, "Thomas M. Cooley and the Interstate Commerce Commission: Continuity and Change in the Doctrine of Equal Rights," *Political Science Quarterly* 81 (1966):602, 622.

through specific provision for the basic rights of criminal defendants and others dealing with law enforcement officials.

ENGLISH LAW COMPARED

To continental thinkers of the day, eighteenth-century England was, of course, considered the very home of constitutional liberty. A contemporary observer, Voltaire, had been sent to the Bastille for a poem he had not written, whose author he did not know, and with whose views he did not agree. When he came to England, his feeling was one of having left the realm of despotism for a land where, though the laws might sometimes be harsh, men were ruled by law and not by caprice. Here, said Voltaire, the very air one breathes is free, for there is no place for arbitrary power.[13]

Yet the England of Voltaire's encomium fell short of the standard set by American bills of rights. The rights protected by the federal Bill of Rights can be grouped into five broad classifications: (1) freedom of religion, (2) the rights of expression and association, (3) the right to privacy, (4) the right to due process, and (5) freedom from arbitrary restraint or trial and from cruel and unusual punishment.[14] By American criteria, these rights were in every case either not protected or inadequately protected in the England of the late eighteenth century.

By the continental standards with which Voltaire was familiar, England of that day might have looked like the home of free reason.[15] But the consequences of the nonconstitutional basis of free expression in England were well illustrated by the libel trial of Thomas Paine, who was prosecuted for publishing the second part of *The Rights of Man*. The trial took place in 1792, the year after the federal Bill of Rights was ratified. Despite an impassioned defense by Thomas Erskine,

---

[13] See Albert Venn Dicey, *An Introduction to the Study of the Law of the Constitution,* 10th ed. (London, 1964), pp. 189–90.

[14] Compare Earl Warren, *A Republic If You Can Keep It* (New York, 1972), p. 112.

[15] Compare Dicey, *Study of the Law,* p. 190.

Paine was found guilty of sedition for his unfavorable contrast of British monarchism with American republicanism. Erskine's final words at the trial set forth the situation facing his client: "I can reason with the people of England but I cannot fight against the thunder of authority." Without constitutional protection basic rights were always subject to governmental "thunder." So strong was the power of authority that, scarcely had Erskine sat down and the attorney general risen to reply, when the Paine jury foreman declared, "'My lord, I am authorized by the jury to inform the Attorney General that a reply is not necessary.' . . . Mr. Attorney General sat down, and the jury gave in their verdict, GUILTY." [16]

The law of seditious libel hung like an albatross on freedom of expression in eighteenth-century England. Overt censorship of speech and press had been replaced by the restrictions imposed by power to prosecute under the law of libel. But even a century after Paine's trial, the leading English text could assert "that the legal definition of a seditious libel might easily be so used as to check a great deal of what is ordinarily considered allowable discussion, and would if rigidly enforced be inconsistent with prevailing forms of political agitation." [17] During the eighteenth century, the English law of libel *was* rigorously enforced. "To speak ill of the government was a crime. . . . Every one was a libeller who outraged the sentiments of the dominant party." [18] The crime of seditious libel was used to prohibit criticisms of government. Freedom of expression in England was thus "neither more nor less than this: that a man may publish anything which twelve of his countrymen think is not blamable." [19]

Freedom of association was even more restricted under English law. Until relatively recently, associations we would

[16] Quoted in Irving Brant, *The Bill of Rights: Its Origin and Meaning* (Indianapolis, 1965), p. 242.

[17] Dicey, *Study of the Law*, p. 243.

[18] Thomas Erskine May, *The Constitutional History of England: Since the Accession of George the Third, 1760–1860*, 2 vols. (Boston, 1863–64), 2:106–7.

[19] *Rex v. Cuthell*, 27 Howell's State Trials 642, 675 (1799).

consider at most venial, including labor unions, benevolent associations, and political clubs, could be condemned as seditious conspiracies.[20] One has only to look at the treatment of the Chartist movement, which sought electoral reforms in nineteenth-century England, to see the reality of English law in this regard.

The situation with regard to freedom of religion was equally unsatisfactory. Freedom of religion in the First Amendment sense was almost totally lacking in the England of that day. The established Church of England was the negation of all James Madison sought to accomplish by the establishment clause, and freedom of conscience meant only the right to free exercise without disabilities.

Similarly, due process in the Fifth Amendment sense was unknown in English law. The very notion of due process as a constitutional restraint is inconsistent with the doctrine of parliamentary supremacy, which has dominated English public law since 1688. English lawyers could scarcely acknowledge a concept like due process, which as Alexander Hamilton noted in a 1787 speech,[21] made clear that fundamental rights could not be taken away even by an act of the legislature.

But it is when we turn to English criminal law that we understand how forward-looking the federal Bill of Rights really was. In large part, American bills of rights sought foremost to correct the deficiencies of English criminal law, a legacy of barbarism that had stretched its long arm across the ocean to touch the colonists time and time again in painful and humiliating ways. In the first place, the right against unreasonable intrusion by governmental agents was made secure. This right had been consistently violated through the general warrants issued toward the end of the colonial period, and "the Warrant Clause [of the Fourth Amendment] was aimed specifically at the evil of the general warrant, [which was] often

[20] See May, *Constitutional History of England,* chap. 10.

[21] Harold A. Syrett and Jacob E. Cooke, eds., *The Papers of Alexander Hamilton,* 27 vols. (New York, 1961–87), 4:35.

regarded as the single immediate cause of the American Revolution."[22] While it is true that the English courts had also started to impose restrictions on the power of the State to obtain evidence of crimes,[23] these restrictions were not nearly so strong as those drafted in the American Bill of Rights.

Some of the other rights—those, for instance, safeguarded in the Fifth and Sixth Amendments—had, to be sure, also been secured in English criminal law by the end of the eighteenth century, notably the right to jury trial and the privilege against self-incrimination. But other basic rights were still not protected. Not until 1837, for example, was the right to counsel fully recognized in English felony cases, and not until 1898 were accused persons given the right to testify in English criminal trials.[24] Without these rights, it is difficult to see how justice could be served. Both were fully guaranteed in the federal Bill of Rights.

In addition, the Eighth Amendment expressly prohibited cruel and unusual punishments. This provision was derived from a similar clause in the English Bill of Rights of 1689, but a reading of William Blackstone tells how barbarous were the punishments still inflicted in English law during the following century.[25] The men who voted for the Eighth Amendment well realized that they were outlawing the cruelties of the eighteenth-century English modes of punishment. We have only to note the complaint of Samuel Livermore during the House debate on the Bill of Rights that "villains often deserve whipping and perhaps having theirs ears cut off, but are we in future to be prevented from inflicting these punishments because they are cruel?"[26]

The Eighth Amendment also illustrates the most important

---

[22] *Lopez* v. *United States,* 373 U.S. 427, 454 (1963) (Brennan dissenting).

[23] Notably in *Entick* v. *Carrington,* 19 Howell's State Trials 1029 (1765).

[24] See Theodore Frank Thomas Plucknett, *A Concise History of the Common Law,* 2d ed. (London, 1936), pp. 386, 388.

[25] William Blackstone, *Commentaries on the Laws of England,* 4 vols. (Oxford, 1765–69), 4:chaps. 1, 6.

[26] See Bernard Schwartz, comp., *The Bill of Rights: A Documentary History,* 2 vols. (New York, 1971), 2:1112.

difference between the English and American systems of protection of individual rights at the end of the eighteenth century. The Bill of Rights of 1689 spoke only the hortatory
words of "ought not" and had only the status of a statute,
which could be abrogated by later laws. The Eighth Amendment spoke the imperative of "shall not" and had the status
of a constitutional command, which could be enforced by the
courts even against the legislature.

The same distinctions applied to the other rights guaranteed by the federal Bill of Rights as compared with the equivalent rights in the English law of the day. Even where similar
rights were recognized in English law, they had nothing like
the status they had in the American system.[27] For them to
have achieved that status, the English would first have had to
do what the so-called Levellers had called for a century and a
half earlier: establish a written constitution as the supreme
law of the land and enforceable as such by the courts against
abridgement by Parliament, the Crown, and the common law,
and the constitution would have had to have a bill of rights
with provisions expressly protecting the rights concerned.[28]
This was, of course, precisely what was done in the United
States through the federal Constitution and Bill of Rights.

AMERICAN EXPERIENCE

Justice Stephen J. Field once said that, so far as protection of
individual rights is concerned, "our country was . . . the heir
of all the ages."[29] In a broad sense, this may be true. Practically speaking, however, the federal Bill of Rights was derived
almost entirely from American experience. Except for the
right of petition and that to bear arms (which were provided
for, albeit only in hortatory form, in the English Bill of
Rights), all the rights safeguarded in the federal Bill of Rights
were first secured in American enactments. To be sure, the

[27] See Brant, *Bill of Rights,* p. 64.

[28] Compare ibid., p. 218.

[29] Stephen J. Field, "The Centenary of the Supreme Court of the United
States," *American Law Review* 24 (1890):351, 355.

rights against illegal seizures of the person and to due process and jury trial may ultimately be traced to Magna Charta. But its Chapter 39 only sowed the seed; centuries of further development were required before the basic rights concerned could attain the status given them by the Fourth, Fifth, and Sixth Amendments. The rudimentary guarantees in Chapter 39 were first given their modern form in the American constitutions and bills of rights of the Revolutionary period.

Indeed, all of the important rights safeguarded by the federal Bill of Rights were first given legal protection by American organic instruments, both during the colonial and Revolutionary periods. These include freedom of religion,[30] freedom of speech,[31] press,[32] and assembly,[33] the prohibition against unreasonable searches,[34] double jeopardy,[35] self-incrimination,[36] the guarantees of due process[37] and just compensation,[38] and those protecting criminal defendants—the right to a speedy public trial by jury,[39] to be informed of the accusa-

[30] First stated in Maryland Act concerning Religion, 1649, in Schwartz, comp., *Bill of Rights*, 1:91.

[31] First stated in Massachusetts Body of Liberties, 1641, ibid., p. 71.

[32] First stated in Address to the Inhabitants of Quebec, 1775, ibid., p. 221.

[33] First stated in Declaration and Resolves of the First Continental Congress, 1774, ibid., p. 215.

[34] First stated in The Rights of the Colonists and a List of Infringements and Violations of Rights, 1772, ibid., p. 200.

[35] First stated in Massachusetts Body of Liberties, 1641, ibid., p. 71.

[36] First stated in Virginia Declaration of Rights, 1776, ibid., p. 234.

[37] First stated in New York Ratifying Convention, Proposed Amendments, 1788, ibid., 2:911.

[38] First stated in Massachusetts Body of Liberties, 1641, ibid., 1:71.

[39] First stated in Virginia Declaration of Rights, 1776, ibid., p. 234; Concessions and Agreements of West New Jersey, 1677, ibid., p. 126; Massachusetts Body of Liberties, 1641, ibid., p. 71. The latter guarantees jury trial far more specifically than Magna Charta, Chapter 39.

tion,[40] to secure witnesses[41] and counsel,[42]—as well as the right to jury trial in civil cases.[43]

It is true that the rights secured by the Eighth Amendment were provided for as well in the English Bill of Rights.[44] But they had also been safeguarded in earlier American colonial enactments—notably the Massachusetts Body of Liberties (1641)[45] and the Pennsylvania Frame of Government (1682).[46]

When Madison drew up the draft that became the federal Bill of Rights he did not have to rely upon abstract theories "derived from the exclusive light of his own reason."[47] Unlike the French, the Americans had had experience with their own representative governments for over a century and a half. For almost the same period, they had provided legal protection for individual rights, starting with the 1606 Virginia Charter[48] and the 1631 Maryland Act for the Liberties of the People.[49] Over the years, similar protection was provided in other colonial enactments. The movement that began with the first colonization culminated in the constitutions and bills of rights adopted by the different states during the Revolutionary period, as well as the amendments proposed by the state ratifying conventions along with their ratifications of the Constitution.

The federal Bill of Rights was derived directly from the American experience during the Revolutionary period and

[40] First stated in Virginia Declaration of Rights, 1776, Schwartz, comp., *Bill of Rights*, 1:234.

[41] First stated in Pennsylvania Charter of Privileges, 1701, ibid., p. 170.

[42] First stated in Massachusetts Body of Liberties, 1641, ibid., p. 71.

[43] First stated ibid.

[44] Ibid., p. 41.

[45] Ibid., p. 71.

[46] Ibid., p. 132.

[47] Tocqueville, *L'Ancien Régime*, p. 232.

[48] Schwartz, comp., *Bill of Rights*, 1:54.

[49] Ibid., p. 68.

the Constitution ratification process—which, in turn, was based upon the American experience with the violation of their rights before Independence. By the time the Constitution was adopted, there was general agreement among Americans on the rights to be protected by an organic instrument, as shown by the state bills of rights and the amendments proposed by the state ratifying conventions. Perhaps the situation was not as simple as George Mason had stated when he had raised the bill of rights issue near the end of the Constitutional Convention: "With the aid of the State declarations, a bill might be prepared in a few hours."[50] But when Madison did draw up the amendments he introduced in the First Congress, he had at hand the compendium contained in the state recommendatory amendments. The state proposals reflected the consensus that had developed among Americans with regard to the fundamental rights that ought to be protected by any bill of rights worthy of the name.

All of the eight states to propose amendments included as one of their provisions a proposal similar in wording and scope to the Tenth Amendment, reserving to the states powers not delegated to the federal government. Seven states recommended a guarantee of jury trial in civil cases. Six urged protection for religious freedom. Five sought guarantees of freedom of the press (with three adding freedom of speech as well), the right to bear arms, trial by jury of the vicinage, and prohibitions against quartering of troops and unreasonable searches and seizures. Four states asked for protection of the right to "the law of the land" or due process, grand jury indictment, speedy public trial, assembly and petition, and against excessive bail and fines and cruel and unusual punishments.[51] Of twenty-two amendments supported by four or more states, fourteen were incorporated by Madison in his recommendations to Congress.[52]

---

[50] Max Farrand, ed., *The Records of the Federal Convention of 1787*, 3 vols. (New Haven, 1911), 2:588.

[51] See Schwartz, comp., *Bill of Rights*, 2:1167 (table).

[52] See Edward Dumbauld, *The Bill of Rights and What It Means Today* (Norman, Okla., 1957), p. 33.

This does not mean that Madison's job as draftsman of the Bill of Rights was that of mere compiler. On the contrary, as will be seen, Madison was able to play a most important creative role. He had to choose from the myriad of state proposals those that were worthy of being raised to the federal constitutional level. He also had to refine their language, so that the Bill of Rights would be, at the same time, both an eloquent inventory of basic rights and a legally enforceable safeguard of those rights.

Yet if the ultimate bill of rights edifice was designed by Madison, it was built from the materials furnished by the state ratifying conventions—themselves derived from the prior American experience demonstrating the need for constitutional protection of basic rights. Now it was plain that, in Thomas Jefferson's phrase, "this security for liberty seems to be demanded by the general voice of America."[53]

The Jefferson estimate was confirmed by Madison, who agreed that "the friends of the Constitution . . . are generally agreed that the system should be revised . . . to supply additional guards for liberty."[54] Looking ahead to the First Congress under the Constitution, which was soon to meet, he predicted that "if the first Congress embrace the policy which circumstances mark out, they will not fail to propose of themselves, every desirable safeguard for popular rights."[55] When the First Congress did meet in New York a few months later, it was Madison who ensured that his prediction would be borne out by serving as the legislative catalyst for the amendments that were to become the Bill of Rights.

MADISON'S CONTRIBUTION

When the First Congress convened in the old City Hall on Wall Street in New York in April 1789, Madison was at the

---

[53] Julian P. Boyd et al., eds., *The Papers of Thomas Jefferson*, 28 vols. to date (Princeton, 1950-), 14:688.

[54] Gaillard Hunt, ed., *The Writings of James Madison*, 9 vols. (New York, 1900–10), 5:311.

[55] Ibid., p. 312.

peak of his powers, both physically and intellectually. He was
a slender, short-statured man of thirty-eight, not yet clothed
in the habitual black that would later rule his dress. His more
likely costume at this earlier period was of ornate blue and
buff, with hair powdered and falling behind in the berib-
boned queue of fashion.[56] "He speaks low," said Fisher Ames,
"his person is little and ordinary."[57] In fact, he was so small
he could not be seen by all the members and his voice was so
weak he could scarcely be heard throughout the hall.[58] This
led Henry Adams to write, "An imposing personality had
much to do with political influence, and Madison labored under serious disadvantages."[59] Yet it was of Madison that John
Marshall once said if eloquence included the art of "persuasion by convincing, Mr. Madison was the most eloquent man
I ever heard."[60] Madison may have spoken so softly at times
that even the reporter could not catch what he said,[61] but the
power of his speeches—in the Philadelphia Convention, in
the Virginia ratifying convention, and in the First Congress—
has, in spite of poor reporting, projected itself through over
two centuries.

It was Madison, acting to fulfill his campaign pledge, who
was the prime mover in the congressional chapter of the Bill
of Rights, as well as its draftsman. That is the case even
though Madison himself had no legal training or experience.
It is true that, soon after he had completed his studies at
Princeton, Madison had considered a legal career, as well as
life as a clergyman. In 1773 he told a friend, "Intend myself

[56] See Irving Brant, *James Madison*, vol. 3, *Father of the Constitution, 1787–1800* (Indianapolis, 1950), p. 14.

[57] Ibid., p. 249.

[58] See Albert J. Beveridge, *The Life of John Marshall*, 4 vols. (Boston, 1916–19), 1:394.

[59] Henry Adams, *History of the United States of America during the Administration of Thomas Jefferson* (New York, 1986), p. 128.

[60] Irving Brant, "The Madison Heritage," in Edmond Nathaniel Cahn, ed., *The Great Rights* (New York, 1963), p. 30.

[61] Beveridge, *Life of Marshall*, 1:394.

to read law occasionally and have procured books for that purpose."[62] After he had struggled for some months over what he called "the coarse and dry study of the law," Madison wrote that though "I keep up my attention to the course of reading . . . I am however far from determined ever to make a professional use of it."[63] Ultimately, Madison decided against a life devoted either to Blackstone or the Bible, and the rest of his life was spent in politics.[64]

To the young Madison, the law may have been a "barren desert," but he soon qualified the characterization: "Perhaps I should not say barren either, because the law does bear fruit, but it is sour fruit, that must be gathered and pressed and distilled before it can bring pleasure or profit."[65] With Madison the "fruit" ultimately borne was distilled from both his reading (particularly in public law—his wish, he once wrote to Jefferson, was to read "whatever may throw light on the general constitution and droit public")[66] and political experience, his own as well as that of other Americans of his day.

To a member of today's lawyer-dominated polity, it must remain a source of wonder that a gentlemen-planter without experience in the law could play the seminal role in drawing up the documents that are the foundation of the American system. Yet Madison was not the only nonlawyer who played the crucial part in the constitution-drafting of the time. George Mason, the principal architect of both the Virginia constitution of 1776 and its Declaration of Rights was,[67] like Madison, only an untutored planter. However, Mason, Madison, and their fellow statesmen knew Locke, Montesquieu, and Sydney—the trio that gave the American Revolution its

[62] Irving Brant, *James Madison*, vol. 1, *The Virginia Revolutionist* (Indianapolis, 1941), pp. 111–12.

[63] Hunt, ed., *Writings of Madison*, 1:19, 2:54.

[64] See Robert Allen Rutland, *James Madison: The Founding Father* (New York, 1987), p. 4.

[65] Hunt, ed., *Writings of Madison*, 1:19–20.

[66] Ibid., 2:43.

[67] Schwartz, comp., *Bill of Rights*, 1:231.

theoretical underpinnings—and were widely read in the classics and English and Continental legal writers, particularly in the field of public law.

On June 8, 1789, Madison rose in the House of Representatives and introduced his draft of the amendments that became the Bill of Rights. He explained his proposal in what is rightly considered one of the great addresses in our history.[68] Madison's own notes for his June 8 speech tell us the object of his proposed amendments: "To limit and qualify powr. by exceptg. from grant cases in wch. it shall not be exercised or exd. in a particular manner." Their primary purpose is to guard "against the legislative, for it is the most powerful, and most likely to be abused," as well as to guard against abuses by the executive and "the body of the people, operating by the majority against the minority." Thus they will guard against what he points to "as the greatest danger which in Rep: is Prerogative of majority."[69]

The Madison amendments cover every one of the articles that eventually became the Bill of Rights. Four of Madison's amendments were eliminated during the congressional debate: his first amendment containing a general declaration of the theory of popular government; his fifth, prohibiting state violations of freedom of conscience, the press, and trial by jury; his sixth, limiting appeals; and eighth, dealing with the separation of powers. Two failed of ratification—his amendments dealing with congressional size and compensation. The other Madison amendments survived substantially in their original form as the Bill of Rights. Every provision of the Bill of Rights is based directly upon Madison's original draft. Where changes were made during the congressional debate, they relate more to form than substance.

The extent of Madison's achievement is not lessened by the fact that he based his draft upon the state recommendatory amendments, especially those of Virginia. "What a cool and exploring sagacity," wrote St. John Crèvecoeur to Jefferson in

---

[68] James Madison's speech is printed in *Annals of Congress,* 1st Cong., 1st sess., 1:448–59.

[69] Hunt, ed., *Writings of Madison,* 5:389–90.

October 1788, "will be wanted in the discussion and accep-
tation of these numberless amendments, which a few of the
States insist upon, in order to please every body, & yet to discriminate the useful from the needless &c." [70] It was Madison
who chose which among the pyramid of state proposals
should be acted upon by Congress and, with the perspective
of two centuries, we can say that he chose remarkably well,
including in his list all the great rights appropriate for constitutional protection—except for equal protection, which was
not thought of as a basic right at the time. It was Madison also
who tightened the constitutional language, substituting the
imperative *shall* for all but one of the flaccid *ought* and *ought
nots* of the state proposals. We can see Madison's contribution
in this respect in the following sequence:

Bill of Rights, 1689: "That excessive bail *ought not* be required, nor excessive fines imposed, nor cruel and unusual
punishments inflicted." [71]

Virginia Declaration of Rights, 1776: "That excessive bail
ought not to be required, nor excessive fines imposed, nor
cruel and unusual punishments inflicted." [72]

Virginia—Proposed Amendments, 1788: "That excessive
bail *ought not* to be required, nor excessive fines imposed, nor
cruel and unusual punishments inflicted." [73]

Amendment proposed by Madison, June 8, 1789: "Excessive bail *shall not* be required, nor excessive fines imposed, nor
cruel and unusual punishments inflicted." [74]

Madison's amendments were based on the understanding that mere declarations and wishful normatives were not
enough—that the situation called for flat commands. In America, as the Virginia-proposed bill of rights had stated expressly,
the people were sovereign and officials their mere trustees

[70] Crèvecoeur quotation in Robert Allen Rutland, *The Birth of the Bill of
Rights, 1776–1791* (Chapel Hill, 1955), p. 191.

[71] Schwartz, comp., *Bill of Rights*, 1:43.

[72] Ibid., p. 238.

[73] Ibid., 2:841.

[74] Ibid., p. 1027. See Cahn, ed., *Great Rights*, p. 5.

and agents. "In Europe," wrote Madison, "charters of liberty have been granted by power"; in America, "charters of power granted by liberty."[75] In Magna Charta, where King John spoke as monarch, "We will not" was deemed proper. In the English Bill of Rights, where William and Mary still spoke as sovereigns, "ought not" was deemed bold enough for the protection of the rights of subjects. Now when the American people prescribed the acts their new federal government was not to do at all or was to do only in a particular manner, it was appropriate to say "shall not"—the language of command. It was Madison who toughened exhortations into law.[76]

In addition, it was Madison who followed the New York proposed amendment and drafted his version of Chapter 39 of Magna Charta in terms of "due process of law," instead of the "law of the land." We do not know what led Madison to use the New York due process language. Perhaps it was Hamilton, with whom he was in close contact at the time, who influenced him in this respect. Hamilton was one of the few men at that early date who realized that the phrase "due process" might make a difference. In a speech in the New York Assembly on February 6, 1787, Hamilton emphasized that the words "due process" in the just enacted "Act concerning the Rights of Citizens of This State" removed any doubt over whether a person might be disfranchised or deprived of any right by an act of the legislature. Only "the process and proceedings of the courts of justice" could, consistently with the due process phraseology, disenfranchise or deprive anyone of a right.[77] At any rate, Madison's change from "the law of the land" to "due process of law" was the origin of the due process clause of the Fifth, and later of the Fourteenth Amendment and was of seminal significance for our subsequent constitutional development—although it may be doubted that Madison (any more than Hamilton in New York before him) realized anything like the full import of what he

[75] Hunt, ed., *Writings of Madison*, 6:83.

[76] Compare Brant, "Madison Heritage," pp. 4–5.

[77] Syrett and Cooke, eds., *Papers of Hamilton*, 4:35.

was doing in writing the due process clause into the Constitution.

MADISON AND JUDICIAL ENFORCEMENT

"What is a right?" asked the Supreme Court over a century and a half ago. "That which may be enforced in a court of justice."[78] The French Declaration of the Rights of Man lays down abstract principles in hortatory terms. It does not contain mandatory prohibitions that can be enforced by the courts in specific cases. Hence, despite its title, it does not declare rights at all since the liberties stated by it are not protected or legally enforceable.

Madison's amendments also sought, in his own words, "to . . . expressly declare the great rights of mankind secured under this constitution."[79] But the American conception of a bill of rights was based not only upon the need to state "the great rights" to be secured but also upon the need to make the constitutional guarantees effective in practice. Their experience had shown Americans that mere declaration without enforcement machinery was what Madison termed only a "paper barrier."[80] His colonial contemporaries may have agreed with the 1761 argument of James Otis that there were fundamental legal principles beyond the power of Parliament to disturb,[81] but the argument could have no legal basis before Independence. Fundamental law may have been the major refuge of the colonists during the Revolutionary struggle. Yet it was a weak ally at best until a new polity was set up in which government was limited by an express fundamental law enforced by the courts.

Madison framed the rights guaranteed by the Bill of Rights in terms of mandatory imperatives that would be enforced by the courts. During the Philadelphia Convention itself, he

[78] *Comegys and Pettit* v. *Vasse*, 1 Pet. 193, 216 (U.S. 1828).

[79] Schwartz, comp., *Bill of Rights*, 2:1024.

[80] Ibid., p. 1030.

[81] Lechmere's Case, 1761, ibid., 1:185.

had declared, "A law violating a constitution established by the people themselves, would be considered by the Judges as null & void."[82] In the Bill of Rights debate, Madison applied this principle to the rights to be guaranteed by his proposed amendments. His June 8 address answered the claim that the Bill of Rights guarantees would not be "effectual" by asserting, "If they are incorporated into the constitution, independent tribunals of justice will consider themselves in a peculiar manner the guardians of those rights; they will be an impenetrable bulwark against every assumption of power in the legislative or executive; they will be naturally led to resist every encroachment upon rights expressly stipulated for in the constitution by the declaration of rights."[83]

This was more than an assertion made to gain supporters in the congressional debate. It was a theory of review power to which Madison adhered during his entire career. Jefferson took every opportunity to criticize *Marbury* v. *Madison*[84] and "the right they [the judges] usurp of exclusively explaining the constitution."[85] Madison never criticized *Marbury* v. *Madison*, for it elevated his view of judicial power to the constitutional plane. The only Supreme Court decision that Madison censured was *McCulloch* v. *Maryland*,[86] and he did so on the ground that the statute there should have been ruled invalid. "Does not the Court," Madison complained, "relinquish by their doctrine, all controul on the Legislative exercise of unconstitutional powers?"[87] The clear implication was that he still considered judicial review as the essential means to "controul . . . unconstitutional powers."

Only once did Madison seemingly waver in his approval of judicial review—in the Virginia Resolutions he drafted in

---

[82] Farrand, *Records of the Convention,* 2:93.

[83] Schwartz, comp., *Bill of Rights,* 2:1031.

[84] 1 Cranch 137 (U.S. 1803).

[85] Paul Leicester Ford, ed., *The Writings of Thomas Jefferson,* 10 vols. (New York, 1892–99), 10:140.

[86] 4 Wheat. 316 (U.S. 1819).

[87] Hunt, ed., *Writings of Madison,* 8:449.

1798.[88] But they were written in the heat of partisan controversy, and it is fair to say that Madison never intended to go so far as some of their unguarded language appears to indicate. The resolutions were prompted by the now-notorious Alien and Sedition Laws of 1798, and their purpose was as much propagandist as was that of the laws they were attacking. Certainly Madison himself was dismayed by the extremes to which his resolutions were carried during the Nullification controversy of the 1830s.

When that controversy was at its peak, he wrote, "With respect to the supremacy of the Judicial power on questions occurring in the course of its functions, . . . I have never ceased to think that this supremacy was a vital principle of the Constitution as it is a prominent feature of its text. A supremacy of the Constitution & laws of the Union, without a supremacy in the exposition & execution of them, would be as much a mockery as a scabbard put into the hand of a Soldier without a sword in it. I have never been able to see, that without such a view of the subject the Constitution itself could be the supreme law of the land; or that . . . anarchy & disunion could be prevented."[89]

One of the last documents left by Madison was his *Notes on Nullification*,[90] written in 1835–36, a lengthy essay designed to emphasize "the forbidding aspect of a naked creed."[91] In it, Madison repeated his denial that his Virginia Resolutions were intended to support any such extreme doctrine as nullification; he gave a detailed analysis of the resolutions to support his position.

Most pertinent for our purposes was Madison's restatement of the essential role of judicial review: "A political system which does not contain an effective provision for a peaceable decision of all controversies arising within itself, would be a Gov in name only. Such a provision is obviously essential; and

[88] Ibid., 6:326.

[89] Ibid., 9:476.

[90] Ibid., p. 573.

[91] Ibid.

it is equally obvious that it cannot be either peaceable or effective by making every part an authoritative umpire."[92]

In such cases, "The final appeal" must be to the courts which have the power of "exposition & execution of . . . the Constitution & laws of the Union."[93] This is the only view consistent with the Constitution itself, as demonstrated by the supremacy clause. "And," Madison concluded with prophetic eloquence, "it may be confidently foretold, that notwithstanding the clouds which a patriotic jealousy or other causes have at times thrown over the subject, it is the view which will be permanently taken of it, with a surprise hereafter, that any other should ever have been contended for."[94]

CONCLUSION

In conclusion, we come back to our comparison between the Bill of Rights and comparable French documents such as the Declaration of the Rights of Man. The American instrument, based upon experience showing the need for specific, legally enforceable guarantees, speaks the language of command in language that can be enforced by the courts. In this, it differs fundamentally from the French document, which is based upon "the same spirit that produced so many abstract books on government."[95] Its framers were more interested in laying down broad hortatory principles deemed universally applicable, rather than to descend to the level of practical enforcement.

There is also a difference in approach to the rights to be protected. The Declaration of the Rights of Man, we saw, lists rights in an abstract manner. But it also leaves out many of the rights which most people consider basic, such as the right against illegal searches and seizures and the right not to be deprived of property arbitrarily. The rights safeguarded by the first ten amendments, on the other hand, include the ba-

[92] Ibid., pp. 606–7.

[93] Ibid., pp. 607, 476.

[94] Ibid., p. 607.

[95] Tocqueville, *L'Ancien Régime*.

sic rights appropriate for protection by constitutional guaranty, at least as they were understood at the end of the eighteenth century.

According to John Rawls, "The basic liberties of citizens are, roughly speaking, political liberty (the right to vote and to be eligible for public office) together with freedom of speech and assembly; liberty of conscience and freedom of thought; freedom of the person along with the right to hold (personal) property; and freedom from arbitrary arrest and seizure."[96] Except for the right to vote and to hold public office (left almost entirely to the states in the original constitutional scheme and hence inappropriate for inclusion in a list of rights that the federal government might not infringe), all the liberties listed by Rawls are safeguarded by the Bill of Rights. Indeed, of the nonpolitical rights that, even today, are deemed suitable for constitutional protection only one important one is omitted by the Bill of Rights—that to equal protection of the laws.

Two things should be borne in mind about the omission. The first is the restricted notion of equality that prevailed at the end of the eighteenth century. However far-reaching the American conception of equality at the time might have seemed to contemporaries, it was, by present-day standards, rather limited: the American Revolution's emphasis on liberty and equality for all must be sharply distinguished from the twentieth-century meaning of "all." To the Framers, "all" did not include blacks and women; their concept was basically governed by the Aristotelian notion of the inherent inequality of persons outside the select circle of full citizenship. Even the basic political right of suffrage was restricted by property qualifications in most of the country. Equality before the law in the equal protection sense had not begun to develop. Nowhere in the document drafted in 1787 or in the Bill of Rights was there any guarantee of equality—or even mention of the concept.

Second, and even more important, the Bill of Rights was drafted in language that could include the new right of equal

---

[96] John Rawls, *A Theory of Justice* (Cambridge, Mass., 1971), p. 61.

445

protection as it began to develop. This, in some ways, was Madison's greatest contribution: he wrote in words that enabled later generations to mold the Bill of Rights to accord with changes in the community sense of justice. In particular, he substituted the due process clause for the "law of the land" phraseology, which had been used in the state declarations of rights and recommended amendments. Due process was a plastic conception that could expand to include new rights that even a Madison could not foresee. When the right to equal protection was made a constitutional right by the Fourteenth Amendment, it was made binding only upon the states. But the due process language proved to be broad enough to include the new right of equality. Hence, the courts have held that a governmental act that violated the equal protection clause of the Fourteenth Amendment if it were taken by a state, violates the due process clause of the Fifth Amendment if it is a federal act.[97]

When Madison wrote "due process" into what became the Fifth Amendment, he ensured that the Bill of Rights could be used to meet future conditions. Due process expresses more than the restricted views of the eighteenth century; it is an enduring reflection of experience with human nature.[98] The due process concept has enabled the Supreme Court to serve as a virtual continuing constitutional convention[99] as it has adapted the black-letter text to the needs of later days.

All of this was possible only because the Bill of Rights was based more upon experience than reason—or, to put it more accurately, upon reason only as codified by experience. We thus end, as we began, by contrasting the Dickinson statement on reason and experience with the Tocqueville emphasis upon the French passion for pure reason, untempered by experience. In another passage, Tocqueville notes that the men of the French Revolution "relied blindly" on "general and abstract theories in matters of government. In the almost infinite distance that they lived from practice, no experience

---

[97] *Bolling* v. *Sharpe*, 347 U.S. 497 (1954).

[98] Compare *Adamson* v. *California*, 332 U.S. 46, 63 (1947).

[99] Compare *Griswold* v. *Connecticut*, 381 U.S. 479, 520 (1965).

moderated their zeal."[100] That was emphatically not true of Madison and his colleagues. The Bill of Rights which they wrote into organic law was based specifically upon their experience—as colonists, as Revolutionaries, and as constitution-makers. That is why the document they drafted has endured two centuries as the classic inventory of "the great rights of mankind,"[101] while the edifying sentiments expressed in the French Declaration of the Rights of Man, had, as Conor Cruise O'Brien recently pointed out, "no influence over the conduct of the French Revolutionaries themselves, or of anybody else."[102]

[100] Tocqueville, *L'Ancien Régime*, p. 232.

[101] Madison, House of Representatives, June 8, 1789, in Schwartz, comp., *Bill of Rights*, 2:1024.

[102] Conor Cruise O'Brien, "A Vindication of Edmund Burke," *National Review* 28 (1990):34.

Contributors

AKHIL REED AMAR is a professor at the Yale Law School. His writings have appeared in the *Harvard Journal of Law and Public Policy,* the *University of Chicago Law Review,* the *Yale Law Journal,* and the *University of Pennsylvania Law Review.*

KENNETH R. BOWLING is coeditor of the *Documentary History of the First Federal Congress, 1789–1791,* at the George Washington University. He teaches an undergraduate research seminar there and documentary editing at George Mason University. He is the author of *The Creation of Washington, D. C.: The Idea and Location of the American Capital* (1991) as well as the author of several scholarly articles including the widely reprinted "'A Tub to the Whale': The Founding Fathers and the Federal Bill of Rights" (1988). He is coauthor of *Birth of the Nation: The First Federal Congress, 1789–1791.* Since 1994 he has moderated the United States Capitol Historical Society's annual conference on Congress in the 1790s.

SAUL CORNELL is associate professor of history at the Ohio State University. In 1995 he held the Thomas Jefferson Chair in American Studies at the University of Leiden, the Netherlands. His articles have appeared in the *Journal of American History,* the *William and Mary Quarterly,* the *American Quarterly,* the *Law History Review, American Studies,* and the *Northwestern University Law Review.* His book, *The Other Founders: Anti-Federalism and the American Constitutional Tradition,* is forthcoming from the Institute of Early American History and Culture. Professor Cornell is currently working on a study of Federalist political and constitutional thought and a volume of essays on the implications of postmodern theory for constitutional history.

CONTRIBUTORS

PAUL FINKELMAN currently holds the Joseph C. Hostetler-Baker and Hostetler Chair at Cleveland Marshall College of Law. He has also taught at Hamline University School of Law, where he was Distinguished Visiting Professor, at the University of Miami, where he was Charlton W. Tebeau Visiting Research Professor, at Brooklyn Law School, and at Virginia Tech. He has published more than sixty scholarly articles and written or edited eleven books, including *Dred Scott v. Sandford: A Brief History with Documents* (1997), *A Brief Narrative of the Tryal of John Peter Zenger* (1997), *Slavery and the Founders: Race and Liberty in the Age of Jefferson* (1996), *Baseball and the American Legal Mind* (with Spencer Waller and Neil Cohen, 1995), *Slavery in the Courtroom* (1985), which won the 1986 Joseph L. Andrews Award from the American Association of Law Libraries, and *An Imperfect Union: Slavery, Federalism, and Comity* (1981). He is currently writing a history of the enforcement of the fugitive slave laws.

MICHAEL LIENESCH is Bowman and Gordon Gray Professor of Political Science at the University of North Carolina at Chapel Hill. He is the author of *New Order of the Ages: Time, the Constitution, and the Making of Modern American Political Thought* (1988), coeditor (with Michael Allen Gillespie) of *Ratifying the Constitution* (1989), and has written articles on early American political thought that have appeared in *American Politics Quarterly, History of Political Thought,* the *Journal of Politics,* the *Review of Politics,* and the *Western Political Quarterly.* His recent research has been on the role of religion in American politics, where his writings include *Redeeming America: Piety and Politics in the New Christian Right* (1993).

DONALD S. LUTZ is professor of political science at the University of Houston where he teaches political philosophy, especially as it relates to constitutional theory in general and American political theory in particular. His most recent books include *The Origins of American Constitutionalism* (1988), *A Preface to American Political Theory* (1993), and *Colonial Origins of the American Constitution: A Documentary History* (1997). He is currently working on his tenth book, entitled *Popular Sovereignty and Principles of Constitutional Design,* which is a comparative study of all the foreign national and American state constitutions ever written. The fourth chapter of

450

this book, "Toward a Theory of Constitutional Amendment," has been published in the *American Political Science Review*.

FORREST MCDONALD is the Distinguished University Research Professor at the University of Alabama. The historian is best known for his *We the People: The Economic Origins of the Constitution* (1958), *Alexander Hamilton: A Biography* (1979), and *Novus Ordo Seclorum: The Intellectual Origins of the Constitution* (1985). His most recent book is *The American Presidency: An Intellectual History* (1994). Currently he is working on a study of international law in the Age of Democratic Revolutions.

WHITMAN H. RIDGWAY is associate professor of history at the University of Maryland, College Park. He has written *Community Leadership in Maryland, 1790–1840: A Comparative Analysis of Power in Society* (1979) and coedited with Joseph Melusky a book of documents, *The Bill of Rights: Our Written Legacy* (1993). He is presently working on a book-length study of the background and adoption of the Bill of Rights.

BERNARD SCHWARTZ is Chapman Distinguished Professor of Law at the University of Tulsa College of Law. He is the author of the definitive judicial biography of Earl Warren and casebooks and treatises on administrative and constitutional law, as well as many books on the Supreme Court, legal and constitutional history, and other subjects.

LOIS G. SCHWOERER is the Elmer Louis Kayser Professor Emeritus of History at the George Washington University. The author of numerous articles and reviews, she has written *"No Standing Armies!" The Antistanding Army Ideology in Seventeenth-Century England* (1974), which won the Berkshire Conference of Women Historians' prize for the best book published by a woman historian in 1974, *The Declaration of Rights, 1689* (1981), which received Honourable Mention in the John Ben Snow Prize Competition (1981–82), and *Lady Rachel Russell: "One of the Best of Women"* (1988), and edited *The Revolution of 1688–89: Changing Perspectives* (1992), a collection of essays to which she contributed. Her articles include

"Seventeenth-Century English Women Engraved in Stone?" (1984), which won the Walter D. Love Prize for the best article in British Studies published by a North American author in 1984, and "Images of Queen Mary II, 1688–95" (1989), which won the prize for the best paper presented at the 1986 annual meeting of the Carolinas Symposium on British Studies.

Schwoerer's current interests include the public political voices of English women, 1640–1740, and a book-length project dealing with the intersections between print culture, law, and ideology in Restoration England, as seen through the life of Henry Care (1646–88), a Restoration polemicist.

Index

INDEX